Real
Estate
Exchange

Using Tax-Deferred
Exchange In Real
Estate Investment
Management

Howard A. Zuckerman
& Rochelle Stone
EDITORS

PROBUS PUBLISHING COMPANY
Chicago, Illinois
Cambridge, England

33 26324

Z94 n

For my wife and partner, Amy, and my three children Lindsey, Carley, and Adam
For my parents and sister
To the memory of Dr. James Graaskamp; may his legacy continue with the
thousands of students he taught
In memory of our family friends, S, S, and W

CONTENTS

ABOUT THE EDITORS

HOWARD A. ZUCKERMAN

Howard A. Zuckerman is president of The Seville Companies, a real estate acquisition and development firm in Atlanta, Georgia.

Since 1976, Mr. Zuckerman has been active in the acquisition, development, financing, and equity placement of income-producing properties valued at over $100,000,000.

His experience covers a wide range of real estate, including syndication of new and existing residential and commercial properties; the development, construction, management, leasing, and resale of residential and commercial properties; and brokerage of residential and commercial properties throughout the Sun Belt. These activities have involved single-family homes, apartments, offices, shopping centers, and mini-warehouses.

The author holds an undergraduate degree in Marketing from Ohio State University and a Masters of Science in Real Estate Urban Land Economics and Appraisal from the University of Wisconsin.

His other business affiliations include memberships in local and regional real estate trade groups, including the Real Estate Securities and Syndication Institute (RESSI), the National Association of Realtors (NAR), the National Association of Home Builders, the National Mini-Storage Institute, and the Urban Land Institute (ULI).

He has been the subject of numerous articles in regional and national trade and business publications and has been included in *Who's Who in Real Estate* and *Who's Who in Finance and Industry*.

Mr. Zuckerman's previous works include:

> *Real Estate Investment & Acquisition Workbook*, published in May 1989 by Prentice Hall.

Real Estate Development Workbook and Manual, published in October 1991 by Prentice Hall.

Real Estate Wealthbuilding: How to Really Make Money in Real Estate, published in October 1991 by Dearborn Financial Publishing Co.

Real Estate Workout Deskbook: How to Restructure, Refinance & Remarket Troubled Commercial Properties, published in April 1992 by Probus Publishing Co.

Problem Real Estate: How to Restructure, Refinance & Remarket Troubled Commercial Properties, published in August 1992 by Probus Publishing Co.

Real Estate Workouts & Asset Management, newsletter, published monthly by Warren, Gorham & Lamont.

ROCHELLE STONE

Rochelle Stone is president and founding partner of Starker Services, Inc., with headquarters in Los Gatos, California. Starker Services, Inc. (SSI) is an exchange facilitation company active on a national level performing simultaneous and delayed exchanges.

Ms. Stone has over 15 years of speaking experience and is listed with the National Speaker's Bureau. An accredited real estate instructor in several states, Ms. Stone has taught exchanging and investment techniques to real estate boards, escrow companies, and investment and professional groups. A partial list of firms she has done regional training for include the Alaska Bar Association, CB Commercial, Century 21, ReMax, United National Realty, Stewart Title, First American Title, Chicago Title, Founders Title, and Bank of Boston. She has also written numerous articles for trade publications including "Commercial Property Guide" and the "National Real Estate Investor."

Prior to co-founding SSI, Ms. Stone worked in real estate as an agent specializing in multiple residential and commercial properties. She was at the same time director for Cambrian Groups asset management company, overseeing up to 1,600 apartment units.

Before becoming involved in real estate, Ms. Stone was a senior account executive and consultant for an international finance and marketing company.

ABOUT THE CONTRIBUTING AUTHORS

Bernardine G. Marvel-Ames, CPA, is a principal in her own accounting firm. Her area of expertise is in real estate taxation and real estate exchanging. She received her B.S. in Business Administration from the University of the Pacific and her M.S. in Taxation from Golden State University.

Dr. Mark Lee Levine, is president of Levine, Ltd., Realtors, and partner in the law firm of Levine and Pitler, P.C. both located in Englewood, Colorado. Dr. Levine is also a professor of real estate at University of Denver. He is widely known as an expert in the field of real estate tax law. In addition to a law degree and a Ph.D., he has a LL.M. in tax from New York University, is a graduate of Northwestern University, and holds the following designations: NASD, SRS, CCIM, CA-C, CRS, GRI, CRB, CRA, APRA, SCV, CPM, AFLM, CLU, ChFC, RFPM/IARFP, MREC, NIREC, DREI, ALC, MAI, and SREA.

James F. Little, MBA, operates a real estate educational seminar and consulting practice, located in Sacramento, California. His area of expertise is as an expert witness and financial analysis. He is the author of a number of articles and a nationally known speaker on real estate exchanging and cash flow analysis. He received his B.S. degree in Finance and his M.B.A. from San Jose State University.

Kevin K. Hereford is a senior vice president of Starker Services, Inc., located in Los Gatos, California. His area of expertise is in structuring tax-deferred exchanges. He received a B.S. in Marketing and Finance from the University of Houston. He is a licensed realtor in California.

Michael J. R. Hoffman, DBA, is an associate professor at Florida Atlantic University, located in Boca Raton, Florida. His area of expertise is federal taxation. He received his B.S. in Accounting from University of Tennessee at Martin, his Masters degree in Business and his Doctors of Business Administration from Indiana University.

Karen S. McKenzie, Ph.D., CPA, is an assistant professor at Florida Atlantic University, located in Boca Raton, Florida. Her area of expertise is governmental and managerial accounting. She received her B.B.A. in Accounting from University of Miami, her M.S. in Accounting from University of Central Florida, and her Doctorate in Accounting from Louisiana State University.

Michael Renfro, is senior account executive with Starker Services, Inc. of Los Gatos, California. His area of expertise is in 1031 exchanging. He received his B.S. in Finance from San Diego State University. He is a licensed California real estate broker and has authored numerous articles on real estate exchanging.

Scott R. Saunders, is Vice President-Marketing for Starker Services, Inc., located in Los Gatos, California. His area of expertise is in investment real estate and tax-deferred exchanging. He received his B.A. in Business Economics from University of California at Santa Barbara. He currently writes for numerous California real estate periodicals and is an active speaker for investor exchange workshops.

Michael M. Smith, is a partner in the Atlanta, Georgia law firm of Gambrell, Clarke, Anderson & Stolz. His area of expertise in in real estate taxation and corporate finance. He received his B.S. in Education from California State University and his J.D. from McGeorge School of Law, University of the Pacific. In addition, he is also a Certified Public Accountant.

William Townsend, is the Northwest Regional Manager for Starker Services, Inc., located in Bellevue, Washington. He is an author, panelist, and guest speaker for Real Estate seminars on the complex and misunderstood tax ramification of entering into completing a successful 1031 Tax Deferred Exchange.

R. Douglas Wright, is a partner in the Atlanta, Georgia law firm of Branch, Pike, Ganz & O'Callaghan. He specializes in federal and state income taxation partnership and corporate investment transactions and employee benefits. He received a B.S. in Mechanical Engineering from Cornell University, his J.D. from Georgetown University Law Center, and his L.L.M. in Taxation from Emory University. He is the author of numerous articles concerning the income tax aspects of real estate and partnership investment transactions.

FOREWORD

The basic concept of real estate exchanging is really quite simple and, if used properly, can be an enormous wealth-builder for the astute real estate investor. In actual practice, however, we have to admit that there is a great deal to know about the subject and that structuring a qualifying real estate exchange poses a worthy challenge. In fact, many otherwise astute real estate professionals and investors have shied away from getting involved in exchanges because of what they perceive as a bewildering maze of potential hazards.

This book will help demystify the process. It has been edited and contributed to by two of the nation's most respected authorities on the subject, Howard Zuckerman and Rochelle Stone. The other professionals who contribute are recognized authorities in their fields and are on the front line of exchanging. The material will serve as an invaluable basic reference and reflects what is going on in the real world.

For the real estate professional delving into new and uncharted waters, there is always the very real potential for "learning just enough to get into trouble." While this book will provide as comprehensive a treatment of exchanging, the prudent real estate practitioner will enlist the aid of competent fellow professionals such as attorneys, accountants, and others in the business who have had long and successful experience in exchanging.

Dr. Kenneth W. Edwards

PREFACE

This book was written for the real estate professional who wants to expand his knowledge in real estate tax-deferred exchange strategies. This book is divided into five sections:

1. An Introduction to Exchanging: This section details the benefits of exchanging and the history of the Internal Revenue Service Code changes.

2. Rules and Regulations: This section describes IRC Sections 1033, 1034, and 1031, as well as how exchanging is accounted for by tax-payers.

3. The Mechanics of Exchanging: This section details the various exchange techniques, dealing with personal and multiple exchanges and how to use seller financing in the exchange process.

4. The Exchange Process: This section reviews the various documents used in the exchange process, as well as how to deal with various types of ownership vehicles in exchanging.

5. The Role of the Professionals: This section reviews how a real estate broker can use IRC Section 1031 to his advantage and what part the exchange intermediary has in this process.

Included in these sections are numerous examples and forms that will enable the reader to workout various exchange scenarios. Included in the Appendix are additional exchange documents, court case listings, and the actual code sections from the Internal Revenue Service.

It is the hope of the authors/editors that this book will demystify the real estate exchange process. The Internal Revenue Service designed this section for investors to use to help create wealth, and we hope that this book will help in that process.

ACKNOWLEDGEMENTS

This book entailed a long process of sifting through old files and note-books in order to guide the reader through the IRC 1031 exchange process. Many long hours were spent on my word processors to complete this publication.

I would like to give special thanks to my wife and kids, who have had to live with my coming home late at night and then sneaking away so that the book could be finished.

I would also like to thank the many other individuals who have given their counsel, information, and encouragement. In addition, special thanks should be given in the memory of Dr. Jim Graaskamp, professor of real estate at the University of Wisconsin, who taught me many years ago the basic concepts of real estate and the value of "stick-to-it-iveness."

Additionally, I would like to thank each and every contributing author for their expertise and time involved in this project. I would especially like to give thanks to Rochelle Stone, who gave more than her share of time on this project.

Finally, I would like to thank: Milton (Gimp) Fromson and Danny Rocker, D.D.S., for giving me the opportunity to start in the real estate field in 1973; Richard Katz for showing me the fundamentals of real estate number crunching; Michael Feiner for informing me about the University of Wisconsin Real Estate Program; Carl Millstein, who sat down with me in 1972 to discuss real estate development; Mike Komppa and Steve Leaffer for spending hours on the telephone discussing "deal philosophy"; Joseph Harman for backing me on my first development deal; and Wayne Pratter for giving me the opportunity to joint venture with his service corporation.

—H.Z.

INTRODUCTION

Since mankind discovered its needs to eat and be sheltered, it has been involved in some type of bartering for daily requirements. During the Age of Discovery, mankind became more sophisticated and traveled long distances to trade for items that were not readily available. By the late nineteenth century, the desire to go beyond the basic three needs (i.e., food, clothing, and shelter) became apparent. During this industrialized period, society developed the taste to create wealth.

As a result of this industrialization, Congress decided to generate additional revenue by taxing the capital gains of investments and businesses upon resale. These taxes changed the way that Americans viewed property ownership. With these changes the prudent investor required a knowledge of the IRS tax codes and how they affected his overall return. In 1921 Congress first originated Section 1031 of the IRS Code that enabled investors and businesses to reinvest their sale proceeds into "like-kind" properties and thus avoid an immediate income tax on their profits. It is with this IRS Code that many investors and business owners were able to pyramid their wealth many fold. Over the last 50 years the IRS Codes have changed many times to help stir the economy and to create new job opportunities.

After the last major Tax Reform Act (1986), many of the benefits of real estate ownership were taken away by the government. Whether these changes were for the better or worse are not in question. What is clear from these changes is that one of the only benefits that did survive was Section 1031 of the IRC. Unfortunately, many individuals and their tax professionals have never been able to fully understand the real benefits of this Code Section. Finally, in June 1991, the IRS issued a new set of regulations regarding this Code Section.

It is based on these new regulations that *Real Estate Exchange* was written. This book will describe the history of Section 1031 of the Internal Revenue Service and the new rules and regulations. It will outline the techniques to be used today to exchange properties or businesses under these current IRS tax codes. It will dispel any and all the myths about exchanging. Finally, the book will describe how the real estate broker can increase his commissions while assisting the investor to increase his wealth through pyramiding his property ownership using the 1031 Code Section.

Although this book was written by competent real estate, legal, and accounting professionals, it should be noted that investors should have their own professionals review their own tax situation prior to making any investment decisions.

part **I**

An Introduction to Exchanging

chapter 1

Exchange Basics

by Rochelle Stone
  Starker Services, Inc.
  Los Gatos, California

William Townsend
  Starker Services, Inc.
  Bellevue, Washington

For most investors, the creation of wealth is a process—not an event. **Real property** is a vehicle to move the owner from point A to point B, whether the ultimate goal is retirement, cash flow, security, diversification, or estate planning. There is no single more important reason to do an exchange than to accelerate or accomplish the objectives of the investor.

Many articles are being written about the advantages of the 1031 tax deferred exchange, particularly after the newest Treasury Regulations of 1991. Most authors stress the **deferment of taxes** as the benefit to be planned by doing the **1031 exchange**. To do so is something akin to calling Van Gogh merely a "painter." Exchanging, if used as an integral part of an investment plan, is the most powerful investment tool available to the real property owner.

REASONS TO EXCHANGE

The following list will give some of the more significant reasons the investor will find an exchange beneficial:

3

Preservation of Equity

The seller of real property who realizes $100,000 in proceeds may pay 30% or more in capital gain taxes. (Capital gain taxes are due on both federal and the state level). The net after paying taxes of about $70,000 significantly reduces the seller's return on investment. The **exchangor**, on the other hand, will keep all of the sales proceeds, moving the entire $100,000 into the next investment. This will significantly increase his return on investment. Preserving equity lends itself to the next and probably most important reason to use the 1031 exchange; that is, the ability to **leverage**.

	Sale of Property	vs.	1031 Exchange
Sales Price	$800,000		$800,000
Less Mortgage	($700,000)		($700,000)
Net Equity	$100,000		$100,000
Less Fed. & St. Taxes @ 30%	($ 30,000)		($ 0)
Net Proceeds to Invest	$ 70,000		$100,000

Leveraging

Preserving equity by exchanging means saving a dollar in taxes. But it is not the dollar saved that is significant. It is what the dollar will buy. The term for this ability to use "one" dollar to purchase "three or four" dollars worth of real property is leveraging. Leveraging is the reason many investors find investment property attractive in the first place.

What is Leverage?

Understanding leverage will set the groundwork to see how leverage is maximized through a 1031 exchange, how it is viewed by the lender, and how this view impacts the lending and borrowing decision. The acquisition of real estate is generally financed by borrowing most of the purchase price from either a financial institution, or the seller of the real estate. When borrowing money, the ratio between dollars belonging to the borrower (which go into the equity of the property) to how many dollars are loaned by the lender, is the leverage ratio. For example:

Borrower's equity	$ 30,000	(A)
Bank $ (borrowing)	+ $ 60,000	(B)
Cost of real estate	$ 90,000	

B/A = Leverage
or 2 to 1 Leverage (2:1)

In the example, for every dollar the borrower contributes to equity (after paying expenses) he gets two dollars from the lender. If the borrower purchases property, with $30,000 equity, the leverage ratio changes proportionally.

Cost of Real Estate	Borrowing	Leverage	
105,000	75,000	2.5:1	(75\30)
120,000	90,000	3.0:1	(90\30)
135,000	105,000	3.5:1	(103\30)
150,000	120,000	4.0:1	(120\30)

As you can see, the more that an investor receives from a lender, the more property he can purchase, and the greater the leverage ratio.

Leverage and the 1031 Exchange

A significant advantage to the 1031 tax-deferred exchange is the leverage benefit that comes from keeping tax dollars for your own use in order to build wealth. Let's compare the investor's position in an exchange versus a sale when the investor leverages with a 3 to 1 ratio. (See Chapter 3 regarding realized versus recognized gain.)

Example #1: Sale

Sales price	$200,000	
Profit		$150,000
Capital gains tax		($ 37,500)
		$112,500 + $37,000 = $450,000
		3:1 (Leverage Ratio Purchase Price of New Real Estate)

Example #2: Exchange

Sales price	$200,000	
Profit		$150,000
Capital gains tax		$ 0
		$150,000 + $450,000 = $600,000
		3:1 (Leverage Ratio Purchase Price of New Real Estate)

Example #2 shows how the tax savings plus leverage equals additional purchasing power of $150,000.

What does this mean later?

Leverage and Appreciation

Let's say that **appreciation** for only one year is five percent. Applying this to our earlier example, let's look at the equity one year after the purchase.

Borrower's equity	$ 30,000	(A)
Bank $ (borrowing)	$ 60,000	(B)
Cost of real estate	$ 90,000	

Purchase Price	Present Value	New Equity	$ Equity Build-Up	Return
90,000	94,500	34,500	4,500	15.0%
105,000	110,250	35,250	5,250	17.5%
120,000	126,000	36,000	6,000	20.0%
135,000	141,750	36,750	6,700	22.5%
150,000	157,500	37,500	7,500	25.0%

The equity (real dollars) build up on the same investment of $30,000 for a 2/1 ratio is $4,500 versus $7,500 for a 4/1 ratio. Imagine the difference over many years and a higher appreciation percentage.

Leverage and Financing

Why doesn't a borrower simply leverage 5:1 or even 10:1? In the real world, the lender has two basic principles: cash flow and collateral. Both are important. All financial institutions insist that the cash flow of the new investment pay all expenses, principal and interest payments, and build reserves. The excess cash flow is the investor's. In today's environment, cash flow determines the ability to leverage.

To determine the maximum leverage, you must adjust the borrowed monies up or down within the project's cash flow. Most likely the range is between 3.0 and 5.0. Any ratio below 3.0 usually means that you have "too much" equity in the project. Any ratio over 5.0 means that you have too little equity and the loan is "risky."

The other aspect of a lending decision is collateral. For most lenders this is the second most important consideration. Remember, if cash flow is not acceptable, then collateral makes no difference. The more equity, the safer the loan. The borrower probably is more optimistic regarding the current value of property and its projected appreciation. Simply put, the higher the leverage ratio, the riskier the loan. Also, most financial institutions will give you a better loan structure for lower leverage ratios because their actual loan losses for lower ratio loans are better than the higher ratio loans.

Increase Cash Flow

In addition to the advantages that increased cash flow will give the investor who is seeking financing, cash flow is also another benefit of ownership of real property that some investors look for. Cash flow is not merely a function of a good investment. Raw land may be a good investment from an appreciation viewpoint; however, seldom does it produce significant cash flow. Trading from a property with little or no cash flow (such as raw land) to a property with a cash flow, such as a shopping center, office building, or multi-family property is another good reason for a 1031 exchange. Again, the preservation of equity in an exchange will increase the potential for income.

Consolidation or Diversification

Multiple properties can be exchanged for one larger property, or a larger property may be exchanged into multiple smaller properties. An investor with four houses used as rentals may wish to exchange into one four unit property for ease of management and consolidation of his investment.

The reverse may be true for the investor at the end of his investment cycle. Moving from one large property into a series of smaller properties may allow him to:

- Divest out of some of his investments, paying taxes, and freeing equity, while deferring the balance of taxes by holding the remaining properties.

- Diversifying his holdings by moving his equity into other types of properties. For example: A personal residence and a 60-acre farm could be sold as business/investment property. The purchase/sale price is allocated to the residence and to the investment under acceptable accounting guidelines.

Relief from Management

Many times the investor's portfolio becomes scattered over a large geographical area or contains many different types and sizes of properties. This type of portfolio can become a management nightmare. By exchanging into a property that is less management intensive, the investor can profit just by more free time to find new investments. For example, an investor may have accumulated six rental homes over a three county area. Rather than spending all week to maintain these small rental properties, he exchanges his equity into a nearby building containing the U.S. Post Office. With this new investment, all the investor has to do is pick up his monthly check from the government and the Postal department maintains the property for him.

Locational Considerations

Investors often move some distance from their investment property. With an exchange, an investor can find the same or better property close to their new residence anywhere in the United States.

Tax Deferment

The concept of the **tax-deferred exchange** is similar to the idea of the IRA account. While taxes are owed by the taxpayer, the government has "agreed" to wait to collect them until the taxpayer receives the cash. The tax owed on the money remains in the IRA account and will earn interest. The deferred taxes are still owed to the government. The significance for the real estate investor, however, is the difference between future values versus present value of the dollar. The investor gains in two ways. A dollar owned in taxes will certainly be worth less in the future and the investor has the use of the capital that would otherwise have been paid to the government.

Other Reasons to Exchange

In addition, the following are other reasons why investors may decide it is advantageous to exchange.

- Increase the depreciable property **basis** with a new property with a larger debt.

- Move from heavy-debt property to low- or no-debt.

- Allow heirs to escape taxes on deferred gains by taking over your property at a **stepped-up basis**.

- Complete a sale that might not be possible due to potential tax ramifications.

- Acquire a property with a shorter **depreciation** schedule.

- Increase equity build-up with a property that debt service is amortizing faster than the original property.

- Reallocate basis with a property that has a different land-to-property ratio.

- Obtain tax-free cash by refinancing into a property that can be refinanced after the exchange.

- Obtain a property that might be easier to sell or refinance in the future.

- Obtain a property with a higher building-to-land ratio.

- Exchange property into another location.

- Convert the nature of your investment.

- Exchange into rental property that may be converted to retirement residence.

- Convert **1034** residence to **1031** property.

- Convert 1034 residence to 1031 property; exchange into two 1031 properties (one which will remain 1031, one which will be converted later to a 1034 property.

- Convert 1034 to 1031 back to 1034 (all within 2 years).

- Exchange from raw land into an income-producing property.

WHEN SHOULD YOU NOT EXCHANGE?

The exchange of investment property should always make good financial sense and have a positive impact on your financial goals. Any time a sale of property is better financially then an exchange, it would be prudent to sell. The most common reasons *not* to perform an exchange are:

Recognition of a Loss

Internal Revenue Code Section 1031 reads that no gain or *loss* will be recognized by effecting a 1031 exchange. If a property is being sold with a loss and the taxpayer wants the loss to be recognized, then they must not do an exchange. To do so means that the loss will not be deductible but will be postponed or deferred. Century Electric Co. v. Commissioner, 51-2 U.S.T.C. para. 9842, 192 F.2d 155 (8th Cir. 1951) denied a taxpayer who was attempting to take a loss deduction on the sale of a manufacturing facility. The court ruled the taxpayer, having sold the manufacturing facility and subsequently leasing back the same facility on a lease plus options totaling over 30 years (essentially a fee interest), had inadvertently performed a 1031 and, therefore, could not recognize a loss.

Tax on Boot Does Not Exceed Capital Gain Due

The taxpayer may elect to perform a **partially deferred exchange**. In this case, it may be that the taxpayer is going to use only some of their proceeds to purchase a replacement property and take some proceeds (cash). For example:

Exchangor, Mr. Bradford, decides to sell his apartment building for $500,000. He purchased the building originally for $400,000. He has equity of $250,000 and an adjusted basis in the building of $350,000. He wants to receive $150,000 in cash from the disposal of the property and intends to reinvest $100,000 in a fourplex near where he lives. If he sells the property, his capital gain will be as follows:

Sales price	$500,000
Adjusted basis	($350,000)
Capital gain	$150,000

Mr. Bradford wants $150,000 to put in his pocket. Tax on capital gain is limited to the amount received. In other words, you cannot be taxed on more than you receive as **boot**. In this example, it makes no sense for the taxpayer to do an exchange. The amount of cash he is pulling from the transaction is large enough to pay any capital gains tax due; therefore, he will owe no more in capital gains tax even if he sells the building. There is no economic benefit to the exchange.

Inherited Property

When real property is inherited and disposed of by the heirs immediately, there is no capital gain. When an estate passes to the successors, the basis of the property is adjusted to current market value. If the property is then sold at market value, there has been no appreciatior..

No Intention to Reinvest the Proceeds

If an investor wants to cash out completely and has no intention to buy replacement property, then there is no reason to exchange. Obviously, this decision should be made with the advice of the investor's tax counsel and careful tax planning.

Minimum Taxes Are Due

Since it costs money to perform an exchange, the investor should review these costs against the amount of taxes that would be due in a straight sale. If the taxes saved are not much more than the taxes due, it might not be worth all the time and effort to find a suitable **replacement property** and then close on it.

EXCHANGE MYTHS

Due to the complexity and unresolved issues pertaining to the IRC 1031, many myths and misconceptions have circulated about exchanging. Some of these myths are:

Exchanges Are Illegal

This is definitely not true. IRC Section 1031 details the handling of exchange transactions.

Exchanges Are Complicated

Exchanges are really nothing more than sales. The only difference is in the tax treatment (i.e., tax-deferral) under IRC Section 1031.

Exchanges Will Trigger Tax Audits

If handled properly by your accountant and exchange **intermediary**, there should be no more chance of getting audited than in the case ofa straight sale.

Taxes Have to Be Paid Sometime

This is true; all taxes have to be paid sometime. IRC Section 1031 provides only for a tax-deferral until the investor decides to take cash in hand from a regular sale.

Like-Kind Exchanges Limit Your Options

Under IRC Section 1031 the only option limits are the property must be "like-kind" and must be purchased in the United States.

Be Completed by Two Parties Who Want Each Other's Properties

These types of exchanges are possible, but simultaneous swaps do not usually occur. Under IRC Section 1031 with the use of a qualified intermediary, the exchangor can sell to one party and then purchase someone else's property.

Title Must Pass Simultaneously During an Exchange

Unless two properties are simultaneously swapped, the exchangor has 180 days to close on a replacement property. During this 180-day period, the title is held by a qualified exchange intermediary. Title on passes back to the exchangor when the second leg of the exchange takes place.

History of Real Estate Exchanging

by Rochelle Stone
Starker Services, Inc.
Los Gatos, California

The concept of the **exchange** is as old as civilization. Commonly known as bartering, it has been practiced for centuries, as a method of trading commodities or services without the use of money. The Department of the Treasury Publication 544 (Rev. Nov. 88) states:

> A sale is a transfer of property for money or for a mortgage, note, or some promise to pay money. An exchange is a transfer of property for other property or for services. The rules for figuring a taxable gain or a deductible loss apply to both sales and exchanges; however, some exchanges are not taxable.

These nontaxable exchanges have existed for many years. No one can say for sure when the concept of the exchange was first applied to real estate. The idea probably evolved from our beginnings as a country used to bartering. For example, farmers often traded land for land or livestock for livestock. Seldom was any cash involved. The Internal Revenue Service (IRS) would have had to confiscate equipment or livestock to be "paid."

Revenue Act of 1918

Proposed as a temporary tax, this act resulted in the imposition of the nation's first income tax. The IRS would now recognize gain or loss on any **disposition of property**, including **like-kind exchanges**. Three years later, Congress modified Internal Revenue Code (IRC) Section 202(c) to read as follows: "while no gain or loss had to be recognized in any exchange of **'like-kind' property**, non-'like-kind' exchanges qualified unless the property acquired has a readily realizable market value."

This change was the precursor to the current 1031 code.

Internal Revenue Code Section 1031

By 1924, Code Section 1031(a) was modified to read "that if property used in a trade or business or held for investment purposes is traded for like-kind property that is also used in a trade or business or held for investment" there will be no recognized gain or loss. The *Revenue Act of 1928*, (26 U.S.C.A. 112b) changed the code further to read that upon the sale or exchange of property, while the gain or loss shall be taken into account for income tax purposes, it shall not be recognized if the exchange is for like-kind property. The most significant investment technique available to investors of real property was now part of the federal tax code and ready to use.

Mercantile Trust

During the 1930s, simultaneity was still necessary for the use of tax deferment. Existing tax law required two owners of real property to essentially do a simultaneous swap of **like-kind investment property**, which was a difficult and unlikely occurrence. The significance of the Mercantile Trust Case (Mercantile Trust Co. of Baltimore et al v. Commissioner 32 B.T.A 82 (1935) was two-fold: First, it established the right of the taxpayer to sell if an exchange became impossible; and second, it introduced the concept of a third party to facilitate the exchange.

This case opened the door for modern exchanges.

The court reviewing the purchase/sale contract challenged the fact that the taxpayer could, if unable to trade for their designated replacement property, receive cash "in lieu" of like-kind property. Did this possibility disallow the exchange? In an attempt to avoid what was clearly intended to be a taxable sale by performing an exchange, could the taxpayer be guilty of fraud? The court concluded that the petitioners had exchanged real property for real property and the possibility of the sale did not disallow the nonrecognition of gain. The taxpayer's option to receive cash if unable to find suitable replacement property did not disallow the exchange because the option was never exercised.

Another important feature of the Mercantile Trust decision was the exchangor's (taxpayers') use of a third party to help complete the transaction. This is the first time an intermediary was made part of an exchange and would further set precedent for the "delayed" or "Starker" exchange.

The Starker Decision

The widely publicized **Starker** decision attracted the attention of the real estate industry when an investor by the name of T.J. Starker and his family challenged the necessity for a simultaneous exchange under the existing 1031 code.

T.J. Starker, his son Bruce, and daughter-in-law Elizabeth owned 1,843 acres of timberland in Columbia County, Oregon. In 1967, two companies, Crown Zellerbach and Longview Fibre, offered to purchase the acreage. The timber companies were anxious to harvest the timber; however, the Starkers had not located suitable replacement property yet. The Starkers were willing to sell but wanted to defer their capital gains on the land. To solve both parties' problems, the Starkers entered a contractual agreement to convey lands to Zellerbach and Longview in exchange for a promise to deliver suitable replacement properties to the Starkers in the future.

On April 1, 1967, Bruce and Elizabeth entered into a "Real Estate Exchange Agreement" with Longview Fibre and conveyed property to them. Longview set up "book credits" of $105,811 in favor of the Starkers, which they referred to as the "Exchange Value" for the timberland. Each year until the credits were spent, the remaining **Exchange Credits** would be increased by a 6% "growth factor" to reflect the growing timber. Under the contract, the Starkers did not have control of any cash. At the same time, T.J., Bruce, and Elizabeth entered into a "Land Exchange Agreement" with Zellerbach and conveyed their timberland. T.J. Starkers' exchange credits with Zellerbach were $1,502,000 and Bruce and Elizabeth's were $73,000. Again, the 6% growth factor applied and there was no control of the cash.

As suitable replacement property was found by the Starkers, Crown Zellerbach and Longview Fibre purchased the property, deeding it to them and reducing the Starkers' "exchange credits." Longview Fibre conveyed eight parcels to Bruce and Elizabeth between 1968 and 1972, reducing their credit balance to zero. Crown Zellerbach conveyed three parcels to Bruce and Elizabeth reducing their balance to zero. T.J., having more credits to spend, did not receive all of his property for almost two years. He received twelve parcels, two of which were actually an assignment of a purchase contract. No cash was paid to the Starkers. The Starkers filed their tax returns for 1967 treating these transactions as tax-exempt transfers. The groundwork was laid for a challenge of the "nonsimultaneous" exchange by the Internal Revenue Service.

The IRS disallowed all of the exchanges. The Starkers paid their taxes and filed suits in the U.S. District Court in Portland, Oregon. Three court cases ensued, tried by District Judge Gus Solomon.

Starker I

The first involved Bruce and Elizabeth Starker (Starker I - 1975). The IRS first filed a deficiency notice against Bruce and Elizabeth Starker. The Starkers paid the tax and sued for a refund. In a very short opinion, the court decided in favor of Bruce and Elizabeth Starker while making no mention of the fact that the exchanges were not simultaneous.

Starker II

In 1977, the government filed against T.J. Starker; with the same court that had heard Starker I rule that a sale and purchase had taken place essentially reversing the first decision. (T.J. Starker v. U.S., 432 F. Supp. 864 D. C. Ore. 1977). Judge Solomon wrote he was mistaken in Starker I and stated "My opinion in Starker I has been given wide publicity. I believe that it is desirable that my opinion in this case be published to prevent the mischief that I believe Starker I has caused." He further wrote that T.J. Starker had exchanged real property for a promise that was not like-kind under the statute. He ruled that the growth factor was taxable as interest.

Starker III

The third and final case was T.J. Starker's appeal. (T.J. Starker v. U.S., 602 F. 2d 1341 9th Cir. 1979). The Ninth Circuit Court ruled that the government was collaterally estopped by Starker I from relitigating nine of the transfers overturned in Starker II.

Regarding the property transferred to Jean Roth, the court found no 1031 exchange because T.J. Starker did not receive the replacement property. The Court also found the contract to purchase investment property to be equivalent of a fee interest, therefore qualifying for an exchange. Finally, and most importantly for investors, the Court could not find any requirement for simultaneity in the 1031 tax code. The court ruled in favor of Starker. The **Starker exchange** was born!

This landmark decision enabled investors in the Ninth Circuit's eleven Western states to perform **delayed exchanges**. No longer did the investor need to struggle to force the simultaneous closing of both their sale and buy side properties for fear of destroying the transaction. The Ninth Circuit Court is an appellate court that establishes legal precedent for Federal District Courts; therefore, the Starker decision attracted national attention. However, it was not until many years later that further changes to the tax code made the Starker or delayed exchange a part of the federal tax code affecting investors on a national level.

Tax Reform

The *1984 Tax Reform Act* provided Congressional approval of the delayed exchange concept by establishing time limits for completing the exchange. Exchangors needed to identify their replacement property within 45 days from the close of escrow on the relinquished property. The entire exchange had to be completed within either 180 days after the date in which the Exchangor transferred the relinquished property, or the due date for the Exchangors' tax return in the taxable year in which the transfer of the relinquished property occurred, whichever came first. The Act also amended Section 1031(a)(2) to disallow exchanges of partnership interests.

With the *Tax Reform Act of 1986*, the loss of capital gains treatment removed all doubt of the value of the tax-deferred exchange. Enactment of the "Passive Loss" and "At Risk" rules substantially changed investors reasons for the purchase of real property.

In 1989, the *Revenue Reconciliation Act* specified that U.S. real property and non-U.S. real property were no longer considered "like-kind." This ended the exchange of real property in the continental United States for foreign property while deferring gain. This Act further imposed a two-year holding period for both parties in an exchange between related-party exchanges. Related parties included members of a family, such as brothers and sisters, spouses, ancestors, and lineal descendants.

Treasury Regulations 1991

Regulations adopted by the Treasury Department effective June 1, 1991, gave the investor an over all acceptance of the delayed or Starker exchange by the Treasury and the Internal Revenue Service, as well as some clarification of procedures and requirements.

The following are some of the highlights of the new proposed regulations affecting delayed or Starker exchanges under Section 1031:

ion

identification of the replacement property must still be made within 45 days. Property must be "designated in a written document signed by the taxpayer and hand delivered, mailed, telecopied, or otherwise sent before the end of the **identification period** to a person involved in the exchange other than the taxpayer or a related party." (Note: Under the new regulations the definition of **related party** and "related person" have been expanded. In some cases only 10% ownership of outstanding stock directly or indirectly may constitute a "prohibited relationship" for purposes of a related party.)

The replacement property must be unambiguously described in a written document or agreement. (A legal description or street address is acceptable.) If the transaction is structured with an Intermediary, the designation would be sent to the Intermediary.

The taxpayer may identify more than one property as replacement property; however, regardless of the number of **relinquished properties** transferred by the taxpayer as part of the same deferred exchange, the maximum number of replacement properties may be identified is either three (3) properties of any **fair market value**, or any number of properties as long as their aggregate fair market value at the end of the identification period does not exceed 200 percent of the fair market value of all the relinquished properties. Obviously, under these proposals it would be beneficial to anyone anticipating an exchange from more than one property to treat them as separate exchanges. It is unclear how this may be accomplished. In an industry meeting in Los Angeles in July 1991, a special assistant to the Associate Chief Counsel with the Internal Revenue Service, Washington, D.C., stated that the IRS can "step" a transaction or treat multiple transactions as one exchange if the purpose seems to be to avoid the restriction in replacement properties. It is not clear whether exchanging at different times through different escrows, different buyers, etc. would alleviate this risk.

If the identification period ends on a weekend or holiday, that is the date it ends, not the following workday. If at the end of the identification period, the taxpayer has identified more properties than permitted, the taxpayer is treated as if no replacement property has been identified. If the taxpayer designates too many replacement properties (either more than three or over 200 percent), the taxpayer is treated as though replacement property was not designed with two exceptions:

1. Property received before the end of the 45-day identification period will be treated as properly identified.

2. Replacement property received after the identification period can qualify as identified but only if the taxpayer receives at least 95% of the aggregate fair market value of all identified properties before the end of the **exchange period.**

Replacement Property

Replacement property must be purchased by the 180th day or the filing of taxes, whichever comes first, or must file an extension of his return to have the full 180 days. The **acquisition property** must be "substantially the same" as the property identified. If an exchangor wants to replace a property they have identified, they must do so by writing a letter of revocation to the third party substituting a qualified "like-kind" property in its place.

Safe Harbors

Cash received by the exchangor prior to completing the exchange will be treated as boot. The proposed regulations describe several **safe harbors** for avoiding actual or constructive receipt of cash proceeds and endangering the exchange:

1. A mortgage, deed of trust, or other security interest other than cash or its equivalent. This security may be a letter of credit.
2. A specific form or "qualified" trust or escrow.

    Note: this does not mean proceeds may be left in escrow after the close. This requires a separate relationship or "qualified escrow account to prevent the constructive receipt" of cash by the exchangor.
3. A **qualified intermediary** (facilitation company), who is not related to the exchangor. This does not mean the exchangor's mother, employee, real estate broker, accountant, or attorney. The intermediary must not be an agent for the exchangor.

Direct Deeding

Direct deeding should save the exchangor some document and recording fees charged in **sequential deeding**; however, some though should be used in making this decision. The paper trail created by direct deeding is not as clear as an audit trail. While many escrow holders are very knowledgeable about exchanges, in many parts of the country the escrow or closing process is handled by less experienced people. The reason for good documentation is to make the exchange obvious and to avoid any risk of misunderstanding by an agent of the IRS.

The new regulations are far more involved than this brief overview. Ironically, omitting simultaneous exchanges from the regulations may have been an oversight. If this is not clarified with the final regulations, it may cause the exchangor to avoid a simultaneous exchange in favor of the delayed exchange. **"Reverse" exchanges** have not yet been addressed. The regulations have introduced the idea of multiple classes of assets in a real property exchange (an idea that will at least mean full employment for accountant!). Regardless of these issues, the government has treated the taxpayer fairly. Finally, the IRS has given the investor some guidelines for a defensible exchange.

part **II**

Rules and Regulations

General Tax Deferrals: IRS Rules and Regulations

by Bernardine G. Marvel-Ames, CPA
Redding, CA

OVERVIEW

Rather than taxing investors on property as it appreciates for income tax purposes, property appreciation is generally taxed when the property is ultimately sold. Due to public policy considerations, the **Internal Revenue Code** carves out a number of exceptions to this general rule. In specific circumstances, property dispositions may be tax-free or tax-deferred. Many of the tax-deferral provisions are based on the premise that the taxpayer has continued his investment in the property or similar property.

Some of the major tax provisions for tax-deferred and tax-free property dispostions include:

TAX DEFERRED

- Installment gains (Section 453).

- Like-kind exchanges (Section 1031).

- Involuntary conversions (Section 1033).

- Rollover of gain on sale of principal residence (Section 1034).

- Property contributions to partnerships and corporations (Sections 751 and 351).

- Corporate mergers or consolidations (Section 368).

TAX FREE

- $125,000 one-time exclusions of gain from sale of principal residence by individual who has attained age 55 (Section 121).

It is beyond the purview of this book to address corporate mergers or partnership and corporate property contributions. Although there are numerous potential alternatives for property transfers, most real estate transfers fall into one of two categories: (1) the sale of a principal residence, or (2) the sale or exchange of property held for investment or used in a trade or business.

This chapter will focus primarily on the fundamental rules for personal residence sales and involuntary conversions in order to correlate these rules to like-kind exchanges.

Gain on Sale—General Property Dispositions

It is important to have a clear understanding of the general tax rules of property sales as a basis for analyzing the tax effects of alternatives. In the absence of a specific deferral or exclusion provision of the Internal Revenue Code, a property sale is taxable when consummated. In order to analyze the alternatives in effective tax planning, the total potential tax for the gain on sale of the property should first be determined. The total tax for a sale of property can then be compared to the tax for a deferral option. In addition to the total tax difference, variables such as timing of tax payments, cash availability, and projected **tax brackets** are all considered in evaluating a taxpayer's options.

As a brief review, IRC Section 1001 governs general property dispositions. The taxable gain on sale of property is defined as the "amount realized" over the "adjusted basis" of the property sold. The **amount realized** is essentially defined as the gross sales price of the property less selling costs such as commissions and escrow fees. The **adjusted basis** rules are contained in IRC Section 1016. In most cases, the adjusted basis is the original cost of the property net of any prior depreciation deductions, plus any capitalizable improvements.

Table 3.1 is a simplified example of a formula approach to determine the taxable gain for a property sale:

Table 3.1

Sales price	$ 200,000	
Less: selling expenses	(10,000)	
"Amount realized"	$ 190,000	$ 190,000
Original cost basis	$ 150,000	
Less: accumulated depreciation	(40,000)	
Adjusted basis	$ 110,000	110,000
Taxable gain on sale		$ 80,000

When property is acquired in a tax-deferred transaction, the adjusted basis is usually determined with reference to the previous property. The basis of the previous property, less any deferred gain becomes the adjusted basis of the new property acquired.

The timing mechanism for many tax-deferral techniques arise as a result of the adjusted basis provisions. Since the prior gain reduces the basis of the new property, the gain is merely deferred, and is ultimately taxable when the new property is sold (unless other exclusion or deferral provisions apply at that time).

SALE OF A PRINCIPAL RESIDENCE

Although this publication is not intended to be an extensive treatise regarding the sales of residences, the rudimentary provisions are outlined here for contrast and comparison to Section 1031 exchanges.

Under the general rules of IRC Section 1001, any resultant gain on the sale of a principal residence is taxable, unless the taxpayer qualifies for a specific exception. The two primary exceptions are (1) IRC Section 121, which allows taxpayers over the age of 55 to make a once-in-a-lifetime election to exclude up to $125,000 of gain, and (2) IRC Section 1034, which allows taxpayers to defer the gain on sale of a principal residence if a replacement residence is acquired within the statutory time limits.

Loss on Sale of a Principal Residence

Although any gain on the sale of a personal residence is potentially taxable, current tax law does not allow the deduction of a loss, unless the loss is a result of a casualty. At the time of this writing, Congress is considering tax bill proposals that would allow the deduction of losses on personal residences.

The loss on a personal residence is not deductible because the property is not used in a trade or business. However, the loss on the sale of a residential rental is deductible. Taxpayers in economically depressed areas who anticipate a large loss, may wish to consider the option of converting their residence to a residential rental. The determination of whether or not a property has been converted to a rental depends on the facts and circumstances, as a result of a long line of test cases. Taxpayers and their advisors who are considering this option should review these factors carefully.

IRC Section 1034 Requirements

Internal Revenue Code Section 1034 governs the taxation of a gain on the sale or transfer of a principal residence. If a replacement residence is acquired and used as a home either two years before or after the sale, the gain can be deferred and "rolled over" into the new residence. Similar to other deferral provisions in the Code, the gain is deferred because the basis of the new residence is reduced by the amount of any gain not recognized. It is important to note that the provisions of IRC Section 1034 are mandatory, not elective, unless an involuntary conversion has occurred (see the analysis for Section 1033 involuntary conversions in this chapter). If an involuntary conversion has occurred with respect to a principal residence, the taxpayer may elect the application of Section 1034 instead of Section 1033.

Commentators sometimes describe a residential reinvestment as a forward or a reverse rollover. With a "forward rollover," the taxpayer sells the old residence first, which must be replaced within a two-year period. In a "reverse rollover," the taxpayer buys a new residence first, and then must sell the old residence within two years.

Section 1034 Minimum Reinvestment Threshold

In order to defer the entire gain on the sale of a residence, a taxpayer must purchase a new residence for a price that equals or exceeds the "adjusted sales price" of the prior residence. The "adjusted sales price" determines the minimum reinvestment threshold. Occasionally, misinformed taxpayers are under the impression that the gain can be deferred if they rollover the equity from the old to the new residence. Unfortunately, this is incorrect. The critical factors in a qualified rollover are price, not equity or cash received.

One confusing aspect of Section 1034 is the application of the term "adjusted sales price." The concept itself is relatively simple: the **adjusted sales price** is the amount realized (sales price less selling expenses) less "qualified fixing up expenses." Fixing up expenses must be for work performed within 90 days before the sale, and must be paid within 30 days after the sale. These expenses must be for repairs, rather than capitalizable improvements.

The term "adjusted sales price" applies only to Section 1034 rollovers. If a residence is sold without any replacement at all, fixing up expenses are nondeductible because the taxpayer is outside of the provisions of Section 1034. When Section 1034 does apply, the effects of fixing up expenses in the formula are:

• A reduction of the minimum reinvestment threshold,

• A reduction of taxable gain in a partially qualified rollover.

Section 1034 Gain Calculations

In order to ascertain the tax effects for a residential rollover, three gain calculations must be performed:

• Total gain realized.

• Taxable gain.

• Gain deferred.

Once the above gain calculations have been performed, the basis for the new residence can be calculated as the purchase price of the new residence less deferred gain.

An example of a formula approach for the gain and adjusted basis calculations is contained in Figure 3.1.

Total Gain Realized

The total **realized gain** determines the total maximum taxable gain on the sale of a residence. If the homeowner does not reinvest within the two-year period, Section 1034 does not apply and the entire gain is taxable. The **total gain realized** on a principal residence is defined as the "amount realized" (sales price less selling expenses) less the adjusted basis of the old residence. The adjusted basis for a residence includes the original cost plus the cost of improvements less any depreciation deductions.

Figure 3.1   Section 1034 Residential Rollovers

Step 1: Total Gain Realized

1.	Sales price of prior residence	$_____
2.	Less: selling expenses	_____
3.	Amount realized	$_____
4.	Less: adjusted basis of residence sold	_____
5.	Total gain realized	$_____

Step 2: Taxable Gain

6.	Amount realized (from Line 3)	$_____
7.	Less: fixing up expenses	_____
8.	Adjusted sales price	$_____

Taxable gain limitation:

9.	Adjusted sales price (from Line 8)	$_____
10.	Purchase price of new residence	_____
11.	Taxable gain	$_____

Note: if the purchase price of the new residence exceeds the adjusted sales price of the prior residence, the taxable gain is zero.

Step 3: Deferred Gain

12.	Total gain realized (from Line 5)	$_____
13.	Less: taxable gain (from Line 11)	_____
14.	Deferred gain	$_____

Step 4: Basis of New Residence

15.	Purchase price of new residence	$_____
16.	Less: deferred gain (from Line 14)	_____
17.	Basis of new residence	$_____

Taxable and Deferred Gain

If the purchase price of the replacement residence exceeds the "adjusted sales price" of the old residence, none of the gain is currently taxable. In this circumstance, all of the gain is deferred and rolled over into the basis of the new residence. To conceptualize these mechanics, the taxpayer has continued his investment. However, because of the differences between loan amounts for the old and new properties, in real life the taxpayer may be in a positive or negative cash position.

When the price of the new residence is less than the adjusted sales price of the prior home, a taxable gain is recognized. However, the taxable gain is limited to the amount that the adjusted sales price of the old residence exceeds the cost of the new residence. For this situation, the deferred gain is the balance of the total gain realized less the taxable gain. Theoretically, the taxpayer has not continued his property investment by the amount of these price differences. Again, it is important to observe that the taxpayer may be in a positive or negative cash position due to differences in the loan amounts.

Example #1: Section 1034 Deferred Gain Calculations

Assume John Smith has sold his residence for $100,000, which had an adjusted basis of $50,000. His expenses to sell the residence amounted to $6,000. He purchases a new home within the two-year replacement period for $91,000 and incurs $1,000 of fixing up expenses. The gain calculations for John Smith are as follows:

Step 1: Total Gain Realized

Sales price	$100,000
Less: selling expenses	(6,000)
Amount realized	$ 94,000
Adjusted basis of residence sold	(50,000)
Total gain realized	$ 44,000

Note: John's fixing up expenses do not reduce the total gain realized.

Step 2: Taxable Gain

In order to determine the total taxable gain and the reinvestment threshold for the new residence, the adjusted sales price must be determined. The adjusted sales price is the amount realized less qualified fixing up expenses, as illustrated below:

Amount realized	$ 94,000
Less: fixing up expenses	(1,000)
Adjusted Sales Price	$ 93,000

Since John has purchased a replacement residence for less than the adjusted sales price of the previous residence, he must recognize a taxable gain. However, of the total gain realized of $44,000, his taxable gain is limited to the excess of the adjusted sales price for the old residence over the purchase price of the new residence:

Adjusted sales price	$ 93,000
Purchase price—new residence	(91,000)
Taxable gain	$ 2,000

Step 3: Deferred Gain

The deferred gain that John may rollover into his new residence is the difference between the total gain realized and the amount which is currently taxable.

Total gain realized	$ 44,000
Less: taxable gain	(2,000)
Deferred gain	$ 42,000

Step 4: Basis of New Residence

John's basis in his new residence is his cost less the deferred gain that has been rolled over from the previous residence:

Purchase price—new residence	$ 91,000
Less: deferred gain	(42,000)
Basis of new residence	$ 49,000

An example of IRS Form 2119 for the above transaction is illustrated as Figure 3.2.

Example #2: Section 1034 Deferred Gain Calculations

Assume the same facts as in Example #1, except that John Smith has acquired a replacement residence for $94,000. Since the price of the new residence exceeds the adjusted sales price for the prior residence ($93,000), all of the gain is deferred and rolled over into the new residence. None of the gain is currently taxable. The basis for the new residence is $50,000 ($94,000 purchase price less deferred gain of $44,000).

An example of IRS Form 2119 for this transaction is illustrated as Figure 3.3.

Other Provisions Under IRC Section 1034

If multiple residences are purchased within two years after a sale, only the last residence will qualify as a replacement residence. If an additional resi-

Figure 3.2 Sale of Your Home (2119) John Smith

Form **2119**	**Sale of Your Home**	OMB No. 1545-0072
Department of the Treasury Internal Revenue Service	▶ Attach to Form 1040 for year of sale. ▶ See separate instructions. ▶ Please print or type.	**1991** Attachment Sequence No. **20**

Your first name and initial. (If joint return, also give spouse's name and initial.) JOHN	Last name SMITH	Your social security number 123 : 45 : 6789
Fill In Your Address Only If You Are Filing This Form by Itself and Not With Your Tax Return	Present address (no., street, and apt. no.; rural route, or P.O. box no. If mail is not delivered to street address) City, town or post office, state, and ZIP code	Spouse's social security number : :

Caution: *If the home sold was financed (in whole or part) from a mortgage credit certificate or the proceeds of a tax-exempt qualified mortgage bond, you may owe additional tax. Get **Form 8828**, Recapture of Federal Mortgage Subsidy, for details.*

Part I   General Information

1a	Date your former main home was sold (month, day, year) . . . . ▶ **1a**	11/30 /91
b	Face amount of any mortgage, note (e.g., second trust), or other financial instrument on which you will get periodic payments of principal or interest from this sale (see instructions) . . . **1b**	-0-
2	Have you bought or built a new main home? . . .	☒ Yes ☐ No
3	Is or was any part of either main home rented out or used for business? (If "Yes," see instructions.) . .	☐ Yes ☒ No

Part II   Gain on Sale (Do not include amounts you deduct as moving expenses.)

4	Selling price of home. (Do not include personal property items that you sold with your home.) **4**	100,000
5	Expense of sale. (Include sales commissions, advertising, legal, etc.). **5**	6,000
6	Amount realized. Subtract line 5 from line 4 . . . . **6**	94,000
7	Basis of home sold (see instructions) **7**	50,000
8a	**Gain on sale.** Subtract line 7 from line 6 . . . . **8a**	44,000

● If line 8a is zero or less, stop here and attach this form to your return.
● If line 2 is "Yes," you **must** go to Part III or Part IV, whichever applies. Otherwise, go to line 8b.

b	If you haven't replaced your home, do you plan to do so within the replacement period (see instructions)?	☐ Yes ☐ No

● If "Yes," stop here, attach this form to your return, and see **Additional Filing Requirements** in the instructions.
● If "No," you **must** go to Part III or Part IV, whichever applies.

Part III   One-Time Exclusion of Gain for People Age 55 or Older (If you are not taking the exclusion, go to Part IV now.)

9a	Who was age 55 or older on date of sale?. . . . . ☐ You ☐ Your spouse	☐ Both of you
b	Did the person who was age 55 or older own and use the property as his or her main home for a total of at least 3 years (except for short absences) of the 5-year period before the sale? (If "No," go to Part IV now.)	☐ Yes ☐ No
c	**If line 9b is "Yes,"** do you elect to take the one-time exclusion? (If "No," go to Part IV now.) . . .	☐ Yes ☐ No
d	At time of sale, who owned the home?. . . . . ☐ You ☐ Your spouse	☐ Both of you
e	Social security number of spouse at time of sale if you had a different spouse from the one above at time of sale. (If you were not married at time of sale, enter "None.") . . . . . ▶ **9e**	: :
f	**Exclusion.** Enter the **smaller** of line 8a or $125,000 ($62,500, if married filing separate return) **9f**	

Part IV   Adjusted Sales Price, Taxable Gain, and Adjusted Basis of New Home

10	Subtract line 9f from line 8a **10**	44,000

● If line 10 is zero, stop here and attach this form to your return.
● If line 2 is "Yes," go to line 11 now.
● If you are reporting this sale on the installment method, stop here and see the line 1b instructions.
● All others, stop here and **enter the amount from line 10 on Schedule D, line 2 or line 9.**

11	Fixing-up expenses (see instructions for time limits) **11**	1,000
12	**Adjusted sales price.** Subtract line 11 from line 6 . . . . **12**	93,000
13a	Date you moved into new home (month, day, year) ▶ 12 /15/ 91 b Cost of new home **13b**	91,000
14a	Add line 9f and line 13b **14a**	91,000
b	Subtract line 14a from line 12. If the result is zero or less, enter -0- **14b**	2,000
c	**Taxable gain.** Enter the **smaller** of line 10 or line 14b **14c**	2,000

● If line 14c is zero, go to line 15 and attach this form to your return.
● If you are reporting this sale on the installment method, see the line 1b instructions and go to line 15.
● All others, **enter the amount from line 14c on Schedule D, line 2 or line 9,** and go to line 15.

15	**Postponed gain.** Subtract line 14c from line 10 . . . . **15**	42,000
16	**Adjusted basis of new home.** Subtract line 15 from line 13b **16**	49,000

Sign Here Only If You Are Filing This Form by Itself and Not With Your Tax Return	Under penalties of perjury, I declare that I have examined this form, including attachments, and to the best of my knowledge and belief, it is true, correct, and complete.		
	Your signature	Date	Spouse's signature	Date
	(If a joint return, both must sign.) ▶		

For Paperwork Reduction Act Notice, see separate instructions.   Cat. No. 11710J   Form **2119** (1991)

Figure 3.3   Sale of Your Home (2119) John Smith

Form **2119**	**Sale of Your Home**	OMB No. 1545-0072
Department of the Treasury Internal Revenue Service	▶ Attach to Form 1040 for year of sale. ▶ See separate instructions. ▶ Please print or type.	**19**91 Attachment Sequence No. **20**

Your first name and initial. (If joint return, also give spouse's name and initial.)	Last name	Your social security number
JOHN	SMITH	123 : 45 : 6789

Fill in Your Address Only If You Are Filing This Form by Itself and Not With Your Tax Return	Present address (no., street, and apt. no., rural route, or P.O. box no. If mail is not delivered to street address)	Spouse's social security number
	City, town or post office, state, and ZIP code	: :

Caution: *If the home sold was financed (in whole or part) from a mortgage credit certificate or the proceeds of a tax-exempt qualified mortgage bond, you may owe additional tax. Get Form 8828, Recapture of Federal Mortgage Subsidy, for details.*

Part I   General Information

1a	Date your former main home was sold (month, day, year) . . . . ▶	**1a**	11 / 30 / 91
b	Face amount of any mortgage, note (e.g., second trust), or other financial instrument on which you will get periodic payments of principal or interest from this sale (see instructions) . . .	**1b**	-0-
2	Have you bought or built a new main home? . . . . ☒ Yes ☐ No		
3	Is or was any part of either main home rented out or used for business? (If "Yes," see instructions.) . . ☐ Yes ☒ No		

Part II   Gain on Sale (Do not include amounts you deduct as moving expenses.)

4	Selling price of home. (Do not include personal property items that you sold with your home.)	**4**	100,000
5	Expense of sale. (Include sales commissions, advertising, legal, etc.)	**5**	6,000
6	Amount realized. Subtract line 5 from line 4	**6**	94,000
7	Basis of home sold (see instructions)	**7**	50,000
8a	Gain on sale. Subtract line 7 from line 6	**8a**	44,000

 • If line 8a is zero or less, stop here and attach this form to your return.
 • If line 2 is "Yes," you **must** go to Part III or Part IV, whichever applies. Otherwise, go to line 8b.
 b If you haven't replaced your home, do you plan to do so within the replacement period (see instructions)? ☐ Yes ☐ No
 • If "Yes," stop here, attach this form to your return, and see **Additional Filing Requirements** in the instructions.
 • If "No," you **must** go to Part III or Part IV, whichever applies.

Part III   One-Time Exclusion of Gain for People Age 55 or Older (If you are not taking the exclusion, go to Part IV now.)

9a	Who was age 55 or older on date of sale? . . . . ☐ You ☐ Your spouse ☐ Both of you		
b	Did the person who was age 55 or older own and use the property as his or her main home for a total of at least 3 years (except for short absences) of the 5-year period before the sale? (If "No," go to Part IV now.) ☐ Yes ☐ No		
c	If line 9b is "Yes," do you elect to take the one-time exclusion? (If "No," go to Part IV now.) . . . ☐ Yes ☐ No		
d	At time of sale, who owned the home? . . . . ☐ You ☐ Your spouse ☐ Both of you		
e	Social security number of spouse at time of sale if you had a different spouse from the one above at time of sale. (If you were not married at time of sale, enter "None.") . . . . . ▶	**9e**	: :
f	**Exclusion.** Enter the **smaller** of line 8a or $125,000 ($62,500, if married filing separate return)	**9f**	

Part IV   Adjusted Sales Price, Taxable Gain, and Adjusted Basis of New Home

10	Subtract line 9f from line 8a	**10**	44,000

 • If line 10 is zero, stop here and attach this form to your return.
 • If line 2 is "Yes," go to line 11 now.
 • If you are reporting this sale on the installment method, stop here and see the line 1b instructions.
 • All others, stop here and **enter the amount from line 10 on Schedule D, line 2 or line 9.**

11	Fixing-up expenses (see instructions for time limits)	**11**	1,000
12	**Adjusted sales price.** Subtract line 11 from line 6	**12**	93,000
13a	Date you moved into new home (month, day, year) ▶ 12/15/91 b Cost of new home	**13b**	94,000
14a	Add line 9f and line 13b	**14a**	94,000
b	Subtract line 14a from line 12. If the result is zero or less, enter -0-	**14b**	-0-
c	**Taxable gain.** Enter the **smaller** of line 10 or line 14b	**14c**	-0-

 • If line 14c is zero, go to line 15 and attach this form to your return.
 • If you are reporting this sale on the installment method, see the line 1b instructions and go to line 15.
 • All others, **enter the amount from line 14c on Schedule D, line 2 or line 9,** and go to line 15.

15	Postponed gain. Subtract line 14c from line 10	**15**	44,000
16	Adjusted basis of new home. Subtract line 15 from line 13b	**16**	50,000

Sign Here Only If You Are Filing This Form by Itself and Not With Your Tax Return	Under penalties of perjury, I declare that I have examined this form, including attachments, and to the best of my knowledge and belief, it is true, correct, and complete.		
	Your signature	Date	Spouse's signature Date
	▶		▶
	(If a joint return, both must sign.)		

For Paperwork Reduction Act Notice, see separate instructions.   Cat. No. 11710J   Form **2119** (1991)

dence is purchased and sold, any gain realized is fully taxable, unless the sale was caused by a job-related move.

For members of the armed forces who are on active duty, the two-year replacement period is suspended, up to a maximum four-year extension period. In some cases, the replacement period may be extended up to an eight year limit for members of the armed forces who are stationed outside of the United States.

Residential Rollovers in Contrast to Like-Kind Exchanges

With a Section 1034 transaction, the taxable gain is calculated without regard to whether the taxpayer ends up in a positive cash position. In contrast, however, cash received in a Section 1031 like-kind exchange results in taxable "boot," which is determined specifically by the amount of cash or other property received. Furthermore, if a taxpayer's equity in the old residence is insufficient for the down payment, the taxpayer may be in a deficit cash position with little or no ability to pay the tax.

Section 1034 allows a taxpayer to reinvest his property by selling the old residence and purchasing a new residence. Like-kind exchanges, however, theoretically constitute a swap of properties. A property sale followed by a purchase of new property will not qualify as a like-kind exchange. However, an exchange can be effectuated with a transfer to an intermediary who subsequently transfer new property to the taxpayer, as long as the taxpayer does not have access to any cash proceeds.

While a reverse rollover is allowed for a principal residence (purchase of new property followed by a sale of the old property), the statute and regulations under Section 1031 specifically do not address a reversed transaction.

IRC Section 121 Requirements

Under IRC Section 121, taxpayers over age 55 may make a once-in-a-lifetime election to exclude a maximum of $125,000 of the gain on sale of a principal residence. In contrast to the rollover roles that function to defer the timing for payment of tax, the over 55 election provides a permanent exclusion of tax.

To qualify for the exclusion election, a taxpayer must be at least age 55. For most tax rules, the taxpayer's age as of the end of the year is the governing factor. However, to qualify for Section 121, it is important to distinguish that although a taxpayer may reach age 55 in a tax year, any sale before the actual birthdate will not qualify for the exclusion election.

Additionally, the taxpayer must own and occupy the home as a principal residence for a total of at least three years out of the five-year period prior to the sale.

Married taxpayers, who file separate tax returns are each allowed an exclusion of up to $62,500 on their respective returns. If a residence that is owned by a married couple is held as joint tenant or community property, both spouses are deemed to satisfy the age, use and holding requirements, as long as one spouse can satisfy these requirements. Generally, the taxpayer's marital status as of the end of the tax year governs marital status treatment for the entire year. However, under Section 121, the taxpayer's marital status is determined as of the date of the sale.

The Tainted Spouse

One of the practical peculiarities of a Section 121 election is the effect on divorced taxpayers. Usually, both spouses are treated as a single taxpayer when filing an exclusion election on a joint return for married couples. With community property, both taxpayers are deemed to qualify and both spouses are deemed to have used the once-in-a-lifetime election, regardless of whether one or both spouses actually qualified. After a Section 121 election has been filed on a joint return, neither spouse may make another election if they are subsequently divorced. Since the elections are denied to these divorced taxpayers, they carry "tax taint" to future marital partners. Future marital partners may only exclude up to $62,500 of gain on a separate tax return.

Section 121 Gain Calculations

The **total gain realized** is determined in the usual manner as: sales price net of selling expenses, less the adjusted basis of the residence sold. If the taxpayer does not acquire a replacement residence, any gain in excess of $125,000 is taxable.

If a taxpayer has realized total gain exceeding the maximum of $125,000 excludable, but has acquired a replacement residence, the taxpayer may take advantage of both the exclusion and deferral provisions of the Internal Revenue Code. All or a portion of the gain in excess of $125,000 may be deferred and rolled over into the new residence.

Example #3: Section 121 Gain Calculations—No Rollover

To illustrate the mechanics of a Section 121 election, assume Mary Marks has sold her residence at a price of $230,000. Her selling expenses were $15,000 and the basis on her prior home was $65,000. She was age 59 on

the date of sale, and has owned and occupied the home as her principal
residence for 25 years. Her taxable gain is calculated below:

Sales price	$ 230,000
Less: selling expenses	(15,000)
Amount realized	215,000
Less: adjusted basis	(65,000)
Total gain realized	150,000
Less: gain excluded under Section 121	(125,000)
Taxable **gain recognized**	$ 25,000

Of Mary Marks' $150,000 of total gain realized, $125,000 of the gain
may be excluded if Mary makes the Section 121 election on her tax return.
The remaining $25,000 of gain is fully taxable, because Mary has not ac-
quired a replacement residence.

Example #4: Section 121 Gain Calculations & Section 1034 Rollover

Bill and Sally Jones both meet the age and holding criteria under Section
121. They sell their home with a basis of $90,000 for $280,000, and incur
$20,000 of selling expenses. They paid for $1,000 of fixing up expenses in
order to facilitate the sale. Their total gain realized is as follows:

Sales price	$ 280,000
Less: selling expenses	(20,000)
Amount realized	$ 260,000
Adjusted basis of residence sold	(90,000)
Total gain realized	$ 170,000

To establish the minimum reinvestment threshold for a Section 1034
rollover combined with a Section 121 exclusion, the adjusted sales price is
reduced by the excluded gain:

Amount realized ($280,000-$20,000) $ 260,000	
Less: fixing up expenses	(1,000)
Section 121 excluded gain	(125,000)
Revised adjusted sales price	$ 134,000

If the Jones reinvest in a replacement residence with a price of at least
$134,000, the gain in excess of $125,000 may be deferred under the rollover rules. If the price of the new residence is less than $134,000, a por-
tion of the gain is taxable. Assuming that the cost of the Jones' new home
is $115,000, their taxable gain is:

Revised adjusted sales price	$ 134,000
Purchase price—new residence	(115,000)
Taxable gain	$ 19,000

The deferred gain that the Jones may rollover into their new residence is the total gain realized adjusted for the Section 121 gain excluded less the current taxable gain:

Total gain realized	$ 170,000
Less: Section 121 gain excluded	(125,000)
Less: taxable gain	(19,000)
Deferred gain	$ 26,000

Step 4: Basis of New Residence

Bill and Sally Jones' basis in their new residence is their cost of the new home reduced by the deferred gain that has been rolled over from the previous residence:

Purchase price - new residence	$ 115,000
Less: deferred gain	(26,000)
Basis of new residence	$ 89,000

An example of IRS Form 2119 for the above transaction is illustrated as Figure 3.4.

Example #5: Section 121 Gain Calculations & Section 1034 Rollover

Assume the same facts as in Example #4, except that Bill and Sally Jones have purchased a replacement residence for $135,000. Since the price of the new residence exceeds the adjusted sales price for the prior residence ($134,000), all of the gain is deferred and rolled over into the new residence. None of the gain is currently taxable. The basis for the new residence is $90,000 ($135,000 purchase price less deferred gain of $45,000). All of the gain in excess of the $125,000 that is excludable under Section 121 is deferred:

Total gain realized	$ 170,000
Less: Section 121 excluded gain	(125,000)
Less: taxable gain	(–0–)
Deferred gain	$ 45,000

An example of IRS Form 2119 for the above transaction is illustrated as Figure 3-5.

Section 1034 and Section 121 Wealth Maximizing Strategies

The gain exclusions under Section 121 do not constitute a tax deferral arising from an exchange. However, the basic requirements have been delineated here to demonstrate one of the most significant wealth maximizing strategies available for average taxpayers. If carefully planned and orchestrated, a taxpayer can rollover gains from each residence sold during

Figure 3.4 Sale of Your Home (2119) Bill and Sally Jones

Form **2119**	Sale of Your Home	OMB No. 1545-0072
Department of the Treasury Internal Revenue Service	▶ Attach to Form 1040 for year of sale. ▶ See separate instructions. ▶ Please print or type.	**1991** Attachment Sequence No. **20**

Your first name and initial. (If joint return, also give spouse's name and initial.)	Last name	Your social security number
BILL & SALLY	JONES	987 : 65 : 4321

Fill In Your Address Only If You Are Filing This Form by Itself and Not With Your Tax Return

Present address (no., street, and apt. no., rural route, or P.O. box no. if mail is not delivered to street address) | Spouse's social security number

City, town or post office, state, and ZIP code

Caution: *If the home sold was financed (in whole or part) from a mortgage credit certificate or the proceeds of a tax-exempt qualified mortgage bond, you may owe additional tax. Get Form 8828, Recapture of Federal Mortgage Subsidy, for details.*

Part I General Information

1a	Date your former main home was sold (month, day, year) . . . . ▶	**1a**	7 / 15 / 91
b	Face amount of any mortgage, note (e.g., second trust), or other financial instrument on which you will get periodic payments of principal or interest from this sale (see instructions) . . .	**1b**	–0–
2	Have you bought or built a new main home?		☒ Yes ☐ No
3	Is or was any part of either main home rented out or used for business? (If "Yes," see instructions.) . .		☐ Yes ☒ No

Part II Gain on Sale (Do not include amounts you deduct as moving expenses.)

4	Selling price of home. (Do not include personal property items that you sold with your home.)	**4**	280,000
5	Expense of sale. (Include sales commissions, advertising, legal, etc.)	**5**	20,000
6	Amount realized. Subtract line 5 from line 4	**6**	260,000
7	Basis of home sold (see instructions)	**7**	90,000
8a	**Gain on sale.** Subtract line 7 from line 6	**8a**	170,000

  • If line 8a is zero or less, stop here and attach this form to your return.
  • If line 2 is "Yes," you **must** go to Part III or Part IV, whichever applies. Otherwise, go to line 8b.

b	If you haven't replaced your home, do you plan to do so within the replacement period (see instructions)?		☐ Yes ☐ No

  • If "Yes," stop here, attach this form to your return, and see **Additional Filing Requirements** in the instructions.
  • If "No," you **must** go to Part III or Part IV, whichever applies.

Part III One-Time Exclusion of Gain for People Age 55 or Older (If you are not taking the exclusion, go to Part IV now.)

9a	Who was age 55 or older on date of sale?	☐ You ☐ Your spouse ☒ Both of you	
b	Did the person who was age 55 or older own and use the property as his or her main home for a total of at least 3 years (except for short absences) of the 5-year period before the sale? (If "No," go to Part IV now.)	☒ Yes ☐ No	
c	If line 9b is "Yes," do you elect to take the one-time exclusion? (If "No," go to Part IV now.) . . .	☒ Yes ☐ No	
d	At time of sale, who owned the home?	☐ You ☐ Your spouse ☒ Both of you	
e	Social security number of spouse at time of sale if you had a different spouse from the one above at time of sale. (If you were not married at time of sale, enter "None.") . . . . . ▶	**9e**	: :
f	**Exclusion.** Enter the **smaller** of line 8a or $125,000 ($62,500, if married filing separate return)	**9f**	125,000

Part IV Adjusted Sales Price, Taxable Gain, and Adjusted Basis of New Home

10	Subtract line 9f from line 8a	**10**	45,000

  • If line 10 is zero, stop here and attach this form to your return.
  • If line 2 is "Yes," go to line 11 now.
  • If you are reporting this sale on the installment method, stop here and see the line 1b instructions.
  • All others, stop here and **enter the amount from line 10 on Schedule D, line 2 or line 9.**

11	Fixing-up expenses (see instructions)	**11**	1,000
12	**Adjusted sales price.** Subtract line 11 from line 6	**12**	259,000
13a	Date you moved into new home (month, day, year) ▶ 8 /27 / 91 **b** Cost of new home	**13b**	115,000
14a	Add line 9f and line 13b	**14a**	240,000
b	Subtract line 14a from line 12. If the result is zero or less, enter -0-	**14b**	19,000
c	**Taxable gain.** Enter the **smaller** of line 10 or line 14b	**14c**	19,000

  • If line 14c is zero, go to line 15 and attach this form to your return.
  • If you are reporting this sale on the installment method, see the line 1b instructions and go to line 15.
  • All others, **enter the amount from line 14c on Schedule D, line 2 or line 9,** and go to line 15.

15	Postponed gain. Subtract line 14c from line 10	**15**	26,000
16	**Adjusted basis of new home.** Subtract line 15 from line 13b	**16**	89,000

Sign Here Only If You Are Filing This Form by Itself and Not With Your Tax Return

Under penalties of perjury, I declare that I have examined this form, including attachments, and to the best of my knowledge and belief, it is true, correct, and complete.

Your signature _____ Date _____ Spouse's signature _____ Date _____

(If a joint return, both must sign.)

For Paperwork Reduction Act Notice, see separate instructions.   Cat. No. 11710J   Form **2119** (1991)

Figure 3.5 Sale of Your Home (2119) Bill and Sally Jones

Form **2119**	**Sale of Your Home**	OMB No. 1545-0072
	▶ Attach to Form 1040 for year of sale.	**1991**
Department of the Treasury Internal Revenue Service	▶ See separate instructions. ▶ Please print or type.	Attachment Sequence No. **20**

Your first name and initial. (If joint return, also give spouse's name and initial.)	Last name	Your social security number
BILL & SALLY	JONES	987 65 : 4321

Fill in Your Address Only If You Are Filing This Form by Itself and Not With Your Tax Return	Present address (no., street, and apt. no., rural route, or P.O. box no. If mail is not delivered to street address)	Spouse's social security number
	City, town or post office, state, and ZIP code	: :

Caution: *If the home sold was financed (in whole or part) from a mortgage credit certificate or the proceeds of a tax-exempt qualified mortgage bond, you may owe additional tax. Get* **Form 8828,** *Recapture of Federal Mortgage Subsidy, for details.*

Part I General Information

1a	Date your former main home was sold (month, day, year) . . . . ▶	1a	7 / 15 / 91
b	Face amount of any mortgage, note (e.g., second trust), or other financial instrument on which you will get periodic payments of principal or interest from this sale (see instructions) . . .	1b	–0–
2	Have you bought or built a new main home?		☒ Yes ☐ No
3	Is or was any part of either main home rented out or used for business? (If "Yes," see instructions.) . .		☐ Yes ☒ No

Part II Gain on Sale (Do not include amounts you deduct as moving expenses.)

4	Selling price of home. (Do not include personal property items that you sold with your home.)	4	280,000
5	Expense of sale. (Include sales commissions, advertising, legal, etc.)	5	20,000
6	Amount realized. Subtract line 5 from line 4	6	260,000
7	Basis of home sold (see instructions)	7	90,000
8a	**Gain on sale.** Subtract line 7 from line 6	8a	170,000

- If line 8a is zero or less, stop here and attach this form to your return.
- If line 2 is "Yes," you **must** go to Part III or Part IV, whichever applies. Otherwise, go to line 8b.

b	If you haven't replaced your home, do you plan to do so within the replacement period (see instructions)?		☐ Yes ☐ No

- If "Yes," stop here, attach this form to your return, and see **Additional Filing Requirements** in the instructions.
- If "No," you **must** go to Part III or Part IV, whichever applies.

Part III One-Time Exclusion of Gain for People Age 55 or Older (If you are not taking the exclusion, go to Part IV now.)

9a	Who was age 55 or older on date of sale? . . . . ☐ You ☐ Your spouse		☒ Both of you
b	Did the person who was age 55 or older own and use the property as his or her main home for a total of at least 3 years (except for short absences) of the 5-year period before the sale? (If "No," go to Part IV now.)		☒ Yes ☐ No
c	If line 9b is "Yes," do you elect to take the one-time exclusion? (If "No," go to Part IV now.) . . .		☒ Yes ☐ No
d	At time of sale, who owned the home? . . . . ☐ You ☐ Your spouse		☒ Both of you
e	Social security number of spouse at time of sale if you had a different spouse from the one above at time of sale. (If you were not married at time of sale, enter "None.") . . . . . . ▶	9e	: :
f	**Exclusion.** Enter the **smaller** of line 8a or $125,000 ($62,500, if married filing separate return)	9f	125,000

Part IV Adjusted Sales Price, Taxable Gain, and Adjusted Basis of New Home

10	Subtract line 9f from line 8a	10	45,000

- If line 10 is zero, stop here and attach this form to your return.
- If line 2 is "Yes," go to line 11 now.
- If you are reporting this sale on the installment method, stop here and see the line 1b instructions.
- All others, stop here and **enter the amount from line 10 on Schedule D, line 2 or line 9.**

11	Fixing-up expenses (see instructions for time limits)	11	1,000
12	**Adjusted sales price.** Subtract line 11 from line 6	12	259,000
13a	Date you moved into new home (month, day, year) ▶	8 / 27 / 91	b Cost of new home	13b	135,000
14a	Add line 9f and line 13b	14a	260,000
b	Subtract line 14a from line 12. If the result is zero or less, enter -0-	14b	–0–
c	**Taxable gain.** Enter the **smaller** of line 10 or line 14b	14c	–0–

- If line 14c is zero, go to line 15 and attach this form to your return.
- If you are reporting this sale on the installment method, see the line 1b instructions and go to line 15.
- All others, **enter the amount from line 14c on Schedule D, line 2 or line 9,** and go to line 15.

15	Postponed gain. Subtract line 14c from line 10	15	45,000
16	**Adjusted basis of new home.** Subtract line 15 from line 13b	16	90,000

Sign Here Only If You Are Filing This Form by Itself and Not With Your Tax Return	Under penalties of perjury, I declare that I have examined this form, including attachments, and to the best of my knowledge and belief, it is true, correct, and complete.		
	Your signature	Date	Spouse's signature	Date
	(If a joint return, both must sign.)	▶		

For Paperwork Reduction Act Notice, see separate instructions. Cat. No. 11710J Form **2119** (1991)

an entire lifetime, each time trading up to a more expensive home and deferring the entire gain. Ultimately, after the age of 55, a taxpayer can exclude up to $125,000 of gain and, if necessary, defer all or a portion of any excess with another rollover residence. The effect of a Section 121 exclusion combined with the Section 1034 rollover provisions potentially saves thousands of tax dollars.

Holding Period

Under current law, capital gains and losses qualify for long-term capital gains and losses, if the property sold has been held by the taxpayer for over a year prior to the sale. For residences that have been acquired in a qualifying Section 1034 rollover, the holding period for the new residence includes the holding period of the prior residence (Section 1223(7)). Thus, if a replacement residence is subsequently sold in a taxable disposition before the taxpayer has held that residence for one year, the holding period of the prior residence may be included in the total holding period. If the total holding period exceeds one year, the taxpayer qualifies for long-term capital gain treatment for the taxable sale.

IRC SECTION 1033:   DEFERRED GAIN FROM INVOLUNTARY CONVERSIONS

Section 1033 provides that taxable gain can be deferred when an involuntary conversion has occurred. Similar to other deferral mechanisms of the Internal Revenue Code, Section 1033 requires that the taxpayer reinvest in other qualifying property; the deferral is created by reducing the cost basis of the new property by the amount of gain that is not currently taxable. When the new property is sold, the deferred gain is eventually taxable.

Under Section 1033, the replacement property for involuntary conversions may be acquired directly or indirectly. In a "direct conversion," the property is compulsorily transferred in exchange for replacement property. In an "indirect conversion," the property is sold; the cash proceeds are then used to acquire the replacement property.

Unlike residential rollovers (Section 1034) and like-kind exchanges (Section 1031), gain deferrals for involuntary conversions under Section 1033 may be elective or mandatory. When a direct property conversion occurs (exchange), the gain deferral is mandatory (Section 1033(a)(1)). With an indirect property conversion, the gain may be deferred only if the taxpayer so elects; in the absence of an election, the gain is fully taxable (Section 1033(a)(2)).

The involuntary conversion statute applies to property that is "compulsorily or involuntarily converted" into other property that is "similar or related in service or use" to the original property. The replacement property must be acquired within the prescribed time frame. Furthermore, the statute applies only to transactions that result in a realized gain. The tax treatment for losses are governed by other sections of the Code—most notably:

1. Section 1231, which encompasses loss dispositions of property used in a trade or business, whether the loss arises as a usual sale or from fire, storm, shipwreck, theft, or other casualty.

2. Section 165, which encompasses loss dispositions of property not associated with a trade or business, when the loss arises from fire, storm, shipwreck, theft, or other casualty exceeding $100. Section 165 applies only to individual taxpayers.

3. Section 1211, which imposes limitations on capital loss deductions for corporate and noncorporate taxpayers.

While it is important to recognize that loss deductions may be allowable as governed by other areas of the statute, this chapter will focus primarily on the aspects of Section 1033 deferred gains.

Section 1033 Criteria: Compulsory or Involuntary Conversion

Section 1033 gains are not defined in the same terminology as casualty gains and losses. While there is some overlap in definitions, it is important to note that these terms are not entirely analogous. As embodied by the statute, Section 1033 involuntary conversions are comprised of property dispositions resulting from its destruction, theft, seizure, requisition, condemnation, or threat or imminence thereof. In broad terms, the compulsory destruction or theft of property is akin to the provisions for casualty gains and losses. However, the compulsory seizure or condemnation of property is generally beyond the general scope of other areas of the Code pertaining to casualties.

The IRS generally interprets Section 1033 to apply to property destruction that is beyond the control of the taxpayer. For example, when a taxpayer hired an arsonist to burn his building, the IRS ruled that Section 1033 did not apply (Rev. Rul. 82-74, 1982-1, C.B.110).

The interpretation of a "threat or imminence" of a condemnation proceeding has been developed over a number of years by case law and IRS rulings. The threat of a condemnation proceeding generally exists, if the taxpayer reasonably believes the condemnation proceeding will take place (Joseph P. Ballistrieri, T.C. Memo, 1979-115). However, in ruling on potential condemnations, the IRS has required that the taxpayer receive a written confirmation from the governmental body to establish that there is a reasonable threat or imminence thereof (Rev. Rul. 63-221, 1963-2 C.B. 332). In another case reviewed by the First Circuit, the taxpayer sold one tract of property under threat of condemnation; the Tax Court held that the second tract did not qualify for Section 1033 because the public authority sought only a voluntary condemnation for the second tract as indicated in its correspondence (*Forest City Chevrolet v. Comr.* 36 T.C. Memo 768 (1977)). Taxpayers and their advisors should carefully evaluate what factors will constitute a satisfactory written confirmation for purposes of Section 1033.

In addition to the general provisions, Section 1033 applies specifically to these circumstances:

- *Involuntary conversions of a principal residence.* If a principal residence has been involuntarily converted and replaced as a result of "seizure, requisition, or condemnation (but not destruction), or the sale or exchange under threat or imminence thereof" the taxpayer may elect to apply the rollover rules as specified by Section 1034 (Reg. Sec.1.1033(a)-3).

- *Property sold pursuant to reclamation laws.* If property within an irrigation project is sold to conform to the acreage limitations of federal reclamation laws, the involuntary conversion rules apply (Section 1033(c)).

- *Livestock destroyed by disease.* If livestock are destroyed by disease or are sold because of the disease, the involuntary conversion rules apply (Section 1033(d)).

- *Livestock sold on account of drought.* Livestock which is held for draft, breeding, or dairy purposes which is sold in excess of usual business practices on account of a drought, qualifies for involuntary conversion treatment (Section 1033(e)).

- *Replacement of livestock with other farm property when environmental contamination has occurred.* If soil or other environmental contamination has occurred, it is not always feasible for a taxpayer to reinvest in property similar or related in use to livestock involuntarily converted. In these circumstances, the taxpayer may reinvest in other property, including real property, used for farming purposes (Section 1033(f)).

Section 1033 Criteria: Similar or Related in Service or Use

When an involuntary conversion has occurred, the taxpayer must acquire replacement property in order to defer the gain. The involuntary conversion rules apply to real or personal property. Qualifying replacement property may be one of two types:

1. *General rule Section 1033(a)(1)*: Property which is "similar or related in service or use" to the original property
2. *Exception for trade or business real property Section 1033(g)*: Property that is like-kind property when an involuntary conversion occurs for trade or business real property.

This section will discuss the general "similar use" test for involuntary conversions. The next section will consider the "like-kind" test for trade or business real property.

The "similar or related in service or use" criteria is a much more narrow qualification for property than the general rules for "like-kind" property. For example, unimproved real estate may generally be transferred for improved real estate and qualify as a like-kind exchange. However, under the strict use test, the IRS takes the position that unimproved real property may not be transferred for improved real property (Reg. Sec. 1.1033(a)-2(c)).

If the original property is actually used by the taxpayer, The Internal Revenue Service will generally seek to apply a "functional use" test. The physical characteristics and use of the replacement property must be closely similar to the converted property. The IRS has ruled that a billiard business does not qualify as replacement property for a bowling center under the "functional use" test (Rev. Rul. 76-319, 1976-2 C.B. 242).

If the taxpayer is an investor in property, rather than its user, the pivoting factor is whether or not the taxpayer's relationship to the property has changed. Some of the key issues to satisfy the similar use tests were outlined in Maloof v. Comr. 65 T.C. 263 1975):

• The reinvestment must be made in substantially similar replacement property.

- The taxpayer should be permitted to return to a position as close as possible to his original position.

- The taxpayer is not required to duplicate the original property; however, the nature of his investment should not be changed.

- The acquisition of replacement property should essentially be a continuation of the prior capital commitment, not a variation from it.

A taxpayer may acquire similar use property indirectly by acquiring stock. That statute provides that a taxpayer may purchase stock in order to acquire control of a corporation that owns qualifying replacement property to satisfy the similar use test (Section 1033(a)(2)(A)). The Code defines "control" as a minimum of at least 80 percent of the total combined voting power all stock entitled to vote, and at least 80 percent of all other classes of stock.

Section 1033 Criteria: Trade or Business Real Property Conversion

Real property that is used in a trade or business or held for investment may be replaced with like-kind property when an involuntary conversion occurs (Section 1033(g)). It is not necessary to meet the requirements of the strict use rules that apply to all other property transfers in an involuntary conversion. The like-kind qualifications are broader in nature than the strict similar use rules.

It is important to emphasize that not all compulsory conversions of real property will qualify for the broader like-kind replacement rules. Most notably, real property that is held as inventory by dealers will not qualify. Generally, qualified trade or business property includes depreciable real property as well as the underlying land. Investment real property that is a capital asset in the hands of the taxpayer will generally qualify.

To determine whether a property is like-kind for a real property involuntary conversion, the IRS indicates that Reg. Sec. 1.1031(a)-1(b) shall apply. Under these regulations, "like-kind" is determined by the character of the property, rather than its grade or quality. The regulations illustrate this concept with the example that improved real property may be exchanged for unimproved real property because they are of like character of property.

For a further discussion, see the analysis of Section 1031, like-kind exchanges in Chapter 4.

Section 1033 Criteria: Statutory Replacement Period

In order to defer the gain on an involuntary conversion, the taxpayer must reinvest in replacement property within the periods prescribed by the statute. For casualties and thefts, the replacement period begins on the date of destruction or the date the property was stolen. For seizures or condemnations, the replacement period begins on the earliest date of: (1) the actual condemnation or seizure of the property, (2) the threat or imminence of the condemnation, or (3) the sale or exchange of the property under the threat of condemnation.

There are essentially two allowable replacement periods for involuntary conversions:

1. *General rule for "similar use" property.* Under the general rule, the replacement period ends two years after the first taxable year in which the gain on conversion is realized.

2. *Exception for trade or business real property.* For real property used in a trade or business or held for investment, the replacement period ends three years after the year in which the conversion is realized.

The taxpayer may request an extension of the replacement period by applying to the district director. The application should be sent to the district in which he filed the tax return containing the deferral election. The extension application should be filed before the replacement period expires and should outline the circumstances whereby he has reasonable cause for being unable to complete the replacement within the prescribed time allowed.

Section 1033 Criteria: Gain Calculations

The total gain realized on an involuntary conversion is calculated in the usual manner for all property dispositions as prescribed by Section 1001. The amount realized (sales price or other proceeds less selling expenses) is reduced by the adjusted basis of the property transferred to establish the total gain realized.

Section 1033 involuntary conversions differ from residential rollovers (Section 1034) because the cash proceeds do not affect the formula to determine the deferred gain for a residential rollover. For an involuntary conversion, the minimum reinvestment threshold is the proceeds from the compulsory sale. If the proceeds are entirely reinvested, the entire gain can be deferred. Any portion of the amount realized which is not reinvested results in taxable gain.

Example #6: Section 1033 Gain Calculations

Mr. Morris receives a condemnation award of $500,000 for property condemned by the city, which he uses to purchase qualifying property at a price of $450,000 within the prescribed period. His adjusted basis in the original property is $300,000. He elects to apply the provisions of Section 1033.

Mr. Morris' total realized gain is as follows:

Amount realized	$ 500,000
Adjusted basis of converted property	300,000
Total gain realized	$ 200,000

Mr. Morris' taxable gain is limited to the amount of the proceeds not reinvested:

Amount realized	$ 500,000
Less: cost of replacement property	450,000
Taxable gain—unused proceeds	$ 50,000

Utilizing the deferral election under Section 1033, Mr. Morris is able to defer $150,000 of gain ($200,000 gain realized less taxable gain of $50,000). The basis of his new property is its cost less the deferred gain:

Purchase price of new property	$ 450,000
Less: deferred gain	150,000
Basis of new property	$ 300,000

An example of a formula approach to determine the gain for involuntary conversions is outlined in Figure 3.6.

Involuntary Conversions in Contrast to Like-Kind Exchanges

Replacement property acquired in an involuntary conversion may be acquired either directly (a reciprocal transfer of property) or indirectly, by selling the old property and purchasing replacement property. Replacement property in a like-kind exchange may be acquired directly (reciprocal transfer of property), in a similar fashion as an involuntary exchange. However, property acquired indirectly in a like-kind exchange must be received via an intermediary; a sale of existing property with a subsequent purchase of replacement property will constitute a fully taxable sale, not a tax-deferred exchange.

Figure 3.6   Section 1033 Involuntary Conversions

Step 1: Total Gain Realized

1.	Sales price of converted property	$_____
2.	Less: selling expenses	_____
3.	Amount realized	$_____
4.	Less: adjusted basis of converted property	_____
5.	Total gain realized	$_____

Step 2: Taxable Gain

6.	Amount realized (from Line 3)	$_____
7.	Less: cost of replacement property	_____
8.	Unused proceeds	$_____

Taxable gain limitation:

9.	Total gain realized (from Line 5)	$_____
10.	Unused proceeds (from Line 8)	_____
11.	Taxable gain (the lessor of Line 9 or 10)	$_____

Note: The gain recognized is limited to the total gain realized or the unused proceeds, whichever is the lessor amount.

Step 3: Deferred Gain

12.	Total gain realized (from Line 5)	$_____
13.	Less: taxable gain (from Line 11)	_____
14.	Deferred gain	$_____

Step 4: Basis of New Property

15.	Purchase price of new property	$_____
16.	Less: deferred gain (from Line 14)	_____
17.	Basis of new property	$_____

Holding Period

The holding period of a capital asset determines whether the asset qualifies for long-term capital gain or loss treatment when the asset is sold. The holding period rules also apply to depreciable business property that qualifies for treatment as Section 1231 gains (analogous to capital gains, but not losses). For property acquired in an involuntary conversion, the holding period for the original property is "tacked on" to the holding period of the replacement property (Section 1223(1)(A)).

Section 1031: IRS Rules and Regulations

by Bernardine G. Marvel-Ames, CPA
Redding, CA

OVERVIEW

Although any gain or loss is generally recognized when a property is sold, not every property transfer is subject to the general rule. The principles embodied by Section 1031 carve out a significant exception whereby certain exchanges of property are tax deferred. Similar to other deferral mechanisms of the Internal Revenue Code, the taxpayer must acquire new property to replace the property transferred. The replacement property theoretically represents a continued investment on the part of the taxpayer.

Frequently presented as an incomprehensible tax gimmick, the fundamental concept of an exchange is uncomplicated. What occurs in a basic exchange is simply a trade of property—a swap. Bartering is a human endeavor that originated centuries before the Internal Revenue Code or the invention of writing. A trade is the most basic form of human economics that was used before money was created as a medium of exchange.

When exchanging like-kind property, a taxpayer may acquire replacement property in a direct trade, or indirectly, from a third-party **facilitator**. Occasionally, taxpayers are under the impression they that may directly sell their existing property and purchase the new property in order to defer any taxable gains under Section 1031. Unfortunately, this idea is incorrect. Although the new property may represent a reinvestment, it does not constitute a "qualified" exchange. Some of the confusion may be caused by the fact that a sale and purchase of reinvestment property is allowed for residential rollovers (Section 1034) and involuntary conversions (Section 1033). Nevertheless, an exchange essentially contemplates a reciprocal transfer of property that can be effectuated with an intermediary, but not a sale followed by a purchase of new property.

STATUTORY REQUIREMENTS FOR IRC 1031

In General

For like-kind exchanges, Section 1031(a)(1) furnishes the statutory authority for the exception from the general rule, which requires the recognition of gain or loss upon the sale or exchange of property. Section 1031(a)(1) provides the following:

"No gain or loss shall be recognized on the exchange of property held for productive use in a trade or business or for investment if such property is exchanged solely for property of like kind which is to be held either for productive use in a trade or business or for investment."

In Reg. Sec. 1.1031(a)-1, the IRS clarifies that property held for productive use in a trade or business may be exchanged for like-kind property held for investment. Similarly, property held for investment may be exchanged for like-kind property that is used in a trade or business.

The primary concepts provided by Section 1031(a)(1) include:

- Section 1031 applies to gain or loss resulting from a like-kind exchange.

- Nonrecognition is mandatory, not elective.

- Section 1031 property must be:

  - Like-kind, and
  - Property used in a trade or business or held for investment.

One often overlooked aspect of like-kind exchanges is that if the qualifying circumstances have transpired, the application of Section 1031 is mandatory, not elective. Furthermore, any losses that result from a like-kind exchange are deferred as well as gains. While deferred gains are not currently taxable under Section 1031, any deferred losses are nondeductible.

Section 1031 qualifying property must be used in a trade or business or be held for investment. An analysis of what constitutes qualifying property is discussed later in this chapter.

Exceptions to the General Rule

There are a number of exceptions to the general rule, whereby the gain may not be deferred in an otherwise qualified exchange. Section 1031(a)(2) specifically enumerates these six exceptions:

1. Stock in trade or other property held primarily for sale.
2. Stocks, bonds, or notes.
3. Other securities or evidence of indebtedness or interest.
4. Interests in a partnership.
5. Certificates of trust or beneficial interests.
6. Choses in action.

Any property that is inventory held for sale to customers will not qualify for like-kind exchange treatment. The determination of whether or not any property is inventory depends on whether the property is held for sale to customers.

Any exchange of an ownership interest in a partnership will not qualify as like-kind, whether they are general or limited partnerships or interests in the same or other partnerships. If a partnership has a valid election defined by Section 761(a) to be excluded from subchapter K, the underlying assets are treated as an interest in the assets and not an interest in the partnership. An exchange of the interest in such a partnership will not qualify for Section 1031, if any of the underlying assets of the partnership will not qualify (Reg. Sec. 1.1031(a)-1).

Basis of Property Received

When property is acquired in an exchange, the basis for the new property is the basis for the relinquished property increased by any gain recognized and decreased by the amount of any money received or loss recognized. If another party in the exchange assumes a liability from the taxpayer, the liability is treated as money received by the taxpayer (Section 1031(d)).

Related Parties

In general, taxpayers may complete tax-deferred, like-kind exchanges with related parties. As a result of tax legislation in 1989, related-party exchanges have been restricted somewhat. Section 1031(f) now mandates that if either party in a related-party exchange disposes of the exchange property within a two-year period, the deferral rules of Section 1031 shall not apply. The two-year period begins on the date of the last transfer. If such exchange property is transferred within the two-year period, the taxable gain will be recognized on the date of disposition.

QUALIFYING PROPERTY

To qualify for the deferral treatment afforded by Section 1031, the property exchanged must be of like-kind. Potentially, real property can be exchanged for real property, and personal property can be exchanged for personal property. However, real property can not be exchanged with personal property, because these properties are of a different kind or class.

Real Property

The regulations under Section 1031 indicate that the term "like-kind" refers to the nature or character of the property, not the quality or grade. Thus, improved real estate may be exchanged for unimproved real estate because they are of the same kind or class. The fact that one property is improved, and another is not describes only grade or quality (Reg. Sec. 1.1031(a)-1(b)).

Although real estate is generally considered to be investment property or held for productive use in a trade or business, such is not always the case. Real estate that is inventory in the hands of a dealer is not qualifying property.

In the examples in the regulations, a leasehold of a fee with 30 years or more to run may be exchanged for real estate, and city real estate may be exchanged with farmland, if the taxpayer is not a dealer. (Reg. Sec. 1.1031(a)-1(c)).

Personal Property

The provisions for like-kind exchanges have been around for many years, but little guidance was available for taxpayers for exchanges of personal property until the new regulations were issued in April 1991. Under these regulations, properties of a **"like class"** may qualify as like-kind. While the IRS did attempt to define "like class" for tangible depreciable personal property, the IRS did not attempt to define this term as it relates to intangible personal property. (Reg. Sec. 1.1031(a)-2(c)).

Tangible Depreciable Personal Property

According to recent regulations, tangible depreciable personal property is of a "like class" if the exchanged properties are of the same "General Asset Class" or "Product Class." A qualified General Asset Class is defined by reference to the depreciation class tables. Specifically, properties that match within the depreciation classes 00.11 through 00.28 and 00.4 of Rev. Proc. 87-56, 1987-2 C.B. 674 may qualify as a "like class." A qualified Product Class is defined as depreciable tangible personal property listed in the 4-digit product class in Division D of the Standard Industrial Classification Manual (Reg. Sec. 1.1031(a)-2(c)).

Intangible Personal Property and Nondepreciable Personal Property

Intangible personal property generally includes assets that are considered to bestow a right upon the owner. Such assets may include copyrights, trademarks, patents, franchises, customer lists, covenants not to compete, goodwill, and lease rights. Some intangibles are depreciable while others are not, depending on the facts and circumstances in each case.

The new regulations for personal property do not provide any definition of like classes for intangible personal property or nondepreciable personal property. These regulations merely indicate that the determination of whether these properties qualify as like-kind is defined by the nature or character of the rights and the nature and or character of the underlying property. However, the examples in the regulations indicate that an exchange of a copyright for a novel is like-kind to an exchange for a copyright for another novel, but not a copyright for a song.

Dealers in Real Property

When property is held as "stock in trade" (inventory) for sale to customers in the ordinary course of business, the property is not qualified for a like-kind exchange. Generally, real property is considered to be investment property, a capital asset, in the hands of the taxpayer. However, when a dealer sells real property in the ordinary course of business (e.g., a subdivision), real property is often characterized as inventory.

The analysis of whether or not a taxpayer is a dealer in real estate is generally tested under the capital gains rules of Section 1221. In some circumstances, a dealer may qualify for the capital gain treatment, although he owns similar property for sale to customers.

The courts have long taken the position that whether or not real property is investment property or inventory is a question of fact, determined on a case-by-case basis. The tax characterization of the property depends on the nature of the property in the hands of the taxpayer, not the nature of the property itself. The primary determinative issue is the intent of the taxpayer—whether the taxpayer intended to hold the property as investment property or for sale to customers.

The Klarkowski Case . . . 11 Points in Determining Dealer Status

As developed by the courts, the following factors affect the determination of whether a taxpayer is a dealer. The first nine characteristics were set forth by the Tax Court in The Klarkowski case. The final two are considered to be additional important factors by the Second Circuit Court.

1. The purpose for which the property was acquired.
2. The purpose for which the property was subsequently held.
3. The nature and extent of improvements made by the taxpayer.
4. The frequency, number, and continuity of sales.
5. The extent and nature of transaction in the property.
6. The ordinary or general business of the taxpayer.
7. The extent of advertising and promotion for sale.
8. Whether the property was listed with a real estate broker or other outlet.
9. The purpose for which the property was held at the time of sale, as opposed to the time of acquisition.
10. Proximity of sale to purchase.
11. Substantiality of income derived from the sale(s), and what percentage it is of taxpayer's total income.

One of the factors that is usually reviewed rather closely is the holding period of the property prior to sale. If the taxpayer has only held the property for a relatively short period of time, the property begins to resemble inventory, in the absence of other factors. In contrast, properties that have been held for several years begin to resemble investment property.

While most case law history for "**dealer**" dispositions relate to real estate transactions, these factors potentially apply to dealers in other property. Although the taxpayer may be a dealer in a specific property, there may be occasional sales, whereby the taxpayer has held the property for investment. In circumstances where the underlying intent for holding property is ambiguous, the previous factors should be reviewed. The critical issue is the nature of the taxpayer's intent for holding the property, not the nature of the property itself.

NONQUALIFYING PROPERTY

Property that does not qualify for tax-deferred like-kind exchange treatment includes:

- Property specifically excluded by the statute.

- Property excluded by recent regulations.

- Taxable "boot": cash or other property received.

1. Property Specifically Excluded by the Statute

As previously addressed, Section 1031(a)(2) lists specific property that is disqualified from like-kind exchange treatment, most notably inventory and stocks and bonds. In addition to these general exclusions, the Internal Revenue Code addresses two other unusual exclusions that apply only in specific circumstances: namely, livestock of different sexes, and real property located outside of the United States.

Generally, livestock that is held for breeding purposes and that is depreciable is exchangeable as like-kind property. However, as delineated by Section 1031(e), "livestock of different sexes are not property of a like-kind."

The *Omnibus Budget Reconciliation Act of 1989* amended the like-kind provisions to address the issue of **foreign property**. Section 1031(h) now mandates that "real property located in the United States and real property located outside the United States are not property of a like-kind." Qualifying real property has been restricted such that only property located in the 50 states and the District of Columbia, but not the U.S. Virgin Islands, Guam, and Puerto Rico, would qualify as like-kind properties in an exchange.

2. Property Excluded by the Regulations

The IRS announced in recent regulations, that the goodwill of a business is not like-kind to the goodwill of another business (Reg. Sec. 1.1031(a)-

2(c)). In the prior version of the proposed regulations issued in 1990, the IRS indicated that their rationale for this position is that the goodwill of any particular business inures to that business and is never like-kind to the goodwill of another business.

3. Taxable Boot

As governed by Section 1031, some exchanges are only partially tax deferred. If money or other property is received in an otherwise qualifying exchange, then taxable gain is recognized. However, the gain recognized is limited to the extent of money and the fair market value of other property received (Section 1031(b)). "Other property" refers to property that is not like-kind to the property exchanged. Taxable boot is any cash or other nonqualifying property received in an exchange. The philosophy for this rule is that the taxpayer has not continued his investment in the underlying property to the extent that he receives other "not like" property.

In an exchange, any liabilities of the taxpayer that are assumed by another party are treated as money received by the taxpayer (Reg. Sec. 1.1031(d)-2). This position is consistent with the treatment of debt relief in other areas of tax law. Under Reg. Sec. 1.61-12, any income from the discharge of indebtedness for a taxpayer is taxable income unless another exclusion applies such as Section 108 or Section 1017 (relating to insolvent and bankrupt taxpayers).

In a like-kind exchange, taxable boot could potentially arise from any of the following:

- Cash received.

- Other nonqualifying (not like) property received.

- Assumption of liabilities by another party.

In the practical application of Section 1031, properties of unequal value are often exchanged. Cash or other nonqualifying property may be transferred in order to balance the unequal values of the like properties. Furthermore, properties that are mortgaged are often transferred. Any party to an exchange may give or receive boot property.

Boot "Netting"

In some exchanges, both the property transferred and the property received are subject to existing mortgages. When the values are unequal, cash is often used to balance the exchange.

Since a taxpayer may both give and receive boot property, a complicated series of boot "netting" rules have been developed by way of the
examples in the regulations (Reg. Sec. 1.1031(d)-2).

In general, if a taxpayer receives **cash boot** in an exchange, he may
offset that boot with cash paid. However, when both the relinquished property and the replacement property are transferred subject to existing mortgages, and other nonqualifying properties are transferred, the equation is
more complex. When a taxpayer is relieved of a mortgage on the property
transferred, he may offset that amount of boot with the mortgage he assumes on the property received and with cash or other boot paid, but not
below zero. If the above netted mortgages and boot paid result in an excess of **mortgage boot** received, the excess plus cash and other boot received are taxable. However, if the above netted mortgages and boot paid
result in an excess of mortgage boot paid, the excess may not offset cash
or other boot received, which are still fully taxable.

Constructive Receipt

Under the general rule, the taxpayer must recognize taxable gain if cash or
other property is actually or constructively received. This issue relates to
the taxable boot in an exchange. In some instances, constructive receipt
can invalidate the entire exchange.

QUALIFIED EXCHANGES

Over the years, like-kind exchanges have evolved as a result of legislative
authorization, IRS controversy, and taxpayer need. Although the original
statute essentially contemplated a simultaneous and reciprocal transfer of
property, a number of variations have developed that have been sanctioned
by the Internal Revenue Code, the courts, and IRS regulations.

There are several primary types of like-kind exchanges:

• Simultaneous exchanges.

• Delayed exchanges.

• Multi-party exchanges.

• Multi-asset exchanges.

The previous types of exchanges could be combined in one transaction.
For example, an exchange comprised of multiple assets may involve multi-

ple parties, whereby the properties are transferred in a qualified delayed exchange.

1. Simultaneous Exchanges

As mentioned in Chapter 1, the IRS originally maintained the posture that a qualified exchange must involve a simultaneous transfer of properties. After a line of several test cases, Congress sanctioned delayed exchanges with the *1984 Tax Reform Act.*

Although a simultaneous exchange is often difficult to achieve with real property, taxpayers often complete a simultaneous exchange without the intention to do so. For example, the IRS indicates that a trade of a business automobile for another business automobile, or a trade of a business truck for another business truck is a like-kind exchange (Reg. Sec. 1.1031(a)-1(c)). These transfers are like-kind exchanges notwithstanding the fact that trade-in values, loans, and cash may be involved. Similarly, a trade in of business equipment for new business equipment is a like-kind exchange, if both properties are of a "like class," as defined in the April 1991 regulations.

2. Delayed Exchanges

In prior years, the time period for completing an exchange was open-ended. As discussed in Chapter 1, the Starkers originally transferred their property to Longview and Zellerbach in 1967, but received replacement property over a period of years from 1968 to 1972. While the IRS focused on the issue that the exchanges were not simultaneous, the replacement period was indefinite.

Specified Time Period—Delayed Exchanges

Section 1031(a)(3) now requires that a delayed exchange must be completed within a specified time period. There are two elements the taxpayer must satisfy: the **45-day identification rule**, and the 180 day replacement rule. The requirements are as follows.

The 45-Day Identification Rule

Replacement property must be identified as property to be received in an exchange on or before 45 days after the disposition date.

The 180-Day Replacement Rule

Replacement property must be acquired before the earliest of either:

- 180 days after the disposition date.

- the due date of the tax return, including extensions, for the tax year of the disposition of the exchange property.

It is important to realize that the basic 45-day identification rule and the 180-day replacement rule are specified in the law, not by regulation. If an exchange fails to meet these requirements, the exchange will fail tax deferral treatment. The IRS will then find that a taxable sale has occurred.

Recent regulations clarify the beginning and ending of the identification and replacement periods. The identification period begins on the date of transfer of the relinquished property and ends at midnight on the 45th day thereafter. The exchange period begins on the date of transfer of the relinquished property and ends on the earlier of the 180th day thereafter or the date of the tax return, including extensions (Reg. Sec. 1.1031(k)-1(b)).

If an exchange occurs late in the year, it will be necessary to do a time line to determine the due date for the acquisition of the replacement property (see Figure 4.1). A taxpayer will never have more than 180 days to complete an exchange, and may have less time, unless a tax return extension is filed. A sample time line for corporate taxpayers is illustrated below. For noncorporate taxpayers, a similar time line should be reviewed, with the applicable tax return due dates and extension due dates, which are different.

Figure 4.1 Sample Time Line

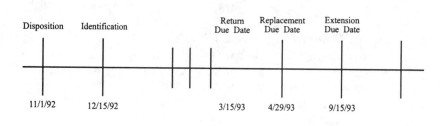

When property is transferred on November 1, 1992, replacement property must be identified no later than December 15, 1992. It should be noted that the replacement property must be acquired by the tax return due date (within 135 days), unless an extension is filed. If a tax return extension is filed, the replacement property must be acquired by April 29, 1993 (within 180 days).

Replacement Property Rules—Delayed Exchanges

Recent regulations specify that the "identification" of replacement property must be in writing. The new regulations are complex; a series of rules have been spelled out whereby alternative and multiple replacement properties may be identified.

Documentation for Identified Properties

In order to meet the regulatory guidelines, the identified properties must be properly documented in writing. The replacement property should be unambiguously described by a legal description, street address, or a distinguishable name, such as The Mayfair Building. As prescribed by Reg. Sec. 1.1031(k)-1(c), the replacement property should be identified in a written document signed by the taxpayer and delivered (hand delivered, mailed, or telecopied) within the 45 day period to either the person obligated to transfer the replacement property to the taxpayer, or any other person involved in the exchange other than the taxpayer or a disqualified person.

The regulations provide that an identification of replacement property may be revoked at any time during the identification period, as long as the revocation is in writing, signed by the taxpayer, and delivered to the person who originally received the identification document (Reg. Sec. 1.1031(k)-1(c)(6)).

Identification of Alternate and Multiple Properties

The new regulations assert a requirement that the taxpayer may identify only a maximum of either (1) three properties of any fair market value, or (2) any number as long as the aggregate fair market value at the end of the identification period does not exceed 200% of the fair market value of all the relinquished properties (Reg. Sec. 1.1031(k)-1(c)(4)(i)).

To illustrate the 200% rule, assume that a taxpayer is exchanging a property with a fair market value of $200,000. During the 45-day period, he identified two lots valued at $30,000 and $20,000, a small office building valued at $150,000, 10 acres of ranch land valued at $70,000, and a duplex valued at $120,000. The total aggregate fair market value identified is $390,000. This amount is $10,000 less than $400,000 (the 200% threshold of the relinquished property with a market value of $200,000).

If the taxpayer has identified more properties than prescribed by the regulations, the taxpayer is treated as if no properties had been identified, except for:

- Any replacement property received before the end of the 45-day identification period, which is treated as identified.

- Any replacement property identified and received before the end of the identification period, if the taxpayer receives identified property with a fair market value of at least 95% of the aggregate fair market value of all identified properties. (Reg. Sec. 1.1031(k)-1(c)(4)(ii)).

The regulations contain extensive examples of the above identification and replacement rules (Reg. Sec. 1.1031(k)-1(c)(7)).

Multiple Party Exchanges

In a **multiple party exchange,** the taxpayer generally transfers his property to an intermediary. The intermediary then acquires replacement property and transfers it to the taxpayer. These transactions are generally known as three-corner or triangular exchanges. The three-corner exchange solves the practical problem most often associated with a reciprocal transfer—the owner of the replacement property sought by the taxpayer wants cash or other property not owned by the taxpayer.

Over the years, the IRS has attacked multiple party exchanges from a variety of focal points: agency issues, constructive receipt issues, and transfer of title issues. The safe harbors discussed later in this chapter address these issues.

Multiple Asset Exchanges

In General

One of the most common forms of a multiple asset exchange is a disposal of an entire business, or segment of a business, followed by a reinvestment in another business. Taxpayers have been struggling for years over the practical application of what constitutes a like-kind exchange for an entire business. For example, if a manufacturer of men's clothing disposes of an entire plant, including land, building, equipment, and all contract rights, and reinvests in another manufacturing facility for men's clothing of similar property components, it appears that at least some of the assets should qualify for like-kind treatment. What if the same taxpayer reinvests in a manufacturing facility for textiles? Or motorcycles? What if the taxpayer receives $900,000 in cash to balance the exchange?

To begin to solve the problem, the real property can most likely be exchanged with other real property. The contract rights will need to be approached on an asset-by-asset basis, analyzing the nature of the rights. Is equipment in a men's clothing plant like-kind to equipment in a textile plant or motorcycle plant? Should the cash be allocable to the property components?

Regulation Section 1.1031(j)-1:

In April 1991, the IRS issued new regulations for exchanges of multiple properties and personal property. The personal property rules have been discussed earlier in this chapter. This section will focus on multiple asset exchanges.

In general, property is analyzed on an asset-by-asset approach to determine whether the property is like-kind and to compute realized gain and any taxable gain from boot received. Reg. Sec. 1.1031(j)-1 provides an exception to the general rule for exchanges of multiple properties. This section will focus on the regulations' requirements for classifying properties.

Definition—Multiple Asset Exchange

The regulations define a multiple asset exchange as (1) an exchange consisting of more than one "exchange group," or (2) an exchange consisting of only one "exchange group," but multiple properties within that group. Most of the operational provisions of these regulations involve the IRS' conception of "exchange groups." An exchange group is comprised only of like-kind or like-class properties.

Exchange Groups

The April 1991 regulations do not address how to match up exchange groups. To do this, the taxpayer will need to review the general rules to determine like-kind properties as defined by the statute, the regulations, and case law. In general, however, real property and intangible personal property can be approached on an asset-by-asset basis, based on the underlying nature of the asset. Tangible depreciable personal property can be analyzed in groups as described under the personal property regulations (Reg. Sec. 1.1031(a)-2).

In example #1 in the regulations, the IRS illustrates the exchange of an automobile and a computer for another automobile and computer printer. Both automobiles are described in General Asset Class 00.22, and qualify as a like-kind exchange group. The computer and computer printer are described in General Asset Class 00.12, and also qualify as a like-kind exchange group. (Reg. Sec. 1.1031(j)-1(d)).

In example #5 of the regulations, real estate and a grader are exchanged for other real estate and a railroad car. The exchange of real estate properties are like-kind and qualify as an exchange group. The grader (SIC Code 3531) is not like-kind to the railroad car (General Asset Class 00.25), and therefore does not qualify to be included in an exchange group.

SALE VS. QUALIFIED EXCHANGE

Constructive Receipt

The IRS has expressed concern that a taxpayer may actually or constructively receive cash in the full amount of the consideration before receiving replacement property. In this instance, the issue is not just the amount of cash boot to equalize the exchange. The new regulations provide that if cash in the full amount of the consideration is actually or constructively received before the replacement property, the transaction will constitute a fully taxable sale, not a deferred exchange (Reg. Sec. 1.1031(k)-1(f)).

A constructive receipt of cash can be created by either an unrestricted access to cash which is credited to the taxpayers account, or actual or constructive receipt by an agent of the taxpayer.

If money or other property is credited to a taxpayer's account or is otherwise made available so that he may draw on it at any time, the taxpayer is in constructive receipt of cash. If the taxpayer's control of funds is subject to substantial restrictions or limitations, the taxpayer is not in constructive receipt, unless the limitations lapse, expire, or are waived (Reg. Sec. 1.1031(k)-1(f)(2)).

Agency Issues

In general terms, an agent is empowered to act for and on behalf of another person, and may be empowered to execute legally binding agreements on behalf of the principal party. In an agency relationship, an agent often "stands in the shoes" of the principal.

Because of the characteristics of an agency relationship, the IRS has often attacked exchanges in the past when the transaction was conducted through an agent. If qualifying property was transferred to an agent, which the agent subsequently sold, the IRS argued that because of the underlying agency relationship, the taxpayer was the underlying principal to the sale. If an agent had actual or constructive receipt of cash proceeds, the IRS argued that the taxpayer had actual or constructive receipt of cash, whereby the transfer was characterized as a sale.

The safe harbor rules in Reg. Sec. 1.1031(k)-1(g) address the agency issue by defining "disqualified persons." Property may not be transferred to an escrow or intermediary who is a "disqualified person." It is interesting to note that their definition below includes not only potential agents, but also "related parties" as defined in other sections of the Internal Revenue Code:

Disqualified Person—Reg. Sec. 1.1031(k)-1(k)

Under the safe harbor rules, a person is a "disqualified person" if:

1. Such person is the agent of the taxpayer.
2. Such person acts as the taxpayer's attorney, accountant, broker, investment banker, or real estate agent, within two years prior to the transfer.
3. Such person bears a relationship to the taxpayer in either Section 267(b) or 707(b) of the IRC determined by substituting "10 percent" for "50 percent" each place it appears.
4. Such person bears a relationship to a person described in (2) above.

Safe Harbors

An actual or constructive receipt of cash can collapse an entire exchange into a fully taxable sale, notwithstanding that all other requirements have been met for a like-kind exchange. For this reason, the new regulations provide several safe harbors. Exchanges that employ any method under the four safe harbors will result in a determination that the taxpayer is not in actual or constructive receipt of cash. Reg. Sec. 1.1031(k)-1(g) provides the following four safe harbors.

1. Security or Guarantee Arrangements.

The first safe harbor rule states that the obligation of the taxpayer's transferee to transfer the replacement property to the taxpayer may be secured or guaranteed by any of the following:

- A mortgage, deed of trust, or other security interest in the property (other than cash or a cash equivalent).

- A standby letter of credit which satisfies all of the requirements of Reg. Sec. 15A.453-1(b)(3)(iii) and which does not allow the taxpayer to draw on the standby letter of credit except upon a default of the transferee's obligation to transfer like-kind replacement property, or

- A guarantee of a third party.

2. Qualified Exchange Escrow Accounts and Trusts

The second safe harbor provides that the obligation of the taxpayer's transferee to transfer the replacement property may be secured by cash or a cash equivalent if such security is held in a qualified escrow or trust. The qualified trust must not be the taxpayer or a "disqualified person." The taxpayer's rights to receive, borrow, pledge, or otherwise obtain the benefits of the cash or the cash equivalent held in escrow must be limited to specified circumstances as described in Reg. Sec. 1.1031(k)-1(g)(6).

3. Qualified Intermediary

The third safe harbor provides that a taxpayer may transfer property to a qualified intermediary if the taxpayer's rights to receive money or other property are limited to specified circumstances. A "qualified intermediary" is defined as a person who:

* Is not the taxpayer or a disqualified person, and

* Entered into a written Exchange Agreement with the taxpayer and as required by the Exchange Agreement:

  – Acquires the relinquished property from the taxpayer,
  – Transfers the relinquished property,
  – Acquires the replacement property, and
  – Transfers the replacement property to the taxpayer.

An intermediary is treated as acquiring and transferring property if the intermediary:

* Acquires and transfers legal title to that property.

* Enters into an agreement with a person other than the taxpayer for the transfer of relinquished property to that person (either on its own behalf or as the agent of any party).

* Enters into an agreement with the owner of replacement property (either on its own behalf or as the agent of any party) for the transfer of that property and pursuant to that agreement, the property is transferred to the taxpayer.

* Accepts the assignment of the rights to an agreement, and all the parties to the agreement are notified in writing of the assignment on or before the date of the relevant transfer of property.

4. Investment Income

The last of the four safe harbor rules states that the taxpayer is allowed to receive interest or a growth factor with respect to the deferred exchange

provided that the taxpayer's rights to receive the interest or growth factor
are limited to specified circumstances. This interest or growth factor will
be treated as interest regardless of whether it is paid in cash or in property.
However, the regulations do not address the proper manner for reporting
interest income that is earned on money held in a qualified escrow account
or a qualified trust. It is also unclear what year the interest income is
reportable.

Restrictions

The taxpayer must not have the right to receive money or other property
until:

- After the end of the identification period if no replacement property is
  identified.

- After the taxpayer has received all of the identified replacement property to which the taxpayer is entitled.

- If the replacement property has been identified but not yet received,
  after the latter of the end of the identification period and the occurrence
  of a material and substantial contingency that relates to the exchange, is
  provided for in writing, and is beyond the control of the taxpayer or a
  related party, or the end of the exchange period.

Items Disregarded in Applying Safe Harbors

The taxpayer's receipt of or right to receive any of the following will be
disregarded in determining whether a safe harbor applies:

- Items that a seller may receive as a consequence of the disposition of
  property that are not included in the amount realized from the disposition of property (e.g., prorated rents).

- Transactional items that relate to the disposition or acquisition of property, appear on the closing statement, and under local practice are the
  responsibility of a buyer or seller (i.e., commissions, prorated taxes, recording charges, transfer taxes, and title company fees).

Holding Period

The **holding period** of any property generally begins when the taxpayer
acquires the property and ends when the taxpayer sells or otherwise dis-

poses of the property. In order to qualify for long-term capital gain (or Section 1231 gain for depreciable business property), an asset must be held by the taxpayer for more than one year. For any property acquired in an exchange, whereby the basis of the replacement property acquires a substituted basis from the original property transferred, the holding period of the replacement property includes the holding period of the exchanged property (Section 1223(1)).

For example, if a taxpayer sells an investment lot that he acquired in a like-kind exchange within eleven months of the acquisition, the taxpayer is allowed to "tack on" the holding period of the prior exchanged property. If the original lot relinquished in the exchange had been held by the taxpayer for five years, the total holding period for the replacement lot would be deemed to be five years and eleven months. Thus, the subsequent disposition of the replacement lot would qualify for long-term capital gain treatment.

Evaluating the Tax Effects of Property Dispositions

by Bernardine G. Marvel-Ames, CPA
  Redding, CA

OVERVIEW

Prior to making a determination of whether to sell or exchange a property, the taxpayer should carefully review the tax effects of the alternatives. As reviewed in previous chapters, the exchange transfers that are available to most taxpayers are: residential rollovers, involuntary conversions, and like-kind exchanges of business or investment property. This chapter will discuss how to how to calculate the tax effects of a like-kind exchange, how to calculate the tax treatment for an installment sale, and an approach to evaluate the alternatives.

The amount and timing of gain recognition for like-kind exchanges and installments are based on separate underlying rules. A fundamental understanding of these rules and their computations is necessary prior to any attempt to evaluate their effects.

LIKE-KIND EXCHANGES: LIMITED GAIN RECOGNITION

In General

As reviewed in Chapter 3, the gain on any property appreciation is generally taxed when the property is sold or disposed; the taxable appreciation is measured as the excess of the amount realized (sales price less selling expenses) less the adjusted basis for the property. Chapter 4 discussed the general statutory and regulatory framework for Section 1031 like-kind exchanges. This chapter will focus on the practical aspects of limited gain recognition under Section 1031.

Single Asset Exchanges

In its most basic form, a like-kind exchange is a "swap" or reciprocal transfer of properties. If the properties transferred qualify as like-kind, and no cash or other property is received, the entire gain is deferred.

Example #1: Basic Exchange Deferral

John Black exchanges an investment lot, A, for another lot, B; both properties are valued at $75,000, and qualify for like-kind treatment. John Black's adjusted basis for the lot is $50,000; therefore, he realizes $25,000 in gain:

Market value, lot B, "Amount realized"	$ 75,000
Adjusted basis, lot A relinquished	(50,000)
Realized gain - deferred	$ 25,000

If John Black had sold his lot for $75,000 in cash, the entire gain of $25,000 is taxable. Because Mr. Black qualifies for a like-kind exchange, the entire gain is deferred. After the exchange, the adjusted basis for the new property, lot B, is $50,000, which is determined in reference to the property relinquished (Section 1031(d)).

Balancing Equities

In an exchange transaction, any consideration that is received other than qualifying like-kind property is referred to as "boot." The amount of taxable gain recognized is limited to the gain realized or boot, whichever is the lessor amount. If money or other property is received in an exchange, a portion of the gain is taxable to the extent of the cash or other boot property received (Section 1031(b)).

In a like-kind exchange, taxable boot may arise from the taxpayer's receipt of cash, nonqualifying property, or debt assumed by another party. Usually, taxable boot is created by exchanging properties of unequal value.

Example #2: Unequal Market Values

The current market value for Mr. Smith's real property is $120,000, but Mr. Johnson's real property is valued at $100,000. Mr. Johnson will have to pay

Mr. Smith $20,000 to equalize their exchange. In essence, Mr. Smith has re-
ceived a $100,000 property and $20,000 cash, "to boot." The cash is nonqualifying property (see Figure 5.1).

Figure 5.1   Unequal Exchange Values of "Taxable Boot"

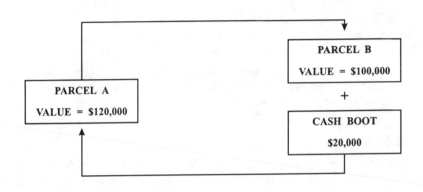

	Smith's Property	Johnson's Property
Market value-qualifying property	$ 120,000	$ 100,000
Cash "boot"	-0-	20,000
Total exchanged	$ 120,000	$ 120,000

It makes sense that above exchange should be partially taxable because
Mr. Smith has "cashed out" $20,000 of his equity.

Alternatively, if Mr. Johnson does not have $20,000 in cash, Mr. Smith
could accept Mr. Johnson's automobile, which they agree is worth
$20,000, instead. The automobile does not qualify for a like-kind exchange
with real estate; it is considered nonqualifying property. Regardless of
whether Mr. Smith receives a $20,000 automobile or $20,000 in cash, he
has "taxable boot" of $20,000.

Example #3: Deferred and Taxable Gain

Assume that Mr. Smith's lot originally cost him $75,000. Of the total
$45,000 of gain realized, $25,000 is deferred because Mr. Smith's taxable
gain is limited to the $20,000 of cash boot received.

Consideration received: Johnson's parcel	
at fair market value	$ 100,000
Cash boot	20,000
Total amount realized	120,000
Less: adjusted basis of property transferred	(75,000)
Total gain realized	45,000
Taxable gain recognized—boot received	(20,000)
Deferred gain	$ 25,000

Mr. Smith's taxable gain is $20,000. The basis in the new property is increased by the gain recognized and decreased by the boot he received. The adjusted basis of Mr. Smith's new property is $75,000:

Adjusted basis of the property relinquished	$ 75,000
Less: boot received	(20,000)
Plus: taxable gain recognized	20,000
Basis of new property	$ 75,000

Liabilities as Boot

When mortgaged property is exchanged, the exchangor is treated as having received cash for the amount of debt assumed by another party. If any property is transferred subject to a debt, the debt assumed by the new party is treated as cash to the taxpayer, even if the taxpayer is not personally liable for the debt secured by the lien. One way to conceptualize this is: if another party assumes the exchangor's mortgage, this assumption relieves the exchangor of the responsibility for the debt, which is similar to a pay-off or capital recovery. Conversely, any liabilities for which the exchangor assumes responsibility is treated as cash boot paid.

A potential trap with mortgages in an exchange is that a taxpayer can have "taxable boot," with no cash to pay the taxes.

Example #4: Liabilities as "Boot"

Mr. White owns real estate with an adjusted basis of $200,000 and a current market value of $350,000 but is subject to a mortgage of $125,000. Mr. White exchanges with Mr. Black for his real estate with a current market value of $250,000 and pays Mr. White $25,000 to equalize the exchange. Mr. Black's adjusted basis is $125,000. If they both effectuate an exchange, the gain calculations are as follows:

	Mr. White	Mr. Black
Market value of the property received	$ 250,000	$ 350,000
Plus: cash "boot" received	0 25,000	
Plus: liabilities to which old property is subject	125,000	0
Total consideration received- amount realized	375,000 375,000	
Less: cash boot paid	(25,000)	0
Less: liability boot paid for property transferred	0 (125,000)	
Less: adjusted basis	(200,000)	(125,000)
Total gain realized	150,000 125,000	
Taxable gain-net boot received	100,000	25,000
Deferred gain	$ 50,000	$ 100,000

Mr. White is relieved of $125,000 of debt that is treated as a cash payment, and included in total consideration received. Mr. White may offset the liability boot received ($125,000) by the amount of cash boot paid ($25,000). Although Mr. White has received no actual cash payment, he will be taxed on the net $100,000 of boot received with no cash to pay his taxes. For Mr. Black the damage is less severe. He will owe tax on $25,000 of the boot that he receives in the exchange; however, he has received $25,000 in cash from Mr. White.

See Figures 5.2 and 5.3. of IRS Form 8824 for Mr. White and Mr. Black. The form for Mr. White illustrates the boot netting error in their formula.

Special rules apply regarding the ability to "net" mortgage liabilities in determining net taxable boot. As discussed in Chapter 4, liability boot received may be "netted" against liability and cash boot paid, but not below zero. The result of netted mortgages plus total cash boot received determines total taxable boot. In any case, taxable cash boot received is not offset with netted mortgages.

The Boot Netting Rules

In an exchange with mortgaged properties, the exchangor may avoid taxable boot if the exchangor does not receive cash or other property, or if the mortgage on property received exceeds the mortgage on the property relinquished.

Figure 5.2   IRS Form 8824 Mr. White

Form **8824**	**Like-Kind Exchanges** (and nonrecognition of gain from conflict-of-interest sales) ▶ See separate instructions. ▶ Attach to your tax return. ▶ Use a separate form for each like-kind exchange.	OMB No. 1545-1190 **1991**
Department of the Treasury Internal Revenue Service		Attachment Sequence No. **49**

Name(s) shown on tax return	Identifying number
MR. WHITE	555-55-9999

Part I   Information on the Like-Kind Exchange

Note: If the property described on line 1 or line 2 is real property located outside the United States, indicate the country.

1   Description of like-kind property given up ▶ REAL PROPERTY -PARCEL A

2   Description of like-kind property received ▶ REAL PROPERTY -PARCEL B

3	Date like-kind property given up was originally acquired (month, day, year)	**3**	12 /15 / 91
4	Date you actually transferred your property to other party (month, day, year)	**4**	12 /15 / 91
5	Date the like-kind property you received was identified (month, day, year). See instructions	**5**	12 /15 / 91
6	Date you actually received the like-kind property from other party (month, day, year)	**6**	12 /15 / 91

7   Was the exchange made with a related party (see instructions)?
  a ☐ Yes, in this tax year   b ☐ Yes, in a prior tax year   c ☒ No (If "No," go to Part II.)
8   Enter the following information about the related party:

Name	Identifying number
Address (no., street, and apt. or suite no., rural route, or P.O. box no. if mail is not delivered to street address)	
City or town, state, and ZIP code	Relationship to you

9   During this tax year, did the related party sell or dispose of the like-kind property received from you in the exchange? . . . . ☐ Yes ☐ No

10   During this tax year, did you sell or dispose of the like-kind property you received? . . . . ☐ Yes ☐ No
  If both lines 9 and 10 are "No," go to Part II. If either line 9 or line 10 is "Yes," the deferred gain or (loss) from line 21 must be reported on your return this tax year, **unless** one of the exceptions on line 11 applies. See instructions.

11   If one of the exceptions below applies to the disposition, check the applicable box:
  ☐ The disposition was after the death of either of the related parties.
  ☐ The disposition was an involuntary conversion, and the threat of conversion occurred after the exchange.
  ☐ You can establish to the satisfaction of the IRS that neither the exchange nor the disposition had tax avoidance as its principal purpose. If this box is checked, attach an explanation. See instructions.

Part II   Realized Gain or (Loss), Recognized Gain, and Basis of Like-Kind Property Received

Caution: If you transferred **and** received **(a)** more than one group of like-kind properties, or **(b)** cash or other (not like-kind) property, see instructions under **Multi-Asset Exchanges.**

Note: Complete lines 12 through 14 ONLY if you gave up property that was not like-kind. Otherwise, go to line 15 now.

12	Fair market value (FMV) of other property given up	**12**	
13	Adjusted basis of other property given up	**13**	
14	Gain or (loss) recognized on other property given up. Subtract line 13 from line 12. See instructions for where to report the gain or (loss) on your tax return	**14**	-0-
15	Cash received, FMV of other property received, plus net liabilities assumed by other party, reduced (but not below zero) by any exchange expenses you incurred (see instructions).	**15**	125,000
16	FMV of like-kind property you received	**16**	250,000
17	Add lines 15 and 16	**17**	375,000
18	Adjusted basis of like-kind property you gave up, net amounts paid to other party, plus any exchange expenses **not** used on line 15 (see instructions) 200,000 + 25,000 . .	**18**	225,000
19	**Realized gain or (loss).** Subtract line 18 from line 17	**19**	150,000
20	**Recognized gain.** Enter the smaller of line 15 or line 19, but not less than zero. Report this amount on the form or schedule on which this exchange is reported. See instructions . . .	**20**	100,000*
21	Deferred gain or (loss). Subtract line 20 from line 19. If a related party exchange, see instructions .	**21**	50,000
22	**Basis of like-kind property received.** Subtract line 15 from the sum of lines 18 and 20 . .	**22**	200,000

For Paperwork Reduction Act Notice, see separate instructions.   Cat. No. 12311A   Form **8824** (1991)

* 125,000 LIABILITY LESS 25,000 CASH PAID
SEE REG. SEC. 1.1031(d)-2, EXAMPLE #2

Figure 5.3   IRS Form 8824 Mr. Black

Form **8824** Department of the Treasury Internal Revenue Service	**Like-Kind Exchanges** **(and nonrecognition of gain from conflict-of-interest sales)** ▶ See separate instructions. ▶ Attach to your tax return. ▶ Use a separate form for each like-kind exchange.	OMB No. 1545-1190 **1991** Attachment Sequence No. **49**

Name(s) shown on tax return	Identifying number
MR. BLACK	999-55-9995

Part I   Information on the Like-Kind Exchange

Note: *If the property described on line 1 or line 2 is real property located outside the United States, indicate the country.*

1 Description of like-kind property given up ▶ REAL PROPERTY - PARCEL B

2 Description of like-kind property received ▶ REAL PROPERTY - PARCEL A

3	Date like-kind property given up was originally acquired (month, day, year)	**3**	12 / 15 / 91
4	Date you actually transferred your property to other party (month, day, year)	**4**	12 / 15 / 91
5	Date the like-kind property you received was identified (month, day, year). See instructions	**5**	12 / 15 / 91
6	Date you actually received the like-kind property from other party (month, day, year)	**6**	12 / 15 / 91

7   Was the exchange made with a related party (see instructions)?
a ☐ Yes, in this tax year   b ☐ Yes, in a prior tax year   c ☒ No *(If "No," go to Part II.)*
8   Enter the following information about the related party:

Name	Identifying number
Address (no., street, and apt. or suite no., rural route, or P.O. box no. if mail is not delivered to street address)	
City or town, state, and ZIP code	Relationship to you

9   During this tax year, did the related party sell or dispose of the like-kind property received from you in the exchange? . . . . . . ☐ Yes ☐No
10 During this tax year, did you sell or dispose of the like-kind property you received? . . . . . . ☐ Yes ☐No
   If both lines 9 and 10 are "No," go to Part II. If either line 9 or line 10 is "Yes," the deferred gain or (loss) from line 21 must be reported on your return this tax year, *unless* one of the exceptions on line 11 applies. See instructions.
11 If one of the exceptions below applies to the disposition, check the applicable box:
   ☐ The disposition was after the death of either of the related parties.
   ☐ The disposition was an involuntary conversion, and the threat of conversion occurred after the exchange.
   ☐ You can establish to the satisfaction of the IRS that neither the exchange nor the disposition had tax avoidance as its principal purpose. If this box is checked, attach an explanation. See instructions.

Part II   Realized Gain or (Loss), Recognized Gain, and Basis of Like-Kind Property Received

Caution: *If you transferred and received (a) more than one group of like-kind properties, or (b) cash or other (not like-kind) property, see instructions under Multi-Asset Exchanges.*

Note: *Complete lines 12 through 14 ONLY if you gave up property that was not like-kind. Otherwise, go to line 15 now.*

12	Fair market value (FMV) of other property given up	**12**	
13	Adjusted basis of other property given up	**13**	
14	Gain or (loss) recognized on other property given up. Subtract line 13 from line 12. See instructions for where to report the gain or (loss) on your tax return	**14**	-0-
15	Cash received, FMV of other property received, plus net liabilities assumed by other party, reduced (but not below zero) by any exchange expenses you incurred (see instructions)	**15**	25,000
16	FMV of like-kind property you received	**16**	350,000
17	Add lines 15 and 16	**17**	375,000
18	Adjusted basis of like-kind property you gave up, net amounts paid to other party, plus any exchange expenses **not** used on line 15 (see instructions) 125,000 + 125,000	**18**	250,000*
19	**Realized gain or (loss).** Subtract line 18 from line 17	**19**	125,000
20	**Recognized gain.** Enter the smaller of line 15 or line 19, but not less than zero. Report this amount on the form or schedule on which this exchange is reported. See instructions . . .	**20**	25,000
21	Deferred gain or (loss). Subtract line 20 from line 19. If a related party exchange, see instructions .	**21**	100,000
22	**Basis of like-kind property received.** Subtract line 15 from the sum of lines 18 and 20 . .	**22**	250,000

For Paperwork Reduction Act Notice, see separate instructions.   Cat. No. 12311A   Form **8824** (1991)

* DEBT 125,000 + PROPERTY 125,000

The netting rules are summarized below:

- Cash paid on the acquisition of replacement property offsets cash received on the disposition of relinquished property.

- Cash paid on the acquisition of replacement property offsets debt relief on the disposition of relinquished property.

- Debt assumed on the acquisition of replacement property offsets debt relief on the disposition of relinquished property.

- Debt assumed on the acquisition of replacement property will not offset cash received on the disposition of relinquished property.

The Exchange Worksheet

To calculate the balancing of equities, an Exchange Worksheet should be prepared. Chapter 7 will discuss this in detail and will include three case studies.

Multiple Asset Exchanges

The April 1991 regulations for multiple asset exchanges require that properties which qualify as like-kind be matched into exchange groups. The principles for matching asset components in a multiple asset exchange are described in Chapter 4. This chapter will focus on the practical aspects of the procedures and computations required for multiple asset exchanges.

Multiple Asset Procedures

1. Segregate Exchange Groups

The regulations first direct the taxpayer to segregate properties transferred and received into exchange groups, matching up like-kind or like class properties. If the total fair market value of properties transferred in the exchange groups do not match, then a "residual group" is created for the difference in values. The residual group, then, is comprised of cash and other property excluded by Section 1031(a)(2) or in the regulations, but only to the extent of the difference in exchange group values (Reg. Sec. 1.1031(j)-1).

2. Netting of Liabilities

The regulations next direct the taxpayer to offset all liabilities assumed by the taxpayer with all liabilities of which he is relieved. This applies to all liabilities involved in the exchange whether they are recourse or nonrecourse debt, and whether or not they are secured by the exchanged properties involved. If there are excess liabilities assumed by the taxpayer, the excess is allocated among the exchange groups in proportion to their relative fair market values. If the taxpayer is relieved of excess liabilities, the excess is treated as cash received. Note that this netting of liabilities is a somewhat different formula from the general boot netting rule.

3. Computation of Gain Realized and Gain Recognized

For each exchange group, an "exchange group surplus" or "exchange group deficiency" is then calculated. A surplus exists if the total fair market value for the properties received exceeds the fair market value for property transferred. A deficit exists if the total fair market value of properties transferred exceed the fair market value of properties received in that group.

The total gain or loss realized is defined as the total market value of properties received for each group net of the adjusted basis of properties in that group. The gain realized is the lesser of either the total gain realized for that exchange group or the exchange group deficiency. Any losses realized are not recognized.

Gain Calculations—Example #6: Multi-Asset Exchange

In example #1 of the regulations, a computer and automobile are exchanged for a printer, automobile, corporate stock, and cash as follows:

	Adjusted Basis	Fair Market Value
Property Relinquished		
Computer A	$ 375	$ 1,000
Automobile A	3,500	4,000
Totals	$ 3,875	$ 5,000
Property Received		
Printer B		$ 800
Automobile B		2,950
Corporate stock		750
Cash		500
Totals		$ 5,000

The regulations analyze the exchange on the basis of fair market values (FMV) of groups created, as follows:

	Exchange Group Computer	Exchange Group Automobile	Residual Group	Total
FMV—property received	$ 800	$ 2,950	$ 1,250	$ 5,000
FMV—property received	1,000	4,000	-0-	5,000
Excess—surplus or deficiency	$ (200)	$(1,050)	$ 1,250	$ 0

The fair market value of property received is less than the fair market value of property relinquished for both exchange groups, thereby creating an exchange group deficiency for both exchange groups.

The gain realized is calculated for each exchange group as the excess of the fair market value of property relinquished over the adjusted basis of property in that group:

	Exchange Group Computer	Exchange Group Automobile	Total
FMV—property received	$ 1,000	$ 4,000	$ 5,000
Less: adjusted basis	(375)	(3,500)	(3,875)
Gain (loss) realized	$ 625	$ 500	$ 1,125
Gain recognized	$ 200	$ 500	$ 700

The taxable gain recognized is limited to the lesser of the gain realized of the exchange group deficiency. If there is an exchange group surplus, the loss is not recognized.

The treatment for the residual group is not clearly explained in the regulations. In this example in the regulations, there is an residual group of $1,250 consisting of cash and stock received. However, the regulations indicate that there is no gain or loss recognized with respect to this residual group, because no property transferred by the exchangor was allocated to the residual group. In the examples in the regulations, the underlying theme appears to be that as long as the total fair market value of exchange group properties transferred exceed the total fair market values of the exchange group properties received, then there is no gain or loss for the residual group.

An extensive set of example calculations including basis calculations are contained in the regulations.

INSTALLMENT GAIN DEFERRALS

Overview

Similar to other timing mechanisms of the Internal Revenue Code, the installment sales rules provide a method to defer the payment of tax into future years. Unlike other "rollover" deferrals, the installment sales rules do not require a reinvestment into replacement property.

The installment sales method may be used as an alternative to a like-kind exchange deferral, or may be used in conjunction with a like-kind exchange.

In general, the tax for the gain on any property sale is due in the year of sale. However, the installment sales rules provide a special tax reporting method. When at least one payment is to be received after the tax year of sale, the installment sales rules apply. Instead of paying the tax all in the year of sale, the tax is due as the payments are received in future years.

The essential aspect of an installment sale is that the tax is deferred. The primary benefits are twofold. First, the taxpayer may avoid paying tax before the cash is received. Second, the taxpayer may be able to reduce the overall tax on the sale.

The installment sales rules were enacted by Congress as Section 453 of the Internal Revenue Code. Due to public policy considerations, Congress sought to relieve the burden and unfairness of collecting the tax before the taxpayer had received the payments for a property sale.

For some taxpayers, a sale that is fully taxed all in one year would result in taxation at a higher marginal tax rate. With an installment sale, a taxpayer can potentially spread the tax over a period of years at a lower marginal tax rate, thereby paying less total tax on the sale overall.

Requirements of Installment Gains: Section 453

In General

An **installment sale** is currently defined by Section 453(b) as a property disposition "where at least one payment is to be received after the close of the taxable year in which the disposition occurs." The current definition is much broader in scope than the law before 1980. Prior to 1980, a taxpayer was not allowed to use the installment sale method if more than 30% of the total sales price was received in cash in the year of the sale. The current law merely requires that at least one cash payment is deferred beyond the year of sale.

The "installment method" provides that income recognition on a property disposition is "that proportion of the payments received in that year which the gross profit bears to the total contract price" (Section 453(c)).

The basic concepts to determine the tax on an installment sale are relatively simple. The essential components are:

- Calculate the total gross profit on the sale.

- Calculate the gross profit percentage on the sale.

- As payments are received, taxable gain is the gross profit percentage represented by each payment.

Instead of taxing the entire proceeds in the year of sale, the gross profit portion of each payment is taxed as it is received.

Example #1

To illustrate the primary concepts, assume that Barney Smith sold land with an adjusted basis of $71,000 for a price of $100,000, which he finances for the buyer. In the year of sale, he received $10,000 in cash from the buyer.

Sales price	$ 100,000
Less: adjusted basis	71,000
Gross profit	$ 29,000
Gross profit percentage	
($29,000/$100,000) =	29%
Payments received - year of sale	$ 10,000
Gross profit percentage	29%
Taxable gain - year of sale	$ 2,900

In the year of sale, Barney Smith will pay tax on $2,900 of gain, instead of $29,000. In subsequent years, as Barney receives the remaining $90,000 of principal, he will report 29% as taxable gain. See Figure 5.4 for an illustration of IRS Form 6252.

Because of the widespread potential application and potential abuses of the installment sales rules, a number of special provisions and exceptions have developed. Furthermore, the installment sales rules contain special traps for accelerating the collection of tax.

Election Out

For any property disposition, the taxpayer may elect not to apply the installment sales rules. This is known as the "election out." The election out of an installment sale may be made only on or before the due date (includ-

Figure 5.4 IRS form 6252 Barney Smith

Form **6252**	**Installment Sale Income**	OMB No. 1545-0228
Department of the Treasury Internal Revenue Service	▶ See separate instructions. ▶ Attach to your tax return. Use a separate form for each sale or other disposition of property on the installment method.	**1991** Attachment Sequence No. **79**

Name(s) shown on return	Identifying number
BARNEY SMITH	XXX-XX-XXXX

A Description of property ▶ .....LAND - 5 ACRES.....

B Date acquired (month, day, and year) ▶ ⌐ 7 / 01 / 70 ⌐ **C** Date sold (month, day, and year) ▶ ⌐ 11 / 12 / 91 ⌐

D Was the property sold to a related party after May 14, 1980? See instructions . . . . ☐ Yes ☒ No

E If the answer to D is "Yes," was the property a marketable security? If "Yes," complete Part III. If "No,"
complete Part III for the year of sale and for 2 years after the year of sale . . . . ☐ Yes ☐ No

Part I Gross Profit and Contract Price (Complete this part for the year of sale only.)

1	Selling price including mortgages and other debts. Do not include interest whether stated or unstated	**1**	100,000
2	Mortgages and other debts the buyer assumed or took the property subject to, but not include new mortgages the buyer got from a bank or other source. .	**2**	-0-
3	Subtract line 2 from line 1	**3**	100,000
4	Cost or other basis of property sold	**4**	71,000
5	Depreciation allowed or allowable	**5**	-0-
6	Adjusted basis. Subtract line 5 from line 4	**6**	71,000
7	Commissions and other expenses of sale.	**7**	-0-
8	Income recapture from Form 4797, Part III. See instructions . .	**8**	-0-
9	Add lines 6, 7, and 8	**9**	71,000
10	Subtract line 9 from line 1. If zero or less, do not complete the rest of this form	**10**	29,000
11	If the property described in question A above was your main home, enter the total of lines 9f and 15 from Form 2119. Otherwise, enter -0-	**11**	-0-
12	**Gross profit.** Subtract line 11 from line 10	**12**	29,000
13	Subtract line 9 from line 2. If zero or less, enter -0-	**13**	-0-
14	**Contract price.** Add line 3 and line 13	**14**	100,000

Part II Installment Sale Income (Complete this part for the year of sale and any year you receive a payment or have certain debts you must treat as a payment on installment obligations.)

15	Gross profit percentage. Divide line 12 by line 14. For years after the year of sale, see instructions	**15**	29%
16	**For year of sale only**—Enter amount from line 13 above; otherwise, enter -0-	**16**	-0-
17	Payments received during year. See instructions. Do not include interest whether stated or unstated	**17**	10,000
18	Add lines 16 and 17	**18**	10,000
19	Payments received in prior years. See instructions. Do not include interest whether stated or unstated . . . . **19** -0-		
20	**Installment sale income.** Multiply line 18 by line 15	**20**	2,900
21	Part of line 20 that is ordinary income under recapture rules. See instructions . . .	**21**	-0-
22	Subtract line 21 from line 20. Enter here and on Schedule D or Form 4797	**22**	2,900

Part III Related Party Installment Sale Income (Do not complete if you received the final payment this tax year.)

F Name, address, and taxpayer identifying number of related party ....

G Did the related party, during this tax year, resell or dispose of the property ("second disposition")? . . . ☐ Yes ☐ No

H **If the answer to question G is "Yes," complete lines 23 through 30 below unless one of the following conditions is
met (check only the box that applies).**

☐ The second disposition was more than 2 years after the first disposition (other than dispositions of
marketable securities). If this box is checked, enter the date of disposition (month, day, year). ▶ ⌐ / / ⌐

☐ The first disposition was a sale or exchange of stock to the issuing corporation.

☐ The second disposition was an involuntary conversion where the threat of conversion occurred after the first disposition.

☐ The second disposition occurred after the death of the original seller or buyer.

☐ It can be established to the satisfaction of the Internal Revenue Service that tax avoidance was not a principal purpose
for either of the dispositions. If this box is checked, attach an explanation. See instructions.

23	Selling price of property sold by related party	**23**	
24	Enter contract price from line 14 for year of first sale	**24**	
25	Enter the **smaller** of line 23 or line 24	**25**	
26	Total payments received by the end of your 1991 tax year. Add lines 18 and 19 . .	**26**	
27	Subtract line 26 from line 25. If zero or less, enter -0-	**27**	
28	Multiply line 27 by the gross profit percentage on line 15 for year of first sale.	**28**	
29	Part of line 28 that is ordinary income under recapture rules. See instructions . . .	**29**	
30	Subtract line 29 from line 28. Enter here and on Schedule D or Form 4797	**30**	

For Paperwork Reduction Act Notice, see separate instructions. Cat. No. 13601R Form **6252** (1991)

ing extensions) for filing the tax return for the year of sale. An election out may only be revoked with the consent of the IRS (Section 453(d)).

Exceptions: Inventory and Dealer Dispositions

Under Section 453(b)(2), the installment sales method does not apply to certain property dispositions. The exceptions are "dealer dispositions" as defined in Section 453(l), and dispositions of personal property that is held by the taxpayer as inventory.

Dealer dispositions are defined separately for personal property and real property in Section 453(l)(1). For personal property, a person who regularly sells personal property on the installment plan is a dealer. For real property, a disposition of real property that is held by the taxpayer for sale to customers in the ordinary course of business is a dealer disposition. Although defined somewhat differently, essentially the excluded target is inventory.

There are specific exceptions to the dealer disposition definitions: (1) certain property used or produced in the business of farming, if sold on the installment plan, and (2) dispositions of timeshares and residential lots. Timeshares and residential lots that qualify are specifically described in Section 453(l)(2)(B)(ii):

1. *Timeshares*—"a timeshare right to use or a timeshare ownership interest in real property for not more than 6 weeks per year, or a right to use specified campgrounds for recreational purposes."
2. *Residential lot*—"any residential lot, but only if the taxpayer (or any related person) is not to make any improvements with respect to such lot."

Since timeshares and residential lots are exceptions to the dealer disposition rules, sales of these properties will qualify for installment gains reporting. However, the taxpayer who sells timeshares and residential lots may only use the installment method if he elects to pay interest on the tax which is deferred (Section 453(l)(2)(C)). Interest is payable at the applicable federal rate.

Exceptions: Revolving Credit Plans & Securities

Certain other property dispositions are excluded from the installment sales provisions. The statute specifically excludes personal property sales under a revolving credit plan. Furthermore, the installment sales rules do not apply to installment obligations arising from sales of stock or securities or to other property that is regularly traded on an established market.

Acceleration of Gain: Depreciation Recapture

In general, the depreciation **recapture** rules serve to convert capital gains (or Section 1231 gains) into ordinary income. Section 453(i) requires that any recapture income is fully recognized in the year of sale, and only the excess gain will qualify for the installment method. For an installment sale, depreciation recapture will accelerate the recognition of gain into the year of sale, regardless of the amount of payments received in that year. Because of this acceleration, if an installment sale is not carefully planned, taxpayers may be in the position of owing tax in the year of sale without sufficient cash to pay the tax.

The depreciation recapture rule is specifically defined as the ordinary income as determined by Section 1245 and 1250. In very broad terms, Section 1245 property is depreciable personal property and certain other specified depreciable property. Section 1250 property is depreciable real property and property that is not included under Section 1245. It is important to note that Section 1245 includes certain types of property that are often classified as real property.

In general, the gain on the sale of Section 1245 property is ordinary income to the extent of previous depreciation deductions allowed or allowable, or the gain on the sale, whichever is the lowest amount. A gain on the sale of Section 1250 property is ordinary income to the extent of accelerated depreciation deductions over the straight line depreciation. Real property acquired prior to 1987 is subject to the recapture rules if depreciated on the accelerated ACRS method. Real property acquired after 1986 is not subject to recapture because current MACRS deductions are limited to straight line.

Example #2

Assume John Miller sells store equipment for $100,000. The adjusted basis of the equipment is $60,000, after previously deducting $15,000 in depreciation. Assume John also sells a building (excluding land) with the same sales price, adjusted basis, and prior depreciation. Assume the building's excess accelerated depreciation over straight line was $4,000. The ordinary recapture amounts are as follows:

	Section 1245 Equipment	Section 1250 Building
Sales price	$100,000	$100,000
Less: adjusted basis	60,000	60,000
Total gain realized	$ 40,000	40,000
Section 1245 ordinary income	$ 15,000	
Section 1250 ordinary income		$ 4,000

Although John will recognize the same total taxable gain for both properties, the ordinary income for the building is less because it is limited to the excess of accelerated depreciation over the straight line amount.

For further information on the depreciation recapture rules, see IRS Publication 544. For information regarding depreciation methods and calculations, see IRS Publication 534.

Acceleration: Related Party Sales

If an installment sale is made to a related party, taxable gain may be accelerated if the related party resells the property before the original installment obligation is paid in full. The amount realized on the second disposition is treated as received by the original seller. The accelerated gain applies to any subsequent dispositions within two years after the date of the first disposition. There is no time limit for the application of this rule for marketable securities (Section 453(e)).

Because the amount realized on the resale is deemed to be received by the original seller, the original seller's taxable gain is accelerated regardless of whether the original seller is paid in full. The amount that is treated as received by the original party is the lesser of (1) the amount realized on the resale, or (2) the total contract price for the first disposition net of total payments treated as received in prior tax years. If the original seller's full amount of gain has not been taxed as a result of the resale, he must recognize the remaining taxable gain; the original seller must continue to report gain on the installment method when total payments actually received exceed previously taxed actual and deemed payments.

The related party resale exception does not apply to: (1) dispositions after the death of either the original buyer or seller, (2) a second disposition resulting from an involuntary conversion. Related parties are defined by Section 453(f) with reference to Section 267(b) and Section 318(a).

Installment Sales Payments

The installment sales rules basically provide that the seller is taxed as payments are received. Most real estate sales involve mortgages and debt. Because of the variety and uses of debt instruments, there are situations whereby debt relief or the debt instrument itself may constitute a payment.

In General

In general, a purchaser's evidence of indebtedness does not constitute a payment (see "Qualifying Indebtedness"). Two exceptions to this general rule are contained in Section 453(f) for purchaser evidences of indebtedness that are 1) payable on demand, or 2) issued by a corporation, government, or political subdivision and are readily tradable. Debt instruments of this nature are treated as payments received for purposes of the installment sales rules.

A purchaser's evidence of indebtedness may be secured by a third-party guarantee (Section 453(f)(3)). Thus, a nonnegotiable, nontransferable standby letter of credit may be used to secure the purchaser's obligation. The regulations stipulate that a letter of credit will not qualify if it may be drawn upon in any circumstance except the default of the underlying obligation (Temp. Reg. Sec. 15A.453-1(b)(3)(iii)).

Qualifying Indebtedness

The temporary regulations define "qualifying indebtedness" for the purpose of clarifying the contract price for an installment sale. The contract price is the selling price reduced by any qualifying indebtedness assumed by the buyer to the extent that it does not exceed the seller's basis in the property.

In an installment sale, any debt that constitutes qualifying indebtedness will not be treated as a payment received by the taxpayer, unless the total liabilities exceed the seller's basis in the property. Qualifying indebtedness includes both mortgages and debt encumbering the property, and any debt that is not secured by the property, but was incurred incident to the purchaser's acquisition (Temp. Reg. Sec. 15A.453-1(b)(2)).

Nondealers in Real Property: Requirements of Section 453A

In General

Special rules apply to nondealers of real property if the total installment obligations arising and outstanding in any tax year exceed $5,000,000. In general, interest must be paid on the deferred tax liability for any obligation if the sales price exceeds $150,000.

Because of the possibility that sales may be split up into separate transactions to avoid the threshold for this rule, Section 453A provides two "aggregation" rules:

1. Any sales, exchanges, or series of related transactions, which are part of the same transaction shall be treated as one sale or exchange (Section 453A(b)(5)), and

2. Any entities which are treated as a single employer shall be treated as one person (Section 453A(b)(2)).

Exceptions

Any sales of personal use property or any property used or produced in the trade or business of farming are exempt from the special rules of Section 453A to pay interest on the deferred tax (Section 453A(b)(3)). Any installment obligations from the sale of residential lots or timeshares, are not subject to Section 453A, but are subject to Section 453(l)(2)(B).

Pledging Rules

Under Section 453A(d)(1), the proceeds of new indebtedness are treated as payments received on an installment obligation if the installment obligation is pledged to secure the new debt. This rule applies to obligations originating from a real estate sale with a price in excess of $150,000. In essence, this rule is another provision to accelerate the recognition of taxable gain with a transaction that Congress perceived as potentially abusive.

The pledging rule is not intended to create a double taxation for any single sale. The total gain that is taxed on an installment sale is limited to the total gain realized on the sale. Subsequent payments on the underlying obligation are not taxable until the total payments exceed the previously taxed amounts.

Installment Sales in Conjunction with Like-Kind Exchanges

When a like-kind exchange occurs with payments to be received over a period of years, receipt of like-kind property will not constitute a payment under the installment sales rules (Section 453(f)(6)(C)). For like-kind exchanges, the contract price is reduced by the amount of like-kind property (Section 453(f)(6)(A)). Similarly, the gross profit from the exchange is reduced by the amount of gain not recognized (Section 453(f)(6)(B)).

Essentially, when taxable boot is received in a like-kind exchange from an installment note, the tax can be deferred. Eventually, the boot (non-qualifying property) is taxable as the cash payments are received.

Installment Gain Calculations

To expand on the basic steps for an installment sale, the taxable gain when a property is sold is determined in the following manner:

1. Calculate the total gross profit on the sale.

2. Calculate the contract price.

3. Calculate the gross profit percentage.

4. Calculate the payments received.

5. Calculate the taxable gain.

Step 1: Calculate the Total Gross Profit on the Sale

This calculation is similar to other types of sales, except that the IRS treats selling expenses as an increase to the basis of nondealer real property (Temp. Reg. Sec. 15A.453-1(b)(2)(v)):

Original cost of the property
+ Capital expenditures
+ Cost of sale
− Accumulated depreciation
= Adjusted cost basis

Gross sales price
− Adjusted cost basis
= Total gross profit (realized gain)

Step 2: Calculate the Contract Price

As defined by the regulations, the contract price is the selling price reduced by qualifying indebtedness assumed by the buyer to the extent that it does not exceed the seller's basis in the property.

Gross sales price
− Qualifying indebtedness,
  limited to seller's basis in property
= Contract price

Step 3: Calculate the Gross Profit Percentage

The formula for this calculation is as follows:

$$\frac{\text{Total gross profit}}{\text{Total contract price}} = \text{Gross profit percentage}$$

Step 4: Calculate the Payments Received

The following items are included as payments received in the year of sale:

1. Down payment.

2. Principal loan payments

3. Excess liabilities assumed by the buyer over the seller's basis in the property.

4. Boot

The down payment is the gross cash paid by the buyer at the closing before any reduction for the seller's closing costs and allocated property taxes. Any principal received from a seller-financed mortgage is included in payments received, but not interest. Liabilities assumed by the buyer in excess of the seller's basis are treated as payments received in the year of sale. This situation may arise if the seller has refinanced the property or simply as a result of depreciation deductions. Boot is any additional consideration (money or property) paid by the purchaser.

The formula for this calculation is as follows:

> Down payment
> +Principal loan payments in the year of sale
> +Excess of loans over basis
> +Boot
> =Total amount received, year of sale

Step 4: Calculate the Taxable Gain

The formula for this calculation is as follows:

> Payments received each year
> × Gross profit percentage
> = Taxable gain

Step 6: Calculate the Tax Due

The formula for this calculation is as follows:

> Taxable gain
> × Taxpayer's marginal tax rate
> = Tax due

Example #3

Mr. Leaffer sold a duplex building for $80,000, and land for $20,000. At the closing he received $10,000 as a down payment. The purchaser assumed a $50,000 first mortgage and received a $40,000 second mortgage made by Mr. Leaffer. The $40,000 note is to be paid over four years with equal principal payments of $10,000 per year, with adequate stated interest. The adjusted basis for the land was $13,000. The adjusted basis for the building after straight line depreciation deductions of $25,000, was $30,000.

The total consideration received for the sale, in the form of loans and the cash down payment are allocated to each respective property on the basis of relative fair market values:

	Land	Building	Total
Cash down payment	$ 2,000	$ 8,000	$ 10,000
Mortgage assumed by buyer	10,000	40,000	50,000
Second mortgage to seller	8,000	32,000	40,000
Total consideration	$20,000	$80,000	$100,000

Step 1: Calculate the Gross Profit

	Land	Building
Gross sales price	$ 20,000	$ 80,000
Less: adjusted basis	(13,000)	(30,000)
Total gross profit	$ 7,000	$ 50,000

Step 2: Calculate the Contract Price

	Land	Building
Gross sales price	$ 20,000	$ 80,000
Qualifying indebtedness	(10,000)	(40,000)
Limited to seller's basis in property	-0-	10,000
Contract price	$ 10,000	$ 50,000

Step 3: Calculate Gross Profit Percentage

	Land	Building
$\dfrac{\text{Gross profit}}{\text{Contract price}}$	$\dfrac{\$\ 7,000}{10,000}$	$\dfrac{\$\ 50,000}{50,000}$
= Gross profit percentage	70%	100%

Step 4: Calculate the Payments Received

For the year of sale, the payments are:

	Land	Building
1. Down payment	$ 2,000	$ 8,000
2. Principal on second mortgage	2,000	8,000
3. Qualifying indebtedness in excess of seller's basis	-0-	10,000
Total payments	$ 4,000	$26,000

In subsequent years, the payments are:
Principal on second mortgage

	Land	Building
Year 2	$ 2,000	$ 8,000
Year 3	2,000	8,000
Year 4	2,000	8,000

Step 5: Calculate the Taxable Gain

For the year of sale:

Payment	$ 4,000	$26,000
Gross profit percentage	70%	100%
Taxable gain	$ 2,800	$26,000

In subsequent years:

Payment	$ 2,000	$ 8,000
Gross profit percentage	70%	100%
Taxable gain	$ 1,400	$ 8,000

The total taxable gain, multiplied by the taxpayer's marginal tax rate for each applicable year, will be the total tax due each year. (See Figures 5.5 and 5.6.)

The table below summarizes the gain to be reported each year for the example above:

Year 1	$ 2,800	$ 26,000
Year 2	1,400	8,000
Year 3	1,400	8,000
Year 4	1,400	8,000
Total taxable gain$	$ 7,000	$ 50,000

EVALUATING PROPERTY DISPOSITION ALTERNATIVES

In General

The federal method of income taxation is based on graduated tax rates. The income tax applicable to any taxpayer is dependent on the type of entity involved, and the tax bracket as determined by the income level for that taxpayer. While there are some overlaps in general rules, taxable income—as defined by the Internal Revenue Code—is determined under a different set of rules for individuals, corporations, trusts and estates. Although partnership and S Corporation income is taxed on a pass-thru basis, in certain cases, tax may be applied to an S Corporation that is otherwise inapplicable to a partnership.

Figure 5.5 IRS form 6252 – Mr. Leaffer

Form **6252**	**Installment Sale Income**	OMB No. 1545-0228
Department of the Treasury Internal Revenue Service	▶ See separate instructions. ▶ Attach to your tax return. Use a separate form for each sale or other disposition of property on the installment method.	**1991** Attachment Sequence No. **79**

Name(s) shown on return	Identifying number
MR. LEAFFER	999-55-5555

A Description of property ▶ DUPLEX BUILDING

B Date acquired (month, day, and year) ▶ 3 / 12 / 82   **C** Date sold (month, day, and year) ▶ 8 / 15 / 91

D Was the property sold to a related party after May 14, 1980? See instructions . . . . ☐ Yes ☒ No

E If the answer to D is "Yes," was the property a marketable security? If "Yes," complete Part III. If "No," complete Part III for the year of sale and for 2 years after the year of sale. . . . . ☐ Yes ☐ No

Part I   **Gross Profit and Contract Price** *(Complete this part for the year of sale only.)*

1	Selling price including mortgages and other debts. Do not include interest whether stated or unstated			**1**	80,000
2	Mortgages and other debts the buyer assumed or took the property subject to, but not new mortgages the buyer got from a bank or other source. .	**2**	40,000		
3	Subtract line 2 from line 1	**3**	40,000		
4	Cost or other basis of property sold	**4**	55,000		
5	Depreciation allowed or allowable	**5**	25,000		
6	Adjusted basis. Subtract line 5 from line 4 . . .	**6**	30,000		
7	Commissions and other expenses of sale.	**7**	-0-		
8	Income recapture from Form 4797, Part III. See instructions . .	**8**	-0-		
9	Add lines 6, 7, and 8			**9**	30,000
10	Subtract line 9 from line 1. If zero or less, do not complete the rest of this form			**10**	50,000
11	If the property described in question A above was your main home, enter the total of lines 9f and 15 from Form 2119. Otherwise, enter -0-			**11**	-0-
12	**Gross profit.** Subtract line 11 from line 10			**12**	50,000
13	Subtract line 9 from line 2. If zero or less, enter -0-			**13**	10,000
14	**Contract price.** Add line 3 and line 13			**14**	50,000

Part II   **Installment Sale Income** *(Complete this part for the year of sale and any year you receive a payment or have certain debts you must treat as a payment on installment obligations.)*

15	Gross profit percentage. Divide line 12 by line 14. For years after the year of sale, see instructions	**15**	100%	
16	**For year of sale only**—Enter amount from line 13 above; otherwise, enter -0-	**16**	10,000	
17	Payments received during year. See instructions. Do not include interest whether stated or unstated	**17**	16,000	
18	Add lines 16 and 17	**18**	26,000	
19	Payments received in prior years. See instructions. Do not include interest whether stated or unstated	**19**	-0-	
20	**Installment sale income.** Multiply line 18 by line 15	**20**	26,000	
21	Part of line 20 that is ordinary income under recapture rules. See instructions . .	**21**	-0-	
22	Subtract line 21 from line 20. Enter here and on Schedule D or Form 4797	**22**	26,000	

Part III   **Related Party Installment Sale Income** *(Do not complete if you received the final payment this tax year.)*

F Name, address, and taxpayer identifying number of related party ....

G Did the related party, during this tax year, resell or dispose of the property ("second disposition")? . . . ☐ Yes ☐ No

H **If the answer to question G is "Yes," complete lines 23 through 30 below unless one of the following conditions is met (check only the box that applies).**

  ☐ The second disposition was more than 2 years after the first disposition (other than dispositions of marketable securities). If this box is checked, enter the date of disposition (month, day, year). . ▶   / /

  ☐ The first disposition was a sale or exchange of stock to the issuing corporation.

  ☐ The second disposition was an involuntary conversion where the threat of conversion occurred after the first disposition.

  ☐ The second disposition occurred after the death of the original seller or buyer.

  ☐ It can be established to the satisfaction of the Internal Revenue Service that tax avoidance was not a principal purpose for either of the dispositions. If this box is checked, attach an explanation. See instructions.

23	Selling price of property sold by related party	**23**	
24	Enter contract price from line 14 for year of first sale	**24**	
25	Enter the **smaller** of line 23 or line 24	**25**	
26	Total payments received by the end of your 1991 tax year. Add lines 18 and 19	**26**	
27	Subtract line 26 from line 25. If zero or less, enter -0-	**27**	
28	Multiply line 27 by the gross profit percentage on line 15 for year of first sale.	**28**	
29	Part of line 28 that is ordinary income under recapture rules. See instructions	**29**	
30	Subtract line 29 from line 28. Enter here and on Schedule D or Form 4797	**30**	

For Paperwork Reduction Act Notice, see separate instructions.   Cat. No. 13601R   Form **6252** (1991)

Figure 5.6   IRS form 6252—Mr. Leaffer

Form 6252

Installment Sale Income

▶ See separate instructions.   ▶ Attach to your tax return.
Use a separate form for each sale or other disposition of
property on the installment method.

OMB No. 1545-0228

1991

Department of the Treasury
Internal Revenue Service

Attachment Sequence No. **79**

Name(s) shown on return: MR. LEAFFER

Identifying number: 999-55-5555

A Description of property ▶ land

B Date acquired (month, day, and year) ▶ 3 / 12 / 85   **C** Date sold (month, day, and year) ▶ 8 / 15 / 91

D Was the property sold to a related party after May 14, 1980? See instructions . . . . ☐ Yes ☒ No

E If the answer to D is "Yes," was the property a marketable security? If "Yes," complete Part III. If "No," complete Part III for the year of sale and for 2 years after the year of sale . . . . ☐ Yes ☐ No

Part I   Gross Profit and Contract Price (Complete this part for the year of sale only.)

1	Selling price including mortgages and other debts. Do not include interest whether stated or unstated	**1** 20,000
2	Mortgages and other debts the buyer assumed or took the property subject to, but not new mortgages the buyer got from a bank or other source.	**2** 10,000
3	Subtract line 2 from line 1	**3** 10,000
4	Cost or other basis of property sold	**4** 13,000
5	Depreciation allowed or allowable	**5** -0-
6	Adjusted basis. Subtract line 5 from line 4	**6** 13,000
7	Commissions and other expenses of sale.	**7** -0-
8	Income recapture from Form 4797, Part III. See instructions	**8** -0-
9	Add lines 6, 7, and 8	**9** 13,000
10	Subtract line 9 from line 1. If zero or less, do not complete the rest of this form .	**10** 7,000
11	If the property described in question A above was your main home, enter the total of lines 9f and 15 from Form 2119. Otherwise, enter -0-	**11** -0-
12	**Gross profit.** Subtract line 11 from line 10	**12** 7,000
13	Subtract line 9 from line 2. If zero or less, enter -0-	**13** -0-
14	**Contract price.** Add line 3 and line 13	**14** 10,000

Part II   Installment Sale Income (Complete this part for the year of sale and any year you receive a payment or have certain debts you must treat as a payment on installment obligations.)

15	Gross profit percentage. Divide line 12 by line 14. For years after the year of sale, see instructions	**15** 70%
16	**For year of sale only**—Enter amount from line 13 above; otherwise, enter -0-	**16** -0-
17	Payments received during year. See instructions. Do not include interest whether stated or unstated	**17** 4,000
18	Add lines 16 and 17	**18** 4,000
19	Payments received in prior years. See instructions. Do not include interest whether stated or unstated	**19** -0-
20	**Installment sale income.** Multiply line 18 by line 15	**20** 2,800
21	Part of line 20 that is ordinary income under recapture rules. See instructions	**21** -0-
22	Subtract line 21 from line 20. Enter here and on Schedule D or Form 4797	**22** 2,800

Part III   Related Party Installment Sale Income (Do not complete if you received the final payment this tax year.)

F Name, address, and taxpayer identifying number of related party

G Did the related party, during this tax year, resell or dispose of the property ("second disposition")? . . . ☐ Yes ☐ No

H If the answer to question G is "Yes," complete lines 23 through 30 below unless one of the following conditions is met (check only the box that applies).

☐ The second disposition was more than 2 years after the first disposition (other than dispositions of marketable securities). If this box is checked, enter the date of disposition (month, day, year). ▶ / /

☐ The first disposition was a sale or exchange of stock to the issuing corporation.

☐ The second disposition was an involuntary conversion where the threat of conversion occurred after the first disposition.

☐ The second disposition occurred after the death of the original seller or buyer.

☐ It can be established to the satisfaction of the Internal Revenue Service that tax avoidance was not a principal purpose for either of the dispositions. If this box is checked, attach an explanation. See instructions.

23	Selling price of property sold by related party	**23**
24	Enter contract price from line 14 for year of first sale	**24**
25	Enter the **smaller** of line 23 or line 24	**25**
26	Total payments received by the end of your 1991 tax year. Add lines 18 and 19	**26**
27	Subtract line 26 from line 25. If zero or less, enter -0-	**27**
28	Multiply line 27 by the gross profit percentage on line 15 for year of first sale	**28**
29	Part of line 28 that is ordinary income under recapture rules. See instructions	**29**
30	Subtract line 29 from line 28. Enter here and on Schedule D or Form 4797	**30**

For Paperwork Reduction Act Notice, see separate instructions.   Cat. No. 13601R   Form **6252** (1991)

Marginal Tax Rates

The marginal tax rate applicable to any taxpayer depends not only on the type of taxable entity and the level of income, but also on the character of income received. At the time of this writing, the maximum tax on capital gains is 28%, whereas the maximum individual tax rate is 31% for ordinary income. Only taxpayers in the highest income tax bracket potentially benefit from the 3% reduction in tax for capital gains.

Some types of property dispositions are characterized as capital gains (Section 1221), while others are classified as ordinary gains. In prior years, individual taxpayers were permitted to exclude 60 percent of net capital gains from taxable income. The capital gains exclusion rules were repealed as a result of the *1986 Tax Reform Act*. However, the legislature did not repeal those sections of the Internal Revenue Code that define capital gains as distinguished from ordinary gains, and those sections that limit the deduction of **capital losses**. Congress is considering the reinstatement of the capital gains exclusion rules, but not to the extent of the former 60 percent exclusion.

Alternative Minimum Tax

An extensive analysis of the alternative minimum tax rules is beyond the scope of this publication. However, it is important to realize that as a result of the *1986 Tax Reform Act*, many more taxpayers are paying alternative minimum tax than in prior years. In the evaluation of any property disposal, the potential application of the alternative minimum tax rules must be considered.

The alternative minimum tax rules currently in effect are essentially an alternate income tax system, in addition to the regular tax system. The current alternative minimum tax rate for corporate taxpayers is 20%, and the current rate for noncorporate taxpayers is 24%. While operative within the same statutory framework of the Internal Revenue Code, taxable income for alternative minimum tax purposes is not defined the same as taxable income for regular tax.

The determination of alternative minimum taxable income begins with regular taxable income, which is adjusted by tax preference items. The nature of the adjustments are primarily:

- Permanent differences from the regular tax system.

- Timing differences from regular taxable income.

A number of tax preference items apply to both corporate and noncorporate taxpayers, while others apply exclusively to corporate or non-corporate taxpayers. Essentially, the permanent differences consist of deductions that are disallowed, and exempt income items that are taxable for alternative minimum tax purposes. The timing differences arise from alternate methods that are specified for calculating deductions or income. Some of the most notable timing differences are depreciation, long-term construction contracts, alternative tax net operating loss, and installment sales.

Alternative Minimum Tax Depreciation

In general, the depreciation deductions allowed for alternative minimum tax purposes are calculated with a slower recovery method and for longer asset lives. In the earlier years of cost recovery, the deduction is less than the regular tax method, which causes an acceleration of taxable income for alternative minimum tax. In later years, this situation eventually reverses, whereby the deduction for alternative minimum tax is more than for regular tax. In essence, this represents a timing difference between the two tax systems. (See Figure 5.7).

Figure 5.7

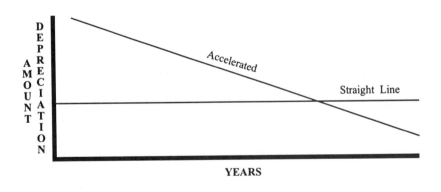

A taxpayer may elect to use the alternate depreciation method for regular tax purposes. Unless this election is made, or the property is fully depreciated, any depreciable property will have a different adjusted tax basis for alternative minimum tax when it is sold.

*In any case where alternative minimum tax potentially applies, two par-
allel sets of calculations must be performed for the disposition of any depreciable property.* The taxable gain for alternative minimum tax purposes
will generally be less than for regular tax. It is also interesting to note that
while the alternative minimum tax rules were designed to be punitive and
accelerate the tax collection process, the current alternative minimum tax
rates are lower than the capital gains rates and higher level income tax
rates for regular tax.

Example

In a simple sale situation, assume that Bill has sold a commercial building
for $400,000, which originally cost $315,000. The prior depreciation for
regular tax was $100,000 (straight line, 31.5 years). The prior depreciation
for alternative minimum tax was $79,000 (straight line, 40 years).

	Regular Tax	Alternative Tax
Original cost basis	$ 315,000	$ 315,000
Less: prior depreciation	100,000	79,000
Adjusted basis	215,000	236,000
Amount realized	400,000	400,000
Less: adjusted basis	215,000	236,000
Taxable gain	$ 185,000	$ 164,000

Projecting Taxable Income

In projecting taxable income, the taxpayer will need to review the primary
factors that affect the determination of taxable income in his particular
case. Because the tax laws and regulations are in a constant state of
change, the taxpayer must keep informed of current legislation that may
affect his position. It is generally considered to be prudent and imperative
to obtain the counsel from an attorney and financial advisor, as necessary.

Potentially, any taxpayer or taxable entity may sell or exchange property. For example, an individual, partnership, corporation, trust, or estate
may all hold property that eventually is sold or exchanged. The entire
body of tax law contained in the Internal Revenue Code that determines
the formulas for taxable income, deductible expenses, and limitations for
each type of taxable entity is beyond the scope of this publication. However, an approach to evaluate any property disposition would generally
include these ten factors:

1. Determine the taxpayer's taxable income from all other sources without regard to the property disposition.

2. Determine taxable income from the sale of property.

3. Determine taxable income for the property disposition under alternative deferral method (i.e., installment gain, residential rollover, involuntary conversion, like-kind exchange, or other provisions in the Internal Revenue Code).

4. Determine taxpayer's total combined taxable income (income from all sources including the property disposition) under the regular tax rules for the sale and all proposed alternatives.

5. Compute the income tax for regular tax purposes.

6. Determine taxpayer's total combined taxable income under the "alternative minimum tax rules," if applicable, for the sale and all proposed alternatives.

7. Compute the income tax for alternative minimum tax purposes.

8. Compare the total tax differences for the year of the proposed property disposition.

9. If a stream of payments will be received in future years, discount the net stream of payments (cash - tax) to present value.

10. Compute the total tax difference.

In situations where an installment sale is not involved, or the interest factor is considered negligible, the last two steps may be disregarded.

In some cases, the taxpayer's marginal tax rate is already a known factor. For example, some high income taxpayers are consistently in the highest tax brackets and are expecting similar levels of income in the current year. If the taxpayer's tax bracket is a known factor, the tax effects of a disposition may be evaluated on the basis of differences in taxable income for a sale or exchange, with proper consideration for potential alternative minimum tax.

Accounting for Real Estate Exchanges under Generally Accepted Accounting Principles

by Michael J.R. Hoffman, DBA
   Karen S. McKenzie, Ph.D., CPA
   Florida Atlantic University
   Boca Raton, Florida

INTRODUCTION[1]

During the several years that have passed since the enactment of the *Tax Reform Act of 1986*, much attention in real estate journals has been paid to the subject of like-kind exchanges.[2] The recent issuance of proposed regulations relating to deferred like-kind exchanges has fanned further interest in the subject.[3] The impact of tax savings or tax costs on the returns from investments in real estate certainly justifies the careful examination of the tax consequences of performing in a like-kind exchange. However, a topic that has been completely overlooked is that of compliance with generally accepted accounting principles (GAAP).[4]

This chapter is reprinted with permission from Warren, Garham & Lamont.

---

[1] This chapter is based on the authors' article "Real Estate Swaps and the Accountant's Dilemma," *Real Estate Review* 21 (Winter 1992), pp. 76-82.

[2] See, for example, Goolsby and Williams [1989], Barrett and Kolbe [1988], and Lindbeck and Edmonds [1987].

[3] See Chane [1990 and 1991].

[4] There is a hierarchy of authoritative guidance, but most authoritative are the pronouncements of the Financial Accounting Standards Board (FASB) and its predecessors.

It is likely that the small real estate investor may not be concerned with GAAP. The investor's bank may be the only external user of the investor's financial statements, and appropriately, the rule of thumb is to make the banker happy. However, if the real estate investment activities are conducted by a publicly traded corporation (subject to SEC regulation) or the investor's financial statements are to be audited (and an unqualified audit opinion is desired), compliance with GAAP becomes more relevant. The tax accounting rules for reporting the results of a like-kind exchange, discussed in detail in other chapters, are quite different from the financial accounting (GAAP) rules relating to exchanges of similar assets.[5]

Although compliance with GAAP has not received attention in the real estate literature, real estate exchanges have received the attention of the group responsible for the promulgation of GAAP.[6] A permanent task force, established by the group with primary responsibility for determining GAAP, has specifically examined the financial reporting version of the like-kind exchange. This task force's selection of real estate exchanges for special attention indicates that it feels that issues relating to such exchanges are material and that the area is in need of additional authoritative guidance. The combination of the lack of attention to the financial reporting implications of real estate exchanges in the literature and the definite interest in such exchanges on the part of the primary financial reporting regulatory group is the reason for including this chapter in this book.

Throughout this chapter, we refer to exchanges of real estate with respect to which gain or loss may not be fully recognized. The label that is attached to such an exchange depends on whether our interest is in the tax consequences or the consequences for financial reporting (e.g., annual reports to shareholders). To facilitate clear communication between the authors and readers, we will attempt to use the following descriptions of the transaction of interest: (1) for financial reporting purposes, the transaction is referred to as the exchange of similar assets; and (2) for tax accounting purposes, the transaction is referred to as the exchange of like-kind property or as a like-kind exchange.

---

5 Accounting Principles Board Opinion Number 29 is the financial accounting authority for exchanges of similar assets. §1031 of the Internal Revenue Code and the Treasury Regulations issued thereunder control the reporting for tax purposes of the results of like-kind exchanges.

6 FASB has published a standard that "establishes standards for recognition of profit on all real estate sales . . ." [FASB, 1982, P 1]. Exchanges subject to APB 29 specifically are not affected by this standard.

This chapter is organized into three major sections. First, the differences between the tax treatment of like-kind exchanges and exchanges of similar assets will be discussed and illustrated by means of a simple example. Since like-kind exchange is the subject of detailed presentations in other chapters, the tax treatment of such exchanges will be described in very basic terms, in order that the provisions of APB 29 might be contrasted. Second, recent deliberations on the part of the Emerging Issues Task Force (EITF) of the Financial Accounting Standards Board (FASB)[7] relating directly to exchanges of real estate will be discussed and illustrated. Finally, the question of how to handle an exchange that includes nonmonetary boot, an issue which has not received either authoritative (i.e., the APB or FASB) or nonauthoritative (i.e., academic and practitioner journals) attention, will be discussed and illustrated.

POINT-BY-POINT COMPARISON OF APB 29 AND IRC §1031

For the purposes of financial reporting under GAAP, APB 29 is the authoritative pronouncement relating to numerous transactions involving nonmonetary assets. In this chapter, only one of these transactions is examined. Of interest here is the exchange of similar assets.[8] For tax purposes, IRC §1031 is the authority. While the basic transaction that is the subject of these provisions is quite similar, the reporting consequences differ greatly. Two principal points of comparison will be examined in this section: (1) the definition of similar assets versus like-kind property for the purpose of determining eligible exchanges, and (2) the extent to which gain or loss is recognized. A third point, the determination of the carrying value of property acquired, will be briefly discussed. The brevity of this final section on carrying value is attributable to the fact that this determi-

---

7   The FASB is the primary source of GAAP. The EITF was established by the FASB as a screening device, which allows pressing issues to be addressed in a timely manner without overburdening the FASB's already overcrowded agenda. Only issues with respect to which the EITF cannot attain a consensus are referred to the FASB for consideration.

8   Other transactions considered by APB 29, but not discussed in this paper, are nonreciprocal transfers with owners (e.g., property dividends), nonreciprocal transfers with other than owners (e.g., charitable contributions of property), and exchanges of nonmonetary assets where fair value is not reasonably determinable.

nation is merely a bookkeeping (account-balancing) consequence of the exchange.

Determination of Eligible Exchanges

Eligibility for both the tax and financial reporting provisions are based primarily on the use to which the properties exchanged are placed. While there is a great deal of overlap between the two rules, there is also a significant difference.

Under APB 29

Regarding exchanges of similar assets, two types of transactions are identified [APB, 1973, ¶ 21]:

1. An exchange of a product or property held for sale in the ordinary course of business for a product or property to be sold in the same line of business to facilitate sales to customers *other than the parties to the exchange* [emphasis added], and

2. An exchange of a productive asset not held for sale in the ordinary course of business for a similar productive asset or an equivalent interest in the same or similar productive asset.

Thus, APB 29 controls the financial reporting for exchanges involving either inventory or productive real estate. However, in the case of real estate held as inventory (i.e., held for sale to customers), there is a qualification that the purpose of the exchange is "to facilitate sales to customers other than the parties to the exchange." This qualification should not pose too great an obstacle to the typical real estate developer. The customers, the sales to whom are facilitated by the exchange, are the individuals who will buy or lease the developed land, not the other party to the exchange (who is probably another developer or investor).

Similar productive assets, referred to in ¶ 21(b) of APB 29, are defined as follows [APB, 1973, ¶ 3(e)]:

> [P]roductive assets that are of the same general type, that perform the same function or that are employed in the same line of business.

By footnote reference, APB 29 indicates eligibility for deferral of tax under IRC §1031 *may indicate* that the assets qualify as similar productive assets as defined in the Opinion.

Under IRC §1031

IRC §1031(a)(1) describes the transactions that qualify tax deferral as follows:

> [T]he exchange of property held for productive use in a trade of business or for investment if such property is exchanged solely for property of a like kind which is to be held either for productive use in a trade or business or for investment.

Thus, in a like-kind exchange, productive real estate may be exchanged for real estate to be held for investment (as well as productive for productive and investment for investment). The Treasury Regulations under IRC §1031 elaborate that the character, quality or grade of the real estate exchanged is not an issue [Reg. §1.1031(a)-1(b)]. Rather, it is the use to which the properties exchanged were and will be put that is important (i.e., productive or investment use). Improved real estate may be exchanged for unimproved real estate or a commercial building may be exchanged for an apartment building. See Chapter 2 for more detail on the technical definition of "like-kind property."

Summary of Differences

While many practitioners believe that the definition of a like-kind exchange under IRC §1031 and an exchange of similar assets under APB 29 are identical, they are not. APB 29 controls the exchange of property held either for sale to customers (i.e., inventory) or for productive use. IRC §1031 controls the tax-deferred exchange of property held for productive or investment use. The overlap between the two authorities is in the area of productive property. APB 29 does not address the exchange of investment property, while IRC §1031 does. IRC §1031 does not permit the tax-deferred exchange of property held for sale to customers, while APB 29 does (with a qualification).

Another distinction between the two provisions is more subtle. Under IRC §1031, a productive owner of real estate may exchange the property for other real estate to be held for investment. That is, the use of property may change as a result of a like-kind exchange. APB 29 does not allow this change of use. Inventory must be exchanged for property to be held as inventory or productive property must be exchanged for property to be held for similar productive use.

Gain or Loss Recognition

Assuming that an exchange is subject to the special nonrecognition provisions of APB 29 for financial reporting and IRC §1031 for tax purposes, many assume the reporting consequences are the same. Again, they are not. After a brief description of what is meant by the term "boot," the different gain and loss recognition rules will be examined.

The Role of Boot in an Exchange

In any exchange of nonmonetary property, the likelihood that the fair market values of the properties exchanged will be equal is very small. This is particularly so in exchanges of real estate. The purpose of boot is to equalize the fair market value being given and received by the parties to the exchange, allowing the transaction to proceed. The portion of the exchange value represented by boot falls outside the definition of either like-kind property or similar assets. At this point, we will make the simplifying assumption that boot will be monetary property. The tax rules relating to giving and receiving boot are discussed in Chapter 3.

Under APB 29

The general rule for nonmonetary exchanges is that gain or loss is recognized in full and the asset acquired is recorded at fair market value [APB, 1973, ¶ 18]. Special treatment of exchanges involving *similar nonmonetary assets* is provided in ¶ 22 of APB 29 as follows:

- If a loss results from the exchange, such loss is recognized in full, regardless of the presence or absence of boot.

- If a gain results from the exchange, such gain is recognized on a prorata basis according to what portion of the exchange value is *received in the form of boot.*

For example, if the real estate exchanged was worth $100 and the real estate acquired was worth $88, $12 worth of boot would equalize the exchange value. In this case, the party receiving the $12 boot would recognize 12 percent ($12 boot/$100 exchange value) of any gain realized. If instead a loss had been realized, the receipt of boot would not affect the full recognition of the loss.

Under IRC §1031

IRC §1031 starts from the position that neither gain nor loss is recognized on an exchange solely in kind [IRC §1031(a)(1)]. IRC §1031(b) and (c) specifically address the impact of boot. IRC §1031 requires that gain be recognized *to the extent* of the value of any other property (i.e., boot) received. Thus, referring to the example used to illustrate the recognition rule of APB 29 above, gain would be recognized for tax purposes *to the extent of $12* (i.e., the smaller of $12 or the gain realized).

If instead a loss had been realized, IRC §1031(c) emphasizes that the loss may not be recognized. That is, the receipt of boot triggers recognition of gain, but not loss.

Summary of Differences

On the side of loss recognition, APB 29 requires that for financial reporting purposes, a loss is recognized in full. Whether or not boot is given or is received is immaterial to this requirement. The tax consequences under IRC §1031(c) are diametrically opposite the full recognition required for financial reporting. Regardless of whether boot is given or received, any loss realized on the like-kind property *must be deferred*. That is, a loss on a like-kind exchange may not be recognized under any circumstances.

If, instead, a gain is realized on the exchange, the difference between tax accounting and financial reporting is less dramatic than with a loss. Under APB 29, the gain is recognized on a prorata basis, according to the relative amount of boot included in the exchange. Under IRC §1031, gain is recognized *to the extent* of the boot received on a dollar-for-dollar basis. Thus, the gain recognized under the tax law will generally be greater than the gain reported on financial statements.

Determination of Carrying Value of Property Acquired

Once the correct amount of gain or loss recognition is determined, the final step is to determine the initial amount at which the like-kind or similar asset acquired is to be recorded. This amount is merely a balancing figure. While the precise amount recorded for tax versus financial reporting purposes may differ, the underlying formula is the same. The determination of the carrying value of the property received in a like-kind exchange is presented in Chapter 3. For the readers convenience, the formulas used to calculate carrying value are presented in Table 6.1.

Table 6.1   Determination of Carrying Value of Property Acquired in a Nonrecognition Exchange

Formula A:		Formula B:	
FMV of like-kind or similar property acquired;		Book value (adjusted basis) of like-kind or similar property surrendered;	
Minus:	Gain postponed	**Plus:**	Book Value (adjusted basis of boot surrendered;
	or		
Plus:	Loss postponed	**Plus:**	Gain recognized;
Equals:	Recorded cost	**Minus:**	Loss recognized;
		Minus:	FMV of boot received
		Equals:	Recorded Cost

ILLUSTRATION COMPARING TAX TREATMENT UNDER IRC §1031 TO FINANCIAL REPORTING TREATMENT UNDER APB 29

The example presented in this section is intended to emphasize the differences between the financial reporting treatment of an exchange of similar real estate under ¶ 22 of APB 29 and the tax treatment of a like-kind exchange of real estate under IRC §1031. The facts presented below will permit the illustration of the basic differences between the two provisions.

Presentation of Facts

The following facts are presented for the reader's consideration:

A and B entered into an exchange of real estate. The exchange qualifies for nonrecognition under both APB 29 and IRC §1031. The property transferred by each party consisted of the following:

Transferred by A (received by B):
Real estate $150 FMV
                                          90 book value

Transferred by B (received by A):
Real estate $120 FMV
                                          135 book value
Cash (boot)   30

The $30 of boot equalizes the exchange value, permitting the transaction to be completed. As discussed in Chapter 3, the same consequences would result if the boot was in the form of a $30 lien on Party A's property that is assumed by Party B (or to which the transferred property is subject).

Consequences to Party A

From the perspective of Party A, $30 (or 20 percent) of the exchange value is received in the form of boot. The consequences of this exchange for Party A is presented in Table 6.2. The tax consequences and financial reporting consequences are presented side-by-side for ease of comparison.

Table 6.2   Comparison of Consequences to Party A

For Financial Reporting		For Tax Purposes
$60	Gain or (loss) **realized**	$60
$12[a]	Gain or (loss) **recognized**	$30[b]
$72[c]	Carrying value	$90[d]

Notes:
[a] $12 = (30/150) × $60
[b] Gain is recognized to extent of $30 worth of boot
[c] $72 = $120 (FMV) − $48 (deferred gain) or
  $72 = $90 (book value given) − $30 (boot received) + $12
  (gain recognized)
[d] $90 = $120 (FMV) − $30 (deferred gain) or
  $90 = $90 (book value given) − $30 (boot received) + $30
  (gain recognized)

Notice that, as expected, the prorata gain recognition rule of APB 29 results in recognition of less gain than the recognition rule of IRC § 1031.

Consequences to Party B

Party B realizes a loss on this exchange; therefore, the receipt or surrender of additional boot will not impact differentially the consequences of the exchange for this party. The tax and financial reporting consequences for Party B are presented in Table 6.3.

Table 6.3 Comparison of Consequences to Party B

For Financial Reporting		For Tax Purposes
$(15)	Gain or (loss) **realized**	$(15)
$(15)[a]	Gain or (loss) **recognized**	$0[b]
$150[c]	Carrying value	$165[d]

Notes:
[a] Loss recognized in full
[b] Loss not recognized per IRC §1031(c)
[c] $150 = $150 (FMV) + $0 (deferred loss) or
$150 = $135 (book value given) + $30 (boot given) − $15
(loss recognized)
[d] $165 = $150 (FMV) + $15 (deferred loss) or
$165 = $135 (book value given) + $30 (boot given) − $0
(loss recognized)

Under APB 29, Party B's loss is recognized in full, while under IRC §1031, no loss is recognized.

IMPACT OF EITF DELIBERATION ON REAL ESTATE SWAPS

As described earlier, the Emerging Issues Task Force (EITF) was formed by the FASB to deal with pressing issues on a timely basis. If the EITF is able to come to a consensus on an issue, the FASB does not have to address the issue. Pronouncements of the EITF are ranked third in terms of authoritative weight in determining GAAP. Accordingly, EITF pronouncements set financial reporting "law" (GAAP) with respect to issues that have not been addressed by a higher authority (e.g., FASB statement or APB opinion).

EITF Issue Nos. 86-29 and 87-29

Had it not been subsequently modified, EITF Issue No. 86-29 would have had a major impact on many exchanges of real estate involving boot. In this pronouncement, the EITF came to a consensus that if an exchange that otherwise was an exchange of similar assets included boot of 25 percent or more, the transaction would be viewed as a *monetary transaction*, rather than a nonmonetary transaction. Classification as a monetary transaction results in the full recognition of gain or loss on the transaction. This outcome would have been advantageous for real estate exchanges. In an exchange in which gain was realized, gain would be recognized in full for financial reporting purposes, while, for tax purposes, not being recognized at all (for the party surrendering boot) or only being partially recognized (for the party receiving boot).

In EITF Issue No. 87-29, an exception to the 25 percent boot rule of Issue No. 86-29 was established for real estate exchanges. Rather than recharacterizing the entire exchange as a monetary transaction, the exchange is to be bifurcated into two separate transactions: (1) the purchase for cash (boot) of a portion of the real estate acquired (i.e., a monetary transaction) and (2) the acquisition of the remainder of the real estate in exchange for similar real estate. Gain or loss is recognized in full on the first part, since it is a monetary transaction. On the second part of the transaction, per ¶ 22 of APB 29, loss is recognized in full and gain is recognized proportionately to the boot value.

While this view of the real estate exchange seems to be different, it merely results in extending the jurisdiction of APB 29 (as it relates to similar asset exchanges) to exchanges that would otherwise be excluded from such treatment. That is, the bifurcated view that is adopted in EITF Issue No. 87-29 has the same results as ¶ 22 of APB 29 would have had in the absence of EITF Issue No. 86-29's 25 percent boot rule.

Illustration

To emphasize the potential impact of EITF Issue No. 86-29 versus the treatment of real estate swaps under EITF Issue No. 87-29, the example from earlier in the chapter is revised such that the boot component of the exchange exceeds the 25 percent threshold of Issue No. 86-29 ($15 of exchange value is shifted from Party B's land to boot). The same side-by-side format employed above is again used in Table 6.4, except that this time the comparison is the difference in the financial reporting treatment resulting from the two pronouncements of the EITF.[9] The revised fact pattern for this illustration is as follows:

---

9 The tax consequences would change due to the increase in the value of the boot. Party A would recognize $45 gain, and the basis of the land received by Party A would remain unchanged at $90. From the perspective of Party B, a smaller loss is realized and deferred, resulting in the basis of the land received by Party B equalling $180, instead of $165 (see Table 6.3). The change in the position of the EITF has no differential effect on these tax consequences.

A and B entered into an exchange of real estate. The nonmonetary property exchanged are similar in nature per ¶ 21 of APB 29. The property transferred by each party consisted of the following:

Transferred by A (received by B):
Real estate $150 FMV
                                          90 book value

Transferred by B (received by A):
Real estate $105 FMV
                                          135 book value

Cash (boot)   45

**Table 6.4   Comparison of Real Estate Swap Under
EITF Issue No. 86-29 Versus 87-29**

Consequences for Party A		
For Financial Reporting		**For Tax Purposes**
$ 60	Gain or (loss) **realized**	$60
$ 60[a]	Gain or (loss) **recognized**	$18[b]
$105[c]	Carrying value	$63[d]

Notes:
[a] Treated as monetary transaction, so gain recognized in full
[b] $18 gain recognized on part of transaction treated as a monetary transaction (i.e., 45/150 = 30%)
[c] $105 = $105 (FMV) – $0 (deferred gain) or
$105 = $90 (book value given) – $45 (boot received) + $60 (gain recognized)
[d] $ 63 = $105 (FMV) – $42 (deferred gain) or
$ 63 = $90 (book value given) – $45 (boot received) + $18 (gain recognized)

Consequences for Party B		
Per EITF Issue No. 86-29		**Per EITF Issue No. 87-29**
$(30)	Gain or (loss) **realized**	$(30)
$(30)[a]	Gain or (loss) **recognized**	$(30)[a]
$150[b]	Carrying value	$150[b]

Notes:
[a] Loss is recognized in full whether transaction is considered monetary or nonmonetary
[b] $150 = $150 (FMV) + $0 (deferred loss) or
$150 = $135 (book value given) + $30 (boot given) – $15 (loss recognized)

It is worth repeating that the practical results of the bifurcated approach taken in EITF Issue 87-29 are exactly the same as if ¶ 22 of APB 29 was held to be applicable to the exchange. Under Issue 87-29, a portion of the transaction is separated and treated as a full recognition transaction (i.e., as a monetary transaction). Precisely the same results derive from recognizing a portion of the gain based on how much boot was received.

Party B realizes a loss on the transaction. A loss would be fully recognized under either ¶ 22 of APB 29, the 25 percent boot rule of EITF Issue 86-29, or the bifurcated approach taken under EITF Issue No. 87-29. Thus, there is no difference between the financial reporting consequences for Party B under the two different treatments examined. Full recognition of Party B's loss results in a recorded carrying value equal to fair market value.

ISSUE OF NONMONETARY BOOT

The final issue relating to the treatment of exchanges of similar assets for financial reporting purposes is that of nonmonetary boot. APB 29 implicitly assumes that boot will always be monetary. EITF Issues No. 86-29 and 87-29 also adopt this view of boot. However, it is not difficult to envision a situation where boot is required to equalize the fair market values being exchanged, but little or no cash (or credit) is available for such purpose. For example, some securities possess a readily determinable and objective market value, and therefore, could substitute very easily for cash boot. However, there is no specific authoritative guidance relating to the financial reporting treatment of nonmonetary boot.[10] Accordingly, one must adopt an approach that keeps faith with the spirit of the expressed provisions of the relevant authoritative pronouncements on the issue (i.e., APB 29 and EITF Issue Nos. 86-29 and 87-29).

---

[10] Nonmonetary boot in a like-kind exchange is not a problem. For tax purposes, boot is described as property other than like-kind. Therefore, if the boot is nonmonetary, it is outside the authority of IRC §1031, resulting in full recognition of gain or loss under IRC §1001.

Discussion and Resolution

As a conceptually consistent approach, we recommend a variation on the bifurcated approach adopted by the EITF in its Issue No. 87-29. In order to properly acknowledge and account for the substantive difference between monetary and nonmonetary boot, we suggest that the exchange be bifurcated into two subparts: (1) the exchange of (nonmonetary) boot for a portion of the nonmonetary property and (2) the exchange of property for the remaining portion of the similar nonmonetary property. With respect to the first subpart, gain or loss would be recognized by both parties under ¶ 18 of APB 29, because the transaction would be considered an exchange of dissimilar assets. The second subpart would be treated as an exchange of *similar* assets subject to the special rules of ¶ 22 of APB 29, which calls for nonrecognition of gain and full recognition of loss.

If any cash boot were included in the exchange (in addition to the nonmonetary boot), we would include it, along with the nonmonetary boot, in the subpart characterized as an exchange of dissimilar assets. Including the cash boot in the subpart treated as a similar assets exchange would have the same results; however, it would make the computations more complicated.

As will be seen in the illustration to follow, the financial reporting consequences of this view for the party receiving boot are identical to a situation involving only cash boot. A difference in form does exist, since the boot is in nonmonetary form and would have to be sold to convert it into cash. However, no gain or loss would be realized on this sale of the nonmonetary boot, since the boot takes a book value equal to its fair market value.

With respect to the party surrendering the boot, gain or loss would be recognized equal to the difference between the fair market value of the boot and its book value in that party's hands. To illustrate this approach, the example presented in Table 6.4 is again modified by changing the boot given from $45 cash to $45 worth of nonmonetary property (e.g., cattle or farm equipment or marketable securities).

Illustration

The following facts are presented for consideration:

A and B entered into an exchange of real estate. The nonmonetary property (other than boot) exchanged are similar in nature per ¶ 21 of APB 29. The property transferred by each party consisted of the following:

Transferred by A (received by B):
Real estate $150 FMV
                                                90 book value

Transferred by B (received by A):
Real estate $105 FMV
                                                135 book value
Cash (boot)   45
                                                37 book value

The two subparts that result from this bifurcated approach and the consequences of each subpart are shown in Table 6.5.

Table 6.5   Exchange Viewed as Two Exchanges

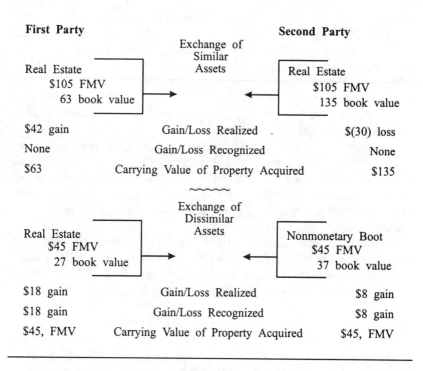

First Party		Second Party
	Exchange of Similar Assets	
Real Estate $105 FMV 63 book value	→ ←	Real Estate $105 FMV 135 book value
$42 gain	Gain/Loss Realized	$(30) loss
None	Gain/Loss Recognized	None
$63	Carrying Value of Property Acquired	$135
	Exchange of Dissimilar Assets	
Real Estate $45 FMV 27 book value	→ ←	Nonmonetary Boot $45 FMV 37 book value
$18 gain	Gain/Loss Realized	$8 gain
$18 gain	Gain/Loss Recognized	$8 gain
$45, FMV	Carrying Value of Property Acquired	$45, FMV

Party A, the party receiving the boot, recognizes exactly the same amount of gain ($18) as when the boot was cash (refer to Table 6.4 for comparison). Since there is no substantive difference between cash boot and nonmonetary boot, this is proper. If Party A were to sell the boot immediately for $45, there would be no gain or loss realized and his or her financial position would be the same as if cash boot had been received. The difference is that Party A has the choice of whether to liquidate the nonmonetary boot. The realized gain on the subpart treated as an exchange of similar assets is not recognized.

From the perspective of Party B, the $8 gain on the subpart treated as an exchange of dissimilar assets is recognized. If there had been a loss on this subpart, it would also have been recognized. The realized loss on the subpart treated as a similar asset exchange is recognized, per ¶ 22 of APB 29.

CONCLUSION

It has been noted by both authoritative and nonauthoritative commentators that the accounting for exchanges of similar assets is "diverse," to use the adjective used by the EITF. A good deal of this diversity in treatment can be attributed to the similarity in the form of the transactions controlled by APB 29 and IRC §1031, respectively. The reporting consequences of these two provisions, however, are not the same. The provisions differ both as to applicability and mechanics. IRC §1031 controls the tax reporting of like-kind exchanges; APB 29 controls the financial reporting of exchanges of similar assets. Except under limited circumstances (gain realized and no boot involved), the two provisions do not provide the same results. This chapter examines real estate exchanges from the perspective of financial reporting. The tax implications of such transactions have received extensive coverage in the real estate literature, and a balancing focus on financial reporting is appropriate.

In the area of real estate, gains and losses are likely to be material in amount. Improper reporting of a material gain or loss on financial statements violates generally accepted accounting principles (GAAP). While the cashflow implications of financial reporting (e.g., impact on earnings per share of a material loss) is not as direct as that associated with tax reporting, such implications must be considered in assessing the attractiveness of a transaction.

The final issue addressed was the treatment of nonmonetary boot, an issue that has received neither authoritative nor nonauthoritative attention. The authors believe that the use of nonmonetary boot may occur with sufficient frequency that some guidance (albeit, nonauthoritative) is needed. An approach is offered that properly ignores formal differences between monetary and nonmonetary boot, while addressing substantive differences.

This chapter is offered on the premise that, for those parties subject to GAAP (e.g., publicly held corporations), ignorance is not bliss. It is better to know the full ramifications of a deal before it is struck, than to discover unpleasant consequences after. Having a basic idea of how a transaction will affect one's earnings per share, and what that might portend for a corporation's stock price, is important.

References

Accounting Principles Board (APB), *Opinion No. 29*, "Accounting for Nonmonetary Transactions" (New York: AICPA 1973).

Barrett, G.V. and P.T. Kolbe, "The Benefits of Tax-Deferred Exchanges Are Often Illusory," *Real Estate Review* 17 (Winter 1988), pp. 56-66.

Chane, L.S., "Recent Developments in the Taxation of Like-Kind Exchanges," *Real Estate Review* 20 (Fall 1990), pp. 13-16.

_____, "Proposed New Regulations to Assist Deferred Like-Kind Exchanges, *Real Estate Review* 20 (Winter 1991), pp. 9-12.

Emerging Issues Task Force, Issue No. 86-29, "Nonmonetary Transactions: Magnitude of Boot and the Exceptions to the Use of Fair Value" (Stamford, Conn.: FASB 1986).

_____, *Issue No. 87-29*, "Exchange of Real Estate Involving Boot" (Stamford, Conn.: FASB 1987).

Financial Accounting Standards Board (FASB), *Statement of Financial Accounting Standards No. 66*, "Accounting for Real Estate Sales" (Stamford, Conn.: FASB 1982).

Goolsby, W.C. and G.D. Williams, "A Reevaluation of the Benefits of Like-Kind Exchanges," *Real Estate Review* 19 (Summer 1989), pp. 40-46.

Lindbeck, R.S. and C.P. Edmonds, "The Advantages of Tax-Free Swaps Under New Tax Law," *Real Estate Review* 17 (Summer 1987), pp. 61-64.

United States Congress, *Internal Revenue Code of 1986* (St. Paul, Minn.: West 1990).

The Exchange Worksheet

by James F. Little, MBA
Sacramento, California

The exchange worksheet, often referred to as the **exchange recapitulation** form, is viewed by many practitioners as one of the most complex forms ever devised. Fear of this form has deprived many of the tremendous satisfaction and reward enjoyed by those who have mastered its use. The goal of this discussion is to assuage the fears of the most apprehensive user by illustrating a simple and enjoyable step-by-step process to completing this form.

The balancing of equities and the determination of cash required to close a two-way exchange is within the grasp of the neophyte practitioner. This process is most often accomplished by setting up a vertical side-by-side "T" comparison, such as the Smith and Jones example below in Table 7.1.

Table 7.1

	Smith (Duplex)	Jones (Fourplex)
Market Value	$100,000	$200,000
Loan(s)	$ 45,000	$130,000
Equity	$ 55,000	$ 70,000

The above example is illustrated in Figure 7.1 on Professional Publishing Corporation's Wainberg Exchange Worksheet to Balance Equities. The reader will readily see that the exchange worksheet is merely a horizontal representation of the above "T" approach.

It is important to note that the NET EFFECTIVE EQUITIES of Smith and Jones represent the "net proceeds" each would receive from a sale escrow — assuming, of course, no commissions, or transaction costs. This is a key concept necessary to understand the exchange worksheet. Since the parties are entitled to receive their NET EFFECTIVE EQUITIES, the maximum Property Equity each party may receive on the GETS line *cannot* exceed the NET EFFECTIVE EQUITY *unless* additional cash is put into the exchange.

In Figure 7.2, the equities are balanced "one at a time," and each of the parties is "taken out" of the exchange. Because of the $15,000 difference in equities, Smith must give an additional $15,000 in cash to Jones. The $15,000 cash in the GIVES column on Smith's GETS Line was determined by subtracting Smith's NET EFFECTIVE EQUITY from the Property Equity Smith will acquire in the fourplex. If Smith sold his property, he would be entitled to $55,000. Since he is adding $15,000 in cash, he is entitled to $70,000 equity in the fourplex. Alternatively, if Smith added $15,000 in paper, in the form of a note secured by a second deed of trust on the fourplex, he would end up with $55,000 equity in the fourplex.

In the following "T" transaction in Table 7.2, costs are added to the exchange.

Table 7.2

	Smith (Duplex)	Jones (Fourplex)
Market Value	$100,000	$200,000
Loan(s)	$ 45,000	$130,000
Equity	$ 55,000	$ 70,000
Cash	$ 15,000	
Transaction Costs1	$ 8,000	$ 14,000
Cash Needed	$ 23,000	$ 14,000

Notes:
1. Assumes a 6% real estate commission and $2,000 in escrow and title fees are incurred by each owner.

The exchange worksheet in Figure 7.3 illustrates the calculation of each party's net effective equity with transaction costs. For purposes of this illustration and ease of understanding, assume that these costs are the same for a sale as an exchange. Thus, the distinction between a sale and an exchange is the receipt of NET EFFECTIVE EQUITY in the acquired property vis-a-vis NET EFFECTIVE EQUITY in the form of "net sale proceeds." In this instance, unless Smith adds cash, Smith will only be entitled to $47,000 equity in the fourplex.

Figure 7.1

THE WAINBERG EXCHANGE WORKSHEET TO BALANCE EQUITIES

1		2	3	4 LOANS EXISTING LOANS	5 LOANS NEW OR ASSUMED LOANS*	6 PROPERTY EQUITIES 3−4	7 ESCROW CASH IN (GIVES)	8 CASH OUT (GETS)	9 PAPER-OTHER BOOT IN (GIVES)	10 PAPER-OTHER BOOT OUT (GETS)	11 GROSS EQUITIES 6+7+9	12 COMMISSION	13 LOAN FEES	14 OTHER COSTS	15 TOTAL OF 13+14	16 NET EFFECTIVE EQUITIES 11−12−15	17 NEW LOANS	18 GROSS LOAN PROCEEDS 17−4
A Smith	GIVES	Duplex	100,000	45,000		55,000			BOOT GOING IN		55,000					55,000		
	GETS					+			PAPER CREATED									
B Jones	GIVES	Fourplex	200,000	130,000		70,000			BOOT GOING IN		70,000					70,000		
	GETS					+			PAPER CREATED									
C	GIVES								BOOT GOING IN									
	GETS					+			PAPER CREATED									
D	GIVES								BOOT GOING IN									
	GETS					+			PAPER CREATED									
E	GIVES								BOOT GOING IN									
	GETS					+			PAPER CREATED									
F	GIVES								BOOT GOING IN									
	GETS					+			PAPER CREATED									
G BROKERS	GET																	

H TRANSACTION COSTS DISBURSED THROUGH ESCROW . . . . .

I LOAN PROCEEDS DISBURSED THROUGH ESCROW . . . . . .

J TOTAL ESCROW ACCOUNTS

(CASH IN must equal CASH OUT) =

(PAPER IN must equal PAPER OUT)

Date: .... Prepared by: .... Office: ....

FORM 122-A

COPYRIGHT © 1987 BY PROFESSIONAL PUBLISHING CORP., 122 PAUL DRIVE, SAN RAFAEL, CALIFORNIA 94903

*Also includes loans taken "Subject To"
†Equity in property acquired = Col. 6 − Col. 9
(But ONLY if Col. 9 represents a purchase-money note on property acquired)

Figure 7.2

THE WAINBERG EXCHANGE WORKSHEET TO BALANCE EQUITIES

			1	2	3	4 (LOANS) EXISTING LOANS	5 NEW OR ASSUMED LOANS*	6 PROPERTY EQUITIES 3-4	7 (ESCROW ACCOUNTS) CASH IN (GIVES)	8 CASH OUT (GETS)	9 PAPER - OTHER BOOT IN (GIVES)	10 PAPER - OTHER BOOT OUT (GETS)	11 GROSS EQUITIES 6-7+9	12 (TRANSACTION COSTS) COMMISSION	13 LOAN FEES	14 OTHER COSTS	15 TOTAL OF 13+14	16 NET EFFECTIVE EQUITIES 11-12-15	17 NEW LOANS	18 GROSS LOAN PROCEEDS 17-4

PARTIES		PROPERTIES	MARKET VALUES	EXISTING LOANS	NEW OR ASSUMED LOANS*	PROPERTY EQUITIES 3-4	CASH IN (GIVES)	CASH OUT (GETS)	PAPER-OTHER BOOT IN (GIVES)	PAPER-OTHER BOOT OUT (GETS)	GROSS EQUITIES 6-7+9	COM-MISSION	LOAN FEES	OTHER COSTS	TOTAL OF 13+14	NET EFFECTIVE EQUITIES 11-12-15	NEW LOANS	GROSS LOAN PROCEEDS 17-4
A	Smith GIVES	Duplex	100,000	45,000		55,000					55,000						55,000	
	GETS	Fourplex	200,000		130,000	70,000	15,000											
B	Jones GIVES	Fourplex	200,000	130,000		70,000					70,000						70,000	
	GETS	Duplex	100,000		45,000	55,000		15,000										
C	GIVES																	
	GETS																	
D	GIVES																	
	GETS																	
E	GIVES																	
	GETS																	
F	GIVES																	
	GETS																	
G	BROKERS GET																	
H	TRANSACTION COSTS DISBURSED THROUGH ESCROW																	
I	CASH PROCEEDS DISBURSED THROUGH ESCROW					(CASH IN must equal CASH OUT)												
J	TOTAL ESCROW ACCOUNTS								(PAPER IN must equal PAPER OUT)									

*Also includes loans taken "Subject To" Col. 6
Equity in property acquired Col. 9 (but ONLY if Col. 9 represents a purchase money note on property acquired)

Figure 7.3

THE WAINBERG EXCHANGE WORKSHEET TO BALANCE EQUITIES

	1 PARTIES	2 PROPERTIES	3 MARKET VALUES	4 EXISTING LOANS	5 NEW OR ASSUMED LOANS*	6 PROPERTY EQUITIES 3-4	7 CASH IN (GIVES)	8 CASH OUT (GETS)	9 PAPER-OTHER BOOT IN (GIVES)	10 PAPER-OTHER BOOT OUT (GETS)	11 GROSS EQUITIES 6+7+9	12 COM-MISSION	13 LOAN FEES	14 OTHER COSTS	15 TOTAL OF 13+14	16 NET EFFECTIVE EQUITIES 11-12-15	17 NEW LOANS	18 GROSS LOAN PROCEEDS 17-4
A	Smith GIVES	Duplex	100,000	45,000		55,000			BOOT GOING IN		55,000	6,000		2,000	2,000	47,000		
	GETS					†			PAPER CREATED									
B	Jones GIVES	Fourplex	200,000	130,000		70,000			BOOT GOING IN		70,000	12,000		2,000	2,000	56,000		
	GETS					†			PAPER CREATED									
C	GIVES					†			BOOT GOING IN									
	GETS								PAPER CREATED									
D	GIVES					†			BOOT GOING IN									
	GETS								PAPER CREATED									
E	GIVES					†			BOOT GOING IN									
	GETS								PAPER CREATED									
F	GIVES					†			BOOT GOING IN									
	GETS								PAPER CREATED									
G	BROKERS GET																	

H TRANSACTION COSTS DISBURSED THROUGH ESCROW . . . . . .

I LOAN PROCEEDS DISBURSED THROUGH ESCROW . . . .

J TOTAL ESCROW ACCOUNTS   (CASH IN must equal CASH OUT)   =   (PAPER IN must equal PAPER OUT)

(CASH IN must equal CASH OUT)   (PAPER IN must equal PAPER OUT)

*Also includes loans taken "Subject To"
†Equity in property acquired = Col. 6 – Col. 9
(But ONLY if Col. 9 represents a purchase-money note on property acquired)

Date: ....   Prepared by: ....   Office: ....

COPYRIGHT © 1987 BY PROFESSIONAL PUBLISHING CORP., 122 PAUL DRIVE, SAN RAFAEL, CALIFORNIA 94903

Before proceeding to balance the equities with the transaction costs for Smith and Jones, a few caveats must be understood:

- Always use a pencil (with a good eraser) when completing any exchange worksheet.

- Only equities in "like-kind" properties may be exchanged on a tax-deferred basis. When equity given exceeds equity received, there may be boot.

- Notes created in the exchange to balance equities encumber the property acquired and reduce its equity.

- Cash deposited or generated through refinancing of loans pays transaction costs, then increases equity.

In Figure 7.4, Smith's NET EFFECTIVE EQUITY is $47,000. He must add $23,000 in cash to the exchange in order to exit the transaction with $70,000 equity in the fourplex. This $23,000 will first pay commissions ($18,000) and costs ($4,000). Since Jones's NET EFFECTIVE EQUITY is $56,000, he is entitled to the $55,000 equity in the duplex, plus the $1,000 cash remaining after the payment of the transaction costs.

Since Jones is trading down, Jones will receive "boot" in the form of cash ($1,000) and net loan relief of $85,000 ($130,000 − $45,000), for a total of $86,000 in boot.

From the above examples it should be apparent that the exchange worksheet enables practitioners to ascertain the following:

- Structure of the exchange.

- Cash required to close by each party.

- Feasibility of the exchange from the perspective of the principals and the broker(s).

- Boot that will be generated in the exchange through net mortgage relief and cash or other nonqualifying property received.

- Structure of the contract between the parties.

Participants at real estate exchange meetings often use exchange worksheets to determine the viability of transactions. Before attending any exchange meeting, the participant should have counselled his client and determined:

Figure 7.4

THE WAINBERG EXCHANGE WORKSHEET TO BALANCE EQUITIES

1 PARTIES	2 PROPERTIES	3 MARKET VALUES	4 EXISTING LOANS	5 NEW OR ASSUMED LOANS*	6 PROPERTY EQUITIES 3-4	7 CASH IN (GIVES)	8 CASH OUT (GETS)	9 PAPER-OTHER BOOT IN (GIVES)	10 PAPER-OTHER BOOT OUT (GETS)	11 GROSS EQUITIES 6+7+9	12 COMMISSION	13 LOAN FEES	14 OTHER COSTS	15 TOTAL OF 13+14	16 NET EFFECTIVE EQUITIES 11-12-15	17 NEW LOANS	18 GROSS LOAN PROCEEDS 17-4
A Smith GIVES	Duplex	100,000	45,000		55,000					55,000	6,000		2,000	2,000			
A Smith GETS	Fourplex	200,000		130,000	70,000†	23,000									47,000		
B Jones GIVES	Fourplex	200,000	130,000		70,000					70,000	12,000		2,000	2,000			
B Jones GETS	Duplex	100,000		45,000	55,000†		1,000								56,000		
C GIVES					†												
C GETS																	
D GIVES					†												
D GETS																	
E GIVES					†												
E GETS																	
F GIVES					†												
F GETS																	
G BROKERS GET							18,000				18,000						

H TRANSACTION COSTS DISBURSED THROUGH ESCROW 18,000

I LOAN PROCEEDS DISBURSED THROUGH ESCROW 4,000

J TOTAL ESCROW ACCOUNTS   (CASH IN must equal CASH OUT) 23,000 = 23,000   (PAPER IN must equal PAPER OUT)

*Also includes loans taken "Subject To"

†Equity in property acquired = Col. 6 − Col. 9 (But ONLY if Col. 9 represents a purchase-money note on property acquired)

Prepared by: ....   Office: ....

Date: ....

FORM 122-A   COPYRIGHT © 1987 BY PROFESSIONAL PUBLISHING CORP., 122 PAUL DRIVE, SAN RAFAEL, CALIFORNIA 94903

- The client's motivation.

- The financing available on the client's property (this is imperative in order to determine the feasibility of the transaction).

- The client's ability to add cash or other boot.

- The type of property the client will accept.

- The acquisition criteria used by the client to evaluate the property.

Now that the exchange worksheet has been introduced, it will be easier to understand the instructions for the use of the form and the more comprehensive examples that follow. The following directions are excerpted, with permission, from Professional Publishing Corporation's instructions for the use of The Wainberg Exchange Worksheet to Balance Equities (Form 122-A).

To balance the equities on Form 122-A, proceed as follows:

1. Inventory the real properties, cash, existing paper (not paper created in the exchange) and other boot going into the exchange by filling in the GIVES LINES of A through F in columns 2,3,4,6,7,9, and 11. (In the event the Brokers have put any real property, cash, existing paper, or other boot into the exchange, use the GIVES line in section F.) Enter any real estate commissions in Column 12.

2. Fill in the maximum potential financing in Column 17 and gross loan proceeds in Column 18.

3. Inventory the real property coming out of the exchange by filling in the GETS LINES of A through F in Columns 2,3,5, and 6. Inventory the boot (e.g., personal property) coming out of the exchange by filling in the GETS lines of A through F in Columns 2,3,5, and 6. Ascertain that all real property and boot have been disposed of; if not, post to "Brokers" in the GETS line of G in Columns 2,3,5, and 6.

4. Charge the loan fee on each new loan to the party doing the refinancing in Column 13 and charge the transaction costs for the properties given and received to each party in Column 14. Then fill in the totals on the GIVES LINES in Column 15.

5. Now fill in the NET EFFECTIVE EQUITIES in Column 16.

6. Any differences between the PROPERTY EQUITIES on the GETS LINES of Column 6 and the NET EFFECTIVE EQUITIES (Column 16) must now be made up in ESCROW ACCOUNTS (Columns 7, 8,

9, or 10). Balance the equities of the party cashing out last, giving him all of the paper first (the grand total of Column 9) and the balance in cash.

7. Total Column 18 and transfer to Column 7-I (see dotted line).
8. Total Column 15 and transfer in Column 8-H (see dotted line).
9. Tentatively total Columns 7,8,9, and 10 on Line J and examine these totals. First ascertain that all of the paper (the grand total of Column 9) has been disposed of; if not, post the balance to the Brokers in Column 10-G. Then determine if any cash is available for commissions; if so, post available cash to 8-G.
10. Re-total Columns 7,8,9, and 10, so that CASH-IN equals CASH-OUT and PAPER IN equals PAPER OUT.

Sample Problems

In the following problems, assume:

1. The party transferring real property will pay a six percent real estate commission (no commissions will be paid on personal property).
2. The party acquiring a property subject to a new loan will pay loan fees equal to two percent of the amount borrowed.
3. The maximum loan-to-value ratio (including paper created) on any acquired property cannot exceed 80% of the value, except for 1-4 unit residential property, where the maximum loan-to-value ratio cannot exceed 85% of the value.

Problem One

Stone owns a fourplex with a FMV (fair market value) of $250,000 subject to a $100,000 loan, which she would like to exchange for a 12-unit apartment complex. A new $200,000 loan is available. Stone's transaction costs, exclusive of the commission and loan fees, are estimated at $1,500.

Hereford owns a luxury 12-unit apartment complex with a FMV of $600,000, encumbered with $270,000 in loans, which he would like to sell. A new $420,000 loan is available. Hereford's transaction costs, exclusive of the commission, are estimated at $2,500.

Dupe has $50,000 in cash that he would like to use to purchase a fourplex. Dupe's transaction costs, exclusive of loan fees, are estimated at $1,000.

Solution

The exchange worksheet in Figure 7.5 illustrates steps 1-2.

The exchange worksheet in Figure 7.6 adds steps 3-5 to the first worksheet. The reader is reminded that the NET EFFECTIVE EQUITIES represent the amount each party is entitled to receive in equity in the properties acquired on the GETS LINE unless cash is added to the exchange.

Steps 6 through 11 are illustrated in Figure 7.7. Step 6 is the critical step that "unlocks" the exchange recapitulation process. Since the party cashing out is the best candidate to "take" the paper created in the exchange (The brokers do not want to get stuck with this), the equities of the party cashing out must be balanced last.

The paper created (and/or cash added) in this step is simply the difference between the NET EFFECTIVE EQUITIES of the properties on the GIVES LINES and the GROSS EQUITIES on the GETS LINES. Stone's NET EFFECTIVE EQUITY of $125,100 is significantly less than the $180,000 equity in the 12-units that she is interested in acquiring. To balance the NET EFFECTIVE EQUITIES, it will be necessary for Stone to execute a $54,900 ($180,000 – $125,100) note secured by a second deed of trust on the 12-units. Since Dupe's transaction costs of $5,000 reduce his cash, he will have to execute a note secured by a second deed of trust on the fourplex for $5,000.

It should be obvious that if Stone had the $54,900 necessary to pay the $24,900 in transaction costs and the $30,000 difference in PROPERTY EQUITIES in cash, she would end up with a NET EFFECTIVE EQUITY of $180,000. (The $125,100 would be increased by the $54,900 in cash.) Similarly, if Dupe had the $5,000 necessary to pay his transaction costs in cash, he would end up with a NET EFFECTIVE EQUITY of $50,000. (The $45,000 would be increased by the $5,000 in cash.)

Hereford will be taken out of the exchange last. He will receive his NET EFFECTIVE EQUITY of $291,500 in the form of a $54,900 second deed of trust on the 12 units, a $5,000 second deed of trust on the fourplex, and $231,600 in cash.

Notice that none of the parties exchanging properties, put any cash into the exchange. The majority of the transaction costs, commissions, and cash paid to Hereford came from the Gross Loan Proceeds. Could this transaction have been structured without Dupe's $50,000 in cash? Yes, if the brokers were interested in the fourplex and agreed to add $4,000 to their $51,000 real estate commission for a total of $55,000 (GROSS EQUITY),

Figure 7.5 (Steps 1–2)

All Numbers in Thousands

1		2	3	4	5	6	7	8	9	10	11	12	13	14	15	16	17	18
				LOANS		PROPERTY	ESCROW ACCOUNTS				GROSS	TRANSACTION COSTS			TOTAL	NET		GROSS
PARTIES		PROPERTIES	MARKET VALUES	EXISTING LOANS	NEW OR ASSUMED LOANS*	EQUITIES 3−4	CASH IN (GIVES)	CASH OUT (GETS)	PAPER - OTHER BOOT IN (GIVES)	PAPER - OTHER BOOT OUT (GETS)	EQUITIES 6+7+9	COM-MISSION	LOAN FEES	OTHER COSTS	OF 13+14	EFFECTIVE EQUITIES 11−12−15	NEW LOANS	LOAN PROCEEDS 17−4
A Stone	GIVES	Fourplex	250	100		150 †			BOOT GOING IN / PAPER CREATED		150	15					200	100
	GETS																	
B Hereford	GIVES	12 units	600	270		330 †			BOOT GOING IN / PAPER CREATED		330	36					420	150
	GETS																	
C Dupe	GIVES	Cash					50		BOOT GOING IN / PAPER CREATED		50							
	GETS					†												
D	GIVES								BOOT GOING IN / PAPER CREATED									
	GETS					†												
E	GIVES								BOOT GOING IN / PAPER CREATED									
	GETS					†												
F	GIVES								BOOT GOING IN / PAPER CREATED									
	GETS					†												
G BROKERS	GET																	
H TRANSACTION COSTS DISBURSED THROUGH ESCROW																		
I LOAN PROCEEDS DISBURSED THROUGH ESCROW																		
J TOTAL ESCROW ACCOUNTS																		

(CASH IN must equal CASH OUT)   (PAPER IN must equal PAPER OUT)

Date:............... Prepared by:................... Office:...................

FORM 122-A

COPYRIGHT © 1987 BY PROFESSIONAL PUBLISHING CORP., 122 PAUL DRIVE, SAN RAFAEL, CALIFORNIA 94903

*Also includes loans taken "Subject To"

†Equity in property acquired = Col. 6 − Col. 9 (But ONLY if Col. 9 represents a purchase-money note on property acquired)

Figure 7.6 (Steps 3–5)

All Numbers in Thousands

THE WAINBERG EXCHANGE WORKSHEET TO BALANCE EQUITIES

	1 PARTIES	2 PROPERTIES	3 MARKET VALUES	4 EXISTING LOANS	5 NEW OR ASSUMED LOANS*	6 PROPERTY EQUITIES 3–4	7 CASH IN (GIVES)	8 CASH OUT (GETS)	9 PAPER-OTHER BOOT IN (GIVES)	10 PAPER-OTHER BOOT OUT (GETS)	11 GROSS EQUITIES 6+7+9	12 COM-MISSION	13 LOAN FEES	14 OTHER COSTS	15 TOTAL OF 13+14	16 NET EFFECTIVE EQUITIES 11-12-15	17 NEW LOANS	18 GROSS LOAN PROCEEDS 17-4
A	GIVES Fourplex		250	100		150			BOOT GOING IN		150	15	8.4	1.5	9.9	125.7	200	100
A	GETS 12 units		600		420	†180			PAPER CREATED									
B	GIVES 12 units		600	270		330			BOOT GOING IN		330	36		2.5	2.5	291.5	420	150
B	GETS out					†			PAPER CREATED									
C	GIVES Cash		250				50		BOOT GOING IN		50					45		
C	GETS Fourplex		250		200	†50			PAPER CREATED				4	1	5			
D	GIVES								BOOT GOING IN									
D	GETS					†			PAPER CREATED									
E	GIVES								BOOT GOING IN									
E	GETS					†			PAPER CREATED									
F	GIVES								BOOT GOING IN									
F	GETS					†			PAPER CREATED									
G	BROKERS GET											51						
H	TRANSACTION COSTS DISBURSED THROUGH ESCROW																	
I	LOAN PROCEEDS DISBURSED THROUGH ESCROW																	
J	TOTAL ESCROW ACCOUNTS						(CASH IN must equal CASH OUT)		(PAPER IN must equal PAPER OUT)									

Date:... Prepared by:... Office:...

FORM 122-A   COPYRIGHT © 1987 BY PROFESSIONAL PUBLISHING CORP. — 122 PAUL DRIVE, SAN RAFAEL, CALIFORNIA 94903

*Also includes loans taken "Subject To"
†Equity in property acquired = Col. 6 – Col. 9
(But ONLY if Col. 9 represents a purchase-money note on property acquired)

Figure 7.7 (Steps 6–11)

All Numbers in Thousands

THE WAINBERG EXCHANGE WORKSHEET TO BALANCE EQUITIES

	1 PARTIES	2 PROPERTIES	3 MARKET VALUES	4 EXISTING LOANS	5 NEW OR ASSUMED LOANS*	6 PROPERTY EQUITIES 3–4	7 CASH IN (GIVES)	8 CASH OUT (GETS)	9 PAPER–OTHER BOOT IN (GIVES)	10 PAPER–OTHER BOOT OUT (GETS)	11 GROSS EQUITIES 6+7+9	12 COMMISSION	13 LOAN FEES	14 OTHER COSTS	15 TOTAL OF 13+14	16 NET EFFECTIVE EQUITIES 11-12-15	17 NEW LOANS	18 GROSS LOAN PROCEEDS 17–4
A	Stone GIVES	Fourplex	250	100		150					150	15	8.4	1.5	9.9		200	100
	GETS	12 units	600		420	†180										125.1		100
B	Hereford GIVES	12 units	600	270		330			BOOT GOING IN		330	36		2.5	2.5		420	150
	GETS	Out				†		231.6	PAPER CREATED 54.9	54.9 / 5.0						291.5		150
C	Dupe GIVES	Cash					50		BOOT GOING IN		50							
	GETS	Fourplex	250		200	†50			PAPER CREATED 5				4	1	5	45		
D	GIVES								BOOT GOING IN									
	GETS					†			PAPER CREATED									
E	GIVES								BOOT GOING IN									
	GETS					†			PAPER CREATED									
F	GIVES								BOOT GOING IN									
	GETS					†			PAPER CREATED									
G	BROKERS GET							51				51						
H	TRANSACTION COSTS DISBURSED THROUGH ESCROW							17.4							17.4			
I	LOAN PROCEEDS DISBURSED THROUGH ESCROW						250											250
J	TOTAL ESCROW ACCOUNTS (CASH IN must equal CASH OUT)						300 = 300	300	59.9 = 59.9	59.9	(PAPER IN must equal PAPER OUT)							

Date: _____ Prepared by: _____ Office: _____

FORM 122 A

*Also includes loans taken "Subject To"

†Equity in property acquired = Col. 6 – Col. 9 (But ONLY if Col. 9 represents a purchase-money note on property acquired)

the Brokers would have a NET EFFECTIVE EQUITY of $50,000 after the $5,000 in transaction costs.

Problem Two

Smith owns a retail building with a FMV of $500,000, subject to a $300,000 loan, which he would like to exchange for an office building. A new $350,000 loan is available. Smith's transaction costs, exclusive of the commission and loan fees, are estimated at $6,000.

Turk owns an office building with a FMV of $900,000, subject to a $550,000 loan, which he would like to exchange for a retail center. A new $630,000 loan is available. Turk's transaction costs, exclusive of the real estate commission and loans fees, are estimated at $7,000.

Finch owns a retail center with a FMV of $1,200,000, subject to a $480,000 loan. Finch, who celebrated his 75th birthday last month, wants to sell his retail center and spend the rest of his years with his fifth wife, a 25-year-old beauty pageant winner. A new $840,000 loan is available. Finch's transaction costs, exclusive of the real estate commission and loan fees, are estimated at $9,000.

The brokers, anxious for a transaction, will accept equity in the retail building (or any property) just to make a deal. They will pay any transaction costs out of their real estate commission and will make up any "equity" by executing a note secured by a second deed of trust on the retail building. The transaction costs on the retail building, exclusive of loans fees, are estimated at $4,500.

Solution

The exchange worksheet in Figure 7.8 illustrates steps 1-2 above.

The exchange worksheet in Figure 7.9 adds steps 3-5 to the first worksheet. The reader is reminded that the NET EFFECTIVE EQUITIES represent the amount each party is entitled to receive in equity in the properties acquired on the GETS LINE unless cash is added to the exchange.

Because the brokers will be receiving the RETAIL BUILDING and paying the loan fees ($7,000) and transaction costs ($3,500) for a total of $10,500, their $156,000 real estate commission (Gross Equity) will be reduced by these transaction costs giving them a NET EFFECTIVE EQUITY of $145,500.

Steps 6 through 11 are completed in Figure 7.10. Since Smith's NET EFFECTIVE EQUITY of $151,400 is $118,600 less than the $270,000 equity in the office building, Smith must add this amount in cash and/or

Figure 7.8 (Steps 1–2)　　　　　　　　　　　　　　All Numbers in Thousands

THE WAINBERG EXCHANGE WORKSHEET TO BALANCE EQUITIES

1		2	3	4	5	6	7	8	9	10	11	12	13	14	15	16	17	18
PARTIES		PROPERTIES	MARKET VALUES	LOANS — EXISTING LOANS	NEW OR ASSUMED LOANS*	PROPERTY EQUITIES 3–4	ESCROW ACCOUNTS — CASH IN (GIVES)	CASH OUT (GETS)	PAPER – OTHER BOOT IN (GIVES)	PAPER – OTHER BOOT OUT (GETS)	GROSS EQUITIES 6+7+9	TRANSACTION COSTS — COMMISSION	LOAN FEES	OTHER COSTS	TOTAL OF 13+14	NET EFFECTIVE EQUITIES 11–12–15	NEW LOANS	GROSS LOAN PROCEEDS 17–4
A Smith	GIVES	Retail	500	300		200			BOOT GOING IN		200	30					350	50
	GETS				350	†			PAPER CREATED									
B Turk	GIVES	Office	900	550		350			BOOT GOING IN		350	54					630	80
	GETS					†			PAPER CREATED									
C Finch	GIVES	Center	1,200	480		720			BOOT GOING IN		720	72					840	360
	GETS					†			PAPER CREATED									
D	GIVES								BOOT GOING IN									
	GETS					†			PAPER CREATED									
E	GIVES								BOOT GOING IN									
	GETS					†			PAPER CREATED									
F	GIVES								BOOT GOING IN									
	GETS					†			PAPER CREATED									
G BROKERS	GET																	
H TRANSACTION COSTS DISBURSED THROUGH ESCROW																		
I LOAN PROCEEDS DISBURSED THROUGH ESCROW																		
J TOTAL ESCROW ACCOUNTS								(CASH IN must equal **CASH OUT**)		(**PAPER IN** must equal **PAPER OUT**)								

Date: .... Prepared by: .... Office: ....

FORM 122-A

COPYRIGHT © 1987 BY PROFESSIONAL PUBLISHING CORP., 122 PAUL DRIVE, SAN RAFAEL, CALIFORNIA 94903

*Also includes loans taken "Subject To."
†Equity in property acquired = Col. 6 – Col. 9 (But ONLY if Col. 9 represents a purchase-money note on property acquired)

Figure 7.9 (Steps 3–5)

All Numbers in Thousands

THE WAINBERG EXCHANGE WORKSHEET TO BALANCE EQUITIES

1 PARTIES		2 PROPERTIES	3 MARKET VALUES	4 EXISTING LOANS	5 NEW OR ASSUMED LOANS*	6 PROPERTY EQUITIES 3-4	7 CASH IN (GIVES)	8 CASH OUT (GETS)	9 PAPER-OTHER BOOT IN (GIVES)	10 PAPER-OTHER BOOT OUT (GETS)	11 GROSS EQUITIES 6+7+9	12 COM-MISSION	13 LOAN FEES	14 OTHER COSTS	15 TOTAL OF 13+14	16 NET EFFECTIVE EQUITIES 11-12-15	17 NEW LOANS	18 GROSS LOAN PROCEEDS 17-4
A Smith	GIVES	Retail	500	300		200			BOOT GOING IN		200	30	12.6	6	18.6	151.4	350	50
	GETS	Office	900		630	†270			PAPER CREATED									
B Turk	GIVES	Office	900	550		350			BOOT GOING IN		350	54	16.8	7	23.8	272.2	630	80
	GETS	Center	1200		840	†720			PAPER CREATED									
C Finch	GIVES	Center	1200	480		720			BOOT GOING IN		720	72		9	9	639	840	360
	GETS	Out				†			PAPER CREATED									
D	GIVES								BOOT GOING IN									
	GETS					†			PAPER CREATED									
E	GIVES								BOOT GOING IN									
	GETS					†			PAPER CREATED									
F Brokers	GIVES	Fees										156	7	3.5	10.5	145.5		
	GETS																	
G BROKERS	GET	Retail	500		350	150												

H TRANSACTION COSTS DISBURSED THROUGH ESCROW . . . . . .   156 / (10.5) = 145.5   Transaction Cost

I LOAN PROCEEDS DISBURSED THROUGH ESCROW . . . . . .   (CASH IN must equal CASH OUT)

J TOTAL ESCROW ACCOUNTS   (CASH IN must equal CASH OUT)   (PAPER IN must equal PAPER OUT)

Date:_____   Prepared by:_____   Office:_____

FORM 122-A

*Also includes loans taken "Subject To"
†Equity in property acquired = Col. 6 — Col. 9
(But ONLY if Col. 9 represents a purchase-money note on property acquired)

Figure 7.10 (Steps 6–11)

All Numbers in Thousands

THE WAINBERG EXCHANGE WORKSHEET TO BALANCE EQUITIES

	1 PARTIES	2 PROPERTIES	3 MARKET VALUES	4 LOANS EXISTING LOANS	5 LOANS NEW OR ASSUMED LOANS*	6 PROPERTY EQUITIES 3−4	7 ESCROW CASH IN (GIVES)	8 ESCROW CASH OUT (GETS)	9 PAPER-OTHER BOOT IN (GIVES)	10 PAPER-OTHER BOOT OUT (GETS)	11 GROSS EQUITIES 6+7+9	12 COMMISSION	13 LOAN FEES	14 OTHER COSTS	15 TOTAL OF 13+14	16 NET EFFECTIVE EQUITIES 11−12−15	17 NEW LOANS	18 GROSS LOAN PROCEEDS 17−4
A	Smith GIVES Retail	500	300		200					200	30	12.6	6	18.6	151.4	350	50
	GETS Office	9000		630	÷270	2.8		90 BOOT GOING IN / PAPER CREATED									
B	Tuck GIVES Office	900	550		350					350	54	16.8	7	23.8	272.2	630	80
	GETS Center	1200		810	÷360			87.8 BOOT GOING IN / PAPER CREATED									
C	Finch GIVES Center	1200	480		720					720	72		9	9	639	840	350
	GETS Out				720		456.7	BOOT GOING IN / PAPER CREATED	90.8 / 84.5								
D	GIVES							BOOT GOING IN									
	GETS							PAPER CREATED									
E	GIVES							BOOT GOING IN									
	GETS							PAPER CREATED									
F	Stckets GIVES Fees				150						156	7	3.5	10.5	145.5		
	GETS																
G	BROKERS GET Retail	500		350	150			4.5									

H TRANSACTION COSTS DISBURSED THROUGH ESCROW 61.9
I LOAN PROCEEDS DISBURSED THROUGH ESCROW 490
J TOTAL ESCROW ACCOUNTS .... 518.6 = 61.9 / 518.6 = 518.6 / 182.3 = 182.3

(CASH IN must equal CASH OUT) 490
(PAPER IN must equal PAPER OUT)

Col. 12: 156.0 / −145.5 = 145.5
Col. 15: 61.9

*Also includes loans taken "Subject To"
†Equity in property acquired = Col. 6. Col. 9 represents a purchase (But ONLY if Col. 9 money note on property acquired).

Date: .... Prepared by: .... Office: ....
FORM 122 A
COPYRIGHT © 1987 BY PROFESSIONAL PUBLISHING CORP., 122 PAUL DRIVE, SAN RAFAEL, CALIFORNIA 94903

paper into the exchange. Inasmuch as the maximum loan-to-value ratio on the office building cannot exceed 80% after the exchange, the maximum loans against the office building cannot exceed $720,000 (80% of $900,000). Subtracting the new loan of $630,000 from the maximum financing gives the maximum second deed of trust of $90,000. Therefore, Smith will need $28,600 in cash to close the exchange.

Turk will need to give a note for $87,800 secured by a second deed of trust on the retail center in order to acquire a NET EFFECTIVE EQUITY of $272,2000 ($360,000 – $87,800).

In order for the brokers to acquire the retail building with their NET EFFECTIVE EQUITY of $145,500, they must execute a $4,500 note secured by a second deed of trust on the retail building.

Finch will receive his $639,000 in NET EFFECTIVE EQUITY (net sale proceeds) in the form of a $90,000 second deed of trust on the office building, an $87,800 second deed of trust on the retail center, a $4,500 second deed of trust on a retail building, for a total of $182,300 in paper, and $456,700 in cash.

The Brokers have earned a NET EFFECTIVE EQUITY of $145,500 in the Retail Building worth $500,000. The brokers' only remaining problem is how they are going to pay the income taxes due on these real estate commissions.

The simple exchange worksheet examples featured in this discussion illustrate the tremendous flexibility of the exchange recapitulation form. Using this worksheet to structure exchanges is a lot of fun and very rewarding. It should now be apparent that the fears of the most apprehensive user can be allayed with a few step-by-step examples on the use of this form.

part **III**

The Mechanics of Exchanging

chapter 8

Types of Exchanges

by *Kevin K. Hereford*
Rochelle Stone
Starker Services, Inc.
Los Gatos, California

The various ways Internal Revenue Code Section 1031 can be used offers investors procedures to accomplish a wide range of investment objectives. Tax deferment through exchanging is only one of the benefits derived. Estate planning, wealth building, relocations, divesting investments, consolidating investments, problem solving are some examples. There are as many reasons to perform an exchange as there are investors. The ultimate investment objectives of the investor will determine the form of the exchange.

All exchanges involve the trade of property for like-kind property. A sale is a simultaneous exchange of real property for cash (or the equivalent of cash). A sale is taxable. The only difference in an exchange is that equity in a replacement property is received by the exchangor in lieu of cash (or the equivalent). The exchange of property for like-kind property is a nontaxable event. The intent of each of the forms of exchange is to prevent the **exchangor** from receiving cash.

Swaps

A real estate trade between two individuals that does not include the concurrent sale of one of the properties is a "two-party" exchange (sometimes called a "swap"). In Figure 8.1, Exchangor "A" has a rental house that is

Figure 8.1 Swaps

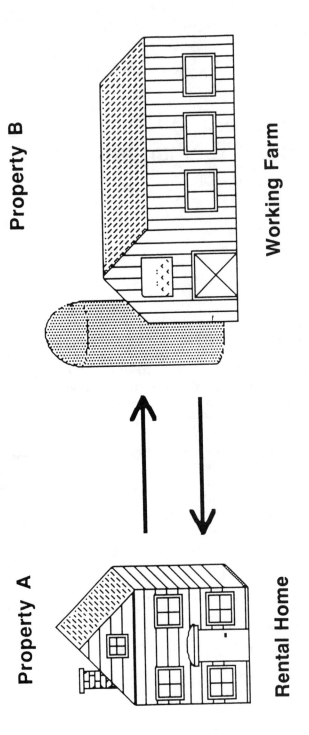

Property A

Property B

Rental Home

Working Farm

to be traded to Exchangor "B" for a working farm. Exchangor "B" wants the rental house in exchange for the working farm. Each party transfers ownership to the other. If both owners agree that the value of their properties are the same, there is no "cash" is this transaction.

Swaps

Two-party exchanges are rare. Seldom do two property owners agree to simply "trade" deeds.

When two owners want to trade properties, there is cash involved in order to balance equities, pay for closing costs such as title insurance or real estate commissions, and one or both of the owners must add cash to the transaction. Often one of the owners has a higher equity position in their property compared to the other party and they must either pay tax on the cash to balance the trade or to acquire another property.

Another form of "swap," which has been restricted under the 1991 Treasury Regulations, is one between related parties. With a couple of exceptions, if an individual swaps with a related party and that related party then sells the property within a two-year period, both parties will incur a taxable liability. Related-party exchanges were restricted to prevent avoidance of tax liability by shifting the tax basis in property.

Example

Exchangor A is the sole stockholder of Corporation B. Exchangor A owns rental property on Green Street, which is valued at $500,000 and has a zero basis. If sold, Green Street would have $500,000 in capital gains. Corporation B owns raw land (a parcel known as Redwood Estates) worth $500,000. Because Redwood is raw land and was never part of an exchange, the basis in Redwood Estates is $500,000. Exchangor A arranges to swap Green Street to Corporation B for Redwood Estates. Exchangor A's basis in the new property is still zero and the corporation's basis in Green Street is $500,000. Corporation B then sells Green Street for $500,000 and because the basis is the same as the sales price, there is no tax to pay. The Exchangor has the use of the funds.

Simultaneous Exchanges

A sale is a simultaneous exchange of real property for cash (or the equivalent). The only difference in an exchange is that equity in a replacement property is received in lieu of cash (or the equivalent).

A **simultaneous exchange** is an exchange in which all parties and properties to be traded are part of the same escrow or closing. Simultaneity refers to the contingency of the transactions, since nothing can actually occur at exactly the same moment. Regardless of whether the entire escrow (closing) is held with one **escrow officer** (closing agent) or separate escrows (closings) with two different closers, the escrows are contingent on each other and must close within a very short period of time. This interval is generally no longer than the time necessary to transfer funds by wire to the second close.

There are three types of simultaneous exchange:

1. Simultaneous Without Accommodator or Intermediary

In this form of exchange, there is no **accommodator** (one of the principals in the transaction), or intermediary (an outside party used to facilitate the exchange). The proceeds from the exchangors' sale property are transferred directly through escrow to the purchase of the replacement property in a concurrent close. Often referred to as the **"pot theory"** because the exchangor places a deed in escrow/the closing (pot) and gets a deed back out the "pot."

This form of an exchange is still commonly performed. It is the least expensive but the most risky. Opponents argue these transactions are nothing more than a sale of property and a simultaneous repurchase of replacement property and thus not an exchange. Under the 1991 Treasury Regulations, this is not considered a form of "safe harbor" for the exchangor. Another problem with this form is that it does not give the exchangor the opportunity to exchange into additional property if the equities are not balanced in the initial transaction.

Example

Exchangor A owns property on Sunny Oaks worth $300,000 with $200,000 in equity and a $100,000 loan. He has contracted to sell the property to Buyer B. He has also arranged to acquire property on Fairway Court from Seller C. The same individual is handling both closings. On the same day Exchangor A executes a deed transferring property Sunny Oaks to Buyer B and Seller C executes a deed transferring property Fairway Court to Exchangor A. There may or may not be a provision for an exchange in the contract and/or closing instructions.

2. Accommodator Exchanges

In this form of exchange either the seller or the buyer is used to accommo-date the exchange for the exchangor.

Baird Exchange—The Seller as the Accommodator

The **Baird exchange**, known as a **"Missouri Waltz"** exchange (J. H. Baird Publishing Co. (1962) 39 TC 608), is a form of simultaneous exchange in which the seller of the property the exchangor wishes to acquire acts as the "accommodator." The seller (accommodator) and exchangor trade proper-ties (property A for property B). (See Figure 8.2.)

Figure 8.2 Baird Exchange

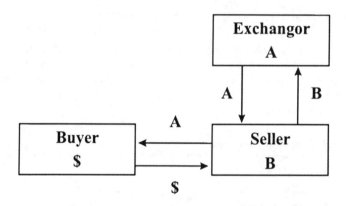

The seller (accommodator) then sells the exchangor's property A to a third-party buyer for cash.

In the Baird exchange, the seller, as the accommodator, assumes the additional liability as the seller of the exchangor's property. The exchange ends when the exchangor holding property A trades for property B and the seller of property B sells to a buyer for cash. Legally, the seller of B has full liability as the seller of property A.

It is extremely important that the seller who is willing to act as the accommodator in a Baird exchange is fully aware of the liability of an

accommodating grantor. Future problems with property A may mean the seller is sued as the seller of property "A." Seller may be indemnified by the exchangor, but the indemnification is only as good as the financial stability of the exchangor at that point in time the indemnification is needed. Furthermore, indemnification does not mean the seller cannot be named in a suit or have to defend themselves as a principle in the transaction.

Occasionally, the seller who is willing to act as the accommodator also desires to perform an exchange. If he does an exchange on the property he received from the first exchangor, his exchange may be disallowed because the property may be deemed as property held for resale, not for investment purposes, and thus not "like-kind."

Alderson Exchange—The Buyer as the Accommodator

In the **Alderson exchange**, sometimes known as a "reverse Missouri Waltz," (Alderson v. Commissioner (9th Circuit 1963) 317 F2d 290), the Buyer wishing to purchase the exchangor's property becomes the accommodator. Instead of purchasing the exchangor's property (property A), the cash buyer (accommodator) uses his cash to purchase the property the exchangor wishes to own (property B) and trades it for the exchangor's property A (see Figure 8.3).

Figure 8.3   Alderson Exchange

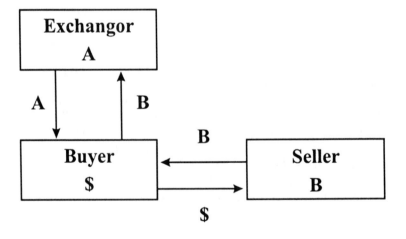

In the Alderson exchange, the buyer assumes the liability for acting in the capacity of both an exchangor and a buyer. Again, the basic exchange is similar to the simultaneous. It is also exactly the same as the Baird with the exception of which party acts as the accommodator. As with the Baird, there are three transfers of property (property B from the seller to the cash buyer, transfer of the replacement property B to the exchangor and exchange of exchangor's property A to the cash buyer).

Again, the buyer must be willing to accept the liability as the accommodator. However, the liability for the buyer is less in an Alderson exchange than for the seller in a Baird exchange. In a Alderson exchange, it is the exchangor who directs the buyer to purchase the target property; therefore, he has less recourse against the buyer. The seller in a Baird exchange does not know what kind of guarantee and warranties the exchangor has made to the ultimate buyer.

3. Simultaneous with a Qualified Intermediary

The **intermediary exchange** involved a fourth-party principal, the intermediary, who is brought into the exchange for the purpose of passing title and cash to the proper parties while insulating the exchangor from constructive receipt. The intermediary becomes the accommodator and assumes the liability of the accommodating grantor. The intermediary exchange protects the buyer, seller, and exchangor from assuming additional liabilities. The intermediary assumes the liability of an exchangor, buyer, and a seller.

There are several advantages when an Intermediary is used. As previously stated, the only safe harbor that applies to a simultaneous exchange is the use of a "qualified intermediary." Many tax authorities still believe an intermediary is not necessary in a simultaneous exchange but prefer to use one if only as an "insurance policy." The use of an intermediary also enables the exchangor to acquire more replacement properties to balance the exchange (see Figure 8.4).

Delayed or "Starker" Exchanges

This is an exchange in which the sale of the exchangors' property and the purchase of an acquisition property occur at separate times and involve separate escrows or closings. Essentially the same as a simultaneous exchange, it is completed in two separate steps.

First, the exchangor transfers ownership of the relinquished property to an intermediary. The intermediary provides a written contract (exchange

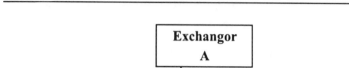

Figure 8.4   Simultaneous with a Qualified Intermediary

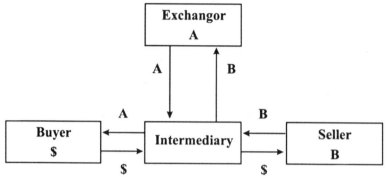

agreement) to the exchangor to sell the exchangors' relinquished property to the buyer and then receives and hold the sale proceeds (net equity). This completes Phase One.

The second step involves the purchase by the intermediary (within 180 days from the sale of the replacement property) to complete the exchange. The intermediary provides the downpayment (net equity) to the owner of the replacement property. The replacement property seller then transfers ownership of the property to the intermediary. The intermediary transfers ownership of the replacement property to the exchangor to satisfy the exchange agreement. This completes Phase Two.

From the closing date of the Phase One sale side, the exchangor has 45 days to identify the replacement property and 180 days to complete the exchange. Under the regulations the exchangor can identify three (3) replacement properties of any value or any number of properties, as long as the aggregate fair market value of those properties does not exceed 200 percent (200%) of the fair market value (sales price) of the property transferred. There are two exceptions: An exchangor can identify any number of properties of any value as long as the exchangor completes the exchange within the 45-day identification period; the exchangor can identify any number of properties of any value as long as the exchangor acquires 95% of the properties identified within 180 days of the close of the relinquished property.

Again, as with the previous examples, the basic exchange is still the same. There are four transfers of property (A transfers to the intermediary and then to buyer, B transfers from seller to intermediary and then to exchangor). Utilizing a "qualified intermediary" is the only safe harbor available for simultaneous exchanges (see Figure 8.5).

Figure 8.5 Delayed Exchange

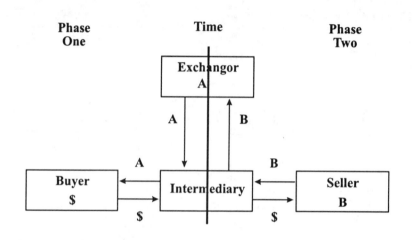

Improvement or Construction Exchanges

Frequently, the exchangor has a buyer for his/her relinquished property and has located the replacement property that he or she wishes to acquire. However, the acquisition property is not equal to or greater in value to the sale property. To complete the Phase two purchase of the replacement property would mean that "boot" would be recognized for the difference in values and taxed.

The key to understanding the improvement exchange is the concept of balancing the exchange. An improvement exchange is a delayed exchange where the intermediary retains ownership to the replacement property (J.H. Baird Publishing Co. v. Commissioner (1962) 39 TC 608 and Coastal Terminals, Inc. v. U.S. (1963) 320 F2d 333/0). While the intermediary has ownership of the replacement property, improvements are made to increase the value until it is worth the same or greater than the sale property. Once this is done, the intermediary transfers the property to the exchangor to complete Phase Two of the exchange. This entire process must take place within the 180-day limit as established in the 1031 regulations. All intended improvements do not need to be finished in order to transfer the property back to the exchangor. As long as the value of the land and improvements made are at a level to defer the taxes, the exchange can be completed. However, the completed project must be substantially the same as what was identified (see Figure 8.6).

Figure 8.6   Improvement Exchange

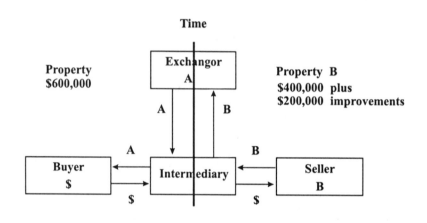

In Figure 8.6, the exchangor disposes of a property valued at $600,000 and wants a replacement property worth $400,000. There is $200,000 worth of taxable boot. The $600,000 cash from the sale of property A is retained by the intermediary. $400,000 is used to buy property B and $200,000 is left for constructing improvements. The intermediary retains ownership of property B and makes the improvements required to bring the value of B to $600,000. Once the work is completed, the exchange is finalized and the property is passed to exchangor A with a value of $600,000.

In performing **Improvement Exchanges,** the escrow holder is often required to maintain a trust account for the cash, which comes from the sale of property A. This cash will be used to make the improvements. The exchangor determines which improvements are desired and makes arrangements for their construction. The exchangor must identify the improvements in as much detail as possible within 45 days of the first closing. The intermediary will then provide written authorization to disburse funds when the work is completed.

The intermediary will usually give the exchangor power of attorney to manage the property and make arrangements for the improvements. Because of the liability, the intermediary will usually require the exchangor to obtain casualty insurance.

In an improvement exchange, financing is an important issue. The general rule is that improvements can only be completed if the property is being purchased with all cash or if the seller is willing to carry financing on the property. Conventional lenders usually will not loan funds to the exchangor if the intermediary is the entity on the title of the property.

Investors incorrectly assume that they can balance their exchange by moving all of their equity into the land and then by obtaining a construction loan to have an equal or greater mortgage. If the exchange is completed in this manner, the exchangor has received real property and a contractual obligation to make the improvements. This obligation is personal property and is not "like-kind." If the exchangor does need to get a loan to do the improvements he can arrange to have the seller finance the property for six months. This arrangement would leave cash in the exchange to make the needed improvements. Once the improvements are made, the exchangor could make arrangements to get permanent financing on the property and pay off the note to the seller.

A situation where an improvement exchange is not possible is when there is conventional financing and the seller does not have a large enough equity position to carry the financing. There are alternatives that allow the exchangor to get all of the equity in the replacement property. The exchangor could contract to acquire the property at a higher value and require the sellers do the improvements. When the seller does not have the cash to make the improvements, the exchangor can have the intermediary loan the needed funds to the seller and secure the loan with a trust deed/mortgage. When the transaction closes, the lien would be removed from the property. The exchangor could also have the intermediary pay contractors for the improvements before escrow closes (improvements must be finished). If the transaction does not close, the exchangor could lose the money advanced to pay for the improvements.

Reverse Exchanges

This is one form of exchange which was not included in the 1991 Treasury Regulations. It is considered a very aggressive form of tax deferment and should not be used unless there is no alternative for the exchangor. The situation, which cases the use of the reverse, is the inability of the exchangor to sell their property while at the same time the exchangor must close on the purchase of the replacement property. An exchangor cannot trade into a property they already own. The "Reverse exchange" is then a way in which the exchangor uses the intermediary to purchase and "warehouse" the replacement property until the sale of the relinquished property is possible. To put it more simply, the Phase Two of the exchange occurs before the Phase One (see Figure 8.7).

Figure 8.7   Reverse Exchange

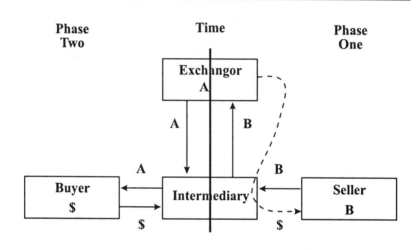

In Figure 8.7, the intermediary is required to buy the replacement property B first, exchange it for property A, and finally sell property A to the buyer. The intermediary must have the cash for a down payment to purchase B. The intermediary generally borrows the funds from the exchangor and the intermediary will execute a note as trustor for the amount of the loan with the exchangor as the beneficiary. This Note will not appear on the settlement statements for the purchase or the exchange of B. The escrow officer will draw the Note to create the loan. (Important: For a completely tax-deferred exchange, it is important to have a down payment at least equal to the value of the net equity from the relinquished property). When Phase One is completed in the future, the exchangor will place a demand into the sale escrow for property A and the escrow holder will repay the note with proceeds from the sale.

Two variations of the Reverse Exchange may be used:

1. Type A: The intermediary buys property B and maintains ownership until a buyer is found for property A. When a buyer is found, the trade is completed as a simultaneous exchange. This format is useful if the exchangor must make renovations on property B before it is delivered to them ("Reverse Improvement Exchange").

   Occasionally, the exchangor is able to negotiate a small down payment on property B with short-term, seller-financing until property A is sold. If the down payment required in Phase One is less than the equity coming from the sale of property A, the exchangor would have a "boot" problem. The Type A format is ideal for this situation. In order to circumvent such potential difficulties, the intermediary maintains ownership of property B until the equity from Phase One is known.

   This format is difficult to administer. Since property A is owned by the intermediary, the exchangor is not allowed to manage or operate the property without being a real estate agent or having the power of attorney from the intermediary. Additional problems can arise if there is an excess or shortage of cash flow. If a loan is needed, it is almost impossible to have a temporary owner, such as the intermediary. Insurance will also have to be obtained to protect the intermediary against liability and loss while they own the property.

2. Type B: The intermediary acquires property B and immediately trades it for property A. Property A is held by the intermediary until a buyer is found (Simultaneous Exchange). This format has many of the same problems as Type A. If the equity in property A is greater than the down payment required to buy property B, this format cannot be used.

   There is no difficulty with a new loan, however, since the exchangor acquires ownership of property B immediately. As in the Type A format, management by the exchangor would still require a real estate license or Power of Attorney. The main advantage of this format is that conventional financing on the replacement property is feasible.

Proponents who argue that this form is a valid form of an exchange often cite Code Section 1034, which deals with a principal residence. Briefly, Section 1034 allows an individual to acquire a new principal residence and have two years to sell the old residence in order to defer the taxes. Because of the high level of risk involved in reverse exchanges, most Intermediaries will not participate.

chapter 9

Personal Property and Multiple Property Exchanges

by Michael Renfro
Starker Services, Inc.
Los Gatos, California

Although Section 1031 is most commonly used for real property, personal property may also be exchanged. As with real property exchanges, the personal property received must be of a like-kind or class and must be used for productive use in a trade or business or for investment. Trucks, tractors, office furniture, and computers are all examples of property that can be exchanged without recognizing a gain on their disposal.

The sale of an entire business will often include items of personal property. The seller of a hotel can exchange furniture, televisions, and laundry and ice machines for items of like-kind or class in another hotel. A liquor store owner, wishing to change locations, can exchange into a new store without being taxed on any gain on the disposition of the original assets. The real property can be exchanged, as well as the store's fixtures, refrigeration units, signs, and other miscellaneous equipment. Each new asset must be of like-class to the one given up.

So, What Is Like-Class?

While like-kind in real property exchanges can vary greatly, like-kind personal property must be of like-class. Treasury Regulations state that depreciable tangible assets will be considered of like-class if they are within the same "General Asset Class" or within the same "Product Class." There are 13 General Asset Classes for property frequently used in many businesses.

1. Office furniture, fixtures and equipment.

2. Information systems.

3. Data handling equipment, except computers.

4. Airplanes (airframes and engines), except those used commercial or contract carrying of passengers and freight, and all helicopters.

5. Automobiles and taxis.

6. Buses.

7. Light general purpose trucks.

8. Heavy general purpose trucks.

9. Railroad cars and locomotives, except those owned by railroad companies.

10. Tractor units for use over the road.

11. Trailer and trailer-mounted containers.

12. Vessels, barges, tugs and similar water-transportation equipment, except those used in marine construction.

13. Industrial steam and electric generation and/or distribution systems.

If the asset in question does not fall under one of these classes, it will be identified by its "Product Code." A property's Product Code is its classification under the *Standard Industrial Classification Manual*. The *SIC Manual* is a commonly used coding system provided by the Office of Management and Budget.

Intangible or Nondepreciable Personal Property

Exchanges of intangible, nondepreciable or investment property may also qualify for nonrecognition treatment under Section 1031. Because of the wide variety of these types of property, no classification system is set up. Qualification will have to be made on an individual basis. For example, the determination as to whether a type of right involved (i.e., a patent or a copyright) qualifies depends not only on the right but also on the nature or type of underlying property to which the intangible personal property relates. Copyrights on two novels may qualify, but a copyright on a novel and a copyright on a song might not qualify because of the difference in the underlying asset. Other examples of nondepreciable or investment property include fine art, gems, stamps, baseball contracts, and Chamber of Commerce memberships. Each type of property must be the same. For example, gold cannot be traded for silver.

Goodwill

In many business transactions, goodwill may account for a substantial proportion of the sales price. Unfortunately, the Internal Revenue Service has concluded that the nature of goodwill and going concern value of a business are so inherently unique and inseparable from the business that goodwill and going concern of two businesses will never be considered like-kind.

Multiple Property Exchanges

If the exchange includes multiple types of real and personal property, each asset must be matched by its specific business or product class (i.e., computers traded for computers, trucks for trucks, real property for real property). "Exchange groups" are created consisting of property all of which is of a like-kind or class. If more than one exchange group is created, the transaction is termed a "multiple property exchange." In these transactions, no gain will be recognized if the aggregate value of the properties in each exchange group transferred equals the aggregate value of the properties received in the same group. Once the exchange groups are created, the rules of Section 1031 are applied to each individual exchange group to determine the gain recognized and the new basis of the property received. The exchange of a business is a common example of a multiple property exchange. Exchanges of apartment buildings will be exchanges of multiple properties if, in addition to real property, personal property is transferred and received by the taxpayer in the exchange.

Treatment of Liabilities

Consideration received in the form of an assumption of liabilities (or a transfer subject to a liability) is to be treated as other property or money for purposes of Section 1031(b). To determine the amount of other property or money in accord with Section 1031(b), consideration given in the form of an assumption of liabilities (or receipt of property subject to a liability) is offset against consideration received in the form of an assumption of liabilities (or a transfer subject to a liability).

All liabilities of which the taxpayer is relieved in the exchange are offset against all liabilities assumed by the taxpayer in the exchange, regardless of whether the liabilities are recourse or nonrecourse and regardless of whether they are secured by either the property transferred or received in the exchange. If there are excess liabilities assumed by the taxpayer, the excess is allocated to the properties received in all the exchange groups, based on their fair market values. This has the effect of preventing liabilities assumed from **offsetting** any **boot** received.

Identification

The identification of personal property generally falls under the same guidelines governing the exchanges of real property. Replacement property must be identified within 45 days after the sale of the disposition property. The task of identifying all like-kind assets may frustrate taxpayers with respect to items that are of little value and size. Think of the work involved in a hotel exchange, where the taxpayer would have to list each lamp, each T.V., or each knife and fork. Fortunately, the regulations allow the taxpayer to disregard the identification of property that is incidental to the exchange of a larger property. Property will be treated as incidental if: (1) in standard commercial transactions, the property is usually transferred with the larger item: and (2) the aggregate fair market value of the incidental property does not exceed 15 percent of the aggregate fair market value of the larger item of property. For example, furniture, laundry machines and other items of personal property will not be treated as separate property from an apartment building worth $1,000,000, if the fair market value of these personal property items does not exceed $150,000. This rule is relevant only to identification of incidental property; exchange groups would still need to be created where the existence of incidental property creates a multiple property exchange.

chapter 10

Seller Financing in an Exchange

by Michael Renfro
  Starker Services, Inc.
  Los Gatos, California

Providing seller financing is one of the most common methods of selling property. Investors frequently ask if it is possible to carry financing and still complete an IRC 1031 tax-deferred exchange. Since the taxpayer cannot act as the seller of the property, often there is confusion as to how the note should be treated and who should be the beneficiary.

Assume that Ms. Johnson, who wishes to complete an exchange, owns a property valued at $200,000. She receives an offer from Mr. Smith for $180,000 cash and an installment note for $20,000, payable over the next five years. Ms. Johnson will be using a qualified intermediary to facilitate a deferred exchange for like-kind property, which she has not yet identified.

In a 1031 exchange, gain is only recognized to the extent of the cash and/or value of nonqualifying property received. If the taxpayer received like-kind property and a note, the note received would be considered taxable boot. The transaction would likely be treated by the IRS as two transactions: an installment sale for the portion of the property, represented by the notes, and a like-kind exchange for the remainder of the property transferred through the qualified intermediary. Since the installment sale treatment will not defer all the gain, this method will only partially defer tax. While this procedure may be advantageous to some investors, there are alternatives that allow the taxpayer to defer the recognition of gain by using their note in the exchange.

Alternatives to the Installment Sale

Like the cash received by the qualified intermediary, a "note" is viewed as additional exchange equity. This equity must be used in the acquisition of the replacement property or it will be treated as boot. If the note is passed through the exchange, the intermediary will act as the beneficiary. This is logical, since the intermediary is acting as the seller of the property. The note is added to the rest of the exchange equity for use in acquiring the replacement property. The taxpayer has several alternatives regarding the use of the note:

Alternative #1

Ms. Johnson can try to locate a seller of a replacement property who is willing to take the note as part of the consideration. If the seller is motivated and the note is well-secured, this could be a viable approach. The intermediary would give the cash and note to the seller in return for the replacement property.

Alternative #2

The intermediary could sell the note to another party (usually at a discount) and apply the cash proceeds towards the acquisition of the like-kind replacement property. The note sale proceeds would be added to the funds the intermediary was holding from the sale of the relinquished property.

Alternative #3

In a separate transaction, Ms. Johnson may purchase the note from the intermediary. The intermediary would, in turn, apply the combined funds from the note sale and the sale of the relinquished property to acquire a replacement property. Care must be taken so that the note sale is indeed a separate transaction. There is a possibility that the IRS could view Ms. Johnson's receipt of the note from the intermediary as boot, or even worse, as constructive receipt, thereby endangering the exchange.

Alternative #4

If Alternative #3 cannot be properly documented, Ms. Johnson may wish to lend $20,000 to Mr. Smith outside of the closing in return for a note and deed of trust to be secured by the property. Mr. Smith would then purchase the property from the intermediary for $200,000 cash. The intermediary now has $200,000 cash to use to acquire the replacement property.

The taxpayer's current financial status will help determine whether they should keep the note. If the note will be used in the exchange, then each of the proceeding alternatives may be explored to find the best available course of action. These alternatives are merely opinions as to the acceptable options to using a note. At the time of this writing, no guidelines addressing the coordination between the deferred exchange rules (IRC 1031) and installment sale rules (IRS 453) were in existence. The IRS has promised to address this issue in forthcoming proposed regulations.

The Exchange Process

chapter 11

Contracting and Closing the Exchange

by Scott R. Saunders
Starker Services, Inc.
Los Gatos, California

Completing a tax-deferred exchange is a relatively simple process from the perspective of a real estate investor. Although an exchange can take place any time before closing on the disposition of the first property, it is most preferable to establish the intention to exchange as early in the transaction as possible.

THE TOOLS OF THE TRADE

In order to complete a successful exchange, the investor will need to have the proper documentation. These tools include the following.

The Listing Agreement

The first step in this process is to include the intention to exchange in the initial "Listing Agreement." The primary intent is to establish the property owner's desire to exchange his property rather than to sell his property. Potential verbiage for an "Exchange Provision" is shown as follows:

> It is the intention of the seller to perform an IRC Section 1031 tax deferred exchange and that the seller's rights and obligations will be assigned to a qualified exchange intermediary to facilitate such exchange.

The Purchase and Sale Agreement

After the investor includes this intention to exchange in the Listing Agreement, the next step is to solicit offers for purchasing the property. Except for the inclusion of an Exchange Provision, the listing will appear identical to any other listing. The property owner will then receive offers and counter-offers until both the seller and buyer have agreed upon the terms and conditions of the sale. At this time, an expanded Exchange Provision should be added to the Purchase and Sale Agreement. An example is reflected below:

> Buyer herein acknowledges that it is the intention of the seller to create an IRC Section 1031 tax-deferred exchange and that the seller's rights and obligations under this agreement will be assigned to (*Name of the Qualified Intermediary*) to facilitate such exchange. Buyer agrees to cooperate with the seller in a manner necessary to enable the seller to qualify for said exchange at no additional cost or liability to the buyer.

The last line in the Exchange Provision will often be required by the buyer's legal counsel. In fact, the wording, "agrees to cooperate" has a significantly different legal interpretation than "agrees to participate." If the latter ("agrees to participate") is incorporated into the final contract, it creates a potential liability for the buyer. Some attorneys have successfully argued this clause requires the buyer to act as the accommodating party to facilitate the exchange transaction. If the buyer acted as the accommodator, they would be required to purchase the exchangor's replacement property and then exchange the replacement property for the property initially held by the exchangor. In this exchange scenario ("Baird" Exchange), the buyer assumes all of the liability and responsibility for acting as the accommodator.

On the other hand, the wording "agrees to cooperate" does not obligate the buyer to have any sort of an active role in the exchange transaction. This language merely states that the buyer will not do anything to prevent the seller from performing an exchange. It is not sufficient to obligate the buyer to function as the accommodator.

Exchange Documents

Once the Purchase and Sale Agreement has been signed, the escrow will be opened. This is the first time that the qualified intermediary officially enters into the transaction. When the qualified intermediary is contacted he forwards the following documents to the closing officer or closing attorney.

Exchange Agreement

This agreement outlines the obligations and responsibilities of the exchange intermediary. Essentially, it states that the exchange intermediary is obligated to give back the to the exchangor the equivalent amount of either property or proceeds that the exchange intermediary has received from the initial disposition of the exchangor's property.

Assignment Agreement

The purpose of the **Assignment Agreement** is to assign the rights under the Purchase and Sale Agreement from the exchangor to the exchange intermediary. This is essential, since in an exchange the exchange intermediary, rather than the exchangor, is truly the Seller of the disposition property. It is preferable to have the Assignment Agreement executed by both the exchangor and the buyer. However, as long as the Purchase and Sale Agreement does not specifically state that the contract is "nonassignable," then an Assignment Agreement executed by the exchangor is sufficient.

Escrow (Closing) Instructions

These are step-by-step instructions to assist the closing officer or the closing attorney in preparing the closing documents and settlement statements. In addition to aiding the closing officer or closing attorney, the Escrow Instructions also help provide a clear paper trail for the exchangor. These instructions clearly delineate the proper sequence of document preparation. For example, they would instruct that an Exchange Settlement Statement be prepared between the exchangor and the exchange intermediary and a Seller's Settlement Statement between the exchange intermediary and the **buyer**. In the event the exchange comes under the scrutiny of the Internal Revenue Service, these instructions will clearly show the specific responsibilities of the closing officer or closing attorney.

Deeding

The Exchange Instructions indicate how the property should be deeded to the buyer. Prior to 1991, most exchange intermediaries utilized "sequential deeding." In sequential deeding, the exchangor deeds the property to the exchange intermediary who then immediately transfers the property to the buyer via a Corporate Deed. The advantage of sequential deeding is that it provides a clear paper trail for the Internal Revenue Service to follow in case of an audit. Unfortunately, the disadvantage of sequential deeding is that in many counties and states, an exchangor is not exempt from "double deed taxation" in exchange transactions where two deeds are recorded concurrently. The exchangor will be required to pay the deed transfer tax twice—once for the transfer to the exchange intermediary and secondly for the transfer from the exchange intermediary to the buyer. In many instances, this additional transfer tax is a substantial percentage of the sales price.

On the other hand, "direct deeding" was officially endorsed under the Treasury Regulations in 1991. This format is the most commonly used approach because it alleviates the "double deed taxation" problem. In "direct deeding," the title passes directly from the exchangor to the buyer. However, ownership to the disposition property still passes through the exchange intermediary as reflected on the two sets of Settlement Statements. The elimination of the extra deed makes the success of the exchange dependent upon the exchange and closing documents. Since title is passing directly, these documents, must prove the exchangor has not acted as the principal. If, inadvertently, the settlement statements are incorrectly prepared, the Internal Revenue Service might view the transaction as a sale regardless of the exchangor's intent.

Phase One: Closing on the Disposition Property

Once the transaction closes, the net proceeds are transferred to the exchange intermediary. The intermediary will generally forward a letter to the exchangor showing the specific account number at the banking institution holding the proceeds, as well as the 45-day and 180-day deadlines. In addition, the exchange intermediary should furnish an Identification Form to the exchangor for specifying the potential replacement properties.

Phase Two: Closing on the Replacement Property

The documents required for the acquisition of the replacement property (or properties) are identical to the disposition phase of the exchange. The exchange intermediary will forward both an Assignment Agreement and the Exchange Instructions to the closing officer or closing attorney. In addition, a document—often called a "Declaration of Satisfactory Performance/Termination of Exchange Agreement"—is prepared. This document essentially wraps-up the exchange by stating that the exchange intermediary has performed all of its obligations under the Exchange Agreement.

Exchanges Involving Different Forms of Ownership

by R. Douglas Wright
  Branch, Pike, Ganz & O'Callaghan
  Atlanta, Georgia

OVERVIEW

As originally enacted, the predecessor to Section 1031 of the Internal Revenue Code was envisioned as a simple, unsophisticated provision to allow two parties to exchange similar properties without recognition of attendant gain for tax purposes. The failure of Congress to anticipate the creativity of the U.S. taxpayer is legendary, however, and the evolution of case and regulatory law under Section 1031 reflects an earnest, albeit belated in many cases, attempt to deal with the myriad forms of ownership of real property and interests therein under various state laws while, at the same time, insuring the integrity of the statute through the disallowance of nonrecognition treatment for disguised exchanges of interests in entities owning like kind properties, rather than the exchange of such properties, or qualified ownership interests therein, themselves.

The essential requirements of Section 1031(a) have existed in their current form since 1924 (except for language addressing delayed exchanges, the exchange of partnership interests and related-party transactions) and such language has been strictly construed as an exception to the general rule under Section 1001 of the Code that all gains (and losses) realized on the exchange of properties shall be recognized.

SPECIFIC REQUIREMENTS OF Section 1031(a)

As noted, Section 1031(a) was enacted specifically as an exception to the general rule that gains must be recognized. With respect to such exceptions, Treasury Regulations provide as follows:

> Exceptions to the general rule are made, for example, by sections 351(a), 354, 361(a), 371(a)(1), 371(b), 721, 1031, 1035 and 1036. These sections describe certain specific exchanges of property in which, at the time of the exchange particular differences exist between the property parted with and the property acquired, but such differences are more formal than substantial. As to these, the Code provides that such differences shall not be deemed controlling, and that gain or loss shall not be recognized at the time of the exchange. The underlying assumption of these exceptions is that the new property is substantially a continuation of the old investment still unliquidated; and, in the case of reorganizations, that the new enterprise, the new corporate structure, and the new property are substantially continuations of the old still unliquidated.[1]

Accordingly, the Internal Revenue Service and courts, alike, have struggled through the years since the enactment of Section 1031(a) to construe the language of the statute in a manner consistent with the underlying purpose thereof as set forth in the Regulations, often with surprising results.

The "Like-Kind" Requirement

The statute provides that no gain or loss shall be recognized on the exchange of property "held for productive use in a trade or business or for investment" for property of a like-kind (which also is to be held either for productive use in a trade or business or for investment). Section 1.1031(a)-1(b) of the Regulations contains the definition of "like-kind" and, with respect to real estate, makes the following points clear.

First, the term refers to the nature of character of property, and not to its grade or quality. Accordingly, the fact that real estate is unimproved or improved is immaterial because such fact relates only to the grade or quality of such property, and not to its nature or classification. Likewise, un-

---

[1] Treas. Reg. § 1.1002-1(c) (1967) (prior to enactment of the Tax Reform Act of 1976 wherein Section 1002 redesignated as Section 1001(c)).

productive property held other than as a "dealer" is the same nature or class as improved, productive real estate. Other examples of like-kind exchanges contained in the Regulations include: the exchange of city real estate for a ranch or a farm; and the exchange of a fee simple interest in real estate for a leasehold of a fee interest in real estate with a remaining term of 30 years or more.[2]

Specifically exempted from the definition of "like-kind" are exchanges of real property for personal property (obviously; *but see* discussion regarding certain contract rights exchanged for interests in real property) and the exchange of real property located in the United States for real property located outside the United States.[3]

OWNERSHIP INTERESTS

The simplest form of a like-kind real property exchange is the simultaneous transfer of unencumbered tracts owned in fee simple by two individuals. The probability of such an exchange in today's environment is effectively zero; hence, taxpayers and the courts have struggled to fit a multitude of ownership forms within the statutory language of Section 1031(a) on the theory that such transactions do not contravene the legislative history or the intent of such Code provisions.

The following discussion will set forth the kinds of real estate and the types of ownership interests therein that can be exchanged on a nonrecognition basis, and the legal authorities supporting characterization under Section 1031(a). It must be emphasized in this regard, however, that where a private letter ruling ("PLR") is cited for authority supporting a particular form of exchange transaction that a taxpayer is well advised to structure with caution because a private letter ruling has no precedential value, nor will it necessarily be afforded any weight as an authority for purposes of avoiding an accuracy-related penalty should an overturned exchange transaction result in a substantial understatement of income tax liability.

Fee Simple Ownership

As noted, the exchange of fee simple ownership interests in real property falls squarely within the language of Section 1031(a). It does not matter

---

2   Treas. Reg. § 1.1031(a)-1(c)(2)(1991).
3   IRC § 1031(h) (effective for transfers after July 10, 1989).

whether such tracts are improved or unimproved[4] or where the property is located (provided, however, that real property located out of the United States is deemed not be of like-kind to U.S. real property per IRC § 1031(h)).

Partial Interests; Leaseholds

An undivided interest in real property held as a tenant-in-common may be exchanged for either (1) a fee simple interest in another real property; (2) an undivided interest in another real property; or (3) in situations where common owners of a single tract seek to rearrange their ownership or to partition their tenancy-in-common.[5]

A fee simple absolute interest may also be separated into temporal interests such as life estates, remainder interests and leasehold interests with possibility of reverter. In this regard, the IRS has ruled privately that the exchange of an indefeasible vested remainder interest in realty for a fee interest in other realty qualifies under Section 1031(a).[6] In ruling favorably on this type of exchange, the IRS emphasized that the taxpayer holding the vested remainder interest was certain to come into possession of such interest in fee simple absolute. Accordingly, the nonpossessory status at the time of the exchange was deemed to be of a lesser grade or quality than a possessory fee interest, but still of the same general character as a fee interest (as required under the Regulations). Moreover, the IRS appears to recognize, at least implicitly, that an exchange of a remainder interest in one piece of real property for a life estate (where the life expectancy of the life tenant exceeds 30 years) in another piece of real property qualifies under Section 1031(a).[7]

With respect to leasehold interests in real property, the Regulations provide specifically that a leasehold having 30 or more years to run is of like-kind to a fee simple interest.[8] The Tax Court has also determined that the owner of a fee interest in real estate subject to a leasehold interest of 99 years is able to exchange such interest under Section 1031(a) for an

---

4   Treas. Reg. § 1.1031(a)-1(b) (1991).
5   *See* Rev. Rul. 73-476, 1973-2 C.B. 300; PLR 8809019 (Dec. 1, 1987); and PLR 8515016 (Jan. 8, 1985).
6   PLR 9143053 (July 30, 1991); PLR 8950034 (Sept. 19, 1989).
7   Rev. Rul. 72-601, 1972-2 C.B. 467. *Cf.* Treas. Reg. § 1.1031(a)-1(c)(2)(1991) (leasehold interests).
8   Treas. Reg. § 1.1031(a)-1(c)(2)(1991).

unencumbered fee interest in other real estate.[9] The IRS argued in the Tax Court case that the owner of the fee simple interest had received in return for the transfer of its real estate only "a lessor's right to receive rent under 99 year condominium leases."[10] The Tax Court determined, however, that the taxpayer's right to rental payments was not separate and distinct from the real property received by the taxpayer, but rather was "part of the bundle of rights incident to the ownership of the fee."[11] Also, as the taxpayer was saddled with the burdens of fee ownership under state law, notwithstanding the pass-through of ad valorem taxes and other responsibilities to the lessee under the terms of the lease agreement, the Tax Court had no trouble dismissing the IRS's argument.

The IRS also argued in the Tax Court that because Treasury Regulations stipulate that the exchange of a leasehold interest with 30 years or more to run for a fee simple interest in land is an exchange of like-kind property, a negative inference is created that a lessor's interest is not of like-kind to a fee interest. The Tax Court pointed out, however, that an interest in real estate need not be equivalent to a fee interest, but merely "like" such interest and the specific approval of a 30-year leasehold interest in the Regulations as of a "like-kind" to a fee interest does no violence to the characterization of a lessor's fee simple interest, which must stand on its own facts, and that there was no logical necessity to deny nonrecognition treatment to a lessor simply because such treatment is granted to the lessee with respect to the same piece of real estate.

It should also be noted that while the regulations specifically acknowledge that a leasehold having 30 years or more to run and a fee interest are of like-kind for purposes of Section 1031(a), the IRS has also ruled that a leasehold of less than 30 years can be exchanged for another leasehold having a term of less than 30 years and be afforded nonrecognition treatment.[12]

When dealing with the proposed exchange of leasehold interests (of whatever duration), a taxpayer should consider carefully the implications of the *Frank Lyon Co.* case[13] and a related series of Revenue Rulings wherein leasehold interests were recharacterized as financing arrangements. In such instances, the "lessee" is deemed to be the owner of the real property in question and the "lessor" is deemed to be a mere "lender,"

9 *Carl E. Koch*, 71 T.C. 54 (1978), acq. 1979-1 C.B. 1.
10 *Id.* at 63, n.5.
11 *Id.* at 66.
12 Rev. Rul. 76-301, 1976-2 C.B. 241.
13 *Frank Lyon Co. v. United States* 435 U.S. 561 (1978).

rather than the owner of an interest in real property eligible for nonrecognition treatment in an exchange transaction pursuant to the authority of the *Carl E. Koch* case.

Condominiums; Cooperatives

Special interests in real estate have been created under various state laws that provide for condominium or cooperative ownership interests.

A cooperative interest is typically that of a stockholder who also owns a long-term (typically in excess of 30 years) leasehold interest in real property. Some states (e.g., New York) have held such an interest to be other than a real property interest, while others (e.g., California) have held such interest to be a real property interest. In the latter case, the IRS has ruled privately that the conversion of an interest in a cooperative to a condominium interest (under relevant state law providing that a condominium interest is also an interest in real estate) pursuant to a liquidation of the stockholder interest and surrender of the leasehold interest in exchange for an undivided interest in land and common areas and a separate interest in space representing the taxpayer's condominium qualifies for nonrecognition treatment under Section 1031(a).[14] Presumably, the exchange of such interests in different pieces of real property would also qualify for nonrecognition treatment in those states which recognize such interests to be "real property interests."

Mineral and Water Rights; Unharvested Crops; Timber

Many times, an interest in the natural resources on a piece of real property will be separated from an interest in the real property, itself, yet the exchange of such an interest may still qualify for nonrecognition treatment under Section 1031(a). On the other hand, minor alterations to the structure of substantially identical transactions may cause recharacterization of an interest in natural resources as an interest in personalty under relevant state law, thereby resulting in disqualification under Section 1031(a).

An early example of this principle is the holding in Revenue Ruling 55-749,[15] wherein the IRS ruled that an exchange of land for perpetual water rights was of "like-kind," provided, however, that such water rights are considered to be an interest in real property under applicable state law.

---

[14] e.g., PLR 8810034 (Dec. 10, 1987); PLR 8445010 (July 30, 1984).
[15] 1955-2 C.B. 295.

A further example is the oft-cited case of *C.I.R. v. P.G. Lake, Inc.*,[16] wherein the United States Supreme Court distinguished a "production payment" from a "royalty interest" in oil or gas production, deeming the former to be merely a temporary right to the mineral produced, therefore, not of a like-kind to rights in real property, while acknowledging the latter to be a continuing investment in the real property from which the minerals are to be extracted, therefore, eligible for nonrecognition treatment under Section 1031(a). On the other hand, taxpayers should be wary of the implications of a recent case wherein the Tax Court recharacterized the attempted exchange of mineral rights underlying one piece of property for a royalty interest and other land as a "lease," rather than an "exchange" potentially subject to nonrecognition treatment under Section 1031(a).[17] Furthermore, the Tax Court has disallowed nonrecognition treatment with respect to an exchange of ranch/business real property for an oil production payment notwithstanding the characterization of the latter as an interest in real estate under state law because the interests exchanged where "intrinsically different."[18]

The importance of the characterization of an interest under state law cannot be overemphasized. For example, the IRS has ruled privately that the exchange of a tree farm for virgin timberland qualifies for nonrecognition treatment under Section 1031(a).[19] On the other hand, the exchange of cut-over timberland for the mere right to cut timber on another's land did not qualify for nonrecognition treatment as the right to cut timber was deemed to be an interest in personalty under applicable state law.[20]

Contract Rights

While the case law and administrative rulings under Section 1031(a) have allowed taxpayers great latitude in structuring exchanges, the "like-kind" requirement is often cited as the reason for disallowing nonrecognition treatment for multi-party or deferred exchanges where real estate (or an exchangeable interest therein) is surrendered for contractual rights. For example, in *Bloomington Coca-Cola Bottling Co. v. C.I.R.*,[21] a taxpayer sur-

---

[16] 356 U.S. 260 (1958).
[17] *Richard W. Crooks*, 92 T.C. 816 (1989).
[18] *William Fleming*, 24 T.C. 818 (1955), *nonacq.* 1965-1 C.B. 6, *aff'd rev'd and rem'd on other issues*, 241 F.2d 78 (5th Cir. 1957), *rev'd*, 356 U.S. 260 (1958).
[19] PLR 8818034 (Feb. 8, 1988).
[20] *Oregon Lumber Co.*, 20 T.C. 192 (1953), *acq.* 1953-2 C.B. 5.
[21] 189 F.2d 14 (7th Cir. 1951).

rendered title to real estate and a manufacturing plant in exchange for a contractor's promise to build a new plant for the taxpayer on land already owned by the taxpayer. The Court had no difficulty in characterizing the consideration to be received as a contractual right, rather than a like-kind interest in real estate and, accordingly, recharacterizing such transaction as a taxable sale of the old plant.

In *J.H. Baird Publishing Co.,*[22] on the other hand, a taxpayer deeded a building to a real estate agent in exchange for the agent's promise to deliver a new building on land acquired from a third party with the proceeds from the sale of the building to yet another unrelated party. The IRS attempted to characterize the real estate agent as the agent of the taxpayer; hence, the transaction as a sale of real property by the taxpayer followed by the purchase of new property and construction of a building thereon. However, the Tax Court determined that the taxpayer's surrender of the building was made in consideration only of the real estate agent's promise to deliver back a lot with a new building constructed on it, not as an "agent" but as a contractual principal, and the transaction was allowed nonrecognition treatment.

The deferred nature of the exchange in the *J.H. Baird Publishing Co.* case was not addressed by the Tax Court, nor was the issue of whether the taxpayer's real estate transfer was in exchange for a contract right, rather than a like-kind interest in real estate. The famous case *Starker v. United States,*[23] seemed to lay this issue to rest, however, when the United States Court of Appeals for the Ninth Circuit stated:

> [A] contractual right to assume the rights of ownership should not, we believe, be treated as any different than the ownership rights themselves. Even if the contract includes the possibility of the taxpayer receiving something other than ownership of like-kind property, we hold that it is still of a like-kind with ownership for tax purposes when the taxpayer prefers property to cash before and through the executory period, and only like-kind property is ultimately received.[24]

Notwithstanding the Starker holding, the IRS thereafter continued to take the position that even though a delayed exchange of improved real property for land plus an exchangor's promise to construct an improvement on such land could result in a Section 1031(a) exchange, that the

---

[22] 39 T.C. 608 (1962).
[23] 602 F.2d 1341 (9th Cir. 1979).
[24] *Id.* at 1355.

exchangor's promise was "boot." Pursuant to the enactment of amendments to the Code specifically authorizing delayed exchanges,[25] Treasury Regulations have now been adopted that provide a rule whereby property relinquished in a deferred exchange transaction can be exchanged for a contractual promise to build improvements on replacement property of a like-kind, but only to the extent such improvements are completed at the time of the consummation of the exchange.[26] The pro rata rule adopted in the regulations apparently removes all controversy with regard to the treatment of exchanges of improved real property for land plus a promise to construct improvements thereon during the period taken to consummate such exchange.[27]

PARTNERSHIP INTERESTS

Code Prohibitions

Prior to the enactment of the *Deficit Reduction Act of 1984*, it was unclear whether the exchange of partnership interests qualified for nonrecognition treatment under Section 1031(a). While the IRS was clearly on record with its position that such exchanges could not qualify,[28] the Tax Court had continually ruled in favor of taxpayers who structured transactions as exchanges of partnership interests, rather than the exchange of properties owned by such partnerships.[29] The Tax Court's approval of such exchanges hinged primarily on its conclusion that the Code's parenthetical exclusion of certain types of property interests from the ambit of Section 1031(a) (wherein "partnership interests" were not excluded specifically) was simply not intended by Congress to apply to partnership interests. The sole limitation on the approval of such exchanges was that the property owned by the partnerships in question had to be of a like-kind.[30] The en-

---

25 IRC § 1031(a)(3).

26 Treas. Reg. § 1.1031(k)-1(e)(4) (1991).

27 *See* Treas. Reg. § 1.1031(k)-1(e)(5), ex. (i)-(iii) (1991).

28 Rev. Rul. 78-135, 1978-1 C.B. 256.

29 e.g., *Est. of Meyer v. C.I.R.*, 58 T.C. 311 (1974), *aff'd*, 503 F.2d 556 (9th Cir. 1974), *nonacq.* 1975-2 C.B. 3; *Peter N. Pappas*, 78 T.C. 1078 (1982); *Arthur E. Long*, 77 T.C. 1045 (1981); *Gulfstream Land & Development*, 71 T.C. 587 (1979).

30 See *Gulfstream Land & Development, supra* at 594.

actment of Section 1031(a)(2)(D) in 1984, however, removed the issue from controversy by specifically including "interests in a partnership" in the definition of those types of property not eligible to be exchanged in a nonrecognition transaction (effective for exchanges occurring after July 17, 1984).[31]

Relief from Prohibitions

Congress provided some relief to taxpayers from the severity of the 1984 legislation in the *Revenue Reconciliation Act of 1990* by providing that an interest in a partnership that has a valid election in effect under Section 761(a) of the Code shall be treated as an interest in each of the assets of the partnership, and not as a partnership interest, for purposes of Section 1031(a).[32] The conditions that must be satisfied in order for the partnership to make a valid election under Section 761(a) limit this exception, however. (Moreover, taxpayers owning undivided interests in property otherwise eligible for exchange in a nonrecognition transaction under Section 1031(a) would be well advised to review the regulations promulgated under Section 761(a) to insure that their common ownership regime is not recharacterized as a "partnership," thereby negating the availability of nonrecognition treatment under Section 1031(a) otherwise afforded to exchanges of such ownership interests.)

Case Law

Taxpayers wishing to withdraw from partnerships or sell their interest in a partnership have gone to great lengths to disguise the transfer of their interest. For example, in *Crenshaw v. United States*,[33] a partner having an

---

[31] The Tax Reform Act of 1984, Pub. L. No. 98-369, 98th Cong., 2d Sess. § 77. Notwithstanding the apparent demise of nonrecognition treatment for exchanges of partnership interests, the IRS ruled privately in 1988 that the exchange of partnership interests in the same partnership qualified under Section 1031(a). PLR 8912023 (Dec. 22, 1988). However, the IRS reversed its position shortly thereafter in favor of a hard and fast rule, notwithstanding legislative history in support of its previous ruling. *See* PLR 8944043 (Aug. 8, 1989) (revoking PLR 8912023).

[32] IRC § 1031(a)(2) (flush language). Section 761(a) provides that certain partnerships may elect to be excluded from the application of the Internal Revenue Code provisions governing partnerships if the partners' income may be adequately determined without the computation of partnership taxable income.

[33] 450 F.2d 472 (5th Cir. 1971).

offer in hand for the cash redemption of her partnership interest restructured the transaction such that she first received a liquidating distribution of an undivided interest in the partnership's apartment building, presumably tax-free under Section 731. She then exchanged such undivided interest for a shopping center owned by the estate of her deceased husband and claimed nonrecognition treatment under Section 1031(a).[34] The estate then sold the undivided interest (having as basis therein the basis of the shopping center stepped up to fair market value as of the husband's date of death) to a corporation owned by the remaining partners for cash in a taxable transaction which resulted in little or no tax due to the "basis swap."[35] The purchasing corporation then re-contributed its undivided interest in the apartments to the partnership, effectively in exchange for the partnership interest redeemed from the taxpayer, also presumably tax-free under Section 721. At the conclusion of these steps, the taxpayer was seen to have transferred a partnership interest through a series of otherwise tax-free transactions which had the same economic result as a sale or a taxable withdrawal. It is not surprising that the Court recharacterized the series of transactions as a sale of a partnership interest followed by a purchase of a shopping center (based primarily on its conclusion that the admission of the corporation to the partnership resulted in the parties being in the identical position they would have been in a two sale scenario). Accordingly, the withdrawing partner recognized income on the deemed sale of her partnership interest.[36]

In a subsequent case,[37] the Tax Court refused to recharacterize a withdrawing partner's transfer of his interest in a partnership as a transfer subject to Section 741 based primarily on the fact that the transferees of an undivided interest in the partnership's shopping center previously distributed to the taxpayer upon his withdrawal from the partnership were never admitted to the partnership (as in the *Crenshaw* case), as they merely

---

34 It is important to note that the IRS attacked the nonrecognition treatment sought by the taxpayer in *Crenshaw* on the step transaction theory and did not argue that the transitory nature of the taxpayer's ownership of an undivided interest in the partnership's real estate could cause the Section 1031 exchange portion of the transaction to fail the "held" test discussed *infra*.

35 Under Section 1031(f) of the Code, effective generally for exchanges made after July 10, 1989, a taxpayer would have been taxable on her exchange due to the disposition of such property by "related party" within two years of the consummation of the exchange.

36 The Court could also have characterized the substance of the transaction as the exchange of a partnership interest for fee ownership of a shopping center; clearly, a non-qualifying exchange.

37 Leon J. Harris, Jr., 61 T.C. 770 (1974).

leased their undivided interest in the property back to the partnership, rather than contributing it to the partnership. This apparent blueprint for nonrecognition treatment should be viewed with extreme caution, however, if the withdrawing partner obtains like-kind property in exchange for his or her undivided interest in partnership property due to the IRS's emphasis on the "held" requirement.[38]

THE "HELD FOR USE OR INVESTMENT" REQUIREMENT

Even if the form of ownership interest in the real estate exchanged qualifies as "like-kind" property with respect to the real estate (or ownership interest therein) received for purposes of Section 1031(a), the Code also requires that such property be "held for productive use in a trade or business or for investment" in order to obtain nonrecognition treatment. Ordinarily, this requirement is satisfied because dispositions of real property are typically contemplated only after a period of use or investment for purposes of realizing the appreciation in value in such property over such period of time. In recent years, however, many investments have been made in the partnership or corporate form, and taxpayers wishing to withdraw such investment from entity-ownership to individual ownership (or to move ownership into an entity for unrelated business reasons) have begun to run afoul of the "held" requirement.

Transfers To and From Corporations

The IRS's position with respect to the "held" requirement is clear-cut and of long standing. In a series of Revenue Rulings in the late 1970s, the IRS took the position that transitory ownership of an interest in real estate does not satisfy the "held" requirement. For example, in a 1975 Revenue Ruling,[39] a corporation contracted to acquire a tract of land and a factory from an unrelated party. Pursuant to an agreement to accommodate the unrelated party's desire to dispose of such property in a nonrecognition transaction, the corporation acquired another tract and built a factory thereon to

---

38 *But see Norman J. Magneson*, 753 F.2d 1490 (9th Cir. 1985) (exchange of property received in liquidation of taxpayer's partnership interest held not to violate "held" requirement).

39 Rev. Rul. 75-291, 1975-2 C.B. 332. *Accord*, Rev. Rul. 77-297, 1977-2 C.B. 304.

the other party's specifications. Immediately upon completion of the factory, the exchange was effectuated. The IRS ruled that while the unrelated third party could avoid the recognition of income under Section 1031(a), the corporation could not because the acquisition of a second tract and the construction of a factory thereon was for the purpose of making the exchange and such property was never to be "held" in the requisite manner. In a companion Ruling,[40] a taxpayer who received property in what would otherwise be considered a tax-free exchange immediately contributed the property received to a newly formed corporation controlled by the taxpayer in hopes of qualifying for nonrecognition treatment under Section 351 of the Code. Again, however, the IRS ruled that the transfer of such property negated an inference that such property was to be held by the taxpayer for productive use in the taxpayer's trade or business or for investment, and the corporation's qualifying use subsequent to the contribution could not be attributed back to the taxpayer.

In 1977, the IRS was confronted with the reverse scenario.[41] An individual owning 100% of a corporation whose only asset was a shopping center, intending to take advantage of provisions then in the Code allowing a tax-free liquidation of a corporation, caused the liquidation of the corporation and the immediate distribution of the shopping center property to himself as the sole shareholder. As part of a pre-arranged plan, however, the taxpayer immediately exchanged the shopping center for like-kind property and claimed nonrecognition treatment under Section 1031(a), taking the position that because the holding period for the shopping center in the taxpayer's hands included the holding period for the stock surrendered by the taxpayer in the liquidation in the taxpayer's hands, that the "held" requirement was satisfied. Notwithstanding the taxpayer's argument, however, the IRS ruled that just as a corporation's productive use of property could not be attributed to its shareholder after an exchange (as in Revenue Ruling 75-292), a corporation's productive use prior to an exchange also could not be attributed to its sole shareholder; hence, the "held" requirement was not satisfied by the taxpayer's transitory ownership preparation to an exchange prearranged with a third party.

In 1985, however, the United States Court of Appeals for the Ninth Circuit held (on facts similar to those of Revenue Ruling 77-337) that the "held" requirement was satisfied by a sole shareholder who received real property in a liquidation of a corporation and, pursuant to a pre-arranged

---

[40] Rev. Rul. 75-292, 1975-2 C.B. 333.
[41] Rev. Rul. 77-337, 1977-2 C.B. 305.

plan, exchanged such property to an unrelated third party.[42] The Court distinguished the Revenue Ruling in two ways. First, the liquidation of the corporation was planned for independent business reasons prior to the formation of an intent to exchange the property, whereas the liquidation in the Revenue Ruling was solely for the purpose of facilitating the exchange. Second, while the exchange in the Revenue Ruling occurred immediately following the liquidation, the taxpayer in the Ninth Circuit case held the property for three months prior to exchanging it. The Court defined the "held" requirement under Section 1031(a) to mean: ". . . that if a taxpayer owns property which he does not intend to liquidate or to use for personal pursuits, he is 'holding' that property for productive use in trade or business or for investment within the meaning of Section 1031(a)."[43]

Clearly, under the *Bolker* standard, possession of property prior to a pre-arranged exchange can be transitory if a taxpayer acquires an ownership interest in the property with no intention of liquidating such investment or converting such property to personal use. Later cases seem to confirm that exchange transactions which culminate in the continuation of an old unliquidated investment in a modified term of ownership can satisfy the "held" requirement of Section 1031(a).[44]

Transfers To and From Partnerships

The "held" requirement has also been construed by the Ninth Circuit Court of Appeals in favor of the taxpayer in the partnership context.[45] In the partnership case, property acquired by an individual in a like-kind exchange transaction was transferred immediately to a newly formed limited partnership in exchange for a general partnership interest. The IRS relied on its determination in Revenue Ruling 75-292, *supra*, in contending that the "held" requirement was not satisfied; however, the Court distinguished the Revenue Ruling by stating first that a corporation is a distinct entity from its shareholders (as opposed to a partnership and its partners under California law) and second, that a like-kind exchange followed by a Section 351 transfer as in the Revenue Ruling could easily be recharacterized as the transfer of real property in exchange for the ultimate receipt of stock, and that in the instant case, the taxpayer's economic situation after

---

[42] *Bolker v. C.I.R.*, 760 F.2d 1039 (9th Cir. 1985).

[43] *Id.* at 1045.

[44] e.g., *Bonny B. Maloney*, 93 T.C. 89 (1989) (exchange by corporation satisfies Section 1031(a) even if immediately followed by tax-free liquidation under old IRC § 333).

[45] *Norman J. Magneson*, 753 F.2d 1490 (9th Cir. 1985).

the transfer of property to the partnership was fundamentally the same as before the transfer.

It is significant to note that the Court relied heavily on state law to justify its assertion that the taxpayer's rights were fundamentally unaltered upon contribution of the property in exchange for a general partnership interest and a similar transaction in another state could alter dramatically the bundle of rights and obligations attendant to ownership of a partnership interest versus ownership of a fee simple interest in real estate. Moreover, the Ninth Circuit case was decided on the law extant prior to the 1984 amendments to Section 1031 that specifically excluded partnership interests from the definition of like-kind property; hence, the court's reliance on pre-1984 case law regarding exchanges of general partnership or joint venture interests would be misplaced today. Taxpayer reliance on the holding in this case outside of the Ninth Circuit is, therefore, suspect.

Taxpayers may take some comfort in this regard, however, from the holdings in *Miles H. Mason*,[46] and *Delwyn G. Chase*,[47] wherein the "held" requirement was implicitly satisfied, although the issue was not discussed specifically by the Tax Court in either instance.

Transfers To and From Trusts

Even though the IRS continued to litigate the "held" requirement in the corporate and partnership context, it offered little resistance to a ruling request made by the **trustees** of a testamentary trust for approval of an exchange of like-kind real properties where shortly after the exchange was consummated, the trust made final distribution of the property received to the trust beneficiaries in accordance with the terms of the trust.[48] In ruling favorably on the issue, the IRS paid lip service to Revenue Rulings 75-292 and 77-337, yet seemed disinclined to extend the holdings therein to a trust created 12 years earlier than the exchange, even though the exchange occurred less than six months prior to the anticipated date of trust termination.

The IRS relied in part on the Tax Court's holding in the case of *Fred S. Wagensen*,[49] wherein a taxpayer, for valid estate planning reasons nonrelated to the transactions entered into for purposes of deferring income taxes under Section 1031(a), gifted property received in an admitted like-

---

[46] 55 T.C.M. (CCH) 1134 (1988), *aff'd in unpub. op.* (11th Cir., June 30, 1989).
[47] 92 T.C. 874 (1989).
[48] PLR 8126070 (Mar. 31, 1981).
[49] 74 T.C. 653 (1980).

kind exchange to his children less than nine months after receiving such property. Accordingly, it can be seen that the IRS was focusing on the intent of the transferor at the time of the exchange and the fact that what otherwise may have been disqualifying dispositions of property following exchanges were not part of prearranged plans.

The Tax Court adopted the IRS's analysis in a later Tax Court case,[50] holding that a taxpayer's gift of property received in an exchange to her children seven months after consummation of the exchange in circumstances where the facts supported an inference that such disposition was part of a prearranged plan, intended at the time of the exchange, caused the exchange to be a taxable event, rather than a nonrecognition event under Section 1031(a).

Related Party Transfers

A primary purpose underlying the enactment of Section 1031 was to avoid the imposition of an income tax on taxpayers who, while changing the form of their ownership, nevertheless continued the nature of their investment.[51] As taxpayer sophistication with respect to exchanges under Section 1031(a) increased, however, Congress began to focus on abuses of the tax deferral rules established by the Code, regulations and case law. Accordingly, recent legislative changes have been directed towards limiting the ability of taxpayers to formally comply with the requirements of Section 1031(a) while, at the same time, cashing out their investment.[52]

The most recent example of such approach was contained in the *Omnibus Budget Reconciliation Act of 1989*[53] wherein Section 1031(f) of the Code was enacted to limit the ability of taxpayers to achieve nonrecognition treatment under Section 1031(a) to the extent that exchanges were consummated with certain "related parties." Although beyond the scope of this discussion, Section 1031(f) effectively eliminates the ability of a taxpayer to effect a "basis swap" or to cash out an investment through the use of a controlled affiliate, unless the taxpayer and the related party are both willing and able to hold their respective properties for a minimum of two

---

50 *Dollie H. Click*, 78 T.C. 225 (1982).

51 H. Rep. No. 704, 73d Cong., 2d Sess. (1934), *reprinted at* 1939-1 C.B. (Part 2) 554, 564.

52 *See* discussion of elimination of nonrecognition treatment under Section 1031(a) for exchanges of partnership interests and endnote 31, *supra*.

53 Pub. L. No. 101-239, 103 Stat. 2106, 101st Cong., 1st Sess. (1989).

years after the exchange, or the statutory exceptions to such holding period, such as death or involuntary concession of a property, apply.[54]

THE "EXCHANGE" REQUIREMENT

A third requirement for nonrecognition treatment under Section 1031(a) is that there be an "exchange" of properties, rather than a series of acquisitions and dispositions with the intent of trading like-kind properties. Taxpayers often run afoul of this requirement in attempting to rearrange ownership interests in like-kind property, even where the "held" requirement is satisfied. The most frequent error made by taxpayers in this regard is to try to characterize two sales of similar property as an exchange after the fact.

For example, in *Charles W. Mars*,[55] the taxpayer contracted to sell a golf course in March 1976 for cash, assumption of existing indebtedness and a promissory note. A deed to the property was executed and delivered to the purchaser on May 14, 1976. Upon the purchaser's notice to the taxpayer thereafter that he would be unable to satisfy the note, the taxpayer purported to cancel the sale; however, no deed of reconveyance of the property was ever executed or delivered by the purchaser. Thereafter, the taxpayer contracted to acquire certain improved real property from the purchaser and, during 1977 and 1978, acquired such properties from the purchaser while, at the same time, accounting for satisfaction of the purchaser's note delivered in connection with his previous acquisition of the golf course property from the taxpayer. The Tax Court had very little difficulty disposing of the taxpayer's arguments that the series of transactions should be recharacterized as an "exchange." Despite thorough and precise documentation of the transaction through the use of legal counsel, no mention was made of an intent to have a tax-free exchange. Furthermore, the transfer of the golf course property was not interdependent upon or necessarily related to the taxpayer's acquisition of the purchaser's admittedly like-kind property. The taxpayer had also reported the transfer of the golf course property for federal income tax purposes as an installment sale, further indicating that characterization as an exchange was an afterthought.

A road map indicating how to blow nonrecognition treatment with respect to an exchange of like-kind properties, even where nonrecognition

---

[54] IRC § 1031(f)(2).
[55] 54 T.C.M. (CCH) 636 (1987).

treatment is clearly intended, is seen in the case of *Garbis S. Bezdjian*.[56] Despite a complicated series of interdependent transactions intended to effectuate an exchange, the Tax Court determined that the taxpayer merely sold real property to a purchaser for a second piece of property acquired in a taxable transaction from a person other than the purchaser. While the substance of the transactions was that the taxpayer parted with ownership of real property and ended up with ownership of a second real property, the conveyances were made with separate persons, and there was no independent agent through which funds were funnelled and title to the two properties was transferred; hence, the formalities of the transaction clearly showed separate purchase and sale, rather than an "exchange."

CONCLUSION

The IRS and the Courts have interpreted Section 1031 and the regulations broadly to allow taxpayers great latitude to structure transfers of real property or interests therein such that no gain need be recognized if the taxpayer's investment continues in substantially the same form as immediately prior to such transfer. As can be seen from the above discussion, however, there are many pitfalls for the unwary, and only scrupulous compliance with the Code, regulations and case authorities extant in a taxpayer's jurisdiction will assure nonrecognition treatment under Section 1031(a).

---

[56] 53 T.C.M. (CCH) 368 (1987), *aff'd* 845 F.2d 217 (9th Cir. 1988).

Problem Areas in Exchanging

13

by Michael M. Smith
  Gambrell, Clarke, Anderson & Stolz
  Atlanta, Georgia

DEFINING INVESTMENT AND PROPERTY USE IN A TRADE OR BUSINESS

Qualified Use

As discussed in Chapter 4, Section 1031(a)(1) requires that both the relinquished and replacement properties of an exchange must be either held (1) for investment, or (2) for productive use in a trade or business. Section 1031 does not define investment or for use in a trade or business, nor do the Treasury Regulations under that section. However, Treasury Regulation 1.1031(a)-1(a) states that a productive property held by a nondealer for future trade or business use or for future appreciation constitutes property held for investment. Presumably then, property held primarily for future appreciation would constitute property held for investment.

The qualified use test is applied with respect to the taxpayer's use. It is not relevant whether the property was held for a nonqualified use in the hands of the other party to the exchange.

Investment or Residence?

A frequent question asked by exchangors is whether they can live in the acquired property after an exchange is completed. The immediate answer seems to be "no" because the intent of an exchange is to go from an investment property into another investment property, not into a residential property. But, the key phrase is "after an exchange." Many Internal Revenue Service Codes allow for and recognize a change in life circumstances that affect your financial circumstances.

> As seen in Revenue Ruling 57-244, this acquisition purpose can change. The IRS considered the circumstances of three taxpayers who purchased property for the construction of homes and later abandoned that purpose for clearly established reasons but continued to hold the property for investment purposes. A subsequent exchange was held to qualify unders IRC Section 1031.

For example, if you exchanged property in 1989 for a rental condominium in Hawaii, then in 1992 you or your spouse had a health condition that required you to live in a warm climate. Can you move into the rental condominium and convert it to your residence? Probably, yes. It is taxable at that time? No. Investment activities, such as depreciation, would stop at that time and a determination of basis would be required to determine the tax base when or if sold at a later date.

What does this all mean? Simply, that at the time of an exchange you must not intend to use the target property for other than investment purposes. If you can demonstrate intent to comply with the spirit of the law along with the technical aspects of the law, you have a valid exchange. If you did an exchange and then within six months moved into the new property, the odds of the IRS believing you intended otherwise is slim. On the other hand, if you had significant time pass (e.g., three years), and had a change in life circumstances, the permissibility of this investment shift is greatly enhanced.

So, the two elements are passage of time and change of life circumstances. Since neither of these elements has been tested in court, exact definitions cannot be found. Each transaction is unique and therefore legal or tax counsel should be sought in these circumstances.

Second Residences

It remains an open question whether a residence used by a taxpayer as a vacation home and not as a principal residence will constitute a qualified-use property within the meaning of Section 1031. Arguably, if the taxpayer can demonstrate that he would not have invested in the vacation home but for its appreciation value, the property will constitute qualified-use property. However, the property would not constitute qualified-use property if the taxpayer could not prove that he still would have purchased the property for his personal use even if there was a substantial likelihood that the property would decrease in value. It is likely that the Internal Revenue Service will disallow an exchange of a vacation home that is used as such by the taxpayer, but the ultimate outcome of whether such an exchange will be respect will depend on the primary intent of the taxpayer in owning that property.

Dealer Property/Inventory

Real estate that is deemed inventory does not constitute qualified-use property. A developer who acquires property, and sub-divides that property into lots for re-sale generally holds this property as inventory. Presumably, it is possible for the dealer in real property to change the character of his property from inventory to a qualified use. The dealer might abandon his original intent and segregate a portion of the property to hold for appreciation or to construct improvements thereon to rent to third parties, which uses would constitute a qualified use within the meaning of Section 1031. Any person who would be deemed a dealer in real estate should exercise caution in utilizing Section 1031 with respect to their exchanges; however, the Treasury Regulations specifically provide that property that is held for investment and not primarily for sale will be characterized as qualified-use property where held by a person other than a dealer in real property. The Treasury Regulations do not address the status of the person who is a dealer but who is holding the property as an investment or in a trade or business. Most likely, the term "dealer" means a dealer with respect to a particular property. However, a dealer desiring to qualify in an exchange under Section 1031 will have the evidentiary burden of proving that his property is qualified use within the meaning of Section 1031.

Property Used by Relatives

Another problem occurs when a relative of the taxpayer moves into a rental house that would otherwise qualify as a qualified use within the meaning of Section 1031, but the relative is not paying any rent. The question becomes whether the taxpayer is holding the property for investment purposes. Presumably, if the taxpayer is holding the property primarily for appreciation and would not otherwise own the property and if there was a substantial likelihood that it would appreciate in value, the property would qualify as a qualified use. However, there may be a difficult evidentiary burden on the owner-taxpayer desiring to qualify under Section 1031 if that property is exchanged. The real risk is proving equitable ownership. It would appear as a gift to that relative although title has not passed.

Depreciation Recapture

All relinquished properties exchanged under Section 1031 need to be reviewed for potential Section 1245 and Section 1250 recapture. If property subject to Section 1250 recapture is exchanged for property that does not constitute Section 1250 property, all of the Section 1250 potential recapture income will be recognized at the time of the exchange. If the potential Section 1250 recapture is greater than the fair market value of the Section 1250 property to be received in the exchange, the taxpayer will be required to recognize as ordinary income on the excess of the potential Section 1250 recapture over the fair market value of the Section 1250 property received in the exchange. See Section 1250(d)(4)(C). Where the Section 1250 property received is greater in fair market value than the Section 1250 appreciation recapture property given up in the exchange, the only gain recognized is gain required to be recognized pursuant to Section 1031. (Under Section 1031, if the fair market value of the relinquished property is greater than the fair market value of the replacement property to an exchange, then gain is recognized to the extent of the difference, subject to the maximum potential gain on the relinquished property as if the exchange were otherwise treated as a fully taxable transaction.) Should the replacement property's fair market value not equal or exceed the relinquished property's fair market value, but the value of the Section 1250 property equals or exceeds the potential Section 1250 appreciation recapture, the taxpayer should consider adding to the exchange as replacement property, another property having a fair market value equal to at least the difference between fair market values of the relinquished and replacement properties in order to avoid gain that will be recognized under Section 1031 upon consummation of the exchange.

Basis

The basis of property received in an exchange is equal to the basis of the property transferred out of the exchange, increased by the amount of the fair market value of the replacement property over the fair market value of the relinquished property. Such increase will be supported by either increased debt assumed in the exchange or additional cash contributed by the taxpayer to effect the exchange. The basis of the replacement property will be decreased by the excess of the relinquished property's fair market value over the fair market value of the replacement property, if the incoming property has a fair market value less than the fair market value of the relinquished property. Such basis decrease will result either from money received by the taxpayer in the exchange or overall debt decrease with respect to the replacement property, as well as the amount of any loss recognized with respect to boot transferred upon the exchange. If more than one property is received in the exchange, the basis of the relinquished property will be allocated to the qualified properties in proportion to their fair market values. The taxpayer who is exchanging out of nondepreciable property, such as land, might consider replacing that property in the exchange with a building or other depreciable property in order to take advantage of the depreciation deductions.

Workouts Via Exchanging: Another Tool

chapter **14**

by Dr. Mark Lee Levine
Levine and Pitler, P.C.
Engelwood, Colorado

WORKOUTS AND DEBT OBLIGATIONS
GENERATE INHERENT PROBLEMS

If a debt obligation is due, the debtor may attempt to work with the creditor. Numerous articles and cases have been examined the potential methods of structuring arrangements between the Debtor and Creditor in order to "work out" the problems between the two parties.

The best solution of settling the problems between the parties is normally cash. However, in many instances in workout settings the ability to obtain cash is extremely difficult, if not impossible.

Given this scenario, the question is whether another tool—namely, a tax-deferred exchange under Code § 1031 (26 U.S.C.A. Section 1031)—may be a means to facilitate a settlement option.

The exchange may involve the Debtor transferring his or her higher-valued and more leveraged property to a creditor in exchange for other property that might also be leveraged, but may facilitate the needs of both debtor and creditor, thus removing each from one property and placing each into another property (properties).

Real World

The real world setting is that the circumstances necessary to arrange an exchange may be extremely difficult. If the debtor and creditor are not on an amiable working basis, certainly the practicalities will dominate the circumstance and any arrangement, aside from cash, may be difficult.

The practical point is that no one should be involved in a tax-deferred exchange unless they meet at least the following four (4) criteria:

1. The debtor must want out of the property.
2. The debtor must want into another property.
3. The debtor must have a large amount of taxable income on the transaction if it was sold.
4. Finally, the debtor must have a large amount of tax that is due.

If all of the four (4) elements are not met, there is not a reason to have the exchange. That is, if the taxpayer-debtor does not want out of the property, there is not a reason for the disposition to be considered in an exchange mode.

If the taxpayer-debtor is willing to move out of the existing property, which apparently is encumbered under the typical scenario with a major debt to a creditor (the workout), the taxpayer must be willing to move into another property.

The requirement to move into another property is necessary, given that Code Section 1031 requires an exchange by a taxpayer moving out of one property and into other "like-kind" property (trade or business or investment property).

From the tax standpoint, the taxpayer may simply sell one property and purchase another. However, if the taxpayer wants to obtain the benefits of a tax-deferred exchange under Code § 1031, the taxpayer must exchange to avoid the current taxable income. Thus, one of the tests is that the taxpayer must have a substantial amount of taxable income from the disposition. If the taxable income does not exist from the disposition, there is not a reason to structure the transaction as an exchange.

Finally, even though a taxpayer may have a substantial amount of taxable income from the sale of property, as opposed to an exchange, the taxpayer may not have tax due. The taxpayer may have sufficient net operating losses that are carried forward to offset any tax due. Tax credits may also offset the tax obligation. Thus, the fourth criteria mentioned is that the amount of tax due must be substantial to encourage a taxpayer to elect an alternative, such as a tax-deferred exchange, to avoid the tax.

Application of Exchanges to Workouts

If the taxpayer could exchange property in a tax-deferred exchange, and if this could meet the desires and needs of both the debtor and creditor, a tax-deferred exchange might facilitate both a workout and avoid the additional tax obligation because of a sale.

One common point often raised in a workout setting is why a taxpayer would be concerned with a "gain," given that it is in a workout. In other words, if the property was valued at $1.5 million, and a loan was taken out at $1 million, one might assume that there is a substantial amount of equity. This could be the case at the time of acquisition. However, if through depreciation the basis of the property falls to say $800,000, and the loan remains at $1 million because of an interest-only loan, there could be $200,000 "gain" if the taxpayer-deeds over (Deed-in-lieu) or otherwise settled the transaction with the creditor by conveying the property to the creditor.

If the taxpayer's adjusted basis is $800,000 and the taxpayer is relieved of debt of $1 million, such relief is the effective sales price of the property, thereby generating $200,000 worth of gain.

Certainly forgiving of debt constitutes taxable income under the Internal Revenue Code. (See Code § 61(a)(12). See also Levine, Mark Lee, *Real Estate Transactions, Tax Planning*, West Publishing Co., St. Paul, Minnesota (1991)).

It is true that in some instances where property is conveyed by a debtor to a creditor, the gain that might be generated, similar to the example, may be avoided if the taxpayer-debtor is insolvent. However, the taxpayer normally, to meet the requirements necessary to exclude gain, must meet an insolvency test under Code § 108 to avoid paying tax on the amount of gain noted in the example. (There are a number of requirements to meet the elements within Code § 108. The purpose of this note is not to discuss these in detail. See the Levine text, cited earlier.)

If a taxpayer will generate a substantial amount of gain as a result of a workout relationship, and if Sections, such as Code § 108, are not available to avoid tax on that gain by excluding it, other alternatives must be considered. The use of the tax-deferred exchange under Code § 1031, where the creditor and debtor can work together in situations that are practical, may work in some settings.

CONCLUSION

Notwithstanding the idealistic approach of a tax-deferred exchange in a workout relationship, it is obvious that such application of Code § 1031 in a workout would be difficult. Exchanges are difficult in most instances, simply because the parties must coordinate that many additional matters, and many parties may not comply with the tax-deferred exchange rules.

It is further complicated by the fact that debtors and creditors normally have a strained relationship. As such, they are not normally willing to work with each other to transfer property to each other in a relationship that will accommodate the needs of both parties.

If there is already a default by the debtor to the creditor, there is also a concern by the creditor to transfer additional property from the creditor to the debtor to work the exchange. However, in some instances even creditors have property that they desire to remove from their portfolio. In such circumstances, a workout may be facilitated by an exchange, even between a debtor and creditor.

As a final and practical note, in many instances there may be debt relief, the concept mentioned earlier when there is an exchange. As such, this may generate a taxable amount of income to the debtor and, therefore, defeat the exchange position. As such, the parties must carefully structure their transaction to meet the needs of both the debtor and creditor, not only on the workout position, but also on the tax issue.

part V

The Role of the Professionals

Building a Career in Exchange Brokerage

by Scott R. Saunders
  Starker Services, Inc.
  Los Gatos, California

  William Townsend
  Starker Services, Inc.
  Bellevue, Washington

CAREER CONTROL

It has been stated that more millionaires have made their money in real estate than any other type of investing. The millionaires referred to are not the general home buying public but investors.

If investors are making money, then so are the real estate brokers servicing them. Most investment transactions revolve around the exchange process. Since an exchange transaction requires two transactions, property to be disposed and property acquired, this usually means two commissions are earned by the broker.

Exchange brokerage is not that much different than listing and selling your clients' personal residences. The job of the broker is still to satisfy the wants and needs of the client. The loan and closing functions remain the same and full commissions are paid just as with a residential sale.

What exchange brokerage can do for the agent is to turn the sales process from a reactive one to a proactive one. Consider the processes that must be undertaken to gain a listing. First, something out of your control must happen. The prospect's family situation changes, (divorce, remarriage, kids move out of the nest, job relocation or the family is growing and needs more room). All these, and probably more, affect the decision to list and sell. There is nothing you, the agent, can say or do to affect this decision. Once an event outside your control happens, then your prior marketing and name awareness might get you a listing appointment, but again, you are not controlling this phase either. You are rather pitted against other agents who also have nothing special to offer and are reacting, just as you, to events outside of their control.

Now envision this. An exchange broker prospecting in a territory, with the help of either an automated data base or help from title records, locates potential clients, because they either live out-of-state, or the tax statements are sent to a different address other than the property address, identifying an absentee landlord. Quickly, easily, a list of potential clients can be gathered and they are well-qualified because they already own real estate. A proactive broker is now ready to control the entire sales process.

Deal Making for Real Estate Agents

There is a fundamental difference, which every real estate agent should understand, in approaching investors in real property rather than homeowners. Real estate investors are not sellers, they are buyers of real property. While a homeowner's primary motivation in buying a home is its aethestic appeal and function, investors are more concerned with the future performance of their investment. Only by emphasizing a trade into a better investment will owners consider "moving" their real estate. All an agent needs to do is to discover what the investor values and help them to acquire more of these benefits.

Home agents sell a "thing"—they sell a house. They understand homeowners have an emotional tie to their property. Home agents can convince an owner to enlist their services only after the owner decides to sell. They are not able to influence the owner's selling decision. Once the property is sold, the home agent has little control over the future resale and cannot expect to resell the home once it meets the new owner's objectives. In addition, potential commissions are lost, since only a few agents are able to find the next property for their client. Even if the client does keep the agent for the acquisition of the replacement property, the cash available is substantially reduced after paying the capital gains tax. In fact, often after paying the capital gains tax, the investor does not even have sufficient equity to repurchase the property that they just sold.

On the other hand, there are real estate agents who actively utilize exchanging ("Exchange" or "Investment" agents) to motivate investment property owners to sell. Exchange agents find that most clients will sell their investment properties if the agent can present a better investment. Exchange agents can create transactions by producing opportunities for clients to obtain more benefits and, subsequently, generate greater commissions for themselves. This larger commission can be created because the exchange agent earns a fee both for the disposition of property and also for the acquisition of a suitable replacement property. Furthermore, the equity is not reduced by taxes so the replacement property is often of higher value.

Investment agents realize investors have an emotional tie, not to the property itself, but to their future wealth. These agents sell the dream of retirement and financial security. They understand the property itself is not as important as the contribution the property gives to obtaining their ultimate financial objectives. The disposition of the property is contemplated as soon as a better investment objective is found.

There are many sources of potential exchange clients. An easy way is to begin with your own office clients. The first obvious source is listed properties. Another lucrative source are FSBO's (For Sale By Owners). FSBO's are already motivated to sell. In many instances, they may have either heard of exchanging or may actually wish to perform one. Checking ownership records at the county assessor's office can also reveal non-owner-occupied properties that have been held for a long time and potentially would have a significant gain.

Real estate investors who own land are another good source of clients, since land often does not produce income. These property owners may be anxious to move into property that generates a cash flow and has greater capital appreciation. In addition, exchanging into improved property that can support a new loan gives the investor the ability to receive cash through a refinance.

Apartments are yet another opportunity for exchanging. Long-term ownership creates high equity. Although a high equity position may generate a large cash flow, it also provides a lower return on investment. These owners may be interested in an opportunity to acquire a larger property with greater leverage, and, subsequently, a higher return on investment. They may instead wish to acquire a different type of property to minimize the headaches often associated with managing a multi-tenant property.

Methods for Obtaining Appointments

One of the most effective methods is making "cold calls." The investment agent should have only one objective of every contact—to get the appointment. Agents should never discuss specifics (such as addresses) over the phone. The main object is to make the appointment and hang up. Failure to get the appointment is usually failure to convey that the investor is the party benefitting from the meeting. To obtain the maximum benefit from each contact, a program of continuous contact must be implemented. One idea is to send investors mailers and information after the cold call. Maintaining a "tickler file" is an effective way to keep in touch with potential exchangors. It is essential to convey the attitude that the investor is losing an opportunity to earn greater profits by not using your services.

The Appointment

Prior to the appointment, check the assessor's records to determine properties already owned by the client. The purpose of the appointment is to perform an exchange. At the appointment they discover the investor's objectives. The first item to address is how the investor can save taxes by performing an exchange. Sample questions might include: "Before we discuss any properties I might have that you may wish to trade for, perhaps you can tell me what you are looking for." "What is your investment objective? What are you trying to accomplish?" "Why did you buy your present property? What are you looking for in your next property?"

Next calculate the investment objective (retirement or cash flow). First, in today's dollars, determine the income that the investor would like to obtain at retirement and enter *present value* (PV). Next, calculate the *future value* (FV) of this amount over the investment period using a mutually agreeable inflation factor. Project an annual cash-on-cash percentage yield, which can be obtained from a quality investment purchased for cash flow, and divide the FV by this percentage. You have now calculated the net equity needed to generate the target cash flow at retirement. Use this new value as a FV and enter the investors' present net equity (investment base) in PV. Solve for "i" to determine the annual return on net equity needed to reach the investment objective. Clients with such a guideline purchase, sell and exchange on the basis of annual yield, not on location, size, color or property type.

Post Appointment

Follow up immediately with a letter outlining the results of your meeting and clarifying the information you obtained. Encourage the investors to contact you with questions. Encourage them to call you if they see an attractive property advertised. Once you begin working with potential exchangors, it is vital to continue to keep in contact with them. While many investors perceive agents as only trying to make a fee at their expense, your clients will see you as an advisor and a valuable resource to the attainment of their financial goals.

How to Sell Exchange Concepts

Once you have arrived at a list of potential clients, the next step is to gain a face-to-face meeting.

> **Key:** The exchange broker is not soliciting a listing presentation but a fact finding session to access the prospect needs and wants.

At this meeting it might be helpful to have some background information on the property, such as loan balance, principal, interest, taxes, and insurance, year purchased, rent roll, and a market analysis of current value. What the exchange broker wants to achieve is a plan of action to follow to remain proactive, not reactive, in the sales process. This plan of action is a Real Estate Investment Plan. Any decisions to sell, buy, or hold should be governed by this plan.

Before we continue with ways to motivate the prospects (investors) goals, let's look at the information we already have amassed.

1. Current market value.
2. Present loan balance.
3. Rent roll.
4. Principal, Interest, Taxes and Insurance (PITI).

With these four items we can approximate the present equity (the down payment available for a future purchase) and current rate of return on this equity (the interest the investor is earning on his equity). A very motivating factor for an investor to dispose of property is because it is a nonperforming asset. However, few investors ever think about what their equity is earning.

Example:

Your current market analysis is $165,000, current rent $1,200.

Mortgage balance is $62,500, and present PITI is $750.

Table 15.1 presents a simple return on equity calculation.

Table 15.1

Present Equities		Cash Flow	
Market value	$165,500	Yearly rents	$13,200
Present loan balance	$ 62,500	($1,200 x 12)	
Equity	$103,000	Yearly PITI	$ 9,000
		($750 × 12)	
		Yearly cash flow	$ 4,200

Return on equity

Cash flow ($4,200) divided by equity ($103,000) = 4%

The easiest way to present this concept to an investor is simply: Mr. Investor, you have approximately $103,000 in equity, which could be used as a down-payment on another investment. As it is presently invested, you are receiving at 4% return. Would you be interested in discussing ways to improve your position?

At this point you have very little time invested and probably a very motivated prospect. I am using "investor" and "prospect" interchangeably because he or she is not your client untill you complete the individual's Real Estate Investment Plan.

The next step in formulating the plan is to ask leading questions and then listen to the answers because they will start to define the true goals (needs and wants) of the investor. The investor will buy property that matches these goals.

Suggested Questions:

1. What do you want to achieve through your investments?
2. With what type of properties do you feel most comfortable?
3. How much time do you want to spend in property management?
4. Is location important or would you consider regional investment?
5. How is the investment going to be monitored?
6. Do you want to diversify your holdings or concentrate on one property?
7. Is this plan designed for income today or retirement needs?
8. What is your return on equity expectations?
9. What role do you want me to take in implementing and operating this plan?

Listening is the key, because once the goals of the investor are written, you have a blueprint for a successful transaction.

How do you turn the prospect into your trusted client?

"Mr. Investor, if I can find you properties that meet the criteria of your Real Estate Investment Plan and if it will cost you no additional money, can we do business?

Property Selection and Comparison

From this point, many real estate agents start farming for the replacement property—property which will meet the objective of the plan. One way to monitor and compare potential replacement and maximize future profit is through the formation of *property analysis*.

While establishing a solid rapport and gaining the confidence of your client is of paramount importance, the skilled agent's immediate task is to review the operating records. One of the best ways to accomplish this is to offer to prepare an analysis of the investment property. When completed, this will become a part of the Real Estate Investment Plan. Most investors report their investment income and expenses on Schedule E to IRS form 1040. This information, along with the property value determined by your market analysis, is all that must be obtained to complete the property analysis.

The operation of the current property can be compared to potential replacement properties. When combined with the goals (needs and wants) established in the Real Estate Investment Plan, it will help to pinpoint the next investment property.

The following case study illustrates the use of a properly constructed property analysis. Mark and Cindy have owned a rental home in Eastgate for 11 years. Through your skillful questioning you learn that:

1. Their gross income is $16,800.

2. Vacancy runs about 3.0% per year.

3. Operating expenses were $2,218 per year.

4. Federal Income tax bracket is 28%.

5. Loan Information:
   - Loan Balance: $76,000
   - Loan payments: $9,686
   - Loan Interest: $7,220

6. Annual depreciation is $2,181.

After reconciling the operating portion of the analysis (see example Phase One), you are now ready to enter your "CMA" value ($211,000), to compute the equity, then complete the ratio analysis and return-on-investment portions (see Figure 15.1).

Mark and Cindy's rental, although appreciating over 11 years to today's value, is really doing very little to return the amount of interest which even a bank would offer. (See line Y)

Phase Two of the property analysis compares the property that meets Mark and Cindy's goals. These goals are the ones that you establish at one of your first meetings. It is a medium-sized apartment building (16 unit), not more than 20 years old in an area which is profiled to appreciate in future years, and has a stable employment base.

The financial data was obtained through careful review of the seller's books.

The South Hill Puyallup property comparison is in the right column of the property analysis. Look at the comparison of "ROE" line Y. With a simple exchange of properties, their return on equity has increased from 4.11% to 11.17%. Do you think you are on your way to convince them it is time to exchange? Compute your commission plan to see how much you would have made with this one exchange transaction.

REAL ESTATE ADVISOR

When the tools mentioned in this book are woven into your selling style, you will realize that you have achieved a new plateau of professionalism. Many agents spend their entire careers merely surviving from one transaction to the next. A few agents, however, generate large and more consistent commissions by concentrating on satisfying the objectives of the clients Real Estate Investment Plan. It has been said that Section 1031 is like an IRA for the real estate economy. As long as dollars are reinvested in real estate, all profits will continue to grow tax free.

Because of this tax burden, exchange professionals often entertain repeat business as the investor's goals change or property characteristics necessitate a change. Also, every seller of replacement property is a potential client. Agents have achieved multiple commissions with multilegged exchanges. Until you write a purchase and sales agreement with a seller who is willing to "pay the tax," a potential client is always close at hand. Ask this question at every contract presentation: "Do you want me to show you what I just did for my client? He saved and leveraged tax dollars which

Figure 15.1   Property Analysis—Mark and Cindy Investor

PROPERTY ANALYSIS

Property Address: 8552 Blvd. S.W.
Prepared for: Mark and Cindy Investor
Prepared by: Exchange Agent

Date Prepared: July 18, 19XX

			PHASE I DISPOSITION	PHASE II ACQUISITION
A	FAIR MARKET VALUE		$211,000	(Plus closing costs)
B	– Loans		($76,000)	
C	EQUITY		$135,000	
	ANNUAL PROPERTY OPERATING STATEMENT			
D	GROSS POTENTIAL INCOME		$16,800	
E	– Vacancy & Credit Loss		($504)	
F	= EFFECTIVE GROSS INCOME		$16,296	
G	– Operating Expenses		($2,218)	
H	= NET OPERATING INCOME (NOI)		$14,078	
I	– Interest		($7,220)	
J	– Depreciation		($2,181)	
K	= TAXABLE INCOME		$4,677	
L	x State & Federal Taxes		28.00%	
M	= TAX LIABILITY (OPERATIONS)		$1,310	
N				
O	NET OPERATING INCOME (NOI)		$14,078	
P	– Annual Debt Service		($9,686)	
Q	= CASH FLOW BEFORE TAXES		$4,392	
R	– Tax Liability		($1,310)	
S	– CASH FLOW AFTER TAXES		$3,082	
	RATIO ANALYSIS			
T	GROSS RENT MULTIPLIER	A/D	12.56	
U	OVERALL CAPITALIZATION RATE (CAP RATE)	H/A	6.67%	
V	DEBT COVERAGE RATIO (DCR)	O/P	1.45	
	RETURN ON INVESTMENT (ROI)			
W	BEFORE TAX "CASH ON CASH" (Equity Dividend)	Q/C	3.25%	
X	AFTER TAX "CASH ON CASH" (Equity Dividend)	S/C	2.28%	
Y	RETURN ON EQUITY (Equity Yield)	(S+(P–I))/C	4.11%	

Figure 15.2   Property Analysis—Mark and Cindy Investor

PROPERTY ANALYSIS

Property Address: 8552 Blvd. S.W.   Date Prepared: July 18, 19XX
Prepared for: Mark and Cindy Investor
Prepared by: Exchange Agent

			PHASE I DISPOSITION	PHASE II ACQUISITION
A.	FAIR MARKET VALUE		$211,000	$485,000
B.	– Loans		($76,000)	($350,000)
C.	EQUITY		$135,000	$135,000
	ANNUAL PROPERTY OPERATING STATEMENT			
D.	GROSS POTENTIAL INCOME		$16,800	$69,120
E.	– Vacancy & Credit Loss		($504)	($3,456)
F.	= EFFECTIVE GROSS INCOME		$16,296	$65,664
G.	– Operating Expenses		($2,218)	($15,200)
H.	= NET OPERATING INCOME (NOI)		$14,078	$50,464
I.	– Interest		($7,220)	($35,000)
J.	– Depreciation		($2,181)	($14,109)
K.	= TAXABLE INCOME		$4,677	$1,355
L.	x State & Federal Taxes		28.00%	28.00%
M.	= TAX LIABILITY (OPERATIONS)		$1,310	$379
N.				
O.	NET OPERATING INCOME (NOI)		$14,078	$50,464
P.	– Annual Debt Service		($9,686)	($36,858)
Q.	= CASH FLOW BEFORE TAXES		$4,392	$13,606
R.	– Tax Liability		($1,310)	($379)
S.	– CASH FLOW AFTER TAXES		$3,082	$13,227
	RATIO ANALYSIS			
T.	GROSS RENT MULTIPLIER	A/D	12.56	7.02
U.	OVERALL CAPITALIZATION RATE (CAP RATE)	H/A	6.67%	10.40%
V.	DEBT COVERAGE RATIO (DCR)	O/P	1.45	1.37
	RETURN ON INVESTMENT (ROI)			
W.	BEFORE TAX "CASH ON CASH" (Equity Dividend)	Q/C	3.25%	10.08%
X.	AFTER TAX "CASH ON CASH" (Equity Dividend)	S/C	2.28%	9.80%
Y.	RETURN ON EQUITY (Equity Yield)	(S+(P–I))/C	4.11%	11.17%

would have otherwise been lost. When can we meet to discuss your Real Estate Investment Plan?"

Figure 15.2 is a graphic example of how investors can leverage equity. Every time equity is freed up, it can be leveraged. Experienced agents should also concentrate on what the investor equity will buy, not necessarily just sale price. The key to getting started is to focus on properties that can be marketed in the shortest period of time. A single family rental may yield more equity than a $400,000 commercial building. Once the first equity is reinvested, another client has a choice to either pay tax or reinvest. As you move up the ladder, so does your client. Each year as your network grows through repeat business and multi-legged exchanges, prospects will search you out for your professionalism and unique exchange knowledge.

Real Estate Exchange Associations

For the investor or real estate agent seeking other potential exchange properties, a directory of exchange groups is published monthly as a public service in *Creative Real Estate Magazine* (619-756-1441). For additional 1031 exchange information, the following two trade associations can be contacted:

- The National Council of Exchangors (**NCE**), 13410 East Cypress Forest, Houston, Texas 77070, 800-324-1031.

- The American Institute of Exchangors, 490 Center Road, Suite D, Buffalo, New York 14224, 716-677-2880.

chapter 16

The Role of the Intermediary

by Kevin K. Hereford
Scott R. Saunders
Rochelle Stone
Starker Services, Inc.
Los Gatos, California

WHAT IS AN INTERMEDIARY?

An "intermediary" is the term used to describe a third party in an exchange who is used to transfer property or money while protecting the exchangor (taxpayer) from control of cash (constructive receipt) or agency issues. An intermediary acts as a "middleman" by interfacing with all entities in the exchange. An intermediary is the entity who holds the money in a delayed exchange. They may be used to pass ownership from one party to another when no cash is generated in a trade. An intermediary is a principal in the transaction and, as such, is obligated to make certain that the exchange closes successfully.

Treasury Regulations issued in June 1991 defined a "qualified intermediary" in Reg. 1.1031(k)-1(g)(4)(iii), as a party that is not the taxpayer or a disqualified person who:

1. Enters into a written agreement with the taxpayer and;

2. As required by an 'Exchange Agreement', acquires the relinquished property from the taxpayer, transfers the relinquished property, acquires the replacement property and transfers the replacement property to the taxpayer.

The Treasury Regulations also specified who cannot function in the capacity of an Intermedairy. A "disqualified" person is defined as:

1. Any person who is an agent of the taxpayer at the time of the transaction or any person who has acted as the taxpayer's employee, attorney, accountant, investment banker or broker, or real estate agent or broker within the two-year period ending on the date of the transfer of the first of the relinquished properties;

2. Any person who is related to the taxpayer including any family members;

3. Any individual, partner or corporation where a related party owns more than 10% of capital or profit interest or stock value, or;

4. Two corporations in a controlled group, a grantor and **fiduciary** in a trust, or any other entity that would appear to be an agent under local law.

An intermediary assumes the liability and obligations of an exchangor, a seller, and a buyer. They act as a substitute seller for the exchangor and the buyer and then later a substitute buyer for the exchangors' replacement property. An intermediary is extremely valuable for every form of exchanging.

WHEN TO USE AN INTERMEDIARY

Simultaneous Exchanges

The 1991 Treasury Regulations do not clarify whether the buyer and seller can act as a qualified intermediary, nor were they mentioned in the safe harbor definitions; however, most tax authorities agree they can be used in an exchange. If the exchange is a simultaneous, the exchange can be structured as a Baird or Alderson if all the parties agree. For example, in the Alderson format, the seller of property A, wanting to perform a tax-deferred exchange and wanting to trade from property A to property B, may ask the buyer of A to use their cash to purchase property B and then trade for A. This makes the buyer the Accommodator. Under the 1991 Treasury Regulations only the qualified intermediary safe harbor is available to the exchangor.

Delayed Exchanges

Most investors do not care to use the buyer or seller on a delayed exchange because of the issues of survivorship. If one of these parties is used in a delayed exchange, there is a chance something may happen to them, making them incapable of finishing the exchange. Another disadvantage is that an individual may die, subsequently causing the estate to go into probate. If this does happen, there is a good chance the exchangor will not be able to complete the exchange.

The other issue is the cooperating party may not act in a manner consistent with the exchangors' best interest. More than once an exchangor has transferred property to the buyer with the agreement that the buyer would purchase replacement property at a future date and transfer it to the exchangor to complete the exchange. When it came time for the buyer to complete the transaction, they decided the replacement property was a great deal and bought it to keep for their own investment.

HOW TO SELECT AN INTERMEDIARY

An intermediary cannot be an agent of the exchangor, nor can they have any fiduciary responsibility to the exchangor if the exchange is to be tax deferred. They should not be the exchangor's real estate agent, attorney, or accountant. The exchangor should not use a close relative. The reason for this "arms length" treatment is to insure that the exchangor never has control over the proceeds from the sale of property. If the intermediary is an agent of the exchangor or can be shown to have a fiduciary responsibility to the exchangor outside of the exchange transaction, the exchangor may have a constructive receipt of any sale proceeds and the exchange would be disallowed.

The intermediary should be carefully chosen so that the exchange is defensible. As a principal in the transaction, the intermediary will be as responsible as the exchangor for performance of contractual obligations in the selling and buying of property. The real estate agent for the exchangor will become the real estate agent for the intermediary and, if the agent is unfamiliar with exchanging, it may be the intermediary's responsibility to insure that the transaction is conducted properly. The following examples represent only two of hundreds of similar situations in which intermediaries provided assistance.

Example #1

An exchangor owned "A," three houses—(1, 2, and 3)—two of which were sold. He wished to trade all three houses to acquire property "B," an eight-unit apartment complex. The enterprising agent for the owner of A convinced the owner of B to trade for property "V" a trailer park. The agent then convinced the owner of V to trade for a small shopping center, property "D." At this point, the agent ran out of steam, and the owner of D simply wished to sell. The D owner insisted on his escrow taking place at a different escrow company.

Problem

The agent requested that the primary escrow company "do an exchange." The escrow officer created an exchange in which the owner of B became the accomodator, who promptly lost his right to exchange (1). The escrow holder did not know how to handle the third unsold house of property A or the interface with the secondary escrow holder.

Solution

The intermediary took title to houses one and two of property A and sold them to the buyers. Cash proceeds went to the intermediary's account. The intermediary took title to B and "C" and used the funds from the sale of houses 1 and 2 plus loan proceeds from the owners of A, B and C to buy property D. The various properties were then given to the appropriate parties. The D escrow was conducted as a straight purchase by the intermediary using funds transferred from the primary escrow holder. The owner of B remained as a part owner of property B until house one was sold by the intermediary and exchanged for the remaining ownership in "B." The initial part of this transaction was conducted as a simultaneous exchange; the latter part was a delayed exchange. The intermediary assisted in negotiations between the parties and provided the escrow holders with detailed instructions and diagrams to perform the procedure.

Example #2

An exchangor wished to acquire California property valued at $400,000— property A; he also wanted to sell his $600,000 one-half ownership interest in property B in New York. The purchase would preceed the sale of the exchangor's property B by several months.

Problem

The closing attorney in New York was unfamiliar with the process (commonly called a "reverse exchange"). Property A, being valued at $200,000 less than property B, would create $200,000 taxable boot unless the value could be increased.

Solution

The exchangor arranged to provide $400,000 to the intermediary to acquire property A. The intermediary retained ownership of property A. Later when property B was ready to close, the exchangor transferred ownership of property B to the intermediary, who promptly sold it to the waiting buyer. With the funds from the sale, the intermediary paid off the $400,000 loan and used the remaining amount to make capital improvements to property A. When the value of property A was increased to $600,000, the property was transferred to the exchangor to complete the trade. This procedure combined a reverse exchange with a "construction exchange."

Clearly, the use of qualified intermediary is a neccessity if real estate professionals are to safely expand their use of exchanging and if investors want to obtain the highest level of flexibility for the creation of future wealth.

An intermediary having specialized training in negotiation, contract law, taxation, investment analysis, and escrow and real estate practice, as well as having a proven success record in the field of investment real estate, is extremely valuable when problems arise. Exchange problems frequently require a knowledge of all of these areas in order to arrive at a solution. The intermediary should have the finest legal and tax counsel available to assist when a problem requires specialized knowledge. An intermediary is a valuable resource to the investor, to the real estate agent, and to the investor's tax and legal counsel. A properly trained intermediary will identify problems before they threaten an exchange.

Given the availability of professional qualified intermediaries who are clearly not agents or fiduciaries outside of any exchange transaction, there is no reason to risk disallowance by using the exchangor's attorney, real estate agent, or any other party who can be construed as having an agency relationship.

CHOOSING A qualified intermediary

Since at the present, the exchange industry is not regulated, there are few barriers to entry. Consequently, any individual or entity that wants to promote themselves as an intermediary can do so. Unfortunately for investors, this means that many of the preported "qualified intermediaries" have little experience directly with exchanging. Even worse, since the industry lacks government regulation, there is a chance an unwary investor could utilize the services of a dishonest intermediary.

HOW TO PROTECT YOURSELF FROM A DISHONEST intermediary

How can an investor be absolutely certain they are using the right intermediary? First, the background of the company should be thoroughly investigated. For example, professional references should be obtained and one should learn how much specific exchange experience the exchange intermediary possesses. Far more important is researching the security of the exchange proceeds. The investor should find out if funds are held in one large comingled account or if they are held in a separate account for each exchange. Futhermore, the investor should verify the relationship between the Exchange intermediary and the banking institution. A copy of this agreement should also be obtained. For even more security, the investor can check to see if additional security devices, such as letters of credit, are available.

COST OF USING A qualified intermediary

The cost of using an exchange intermediary ranges from one end of the continuum at $500 to the other extreme, which can be as high as $10,000. Many exchange Intermediaries base their fees on a flat rate plus a percentage of the total deal or of the equity held. Additionally, complex transactions, such as improvement or reverse exchanges, could have additional fees added to the base charge. It should be noted that when it comes to pricing, it is important to remember the old adage "you get what you pay for." Investors who base their decision solely on price often overlook some of the most important aspects of exchanging. It is analogous to being diagnosed with a serious illness and choosing a medical specialist based solely on his or her fees. The level of expertise, technical competence, service, reliability, and a myriad of other factors should influence your eventual decision. By the same token, the fees charged by the exchange intermediary will generally reflect the overall quality and reliability of the service provided.

GLOSSARY

Accommodating Grantor   Same as an intermediary. This party allows ownership to pass through them to effect a Section 1031 exchange. Hence, the description as a "grantor."

Accommodator   See "Intermediary."

Acquisition Property   See "Replacement Property."

Actual Receipt   When the exchangor receives the proceeds from the sale of his or her property, he or she has actual receipt of the funds (can be either cash or notes).

Adjusted Basis   Calculated by taking the Original Basis and adding the following: (1) Capitalized Carrying Expenses (2) Capital Improvements (3) Acquisition; then subtracting the following: (4) Cost Recovery (Depreciation, Amortization, Depletion) (5) Unreimbursed Casualty Loss (6) Divestments.

Alderson Exchange   Refers to a form of exchange based upon James Alderson vs. Commissioner, 63-2 U.S.T.C. para. 9499, 317 F. 2d 790 (5th Cir. 1963) in which the Buyer of the exchangor's property is the accommodator. The accommodator first purchases the replacement property, then trades it for the exchangor's disposition property.

Appreciation   The increase in value of a property over its adjusted initial cost.

Assignment Agreement   A document used to transfer contractual rights (but not necessarily obligations) to a third party. Often used to assign the purchase/sales contract between the exchangor and their buyer or seller. The cooperation of the consenting party (either the buyer or the

215

seller) is requested but not required to allow the assignment of the contract unless the contract specifically states it is not assignable.

Assumption of Liability   This is when the buyer assumes the mortgage liability on a property from the seller.

Baird Exchange   Refers to a form of exchange based upon J.H. Baird Publishing Co. vs. Commission, 39 T.C. 608 (1962) where the seller of the replacement property acts as the accommodator. The accommodator swaps their property with the exchangor and then sells the exchangor's former property to the ultimate buyer and pays tax on the transaction. The result is a simultaneous exchange for the exchangor and a taxable sale for the accommodator.

Balancing Equities   The technique in which an investor with a small equity in an exchange property adds something of value to the difference in equities caused by the exchange.

Basis   Commonly referred to as the purchase price of a property. Property received by gift, inheritance or in some other way received without a purchase has a basis equivalent to the fair market value at the time it was received.

Boot   In terms of IRC 1031, boot is property that is not considered like-kind. Boot may be given or received. If the exchangor receives cash or property other than "like-kind" real estate, they have received boot. If an exchangor gives these items, they are giving boot.

> **Cash Boot**   All non like-kind property which is not mortgage boot.

> **Mortgage Boot**   The difference between the mortgage debt and the exchangor has on the relinquished property and the amount they have on the replacement property. If the exchangor increases the debt, they give mortgage boot. If they decrease the debt, they receive mortgage boot.

Buyer   The individual who is purchasing a property.

Buyer's Broker   An agent who represents the buyer. The agent has a fiduciary relationship with the client and does not receive any commissions or fees from any other party in the transaction.

Capital Gain   The excess of the amount received from the sale or exchange over the adjusted basis of the relinquished property.

Capital Loss   The sale, exchange, or other form of disposition of a capital asset at an amount less than the adjusted basis of the property.

Capitalized Expense   An amount of money that is spent to increase the useful life of a capital asset.

Code Section 1031   The Internal Revenue Code section which refers to the deferral of the recognition of gain or loss on the exchange of property held for investment, trade, or business.

Community Property   A form of property relationship between husband and wife in states that recognize a commonality of ownership under specific circumstances.

Concurrent Exchange   See "Simultaneous Exchange."

Constructive Receipt   When the exchangor is considered to have received the proceeds from the sale of their former property even though the funds have not come directly to them. If the sale is complete and the escrow holder retains the proceeds in the same escrow account, the exchangor is considered to have constructive receipt. If any agent (i.e., the exchangor's accountant, attorney, escrow officer, or real estate agent) or party related to the exchangor receives the funds, the exchangor has constructive receipt. If the exchangor controls the funds, receives the benefits associated with these funds, then or if the funds do not have significant restrictions placed upon them preventing the exchangor from receiving them, the exchangor has constructive receipt.

Dealer   A person holding a property as inventory or for resale as opposed to holding a property for productive use in a trade or business or for investment. Developers are examples of real estate dealers. Multiple sales of property in a given time or rapid turnover of properties may qualify a person as a dealer.

Deeding:

  Sequential Deeding   Title (deeds) to the property pass from the principals to the accommodator and to the ultimate owners.

  Direct Deeding   Title passes directly from the exchangor or seller to the ultimate owners without passing through the accommodator.

Deferral of Tax   This refers to a postponement of a possible tax due on potentially taxable income.

Delayed Exchange   A tax-deferred exchange where the replacement property is not acquired at the same time the exchangor transfers the disposition property to another party. This is also called a "1031 Tax Deferred Exchange" or "Starker Exchange."

Depreciation   An expense reflecting the loss in value of the improvements to real estate.

Disposition of Property   Property to be transferred from the exchangor to the intermediary, the other exchangor, etc. "Phase One" or "relinquished property."

Down-leg   The property relinquished by the exchangor in Phase One. also known as "relinquished property," "Phase One property," "sale side," "disposition property."

Earnest Money   The deposit that is made by the purchaser when a purchase contract is made, evidencing the purchaser's serious intent.

Escrow Officer   An individual who holds an escrow payment. One who acts as an agent for all parties to a transaction and incorporates its various instructions into one agreed upon form.

Escrow Terms:

   Phase One   Describes the transfer of property from the exchangor to the intermediary and from the intermediary to the ultimate buyer. Phase One property can be called "sale side," "disposition property," "transferred property," "1st property," or "down-leg" transaction.

   Phase Two   Describes the transfer of property from the seller to the intermediary and from the intermediary back to the exchangor. Phase Two property can be labeled "buy side," "relinquished property," "acquisition property," "2nd property," or "up-leg." In a reverse exchange in which the property to be acquired is transferred to the exchangor first and his property transferred later, Phase Two is still used as a matter of convenience.

Exchange Agreement   A document used to establish the contractual relationship between the parties to an exchange and to prevent the exchangor form having constructive receipt of the cash proceeds.

Exchange Credits   The term used on the settlement statement between the exchangor and the intermediary to refer to the net equity from the disposition of the original exchange property. This term also represents the net equity applied to the replacement property.

Exchange Period   In a deferred exchange, the period during which the exchangor has to acquire all the replacement property. The exchange period begins on the date the taxpayer transfers the relinquished property and ends on the earlier of (1) 180 days or (2) the due date (including extensions) for the exchangor's tax return for the taxable year in which the transfer of the relinquished property occurs.

Exchangor   A principal who performs an IRC 1031 exchange.

Facilitator   See "Intermediary."

Fair Market Value (FMV)   The value of a property at a given time period.

Fiduciary   A fiduciary is the same as a trustee. The fiduciary acts not for their own benefit but for the benefit of another person. This is the highest form of agency.

FIRPTA   Foreign Investor Real Property Tax.

First Party   In a exchange transaction, the party who initiates the exchange.

Foreign Property   Property which is not considered domestic (property not located in the United States).

Fully Taxable Exchange   An exchange in which the taxpayer must recognize all of the indicated gain. No taxes will be deferred by the exchange transaction.

Holding Period   This is the time period in which a taxpayer has owned a property.

Identification Period   In a deferred exchange, the period during which the exchangor has to identify the replacement property. The identification period begins on the date the exchangor transfers the relinquished property and ends 45 days thereafter. (The identification period is not extended if it ends on a holiday or a weekend).

Improvement Exchange   Describes an exchange in which the exchangor transfers relinquished property priced at a higher fair market value than the replacement property. The intermediary retains ownership to the replacement property until capital improvements are made to increase the value (property is improved) at which time it is traded to the exchangor to complete the exchange.

Indemnify   To protect another individual against damage or loss.

Installment Sale   A sale in which the proceeds are paid in installments over a fixed period of time, allowing the capital gains to be paid over a number of years. (See Code Section 453)

Intermediary   A party to the transaction who assumes the liability of exchangor, seller and/or buyer. The intermediary serves as the conduit to acquire, sell, buy, and dispose of property in order to effect a tax deferred exchange for the exchangor. The intermediary isolates the exchangor from buying and selling activity. The intermediary is not an agent of the exchangor and has no fiduciary responsibility to the exchangor. The intermediary receives a profit from the transaction. This party has an independent business relationship and derives an economic benefit from acting as a party to the exchange.

Intermediary Exchange   Refers to an exchange in which an intermediary is used to transfer ownership, title, and funds in order to provide for a tax-deferred exchange in favor of the exchangor. The intermediary enters the transaction as an independent entity assuming all of the risks of ownership in the various stages of the exchange.

Internal Revenue Code (IRC)   A law that is passed by the United States Congress that specifies how income is to be taxed and how it may be deducted from a taxpayer's taxable income.

Internal Revenue Service (IRS)   The governmental agency that administers the collection of federal income taxes.

Involuntary Conversion (IRC Code 1033)   When a property is acquired as a result of an involuntary exchange, i.e., a casualty, theft, eminent domain, or condemnation, the basis of the replacement property acquired may be calculated using the basis of the property exchanged. (See IRC 1033)

Leasehold   An interest in a property that is not freehold. In real estate it would be less than fee simple ownership.

Leasehold Exchange   A leasehold interest in real estate with more than 30 years remaining can be exchanged under IRC 1031.

Leverage   The use of borrowed capital to make an investment.

Like Classes   Classes of assets as described by the U.S. government, used for personal property exchanges.

Like-Kind Property   Refers to the nature of the property the exchangor receives. Property used for productive use in a trade or business or for investment is like-kind. The nature of the property determines if it is like-kind. Examples can include: single-family residential, multi-family residential, retail, manufacturing, condominiums, offices, lodging facilities, and industrial warehouses.

Like-Kind Exchanges   According to the Department of the Treasury nontaxable property must meet six considerations: (1) Property must be business or investment property, (2) the property must be held for sale, (3) there must be an exchange of like-kind property, (4) the property must be tangible property (i.e., not bonds, stocks, etc.), (5) the property must meet the identification requirements ("45 day rule"), and (6) the exchange must meet the completed transaction requirements ("180 day rule").

Missouri Waltz   An exchange technique in which two parties plus a buyout of one of the properties owed by a third party. (See Baird Exchange)

Moderator   An exchangor who directs the presentation of exchange counselors in the marketing of exchange properties at a property exchange meeting.

Mortgage in Excess of Basis   Sometimes called mortgage over basis. When the debt on the subject property exceeds the basis in the property.

Mortgage Relief   Being relieved of the liabilities and responsibilities of a existing mortgage loan, through a sale or exchange of a property through the assumption or payoff of that loan. Under certain situations, this may result in a tax liability. Mortgage relief is considered boot.

Multiple Party Exchange   An exchange transaction that involves three or more parties.

Napkin Test   A simple test for determining if the exchangor is trading "across" or "up" in equity and value. The following examples illustrate the Napkin Test. They show exchangor's property as "A" and the property to be acquired as "B".

Example 1
exchangor goes "across" with equity and "up" in value.

	Property "A"	Property "B"
Value:	$350,000	$450,000
Equity:	$200,000	$200,000
Mortgage:	$150,000	$250,000

222 Glossary

Example 2
exchangor keeps $50,000 of net proceeds, $50,000 is taxable Cash Boot

	Property "A"	Property "B"
Value:	$350,000	$450,000
Equity:	$200,000	$150,000
Mortgage:	$150,000	$300,000

Example 3
The exchangor goes down in value $50,000. The $50,000 debt relief is taxable Mortgage Boot

	Property "A"	Property "B"
Value:	$350,000	$300,000
Equity:	$200,000	$200,000
Mortgage:	$150,000	$100,000

National Council of exchangors (NCE)   A professional organization of exchange counselors that sponsors marketing sessions and educational courses.

Net Mortgage Relief   The netting of mortgages in an exchange transaction, subtracting the mortgages assumed from the mortgages relieved.

Novation Agreement   This document transfers contractual rights and obligations to a third party and is often used to assign the purchase/sales contract. The signature of the consenting party (either the buyer or seller) is required to allow the novation of the contract. When a contract is novated, it becomes a new contract.

Offsetting Boot   When a taxpayer uses boot to pay to offset boot that he receives to reduce his tax liability.

Overtrade Formula   In an exchange transaction, when a property with a larger equity than the one received in return required cash or unlike-kind property in return to balance the equities.

Partially Deferred Exchange   An exchange in which some of the indicated gain is realized in the tax year of the transaction and part of it is deferred.

Phase One   Describes the transfer of property from the exchangor to the intermediary and from the intermediary to the ultimate buyer. Phase One property can be called "sale side," "disposition property," "relinquished property," "conveyed property," "disposed property," "transferred property," "first property," or "down-leg."

Phase Two   Describes the transfer of property from the seller to the intermediary and from the intermediary back to the exchangor. Phase Two property can be called "buy side," "replacement property," "acquisition property," "second property," or "up-leg." In a reverse exchange where the property to be acquired is transferred to the exchangor first and his property transferred later, Phase Two is still used as a matter of convenience.

Pot Theory   An escrow that deeds the property directly to the party who will finally receive them in the exchange as oppose to using the sequential deeding method. This technique enables the parties to avoid paying multiple transfer fees.

Pyramiding   An investment technique in which the objective is to build equities as quickly as possible. This technique usually requires high leverage and the use of the IRC Section 1031.

Qualified Intermediary

Recapture   Recognition as ordinary income of gains created by accelerated depreciation (cost recovery) deductions in excess of straight-line depreciation.

Real Property   Generally described as real estate, improved, or unimproved. Appurtenances to real property are considered in most states to also be real property.

Realized Gain   Refers to the capital gain or loss but is not taxed. Gain or loss in an exchange may be realized, but not recognized.

Recapitulation   A worksheet used to balance equities, in an exchange that provides a complete accounting of transaction costs, existing and potential financing, the payor and payee of any purchase money notes required, and the potential "boot" given and received by the parties, which serves as a map of the transaction.

Recognized Gain   The portion, if any, of the realized gain that is taxable.

Related Parties   In a 1031 exchange, related parties include: family members, a corporation or partnership in which the exchangor has more than a 50% interest. A related party does not include relatives by marriage, i.e., sister-in-law.

Relinquished Property   The property that is sold by the exchangor. Also known as "outgoing property" or "Phase One property."

Replacement Property   Property to be acquired to complete the exchange. Also known as "incoming property" or "Phase Two property."

Revenue Ruling   An official Internal Revenue Service interpretation that is published in the Internal Revenue Bulletin.

Reverse Exchange   A tax-deferred exchange in which the Phase One property (replacement property) is acquired first and the exchangor disposes of their property at a later date.

Round Table   A marketing technique in which five or more exchangors sit around a large table to discuss and present properties for exchange.

Safe Harbor Rules   These are the four guidelines that the IRS established in 1991 for tax deferred exchanges. They are: 1) Use of a Qualified intermediary, 2) Security or Guarantee Arrangements, 3) Qualified Escrow Accounts and Qualified Trusts, and 4) Interest and Growth Factors.

Secured Letter of Credit   A security device in which a depository (bank) uses the proceeds from the sale of the exchangor's property as collateral for a credit account in the amount of the proceeds. The letter of credit is held by the exchangor. This is a form of third-party guarantee and will not endanger an exchange if drafted properly. Usually costs up to two percent of the funds used as collateral. Must be applied for in the same manner as a loan.

Simultaneous Exchange   When the property to be disposed of and the property to be acquired are in escrow or closed at the same time.

Starker   Three famous court cases that dealt with delayed exchanges. These court cases established the basis for the delayed exchange procedure.

Starker Exchange   Popular term for a deferred exchange. See "Delayed Exchange."

Strawman   Sometimes incorrectly used to describe an intermediary. A strawman actually describes an agent of the exchangor and is an entity who purchases a property that is then conveyed to another for the purposes of concealing the true identity of the actual purchaser.

Stepped-up Basis An accounting term used to describe a change in the adjusted tax basis of property, allowed for certain transactions.

Taker An individual who will purchase or exchange for a property.

Target Property Replacement property.

Tax Bracket An accounting term that describes the marginal tax rate that is assessed by the Internal Revenue Service to a taxpayer, based on a percentage of each additional dollar of income required to be paid as income taxes in a given tax year.

Trustee One of the highest levels of a fiduciary relationship. A trustee of a trust is the direct representative of the exchangor. A trustee holding funds in a trust which benefits the exchangor is not a tax-deferred exchange.

Unrecognized Gain The portion, if any, of the realized gain that is not taxable. Also called the deferred gain.

Up-leg Replacement property. Also known as "buy side," "acquisition," or "Phase Two property."

Want At a marketing exchange meeting, that property type that an individual is seeking.

Zander Board A method used by Exchange Clubs to exchange properties. A moderator starts with a property, service, or product at the top of the board in various boxes. The moderator then describes each item and offers are made.

1031 Exchange An exchange of like-kind business or investment property which qualifies for deferment of capital gains tax. Also known as a "tax-deferred exchange."

1034 Exchange An exchange of a principal residence which qualifies for deferment of capital gains tax.

45-Day Identification Rule That period of time that is required by the Internal Revenue Service to identify a suitable exchange property. This time period starts from the day of closing in the exchange transaction.

180-Day Replacement Rule That period of time that is required by the Internal Revenue Service to close the target property in an exchange transaction. This time period starts from the day of closing in the exchange transaction.

Appendices

Section 1031 of the Internal Revenue Code

APPENDIX

Section 1031 of the Internal Revenue Code

Sec. 1031 [1986 Code].

(a) Nonrecognition of Gain or Loss From Exchanges Solely in Kind.-

(1) IN GENERAL.-No gain or loss shall be recognized on the exchange of property held for productive use in a trade or business or for investment if such property is exchanged solely for property of like kind which is to be held either for productive use in a trade or business or for investment.

(2) EXCEPTION.--This subsection shall not apply to any exchange of--

(A) stock in trade or other property held primarily for sale,

(B) stocks, bonds, or notes,

(C) other securities or evidences of indebtedness or interest,

(D) interests in a partnership,

(E) certificates of trust or beneficial interests, or

(F) choses in action.

For purposes of this section, an interest in a partnership which has in effect a valid election under section 761(a) to be excluded from the application of all subchapter K shall be treated as an interest in each of the assets of such partnership and not as an interest in a partnership.

(3) REQUIREMENT THAT PROPERTY BE IDENTIFIED AND THAT EXCHANGE BE COMPLETED NOT MORE THAN 180 DAYS AFTER TRANSFER OF EXCHANGED PROPERTY.-For purposes of this subsection, any property received by the taxpayer shall be treated as property which is not like-kind property if-

(A) such property is not identified as property to be received in the exchange on or before the day which is 45 days after the date on which the taxpayer transfers the property relinquished in the exchange or

(B) such property is received after the earlier of-

(i) the day which is 180 days after the date on which the taxpayer transfers the property relinquished in the exchange or

(ii) the due date (determined with regard to extension) for the transferor's return of the tax imposed by this chapter for the taxable year in which the transfer of the relinquished property occurs.

(b) GAIN FROM EXCHANGES NOT SOLELY IN KIND.--If an exchange would be within the provisions of subsection (a), of section 1035(a), of section 1036(a), or of section 1037(a), if it were not for the fact that the property received in exchange consists not only of property permitted by such provisions to be received without the recognition of gain, but also of other property or money, then the gain, if any, to the recipient shall be recognized, but in an amount not in excess of the sum of such money and the fair market value of such other property.

(c) LOSS FROM EXCHANGES NOT SOLELY IN KIND.-If an exchange would be within the provisions of subsection (a), of section 1035(a), of section 1036(a), or of section 1037(a), if it were not for the fact that the property received in exchange consists not only of property permitted by such provisions to be received without the recognition of gain or loss, but also of other property or money, then no loss from the exchange shall be recognized.

(d) BASIS.-If a property was acquired in an exchange described in this section, section 1035(a), section 1036(a), or section 1037(a), then the basis shall be the same as that of the property exchanged, decreased in the amount of any money received by the taxpayer and increased in the amount of gain or decreased in the amount of loss to the taxpayer that was recognized on such exchange. If the property so acquired consisted in part of the type of property permitted by this section, section 1035(a), or section 1037(a), to be received without the recognition of gain or loss, and in part of other property, the basis provided in this subsection shall be allocated between the properties

APPENDIX

Section 1031 of the Internal Revenue Code

(other than money) received, and for the purpose of the allocation there shall be assigned to such other property an amount equivalent to its fair market value at the date of the exchange. For purposes of this section, section 1035(a), and section 1036(a), where as part of the consideration to the taxpayer another party to the exchange assumed a liability of the taxpayer or acquired from the taxpayer property subject to the liability, such assumption or acquisition (in the amount of the liability) shall be considered as money received by the taxpayer on the exchange.

(e) EXCHANGES OF LIVESTOCK OF DIFFERENT SEXES.-For purposes of this section, live-stock of different sexes are not property of a like kind.

(f) SPECIAL RULES FOR EXCHANGES BETWEEN RELATED PERSONS.-

(1) IN GENERAL.-If-

(A) a taxpayer exchanges property with a related person,

(B) there is nonrecognition of gain or loss to the taxpayer under this section with respect to the exchange of such property (determined without regard to this subsection), and

(C) before the date 2 years after the date of the last transfer which was part of such exchange-

(i) the related person disposes of such property, or

(ii) the taxpayer disposes of the property received in the exchange from the related person which was of like kind to the property transferred by the taxpayer,

there shall be no nonrecognition of gain or loss under this section to the taxpayer with respect to such exchange; except that any gain or loss recognized by the taxpayer by reason of this subsection shall be taken into account as of the date on which the disposition referred to in subparagraph (c) occurs.

(2) CERTAIN DISPOSITIONS NOT TAKEN INTO ACCOUNT.-For purposes of paragraph (1)(C), there shall not be taken into account any disposition-

(A) after the earlier of the death of the

taxpayer or the death of the related person,

(B) in a compulsory or involuntary conversion (within the meaning of section 1033) if the exchange occurred before the threat or imminence of such conversion or

(C) with respect to which it is established to the satisfaction of the Secretary that neither the exchange nor such disposition had as one of its principal purposes the avoidance of Federal income tax.

(3) RELATED PERSON.-- For purposes of this subsection, the term "related person" means any person bearing a relationship to the taxpayer described in section 267(b) or 707(b)(1).

(4) TREATMENT OF CERTAIN TRANSACTIONS.--This section shall not apply to any exchange which is part of a transaction (or series of transactions) structured to avoid the purposes of this subsection.

(g) SPECIAL RULE WHERE SUBSTANTIAL DIMINUTION OF RISK.-

(1) IN GENERAL.-- If paragraph (2) applies to any property for any period, the running of the period set forth in subsection (f)(1)(C) with respect to such property shall be suspended during such period.

(2) PROPERTY TO WHICH SUBSECTION APPLIES.-This paragraph shall apply to any property for any period during which the holder's risk of loss with respect to the property is substantially diminished by-

(A) the holding of a put with respect to such property,

(B) the holding by another person of a right to acquire such property or

(C) a short sale or any other transaction.

(h) SPECIAL RULE FOR FOREIGN REAL PROPERTY.-For purposes of this section, real property located in the United States and real property located outside the United States are not property of a like kind.

IRS Issues Final Regulations on Deferred Like-Kind Exchanges (T.D. 8346)

appendix B

SUPPLEMENTARY INFORMATION:

Background

On May 16, 1990, the Federal Register published a notice of proposed rulemaking (IA-237-84) under section 1031 of the Internal Revenue Code. The notice proposed to add regulations relating to deferred exchanges and exchanges of partnership interests. Pursuant to section 7805(f) of the Code, these regulations were submitted to the Administrator of the Small Business Administration for comment on their impact on small business. The Internal Revenue Service received public comments on the proposed regulations and held a public hearing on September 5, 1990. After full consideration of the public comments and statements regarding the proposed regulations, the Service adopts the proposed regulations as revised by this Treasury decision. Descriptions of the revisions to the proposed regulations are included in the discussion of the public comments below. A more complete explanation of the provisions common to the proposed and final regulations, and of the policy reasons underlying those provisions, is set forth in the preamble to the proposed regulations.

Deferred Exchanges

Exchanges in Which Receipt of Replacement Property Precedes Transfer of Relinquished Property

Section 1031(a) of the Code and § 1.1031(a)-3 of the proposed regulations apply to deferred exchanges. The proposed regulations define a deferred exchange as an exchange in which, pursuant to an agreement, the taxpayer transfers property held for productive use in a trade or business or for investment (the "relinquished property") and subsequently receives property to be held either for productive use in a trade or business or for investment (the "replacement property"). The proposed regulations do not apply to transactions in which the taxpayer receives the replacement property prior to the date on which the taxpayer transfers the relinquished property (so-called "reverse-*Starker*" transactions). See *Starker* v. *United States*, 602 F.2d 1341 (9th Cir. 1979).

The Service requested comments on whether reverse-*Starker* transactions should qualify for tax-free exchange treatment under any provision of section 1031. The comments received ranged from advocating the application of the deferred exchange provisions of section 1031(a)(3) to these transactions to advising that these transactions should not qualify for tax-free exchange

treatment under either the general rule set forth in section 1031(a)(1) or section 1031(a)(3). After reviewing the comments and applicable law, the Service has determined that the deferred exchange rules of section 1031(a)(3) do not apply to reverse-*Starker* transactions. Therefore, the final regulations, like the proposed regulations, do not apply to reverse-*Starker* transactions. However, the Service will continue to study the applicability of the general rule of section 1031(a)(1) to these transactions.

Identification and Receipt Requirements

In general

Section 1031(a)(3) provides that any property received by the taxpayer in a deferred exchange is treated as property that is not like-kind property if (a) the property is not identified as property to be received in the exchange on or before the day that is 45 days after the date on which the taxpayer transfers the property relinquished in the exchange (the "identification period"), or (b) the property is received after the earlier of (1) the day that is 180 days after the date on which the taxpayer transfers the property relinquished in the exchange, or (2) the due date (including extensions) of the taxpayer's tax return for the taxable year in which the transfer of the relinquished property occurs (the "exchange period"). The proposed and final regulations provide additional guidance with respect to these requirements.

Application of section 7503

The proposed regulations provide that in determining the dates on which the identification and exchange periods end, section 7503 does not apply. Section 7503 provides that where the last day for performance falls on a Saturday, Sunday, or legal holiday, performance on the next succeeding day that is not a Saturday, Sunday, or legal holiday will be considered timely.

Some commentators suggested that the proposed regulations should be revised to provide that section 7503 does apply in determining the dates on which the identification and exchange periods end. However, Rev. Rul. 83-116, 1983-2 C.B. 264, provides that secion 7503 is limited to procedural acts required to be performed in connection with the determination, collection, or refund of taxes. Because it is unnecessary to state a special rule for the application of section 7503 to deferred exchanges, the provision regarding application of section 7503 to section 1031 deferred exchanges has been deleted from the

---

DEPARTMENT OF THE TREASURY

Internal Revenue Service

26 CFR Part 1

[T.D. 8346]

RIN 1545-AH43

Like-kind Exchanges—Limitations on Deferred Exchanges; and Inapplicability of Section 1031 to Exchanges of Partnership Interests

AGENCY: Internal Revenue Service, Treasury.

ACTION: Final regulations.

SUMMARY: This document contains final regulations relating to limitations on deferred exchanges under section 1031(a)(3) of the Internal Revenue Code of 1986 and to the inapplicability of section 1031 to exchanges of interests in a partnership under section 1031(a)(2)(D). The regulations provide the public with the guidance needed to comply with the Tax Reform Act of 1984 and 1986.

EFFECTIVE DATES: Sections 1.1031-0, 1.1031(b)-2 and 1.1031(k)-1 are effective for transfers of property made by taxpayers on or after June 10, 1991. The amendments to § 1.1031(a)-1 are effective for transfers of property made by taxpayers on or after April 25, 1991.

FOR FURTHER INFORMATION CONTACT:
_____ 202-343-2380, or
_____ 202-343-2382 (not toll-free numbers).

final regulations. In addition, because the timing requirements relating to the identification and exchange periods are statutory, requests for extension of the identification period or the exchange period through administrative relief under § 1.9100 will not be granted.

Identification of Alternative Properties

When section 1031(a)(3) was added to the Code in 1984, Congress was concerned that the greater the discretion a taxpayer has to vary the replacement property that will ultimately be received in a transaction, the more the transaction appears to be a sale rather than an exchange. *See* H.R. Rep. No. 432, 98th Cong., 2d Sess., pt. 2, at 1232; Staff of Committee on Finance, 98th Cong., 2d Sess., Explanation of the Deficit Reduction Act of 1984 (Comm. Print 1984) at 242. On the other hand, a taxpayer may encounter practical difficulties in trying to identify with precision the replacement property that the taxpayer will ultimately receive. The identification rules provided by the proposed regulations balance these competing concerns in several ways. Under these rules, the maximum number of replacement properties that a taxpayer may identify is (a) three properties of any fair market value (the "3-property rule"), or (b) any number of properties as long as their aggregate fair market value as of the end of the identification period does not exceed 200 percent of the aggregate fair market value of all the relinquished properties (the "200-percent rule"). The proposed regulations also provide that the fair market value of property for purposes of the deferred exchange rules is the property's fair market value without regard to liabilities secured by the property.

Commentators suggested that both the 3-property rule and the 200-percent rule be expanded to give taxpayers more discretion in identifying replacement property in deferred exchanges. To do so, however, would give these transactions more of the character of sales rather than exchanges and therefore would be less consistent with congressional intent. Accordingly, these rules have not been changed in the final regulations.

Commentators also suggested that the fair market value of property for purposes of the 200-percent rule should be its fair market value less liabilities secured by the property (i.e., its net equity value). Use of net equity value would create practical problems, however, because the 200-percent rule is applied at the end of the identification period. At that time, a taxpayer may not know or be able to control unilaterally

the amount of the liabilities to which the replacement property will be subject when that property is ultimately received. For this reason, the final regulations, like the proposed regulations, provide that for purposes of the deferred exchange rules the fair market value of property is determined without regard to liabilities secured by the property.

Rules Regarding Safe Harbors

In General

Because taxpayers typically are unwilling to rely on a transferee's unsecured promise to transfer the like-kind replacement property, the use of various guarantee or security arrangements is common in deferred exchanges. In addition, because persons who want to purchase the relinquished property may be unwilling or unable to acquire the replacement property, taxpayers often retain an intermediary to facilitate the exchange. Use of these arrangements, however, raises issues concerning actual receipt, constructive receipt, and agency.

Section 1031(a)(3) leaves unclear the application of the rules of actual and constructive receipt and the implications of the taxpayer's possible agency relationship with an intermediary in deferred exchange transactions. Therefore, the proposed regulations provide taxpayers with four safe harbors based on commonly used security, guarantee, and intermediary arrangements. The first safe harbor permits certain security arrangements. The second permits the use of a qualified escrow account or a qualified trust. The third permits the use of a qualified intermediary, and the fourth permits the taxpayer to receive interest or a growth factor to compensate for the time value of money during the period between transfer of the relinquished property and receipt of the replacement property. Use of these safe harbors will result in a determination that a taxpayer is not, either directly or through an intermediary that may be an agent, in actual or constructive receipt of money or other property for purposes of these regulations. The final regulations retain these four safe harbors, but with certain modifications and clarifications.

Rights to Money or Other Property Outside of Safe Harbors

Under the proposed regulations, the safe harbors generally apply only if the taxpayer has no right to receive, pledge, borrow, or otherwise obtain the benefits of the funds or interest in escrow or trust or held by an intermediary before

the occurrence of certain enumerated circumstances. The final regulations clarify that the limitations on a taxpayer's rights to receive, pledge, borrow, or otherwise obtain the benefits of the funds apply only to the money or other property in a qualified escrow account or qualified trust, or held by the qualified intermediary. Under the final regulations, a taxpayer may receive money or other property directly from another party to the transaction, but not from a qualified escrow account, a qualified trust, or a qualified intermediary, without affecting the application of a safe harbor.

Rights Under State Law to Money or Other Property

Some commentators expressed concern that, as a result of certain rights under state law, a taxpayer may be treated as having the immediate right to receive money or other property in an escrow or trust or held by a qualified intermediary. For example, commentators questioned whether a taxpayer would be treated as having the immediate right to receive money or other property held by an intermediary if, under state agency law, the intermediary is the agent of the taxpayer and the taxpayer has the right to dismiss an agent and thereby obtain property held for the taxpayer by the agent.

To assure taxpayers who use the safe harbors that the federal tax treatment of deferred exchanges is not intended to be dependent in this respect upon state law, the final regulations clarify that the terms of the applicable agreement, rather than state law, will determine whether the limitations imposed by a safe harbor with respect to a taxpayer's rights to receive, pledge, borrow, or otherwise obtain the benefit of money or other property are satisfied. Thus, the safe harbors require that the applicable agreement expressly limits the taxpayer's rights to receive, pledge, borrow, or otherwise obtain the benefits of the money or other property before the end of the exchange period. The applicable agreement may, but need not, give a taxpayer rights to receive, pledge, borrow, or otherwise obtain the benefits of the money or other property before the end of the exchange period if the exchange is completed or the requirements of section 1031(a)(3) can no longer be met.

The final regulations also provide that rights conferred upon a taxpayer under state agency law to dismiss an escrow holder, trustee, or intermediary will be disregarded in determining whether the taxpayer has the ability to receive or otherwise obtain the benefits of money

Federal Register / Vol. 56, No. 84 / Wednesday, May 1, 1991 / Rules and Regulations   19935

or other property held by the escrow holder, trustee, or intermediary. Actual or constructive receipt necessarily will occur at the time the taxpayer exercises these rights.

Special Rule for Certain Acquisition and Closing Costs

Commentators pointed out that funds in a qualified escrow account or qualified trust, or held by a qualified intermediary, may be needed to pay closing costs for which the taxpayer is responsible. The taxpayer is in receipt of the funds to the extent the funds are used to pay the taxpayer's closing costs. Commentators questioned whether paying closing costs out of these funds also results in actual or constructive receipt of the remaining funds. The final regulations provide that the use of money or other property in a qualified escrow account or qualified trust, or held by a qualified intermediary, to pay certain specified items will not result in actual or constructive receipt of the remaining funds and, furthermore, will be disregarded in determining whether the applicable agreement properly limits the taxpayer's rights to receive, borrow, pledge, or otherwise obtain the benefits of money or other property. The specified items are transactional items that (a) relate to the disposition of the relinquished property or to the acquisition of the replacement property and (b) are listed as the responsibility of a buyer or seller in the typical closing statement under local standards. Examples of these transactional items include commissions, prorated taxes, recording or transfer taxes, and title company fees. In addition, under the final regulations, a taxpayer's rights to receive items (such as prorated rents) that a seller may receive as a consequence of the disposition of property and that are not included in the amount realized from the disposition of property are disregarded.

Definition of Qualified Intermediary

Under the proposed regulations, a qualified intermediary is defined as a person who is not the taxpayer or a related party and who acts to facilitate a deferred exchange by entering into an agreement with the taxpayer for the exchange of properties. The proposed regulations also require that the qualified intermediary acquire the relinquished property from the taxpayer, acquire the replacement property, and transfer the replacement property to the taxpayer. The final regulations provide that the qualified intermediary must also transfer the relinquished property.

Commentators requested clarification as to what an intermediary must do to

acquire property. In response, the final regulations describe limited circumstances under which an intermediary is treated as acquiring and transferring property regardless of whether, under general tax principles, the intermediary actually acquires and transfers the property. First, an intermediary is treated as acquiring and transferring property if the intermediary acquires and transfers legal title to that property. In addition, an intermediary is treated as acquiring and transferring the relinquished property if the intermediary (either on its own behalf or as the agent of any party to the transaction) enters into an agreement with a person other than the taxpayer for the transfer of the relinquished property to that person and, pursuant to that agreement, the relinquished property is transferred to that person. Finally, an intermediary is treated as acquiring and transferring replacement property if the intermediary (either on its own behalf or as the agent of any party to the transaction) enters into an agreement with the owner of the replacement property for the transfer of that property and, pursuant to that agreement, the replacement property is transferred to the taxpayer. Solely for these purposes, an intermediary is treated as entering into an agreement if the rights of a party to the agreement are assigned to the intermediary and all parties to that agreement are notified in writing of the assignment on or before the date of the relevant transfer of property.

Definition of "Related Party"

Under the proposed regulations, a party that is related to the taxpayer cannot be the escrow holder of a qualified escrow account, the trustee of a qualified trust, or a qualified intermediary. The proposed regulations define a person as a related party if: (i) The person and the taxpayer bear a relationship described in section 267(b) or section 707(b) (applied by substituting in each section "10 percent" for "50 percent" each place it appears); (ii) the person acts as the taxpayer's agent (including, for example, by performing services as the taxpayer's employee, attorney, or broker); or (iii) the person and a person who acts as the taxpayer's agent bear a relationship described in section 267(b) or 707(b) (again, substituting in each section "10 percent" for "50 percent" each place it appears). The proposed regulations further provide that, in determining whether a person acts as the taxpayer's agent, the performance of services with respect to exchanges intended to qualify under section 1031 and the performance of

routine financial services by a financial institution are not taken into account.

Commentators suggested several changes to the above definition of related party. They pointed out that the term "related party" as used in the proposed regulations is defined differently than the term "related person" as used in section 1031(f). To avoid confusion, they suggested using the section 1031(f) definition. The Services believes that the section 1031(f) related person definition is too narrow for purposes of the safe harbors contained in the deferred exchange regulations. To alleviate any potential confusion, the final regulations substitute the term "disqualified person" for the term "related party."

Commenters also asked for clarification regarding when certain persons, such as attorneys, would be treated as acting as a taxpayer's agent. In this regard, commentators suggested that a person who has not recently acted as the taxpayer's agent should not be disqualified from performing exchange-related services for the taxpayer. Finally, commentators requested that the status of title insurance companies, escrow companies, and certain other persons be clarified.

The final regulations have been revised to address these concerns. Under the final regulations, a person is a disqualified person if: (i) The person is an agent of the taxpayer at the time of the transaction; (ii) the person and the taxpayer bear a relationship described in section 267(b) or section 707(b) (applied by substituting "10 percent" for "50 percent" each time it appears in those sections); or (iii) the person and a person who is an agent of the taxpayer at the time of the transaction bear a relationship described in section 267(b) or 707(b) (again, substituting "10 percent" for "50 percent" in applying those sections). A person who has acted as the taxpayer's employee, attorney, accountant, investment banker or broker, or real estate agent or broker within the 2-year period ending on the date of the transfer of the first of the relinquished properties is treated as an agent of the taxpayer at the time of the transaction.

In addition, the final regulations broaden somewhat the services that are disregarded for purposes of determining if an agency relationship exists. In determining whether a person is an agent of the taxpayer or has acted within the preceding 2-year period as the taxpayer's employee, attorney, accountant, investment banker or broker, or real estate agent or broker, the performance of services with respect to exchanges intended to qualify under section 1031 is not taken into account. Furthermore, for these purposes, the performance of routine financial, title insurance, escrow, or trust services by a financial institution, title insurance company, or escrow company is not taken into account.

Extension of Safe Harbor Rules to Simultaneous Exchanges

The rules in the proposed regulations, including the safe harbors, apply only to deferred exchanges. Commentators noted that the concerns relating to actual or constructive receipt and agency also exist in the case of simultaneous exchanges. They requested that the safe harbors be made available for simultaneous exchanges. Upon review, the Service has determined it necessary to make only the qualified intermediary safe harbor available for simultaneous exchanges.

The final regulations provide, therefore, that in the case of simultaneous transfers of like-kind properties involving a qualified intermediary, the qualified intermediary will not be considered the agent of the taxpayer for purposes of section 1031(a). Thus, in such a case the transfer and receipt of property by the taxpayer will be treated as an exchange. This provision is set forth in new § 1.1031(b)–2 of the final regulations and is effective for transfers of property made by taxpayers on or after June 10, 1991.

Application of Section 468B(g) Rules Regarding Interest

Section 468B(g) provides that nothing in any provision of law will be construed as providing that an escrow account, settlement fund, or similar fund is not subject to current income tax. It also directs the Secretary to prescribe regulations relating to the taxation of these accounts or funds whether as a grantor trust or otherwise.

The fourth safe harbor provided by the proposed regulations permits taxpayers to receive interest or a growth factor with respect to the deferred exchange, provided that the taxpayer's rights to receive the interest or growth factor are limited to certain specified circumstances. Although the proposed regulations require the interest or growth factor to be treated as interest, regardless of whether it is paid in cash or in property, they do not address the proper manner for reporting interest income earned on money held in an escrow account or trust. Comments were requested concerning whether the Service should exercise its regulatory authority under section 468B(g) with respect to interest earned on escrow

accounts and trusts used in deferred exchanges.

After considering the comments on this issue, the Service has concluded that guidance on interest reporting should be provided not in piecemeal fashion under a number of Code sections, but rather in general, comprehensive regulations issued under section 468B(g). Accordingly, the final regulations do not address this issue. Guidance will be published in regulations under section 468B(g).

Coordination with Section 453 Installment Sale Rules

The section of the proposed regulations that coordinates the deferred exchange rules and the installment sale rules is reserved. Commentators suggested that this issue should be addressed in the near future because the two sets of rules often apply to the same transactions. The Service agrees this issue merits prompt attention. The issue remains reserved in the final regulations but will be addressed in forthcoming proposed regulations.

Effective Date Relating to Deferred Exchange Provisions

Section 1.1031(k)–1 of the final regulations applies to transfers of property made by taxpayers on or after June 10, 1991. Transfers of property made by taxpayers after May 16, 1990, but before June 10, 1991, will be treated as complying with section 1031(a)(3) and this section if either the provisions of this section or the provisions of the notice of proposed rulemaking published in the Federal Register on May 16, 1990 (55 FR 20278) are satisfied.

Exchanges of Partnership Interests

In General

Section 1031(a)(2)(D) provides that section 1031(a) does not apply to any exchange of interests in a partnership. The Service requested comments on whether an exchange of an interest in an organization which has elected under section 761(a) to be excluded from the application of subchapter K is eligible for nonrecognition of gain or loss under section 1031(a).

Section 11703(d) of the Omnibus Budget Reconciliation Act of 1990, Public Law 101–503, amended section 1031(a)(2) to provide that an interest in a partnership that has in effect a valid election under section 761(a) to be excluded from the application of all of subchapter K is treated for purposes of section 1031 as an interest in each of the assets of the partnership and not as an interest in a partnership. The final

regulations have been revised to reflect the amendment to section 1031(a)(2).

The final regulations otherwise retain the provisions of the proposed regulations regarding exchanges of interests in a partnership. Under the proposed and final regulations, an exchange of partnership interests will not qualify for nonrecognition of gain or loss under section 1031(a) regardless of whether the interests exchanged are general or limited partnership interests or are interests in the same partnership or different partnerships. No inference is to be drawn from these regulations, however, with respect to the application of other Code sections that allow nonrecognition of gain of loss in an exchange of interests in a partnership. For example, as stated in the preamble to the proposed regulations, these regulations are not intended to affect the applicability of Rev. Rul. 84–52, 1984–1 C.B. 157, concerning conversions of partnership interests. More generally, the regulations are not intended to restrict in any way the application of the rules of subchapter K of the Code to exchanges of partnership interests.

Effective Date Relating to Exchanges of Partnership Interests

The amendments to § 1.1031(a)–1 made in the final regulations with respect to exchanges of partnership interests are effective for transfers of property made by taxpayers on or after April 25, 1991.

Special Analyses

It has been determined that these rules are not major rules as defined in Executive Order 12291. Therefore, a Regulatory Impact Analysis is not required. It has also been determined that section 553(b) of the Administrative Procedure Act (5 U.S.C. chapter 5) and the Regulatory Flexibility Act (5 U.S.C. chapter 6) do not apply to these regulations, and therefore an initial Regulatory Flexibility Analysis is not required.

Drafting Information

The principal author of these regulations is D. Lindsay Russell of the Office of Assistant Chief Counsel (Income Tax & Accounting), Internal Revenue Service. However, personnel from other offices of the Internal Revenue Service and Treasury Department participated in developing these regulations, on matters of both substance and style.

List of Subjects in 26 CFR 1.1031(a)-1 through 1.1042-1T

Income taxes, Reporting and recordkeeping requirements.

Adoption of Amendments to the Regulations

The amendments to 26 CFR part 1 are as follows:

PART 1—INCOME TAX; TAXABLE YEARS BEGINNING AFTER DECEMBER 31, 1953

Paragraph 1. The authority for part 1 continues to read in part:

Authority: 26 U.S.C. 7805 * * *

Par. 2. A new § 1.1031-0 is added to read as follows:

§ 1.1031-0 Table of contents.

This section lists the captions that appear in the regulations under section 1031.

§ 1.1031(a)-1 Property held for productive use in a trade or business or for investment.

(a) In general.
(b) Definition of "like kind."
(c) Examples of exchanges of property of a "like kind."
(d) Examples of exchanges not solely in kind.
(e) Effective date.

§ 1.1031(a)-2 Additional rules for exchanges of personal property.

(a) Introduction.
(b) Depreciable tangible personal property.
(c) Intangible personal property and nondepreciable personal property.

§ 1.1031(b)-1 Receipt of other property or money in tax-free exchange.

§ 1.1031(b)-2 Safe harbor for qualified intermediaries.

§ 1.1031(c)-1 Nonrecognition of loss.

§ 1.1031(d)-1 Property acquired upon a tax-free exchange.

§ 1.1031(d)-1T Coordination of section 1060 with section 1031 (temporary).

§ 1.1031(d)-2 Treatment of assumption of liabilities.

§ 1.1031(e)-1 Exchanges of livestock of different sexes.

§ 1.1031(j)-1 Exchanges of multiple properties.

(a) Introduction.
(b) Computation of gain recognized.
(c) Computation of basis of properties received.
(d) Examples.
(e) Effective date.

§ 1.1031(K)-1 Treatment of deferred exchanges.

(a) Overview.

(b) Identification and receipt requirements.
(c) Identification of replacement property before the end of the identification period.
(d) Receipt of identified replacement property.
(e) Special rules for identification and receipt of replacement property to be produced.
(f) Receipt of money or other property.
(g) Safe harbors.
(h) Interest and growth factors.
(i) [Reserved]
(j) Determination of gain or loss recognized and the basis of property received in a deferred exchange.
(k) Definition of disqualified person.
(l) [Reserved]
(m) Definition of fair market value.
(n) No inference with respect to actual or constructive receipt rules outside of section 1031.
(o) Effective date.

Par. 3. Section 1.1031(a)-1 is amended by adding headings for paragraphs (a), (b), (c), and (d), by revising paragraph (a), and by adding paragraph (e) to read as follows:

§ 1.1031(a)-1 Property held for productive use in a trade or business or for investment.

(a) In general—(1) Exchanges of property solely for property of a like kind. Section 1031(a)(1) provides an exception from the general rule requiring the recognition of gain or loss upon the sale or exchange of property. Under section 1031(a)(1), no gain or loss is recognized if property held for productive use in a trade or business or for investment is exchanged solely for property of a like kind to be held either for productive use in a trade or business or for investment. Under section 1031(a)(1), property held for productive use in a trade or business may be exchanged for property held for investment. Similarly, under section 1031(a)(1), property held for investment may be exchanged for property held for productive use in a trade or business. However, section 1031(a)(2) provides that section 1031(a)(1) does not apply to any exchange of—
(i) Stock in trade or other property held primarily for sale;
(ii) Stocks, bonds, or notes;
(iii) Other securities or evidences of indebtedness or interest;
(iv) Interests in a partnership;
(v) Certificates of trust or beneficial interests; or
(vi) Choses in action.
Section 1031(a)(1) does not apply to any exchange of interests in a partnership regardless of whether the interests exchanged are general or limited partnership interests or are interests in the same partnership or in different partnerships. An interest in a partnership that has in effect a valid

election under section 761(a) to be excluded from the application of all of subchapter K is treated as an interest in each of the assets of the partnership and not as an interest in a partnership for purposes of section 1031(a)(2)(D) and paragraph (a)(1)(iv) of this section. An exchange of an interest in such a partnership does not qualify for nonrecognition of gain or loss under section 1031 with respect to any asset of the partnership that is described in section 1031(a)(2) or to the extent the exchange of assets of the partnership does not otherwise satisfy the requirements of section 1031(a).

(2) Exchanges of property not solely for property of a like kind. A transfer is not within the provisions of section 1031(a) if, as part of the consideration, the taxpayer receives money or property which does not meet the requirements of section 1031(a), but the transfer, if otherwise qualified, will be within the provisions of either section 1031 (b) or (c). Similarly, a transfer is not within the provisions of section 1031(a) if, as part of the consideration, the other party to the exchange assumes a liability of the taxpayer (or acquires property from a taxpayer that is subject to a liability), but the transfer, if otherwise qualified, will be within the provisions of either section 1031 (b) or (c). A transfer of property meeting the requirements of section 1031(a) may be within the provisions of section 1031(a) even though the taxpayer transfers in addition property not meeting the requirements of section 1031(a) or money. However, the nonrecognition treatment provided by section 1031(a) does not apply to the property transferred which does not meet the requirements of section 1031(a).

(b) Definition of "like kind." * * *
(c) Examples of exchanges of property of a "like kind." * * *
(d) Examples of exchanges not solely in kind. * * *
(e) Effective date relating to exchanges of partnership interests. The provisions of paragraph (a)(1) of this section relating to exchanges of partnership interests apply to transfers of property made by taxpayers on or after April 25, 1991.

Par. 3a. A new § 1.1031(b)-2 is added to read as follows:

§ 1.1031(b)-2 Safe harbor for qualified intermediaries.

(a) In the case of simultaneous transfers of like-kind properties involving a qualified intermediary (as defined in § 1.1031(k)-1(g)(4)(iii)), the qualified intermediary is not considered the agent of the taxpayer for purposes of section 1031(a). In such a case, the transfer and receipt of property by the taxpayer is treated as an exchange.

(b) This section applies to transfers of property made by taxpayers on or after June 10, 1991.

Par. 4. A new § 1.1031(k)-1 is added to read as follows:

§ 1.1031(k)-1 Treatment of deferred exchanges.

(a) *Overview.* This section provides rules for the application of section 1031 and the regulations thereunder in the case of a "deferred exchange." For purposes of section 1031 and this section, a deferred exchange is defined as an exchange in which, pursuant to an agreement, the taxpayer transfers property held for productive use in a trade or business or for investment (the "relinquished property") and subsequently receives property to be held either for productive use in a trade or business or for investment (the "replacement property"). In the case of a deferred exchange, if the requirements set forth in paragraphs (b), (c), and (d) of this section (relating to identification and receipt of replacement property) are not satisfied, the replacement property received by the taxpayer will be treated as property which is not of a like kind to the relinquished property. In order to constitute a deferred exchange, the transaction must be an exchange (i.e., a transfer of property for property, as distinguished from a transfer of property for money). For example, a sale of property followed by a purchase of property of a like kind does not qualify for nonrecognition of gain or loss under section 1031 regardless of whether the identification and receipt requirements of section 1031(a)(3) and paragraphs (b), (c), and (d) of this section are satisfied. The transfer of relinquished property in a deferred exchange is not within the provisions of section 1031(a) if, as part of the consideration, the taxpayer receives money or property which does not meet the requirements of section 1031(a), but the transfer, if otherwise qualified, will be within the provisions of either section 1031 (b) or (c). See § 1.1031(a)-1(a)(2). In addition, in the case of a transfer of relinquished property in a deferred exchange, gain or loss may be recognized if the taxpayer actually or constructively receives money or property which does not meet the requirements of section 1031(a) before the taxpayer actually receives like-kind replacement property. If the taxpayer actually or constructively receives money or property which does not meet the requirements of section 1031(a) in the full amount of the consideration for the relinquished

property, the transaction will constitute a sale, and not a deferred exchange, even though the taxpayer may ultimately receive like-kind replacement property. For purposes of this section, property which does not meet the requirements of section 1031(a) (whether by being described in section 1031(a)(2) or otherwise) is referred to as "other property." For rules regarding actual and constructive receipt, and safe harbors therefrom, see paragraphs (f) and (g), respectively, of this section. For rules regarding the determination of gain or loss recognized and the basis of property received in a deferred exchange, see paragraph (j) of this section.

(b) *Identification and receipt requirements*—(1) *In general.* In the case of a deferred exchange, any replacement property received by the taxpayer will be treated as property which is not of a like kind to the relinquished property if—

(i) The replacement property is not "identified" before the end of the "identification period," or

(ii) The identified replacement property is not received before the end of the "exchange period."

(2) *Identification period and exchange period.* (i) The identification period begins on the date the taxpayer transfers the relinquished property and ends at midnight on the 45th day thereafter.

(ii) The exchange period begins on the date the taxpayer transfers the relinquished property and ends at midnight on the earlier of the 180th day thereafter or the due date (including extensions) for the taxpayer's return of the tax imposed by chapter 1 of subtitle A of the Code for the taxable year in which the transfer of the relinquished property occurs.

(iii) If, as part of the same deferred exchange, the taxpayer transfers more than one relinquished property and the relinquished properties are transferred on different dates, the identification period and the exchange period are determined by reference to the earliest date on which any of the properties are transferred.

(iv) For purposes of this paragraph (b)(2), property is transferred when the property is disposed of within the meaning of section 1001(a).

(3) *Example.* This paragraph (b) may be illustrated by the following example.

Example. (i) M is a corporation that files its Federal income tax return on a calendar year basis. M and C enter into an agreement for an exchange of property that requires M to transfer property X to C. Under the agreement, M is to identify like-kind replacement property which C is required to

purchase and to transfer to M. M transfers property X to C on November 16, 1992.

(ii) The identification period ends at midnight on December 31, 1992, the day which is 45 days after the date of transfer of property X. The exchange period ends at midnight on March 15, 1993, the due date for M's Federal income tax return for the taxable year in which M transferred property X. However, if M is allowed the automatic six-month extension for filing its tax return, the exchange period ends at midnight on May 15, 1993, the day which is 180 days after the date of transfer of property X.

(c) *Identification of replacement property before the end of the identification period*—(1) *In general.* For purposes of paragraph (b)(1)(i) of this section (relating to the identification requirement), replacement property is identified before the end of the identification period only if the requirements of this paragraph (c) are satisfied with respect to the replacement property. However, any replacement property that is received by the taxpayer before the end of the identification period will in all events be treated as identified before the end of the identification period.

(2) *Manner of identifying replacement property.* Replacement property is identified only if it is designated as replacement property in a written document signed by the taxpayer and hand delivered, mailed, telecopied, or otherwise sent before the end of the identification period to either—

(i) The person obligated to transfer the replacement property to the taxpayer (regardless of whether that person is a disqualified person as defined in paragraph (k) of this section); or

(ii) Any other person involved in the exchange other than the taxpayer or a disqualified person (as defined in paragraph (k) of this section).

Examples of persons involved in the exchange include any of the parties to the exchange, an intermediary, an escrow agent, and a title company. An identification of replacement property made in a written agreement for the exchange of properties signed by all parties thereto before the end of the identification period will be treated as satisfying the requirements of this paragraph (c)(2).

(3) *Description of replacement property.* Replacement property is identified only if it is unambiguously described in the written document or agreement. Real property generally is unambiguously described if it is described by a legal description, street address, or distinguishable name (e.g., the Mayfair Apartment Building). Personal property generally is unambiguously described if it is

Federal Register / Vol. 56, No. 84 / Wednesday, May 1, 1991 / Rules and Regulations   **19939**

described by a specific description of the particular type of property. For example, a truck generally is unambiguously described if it is described by a specific make, model, and year.

(4) *Alternative and multiple properties.* (i) The taxpayer may identify more than one replacement property. Regardless of the number of relinquished properties transferred by the taxpayer as part of the same deferred exchange, the maximum number of replacement properties that the taxpayer may identify is—

(A) Three properties without regard to the fair market values of the properties (the "3-property rule"), or

(B) Any number of properties as long as the aggregate fair market value as of the end of the identification period does not exceed 200 percent of the aggregate fair market value of all the relinquished properties as of the date the relinquished properties were transferred by the taxpayer (the "200-percent rule").

(ii) If, as of the end of the identification period, the taxpayer has identified more properties as replacement properties than permitted by paragraph (c)(4)(i) of this section, the taxpayer is treated as if no replacement property had been identified. The preceding sentence will not apply, however, and an identification satisfying the requirements of paragraph (c)(4)(i) of this section will be considered made, with respect to—

(A) Any replacement property received by the taxpayer before the end of the identification period, and

(B) Any replacement property identified before the end of the identification period and received before the end of the exchange period, but only if the taxpayer receives before the end of the exchange period identified replacement property the fair market vlaue of which is at least 95 percent of the aggregate fair market value of all identified replacement properties (the "95-percent rule").

For this purpose, the fair market value of each identified replacement property is determined as of the earlier of the date the property is received by the taxpayer or the last day of the exchange period.

(iii) For purposes of applying the 3-property rule, the 200-percent rule, and the 95-percent rule, all identifications of replacement property, other than identifications of replacement property that have been revoked in the manner provided in paragraph (c)(6) of this section, are taken into account. For example, if, in a deferred exchange, B transfers property X with a fair market

value of $100,000 to C and B receives like-kind property Y with a fair market value of $50,000 before the end of the identification period, under paragraph (c)(1) of this section, property Y is treated as identified by reason of being received before the end of the identification period. Thus, under paragraph (c)(4)(i) of this section, B may identify either two additional replacement properties of any fair market value or any number of additional replacement properties as long as the aggregate fair market value of the additional replacement properties does not exceed $150,000.

(5) *Incidental property disregarded.* (i) Solely for purposes of applying this paragraph (c), property that is incidental to a larger item of property is not treated as property that is separate from the larger item of property. Property is incidental to a larger item of property if—

(A) In standard commercial transactions, the property is typically transferred together with the larger item of property, and

(B) The aggregate fair market value of all of the incidental property does not exceed 15 percent of the aggregate fair market value of the larger item of property.

(ii) This paragraph (c)(5) may be illustrated by the following examples.

Example 1. For purposes of paragraph (c) of this section, a spare tire and tool kit will not be treated as separate property from a truck with a fair market value of $10,000, if the aggregate fair market value of the spare tire and tool kit does not exceed $1,500. For purposes of the 3-property rule, the truck, spare tire, and tool kit are treated as 1 property. Moreover, for purposes of paragraph (c)(3) of this section (relating to the description of replacement property), the truck, spare tire, and tool kit are all considered to be unambiguously described if the make, model, and year of the truck are specified, even if no reference is made to the spare tire and tool kit.

Example 2. For purposes of paragraph (c) of this section, furniture, laundry machines, and other miscellaneous items of personal property will not be treated as separate property from an apartment building with a fair market value of $1,000,000, if the aggregate fair market value of the furniture, laundry machines, and other personal property does not exceed $150,000. For purposes of the 3-property rule, the apartment building, furniture, laundry machines, and other personal property are treated as 1 property. Moreover, for purposes of paragraph (c)(3) of this section (relating to the description of replacement property), the apartment building, furniture, laundry machines, and other personal property are all considered to be unambiguously described if the legal description, street address, or distinguishable name of the apartment building is specified, even if no reference is

made to the furniture, laundry machines, and other personal property.

(6) *Revocation of identification.* An identification of replacement property may be revoked at any time before the end of the identification period. An identification of replacement property is revoked only if the revocation is made in a written document signed by the taxpayer and hand delivered, mailed, telecopied, or otewise sent before the end of the identification period to the person to whom the identification of the replacement property was sent. An identification of replacement property that is made in a written agreement for the exchange of properties is treated as revoked only if the revocation is made in a written amendment to the agreement or in a written document signed by the taxpayer and hand delivered, mailed, telecopied, or otewise sent before the end of the identification period to all of the parties to the agreement.

(7) *Examples.* This paragraph (c) may be illustrated by the following examples. Unless otherwise provided in an example, the following facts are assumed: B, a calendar year taxpayer, and C agree to enter into a deferred exchange. Pursuant to their agreement, B transfers real property X to C on May 17, 1991. Real property X, which has been held by B for investment, is unencumbered and has a fair market value on May 17, 1991, of $100,000. On or before July 1, 1991 (the end of the identification period), B is to identify replacement property that is of a like kind to real property X. On or before November 13, 1991 (the end of the exchange period), C is required to purchase the property identified by B and to transfer that property to B. To the extent the fair market value of the replacement property transferred to B is greater or less than the fair market value of real property X, either B or C, as applicable, will make up the difference by paying cash to the other party after the date the replacement property is received by B. No replacement property is identified in the agreement. When subsequently identified, the replacement property is described by legal description and is of a like kind to real property X (determined without regard to section 1031(a)(3) and this section). B intends to hold the replacement property received for investment.

Example 1. (i) On July 2, 1991, B identifies real property E as replacement property by designating real property E as replacement property in a written document signed by B and personally delivered to C.

(ii) Because the identification was made after the end of the identification period, pursuant to paragraph (b)(1)(i) of this section (relating to the identification requirement), real property E is treated as property which is not of a like kind to real property X.

Example 2. (i) C is a corporation of which 20 percent of the outstanding stock is owned by B. On July 1, 1991, B identifies real property F as replacement property by designating real property F as replacement property in a written document signed by B and mailed to C.

(ii) Because C is the person obligated to transfer the replacement property to B, real property F is identified before the end of the identification period. The fact that C is a "disqualified person" as defined in paragraph (k) of this section does not change this result.

(iii) Real property F would also have been treated as identified before the end of the identification period if, instead of sending the identification to C, B had designated real property F as replacement property in a written agreement for the exchange of properties signed by all parties thereto on or before July 1, 1991.

Example 3. (i) On June 3, 1991, B identifies the replacement property as "unimproved land located in Hood County with a fair market value not to exceed $100,000." The designation is made in a written document signed by B and personally delivered to C. On July 8, 1991, B and C agree that real property G is the property described in the June 3, 1991 document.

(ii) Because real property G was not unambiguously described before the end of the identification period, no replacement property is identified before the end of the identification period.

Example 4. (i) On June 28, 1991, B identifies real properties H, J, and K as replacement properties by designating these properties as replacement properties in a written document signed by B and personally delivered to C. The written document provides that by August 1, 1991, B will orally inform C which of the identified properties C is to transfer to B. As of July 1, 1991, the fair market values of real properties H, J, and K are $75,000, $100,000, and $125,000, respectively.

(ii) Because B did not identify more than three properties as replacement properties, the requirements of the 3-property rule are satisfied, and real properties H, J, and K are all identified before the end of the identification period.

Example 5. (i) On May 17, 1991, B identifies real properties L, M, N, and P as replacement properties by designating these properties as replacement properties in a written document signed by B and personally delivered to C. The written document provides that by July 2, 1991, B will orally inform C which of the identified properties C is to transfer to B. As of July 1, 1991, the fair market values of real properties L, M, N, and P are $30,000, $40,000, $50,000, and $60,000, respectively.

(ii) Although B identified more than three properties as replacement properties, the aggregate fair market value of the identified properties as of the end of the identification period ($180,000) did not exceed 200 percent of the aggregate fair market value of real property X (200% × $100,000 = $200,000). Therefore, the requirements of the 200-percent rule are satisfied, and real properties

L, M, N, and P are all identified before the end of the identification period.

Example 6. (i) On June 21, 1991, B identifies real properties Q, R, and S as replacement properties by designating these properties as replacement properties in a written document signed by B and mailed to C. On June 24, 1991, B identifies real properties T and U as replacement properties in a written document signed by B and mailed to C. On June 28, 1991, B revokes the identification of real properties Q and R in a written document signed by B and personally delivered to C.

(ii) B has revoked the identification of real properties Q and R in the manner provided by paragraph (c)(6) of this section. Identifications of replacement property that have been revoked in the manner provided by paragraph (c)(6) of this section are not taken into account for purposes of applying the 3-property rule. Thus, as of June 28, 1991, B has identified only replacement properties S, T, and U for purposes of the 3-property rule. Because B did not identify more than three properties as replacement properties for purposes of the 3-property rule, the requirements of that rule are satisfied, and real properties S, T, and U are all identified before the end of the identification period.

Example 7. (i) On May 20, 1991, B identifies real properties V and W as replacement properties by designating these properties as replacement properties in a written document signed by B and personally delivered to C. On June 4, 1991, B identifies real properties Y and Z as replacement properties in the same manner. On June 5, 1991, B telephones C and orally revokes the identification of real properties V and W. As of July 1, 1991, the fair market values of real properties V, W, Y, and Z are $50,000, $70,000, $90,000, and $100,000, respectively. On July 31, 1991, C purchases real properties Y and Z and transfers them to B.

(ii) Pursuant to paragraph (c)(6) of this section (relating to revocation of identification), the oral revocation of the identification of real properties V and W is invalid. Thus, the identification of real properties V and W is taken into account for purposes of determining whether the requirements of paragraph (c)(4) of this section (relating to the identification of alternative and multiple properties) are satisfied. Because B identified more than three properties and the aggregate fair market value of the identified properties as of the end of the identification period ($310,000) exceeds 200 percent of the fair market value of real property X (200% × $100,000 = $200,000), the requirements of paragraph (c)(4) of this section are not satisfied, and B is treated as if B did not identify any replacement property.

(d) *Receipt of identified replacement property*—(1) *In general.* For purposes of paragraph (b)(1)(ii) of this section (relating to the receipt requirement), the identified replacement property is received before the end of the exchange period only if the requirements of this paragraph (d) are satisfied with respect to the replacement property. In the case of a deferred exchange, the identified

replacement property is received before the end of the exchange period if—

(i) The taxpayer receives the replacement property before the end of the exchange period, and

(ii) The replacement property received is substantially the same property as identified.

If the taxpayer has identified more than one replacement property, section 1031(a)(3)(B) and this paragraph (d) are applied separately to each replacement property.

(2) *Examples.* This paragraph (d) may be illustrated by the following examples. The following facts are assumed: B, a calendar year taxpayer, and C agree to enter into a deferred exchange. Pursuant to their agreement, B transfers real property X to C on May 17, 1991. Real property X, which has been held by B for investment, is unencumbered and has a fair market value on May 17, 1991, of $100,000. On or before July 1, 1991 (the end of the identification period), B is to identify replacement property that is of a like kind to real property X. On or before November 13, 1991 (the end of the exchange period), C is required to purchase the property identified by B and to transfer that property to B. To the extent the fair market value of the replacement property transferred to B is greater or less than the fair market value of real property X, either B or C, as applicable, will make up the difference by paying cash to the other party after the date the replacement property is received by B. The replacement property is identified in a manner that satisfies paragraph (c) of this section (relating to identification of replacement property) and is of a like kind to real property X (determined without regard to section 1031(a)(3) and this section). B intends to hold any replacement property received for investment.

Example 1. (i) In the agreement, B identifies real properties J, K, and L as replacement properties. The agreement provides that by July 26, 1991, B will orally inform C which of the properties C is to transfer to B.

(ii) As of July 1, 1991, the fair market values of real properties J, K, and L are $75,000, $100,000, and $125,000, respectively. On July 26, 1991, B instructs C to acquire real property K. On October 31, 1991, C purchases real property K for $100,000 and transfers the property to B.

(iii) Because real property K was identified before the end of the identification period and was received before the end of the exchange period, the identification and receipt requirements of section 1031(a)(3) and this section are satisfied with respect to real property K.

Example 2. (i) In the agreement, B identifies real property P as replacement property. Real property P consists of two acres of unimproved land. On October 15, 1991, the owner of real property P erects a fence on the property. On November 1, 1991, C purchases real property P and transfers it to B.

(ii) The erection of the fence on real property P subsequent to its identification did not alter the basic nature or character of real property P as unimproved land. P is considered to have received substantially the same property as identified.

Example 3. (i) In the agreement, B identifies real property Q as replacement property. Real property Q consists of a barn on two acres of land and has a fair market value of $250,900 ($187,500 for the barn and underlying land and $87,500 for the remaining land). As of July 26, 1991, real property Q remains unchanged and has a fair market value of $250,000. On that date, at B's direction, C purchases the barn and underlying land for $187,500 and transfers it to B, and B pays $87,500 to C.

(ii) The barn and underlying land differ in basic nature or character from real property Q as a whole. B is not considered to have received substantially the same property as identified.

Example 4. (i) In the agreement, B identifies real property R as replacement property. Real property R consists of two acres of unimproved land and has a fair market value of $250,000. As of October 3, 1991, real property R remains unimproved and has a fair market value of $250,000. On that date, at B's direction, C purchases 1½ acres of real property R for $187,500 and transfers it to B, and B pays $87,500 to C.

(ii) The portion of real property R that B received does not differ from the basic nature or character of real property R as a whole. Moreover, the fair market value of the portion of real property R that B received ($187,500) is 75 percent of the fair market value of real property R as of the date of receipt. Accordingly, B is considered to have received substantially the same property as identified.

(e) *Special rules for identification and receipt of replacement property to be produced*—(1) *In general.* A transfer of relinquished property in a deferred exchange will not fail to qualify for nonrecognition of gain or loss under section 1031 merely because the replacement property is not in existence or is being produced at the time the property is identified as replacement property. For purposes of this paragraph (e), the terms "produced" and "production" have the same meanings as provided in section 263A(g)(1) and the regulations thereunder.

(2) *Identification of replacement property to be produced.* (i) In the case of replacement property that is to be produced, the replacement property must be identified as provided in paragraph (c) of this section (relating to identification of replacement property). For example, if the identified replacement property consists of improved real property where the improvements are to be constructed, the description of the replacement property

satisfies the requirements of paragraph (c)(3) of this section (relating to description of replacement property) if a legal description is provided for the underlying land and as much detail is provided regarding construction of the improvements as is practicable at the time the identification is made.

(ii) For purposes of paragraphs (c)(4)(i)(B) and (c)(5) of this section (relating to the 200-percent rule and incidental property), the fair market value of replacement property that is to be produced is its estimated fair market value as of the date it is expected to be received by the taxpayer.

(3) *Receipt of replacement property to be produced.* (i) For purposes of paragraph (d)(1)(ii) of this section (relating to receipt of the identified replacement property), in determining whether the replacement property received by the taxpayer is substantially the same property as identified where the identified replacement property is property to be produced, variations due to usual or typical production changes are not taken into account. However, if substantial changes are made in the property to be produced, the replacement property received will not be considered to be substantially the same property as identified.

(ii) If the identified replacement property is personal property to be produced, the replacement property received will not be considered to be substantially the same property as identified unless production of the replacement property received is completed on or before the date the property is received by the taxpayer.

(iii) If the identified replacement property is real property to be produced and the production of the property is not completed on or before the date the taxpayer receives the property, the property received will be considered to be substantially the same property as identified only if, had production been completed on or before the date the taxpayer receives the replacement property, the property received would have been considered to be substantially the same property as identified. Even so, the property received is considered to be substantially the same property as identified only to the extent the property received constitutes real property under local law.

(4) *Additional rules.* The transfer of relinquished property is not within the provisions of section 1031(a) if the relinquished property is transferred in exchange for services (including production services). Thus, any additional production occurring with respect to the replacement property

after the property is received by the taxpayer will not be treated as the receipt of property of a like kind.

(5) *Example.* This paragraph (e) may be illustrated by the following example.

Example. (i) B, a calendar year taxpayer, and C agree to enter into a deferred exchange. Pursuant to their agreement, B transfers improved real property X and personal property Y to C on May 17, 1991. On or before November 13, 1991 (the end of the exchange period), C is required to transfer to B real property M, on which C is constructing improvements, and personal property N, which C is producing. C is obligated to complete the improvements and production regardless of when properties M and N are transferred to B. Properties M and N are identified in a manner that satisfies paragraphs (c) (relating to identification of replacement property) and (e)(2) of this section. In addition, properties M and N are of a like kind, respectively, to real property X and personal property Y (determined without regard to section 1031(a)(3) and this section). On November 13, 1991, when construction of the improvements to property M is 20 percent completed and the production of property N is 90 percent completed, C transfers to B property M and property N. If construction of the improvements had been completed, property M would have been considered to be substantially the same property as identified. Under local law, property M constitutes real property to the extent of the underlying land and the 20 percent of the construction that is completed.

(ii) Because property N is personal property to be produced and production of property N is not completed before the date the property is received by B, property N is not considered to be substantially the same property as identified and is treated as property which is not of a like kind to property Y.

(iii) Property M is considered to be substantially the same property as identified to the extent of the underlying land and the 20 percent of the construction that is completed when property M is received by B. However, any additional construction performed by C with respect to property M after November 13, 1991, is not treated as the receipt of property of a like kind.

(f) *Receipt of money or other property*—(1) *In general.* A transfer of relinquished property in a deferred exchange is not within the provisions of section 1031(a) if, as part of the consideration, the taxpayer receives money or other property. However, such a transfer, if otherwise qualified, will be within the provisions of either section 1031 (b) or (c). See § 1031(a)–1(a)(2). In addition, in the case of a transfer of relinquished property in a deferred exchange, gain or loss may be recognized if the taxpayer actually or constructively receives money or other property before the taxpayer actually receives like-kind replacement property. If the taxpayer actually or constructively receives money or other property in the

19942   **Federal Register** / Vol. 56, No. 84 / Wednesday, May 1, 1991 / Rules and Regulations

full amount of the consideration for the relinquished property before the taxpayer actually receives like-kind replacement property, the transaction will constitute a sale and not a deferred exchange, even though the taxpayer may ultimately receive like-kind replacement property.

(2) *Actual and constructive receipt.* Except as provided in paragraph (g) of this section (relating to safe harbors), for purposes of section 1031 and this section, the determination of whether (or the extent to which) the taxpayer is in actual or constructive receipt of money or other property before the taxpayer actually receives like-kind replacement property is made under the general rules concerning actual and constructive receipt and without regard to the taxpayer's method of accounting. The taxpayer is in actual receipt of money or property at the time the taxpayer actually receives the money or property or receives the economic benefit of the money or property. The taxpayer is in constructive receipt of money or property at the time the money or property is credited to the taxpayer's account, set apart for the taxpayer, or otherwise made available so that the taxpayer may draw upon it at any time or so that the taxpayer can draw upon it if notice of intention to draw is given. Although the taxpayer is not in constructive receipt of money or property if the taxpayer's control of its receipt is subject to substantial limitations or restrictions, the taxpayer is in constructive receipt of the money or property at the time the limitations or restrictions lapse, expire, or are waived. In addition, actual or constructive receipt of money or property by an agent of the taxpayer (determined without regard to paragraph (k) of this section) is actual or constructive receipt by the taxpayer.

(3) *Example.* This paragraph (f) may be illustrated by the following example.

Example. (i) B, a calendar year taxpayer, and C agree to enter into a deferred exchange. Pursuant to the agreement, on May 17, 1991, B transfers real property X to C. Real property X, which has been held by B for investment, is unencumbered and has a fair market value on May 17, 1991, of $100,000. On or before July 1, 1991 (the end of the identification period), B is to identify replacement property that is of a like kind to real property X. On or before November 13, 1991 (the end of the exchange period), C is required to purchase the property identified by B and to transfer that property to B. At any time after May 17, 1991, and before C has purchased the replacement property, B has the right, upon notice, to demand that C pay $100,000 in lieu of acquiring and transferring the replacement property. Pursuant to the agreement, B identifies replacement property,

and C purchases the replacement property and transfers it to B.

(ii) Under the agreement, B has the unrestricted right to demand the payment of $100,000 as of May 17, 1991. B is therefore in constructive receipt of $100,000 on that date. Because B is in constructive receipt of money in the full amount of the consideration for the relinquished property before B actually receives the like-kind replacement property, the transaction constitutes a sale, and the transfer of real property X does not qualify for nonrecognition of gain or loss under section 1031. B is treated as if B received the $100,000 in consideration for the sale of real property X and then purchased the like-kind replacement property.

(iii) If B's right to demand payment of the $100,000 were subject to a substantial limitation or restriction (e.g., the agreement provided that B had no right to demand payment before November 14, 1991 (the end of the exchange period)), then, for purposes of this section, B would not be in actual or constructive receipt of the money unless (or until) the limitation or restriction lapsed, expired, or was waived.

(g) *Safe harbors*—(1) *In general.* Paragraphs (g)(2) through (g)(5) of this section set forth four safe harbors the use of which will result in a determination that the taxpayer is not in actual or constructive receipt of money or other property for purposes of section 1031 and this section. More than one safe harbor can be used in the same deferred exchange, but the terms and conditions of each must be separately satisfied. For purposes of the safe harbor rules, the term "taxpayer" does not include a person or entity utilized in a safe harbor (e.g., a qualified intermediary). See paragraph (g)(8), *Example 3(v),* of this section.

(2) *Security or guarantee arrangements.* (i) In the case of a deferred exchange, the determination of whether the taxpayer is in actual or constructive receipt of money or other property before the taxpayer actually receives like-kind replacement property will be made without regard to the fact that the obligation of the taxpayer's transferee to transfer the replacement property to the taxpayer is or may be secured or guaranteed by one or more of the following—

(A) A mortgage, deed of trust, or other security interest in property (other than cash or a cash equivalent),

(B) A standby letter of credit which satisfies all of the requirements of § 15A.453–1 (b)(3)(iii) and which may not be drawn upon in the absence of a default of the transferee's obligation to transfer like-kind replacement property to the taxpayer, or

(C) A guarantee of a third party.

(ii) Paragraph (g)(2)(i) of this section ceases to apply at the time the taxpayer has an immediate ability or unrestricted

right to receive money or other property pursuant to the security or guarantee arrangement.

(3) *Qualified escrow accounts and qualified trusts.* (i) In the case of a deferred exchange, the determination of whether the taxpayer is in actual or constructive receipt of money or other property before the taxpayer actually receives like-kind replacement property will be made without regard to the fact that the obligation of the taxpayer's transferee to transfer the replacement property to the taxpayer is or may be secured by cash or a cash equivalent if the cash or cash equivalent is held in a qualified escrow account or in a qualified trust.

(ii) A qualified escrow account is an escrow account wherein—

(A) The escrow holder is not the taxpayer or a disqualified person (as defined in paragraph (k) of this section), and

(B) The escrow agreement expressly limits the taxpayer's rights to receive, pledge, borrow, or otherwise obtain the benefits of the cash or cash equivalent held in the escrow account as provided in paragraph (g)(6) of this section.

(iii) A qualified trust is a trust wherein—

(A) The trustee is not the taxpayer or a disqualified person (as defined in paragraph (k) of this section, except that for this purpose the relationship between the taxpayer and the trustee created by the qualified trust will not be considered a relationship under section 267(b)), and

(B) The trust agreement expressly limits the taxpayer's rights to receive, pledge, borrow, or otherwise obtain the benefits of the cash or cash equivalent held by the trustee as provided in paragraph (g)(6) of this section.

(iv) Paragraph (g)(3)(i) of this section ceases to apply at the time the taxpayer has an immediate ability or unrestricted right to receive, pledge, borrow, or otherwise obtain the benefits of the cash or cash equivalent held in the qualified escrow account or qualified trust. Rights conferred upon the taxpayer under state law to terminate or dismiss the escrow holder of a qualified escrow account or the trustee of a qualified trust are disregarded for this purpose.

(v) A taxpayer may receive money or other property directly from a party to the exchange, but not from a qualified escrow account or a qualified trust, without affecting the application of paragraph (g)(3)(i) of this section.

(4) *Qualified intermediaries.* (i) In the case of a taxpayer's transfer of relinquished property involving a qualified intermediary, the qualified

intermediary is not considered the agent of the taxpayer for purposes of section 1031(a). In such a case, the taxpayer's transfer of relinquished property and subsequent receipt of like-kind replacement property is treated as an exchange, and the determination of whether the taxpayer is in actual or constructive receipt of money or other property before the taxpayer actually receives like-kind replacement property is made as if the qualified intermediary is not the agent of the taxpayer.

(ii) Paragraph (g)(4)(i) of this section applies only if the agreement between the taxpayer and the qualified intermediary expressly limits the taxpayer's rights to receive, pledge, borrow, or otherwise obtain the benefits of money or other property held by the qualified intermediary as provided in paragraph (g)(6) of this section.

(iii) A qualified intermediary is a person who—

(A) Is not the taxpayer or a disqualified person (as defined in paragraph (k) of this section), and

(B) Enters into a written agreement with the taxpayer (the "exchange agreement") and, as required by the exchange agreement, acquires the relinquished property from the taxpayer, transfers the relinquished property, acquires the replacement property, and transfers the replacement property to the taxpayer.

(iv) Regardless of whether an intermediary acquires and transfers property under general tax principals, solely for purposes of paragraph (g)(4)(iii)(B) of this section—

(A) An intermediary is treated as acquiring and transferring property if the intermediary acquires and transfers legal title to that property,

(b) An intermediary is treated as acquiring and transferring the relinquished property if the intermediary (either on its own behalf or as the agent of any party to the transaction) enters into an agreement with a person other than the taxpayer for the transfer of the relinquished property to that person and, pursuant to that agreement, the relinquished property is transferred to that person, and

(C) An intermediary is treated as acquiring and transferring replacement property if the intermediary (either on its own behalf or as the agent of any party to the transaction) enters into an agreement with the owner of the replacement property for the transfer of that property and, pursuant to that agreement, the replacement property is transferred to the taxpayer.

(v) Solely for purposes of paragraphs (g)(4)(iii) and (g)(4)(iv) of this section, an intermediary is treated as entering into an agreement if the rights of a party to the agreement are assigned to the intermediary and all parties to that agreement are notified in writing of the assignment on or before the date of the relevent transfer of property. For example, if a taxpayer enters into an agreement for the transfer of relinquished property and thereafter assigns its rights in that agreement to an intermediary and all parties to that agreement are notified in writing of the assignment on or before the date of the transfer of the relinquished property, the intermediary is treated as entering into that agreement. If the relinquished property is transferred pursuant to that agreement, the intermediary is treated as having acquired and transferred the relinquished property.

(vi) Paragraph (g)(4)(i) of this section ceases to apply at the time the taxpayer has an immediate ability or unrestricted right to receive, pledge, borrow, or otherwise obtain the benefits of money or other property held by the qualified intermediary. Rights conferred upon the taxpayer under state law to terminate or dismiss the qualified intermediary are disregarded for this purpose.

(vii) A taxpayer may receive money or other property directly from a party to the transaction other than the qualified intermediary without affecting the application of paragraph (g)(4)(i) of this section.

(5) *Interest and growth factors.* In the case of a deferred exchange, the determination of whether the taxpayer is in actual or constructive receipt of money or other property before the taxpayer actually receives the like-kind replacement property will be made without regard to the fact that the taxpayer is or may be entitled to receive any interest or growth factor with respect to the deferred exchange. The preceding sentence applies only if the agreement pursuant to which the taxpayer is or may be entitled to the interest or growth factor expressly limits the taxpayer's rights to receive the interest or growth factor as provided in paragraph (g)(6) of this section. For additional rules concerning interest or growth factors, see paragraph (h) of this section.

(6) *Additional restrictions on safe harbors under paragraphs (g)(3) through (g)(5).* (i) An agreement limits a taxpayer's rights as provided in this paragraph (g)(6) only if the agreement provides that the taxpayer has no rights, except as provided in paragraph (g)(6)(ii) and (g)(6)(iii) of this section, to receive, pledge, borrow, or otherwise obtain the benefits of money or other property before the end of the exchange period.

(ii) The agreement may provide that if the taxpayer has not identified replacement property by the end of the identification period, the taxpayer may have rights to receive, pledge, borrow, or othewise obtain the benefits of money or other property at any time after the end of the identification period.

(iii) The agreement may provide that if the taxpayer has identified replacement property, the taxpayer may have rights to receive, pledge, borrow, or otherwise obtain the benefits of money or other property upon or after—

(A) The receipt by the taxpayer of all of the replacement property to which the taxpayer is entitled under the exchange agreement, or

(B) The occurrence after the end of the identification period of a material and substantial contingency that—

(1) Relates to the deferred exchange,

(2) Is provided for in writing, and

(3) Is beyond the control of the taxpayer and of any disqualified person (as defined in paragraph (k) of this section), other than the person obligated to transfer the replacement property to the taxpayer.

(7) *Items disregarded in applying safe harbors under paragraphs (g)(3) through (g)(5).* In determining whether a safe harbor under paragraphs (g)(3) through (g)(5) of this section ceases to apply and whether the taxpayer's rights to receive, pledge, borrow, or otherwise obtain the benefits of money or other property are expressly limited as provided in paragraph (g)(6) of this section, the taxpayer's receipt of or right to receive any of the following items will be disregarded—

(i) Items that a seller may receive as a consequence of the disposition of property and that are not included in the amount realized from the disposition of property (e.g., prorated rents), and

(ii) Transactional items that relate to the disposition of the relinquished property or to the acquisition of the replacement property and appear under local standards in the typical closing statements as the responsibility of a buyer or seller (e.g., commissions, prorated taxes, recording or transfer taxes, and title company fees).

(8) *Examples.* This paragraph (g) may be illustrated by the following examples. Unless otherwise provided in an example, the following facts are assumed: B, a calendar year taxpayer, and C agree to enter into a deferred exchange. Pursuant to their agreement, B is to transfer real property X to C on May 17, 1991. Real property X, which has been held by B for investment, is unencumbered and has a fair market value on May 17, 1991, of $100,000. On or

19944   **Federal Register** / Vol. 56, No. 84 / Wednesday, May 1, 1991 / Rules and Regulations

before July 1, 1991 (the end of the identification period), B is to identify replacement property that is of a like kind to real property X. On or before November 13, 1991 (the end of the exchange period), C is required to purchase the property identified by B and to transfer that property to B. To the extent the fair market value of the replacement property transferred to B is greater or less than the fair market value property X, either B or C, as applicable, will make up the difference by paying cash to the other party after the date the replacement property is received by B. The replacement property is identified as provided in paragraph (c) of this section (relating to identification of replacement property) and is of a like kind to real property X (determined without regard to section 1031(a)(3) and this section). B intends to hold any replacement property received for investment.

Example 1. (i) On May 17, 1991, B transfers real property X to C. On the same day, C pays $10,000 to B and deposits $90,000 in escrow as security for C's obligation to perform under the agreement. The escrow agreement provides that B has no rights to receive, pledge, borrow, or otherwise obtain the benefits of the money in escrow before November 14, 1991, except that:

(A) if B fails to identify replacement property on or before July 1, 1991, B may demand the funds in escrow at any time after July 1, 1991; and

(B) if B identifies and receives replacement property, then B may demand the balance of the remaining funds in escrow at any time after B has received the replacement property.

The funds in escrow may be used to purchase the replacement property. The escrow holder is not a disqualified person as defined in paragraph (k) of this section. Pursuant to the terms of the agreement, B identifies replacement property, and C purchases the replacement property using the funds in escrow and tranfers the replacement property to B.

(ii) C's obligation to transfer the replacement property to B was secured by cash held in a qualified escrow account because the escrow holder was not a disqualified person and the escrow agreement expressly limited B's rights to receive, pledge, borrow, or otherwise obtain the benefits of the money in escrow as provided in paragraph (g)(6) of this section. In addition, B did not have the immediate ability or unrestricted right to receive money or other property in escrow before B actually received the like-kind replacement property. Therefore, for purposes of section 1031 and this section, B is determined not to be in actual or constructive receipt of the $90,000 held in escrow before B received the like-kind replacement property. The transfer of real property X by B and B's acquisition of the replacement property qualify as an exchange under section 1031. See paragraph (j) of this section for determining the amount of gain or loss recognized.

Example 2. (i) On May 17, 1991, B transfers real property X to C, and C deposits $100,000 in escrow as security for C's obligation to perform under the agreement. Also on May 17, B identifies real property J as replacement property. The escrow agreement provides that no funds may be paid out without prior written approval of both B and C. The escrow agreement also provides that B has no rights to receive, pledge, borrow, or otherwise obtain the benefits of the money in escrow before November 14, 1991, except that:

(A) B may demand the funds in escrow at any time after the agreement of July 1, 1991, and the occurrence of any of the following events—

(1) real property J is destroyed, seized, requisitioned, or condemned, or

(2) a determination is made that the regulatory approval necessary for the transfer of real property J cannot be obtained in time for real property J to be transferred to B before the end of the exchange period;

(B) B may demand the funds in escrow at any time after August 14, 1991, if real property J has not been rezoned from residential to commercial use by that date; and

(C) B may demand the funds in escrow at the time B receives real property J or any time thereafter.

Otherwise, B is entitled to all funds in escrow after November 13, 1991. The funds in escrow may be used to purchase the replacement property. The escrow holder is not a disqualified person as described in paragraph (k) of this section. Real property J is not rezoned from residential to commercial use on or before August 14, 1991.

(ii) C's obligation to transfer the replacement property to B was secured by cash held in a qualified escrow account because the escrow holder was not a disqualified person and the escrow agreement expressly limited B's rights to receive, pledge, borrow, or otherwise obtain the benefits of the money in escrow as provided in paragraph (g)(6) of this section. From May 17, 1991, until August 15, 1991, B did not have the immediate ability or unrestricted right to receive money or other property before B actually received the like-kind replacement property. Therefore, for purposes of section 1031 and this section, B is determined not to be in actual or constructive receipt of the $100,000 in escrow from May 17, 1991, until August 15, 1991. However, on August 15, 1991, B had the unrestricted right, upon notice, to draw upon the $100,000 held in escrow. Thus, the safe harbor ceased to apply and B was in constructive receipt of funds held in escrow. Because B constructively received the full amount of the consideration ($100,000) before B actually received the like-kind replacement property, the transaction is treated as a sale and not as a deferred exchange. The result does not change even if B chose not to demand the funds in escrow and continued to attempt to have real property J rezoned and to receive the property on or before November 13, 1991.

(iii) If real property J had been rezoned on or before August 14, 1991, and C had purchased real property J and transferred it to B on or before November 13, 1991, the transaction would have qualified for nonrecognition of gain or loss under section 1031(a).

Example 3. (i) On May 1, 1991, D offers to purchase real property X for $100,000. However, D is unwilling to participate in a like-kind exchange. B thus enters into an exchange agreement with C whereby B retains C to facilitate an exchange with respect to real property X. C is not a disqualified person as described in paragraph (k) of this section. The exchange agreement between B and C provides that B is to execute and deliver a deed conveying real property X to C who, in turn, is to execute and deliver a deed conveying real property X to D. The exchange agreement expressly limits B's rights to receive, pledge, borrow, or otherwise obtain the benefits of money or other property held by C as provided in paragraph (g)(6) of this section. On May 3, 1991, C enters into an agreement with D to transfer real property X to D for $100,000. On May 17, 1991, B executes and delivers to C a deed conveying real property X to C. On the same date, C executes and delivers to D a deed conveying real property X to D, and D deposits $100,000 in escrow. The escrow holder is not a disqualified person as defined in paragraph (k) of this section and the escrow agreement expressly limits B's rights to receive, pledge, borrow, or otherwise obtain the benefits of money or other property in escrow as provided in paragraph (g)(6) of this section. However, the escrow agreement provides that the money in escrow may be used to purchase the replacement property. On June 3, 1991, B identifies real property K as replacement property. On August 9, 1991, E executes and delivers to C a deed conveying real property K to C and $80,000 is released from the escrow and paid to E. On the same date, C executes and delivers to B a deed conveying real property K to B, and the escrow holder pays B $20,000, the balance of the $100,000 sale price of real property X remaining after the purchase of real property K for $80,000.

(ii) B and C entered into an exchange agreement that satisfied the requirements of paragraph (g)(4)(iii)(B) of this section. Regardless of whether C may have acquired and transferred real property X under general tax principles, C is treated as having acquired and transferred real property X because C acquired and transferred legal title to real property X. Similarly, C is treated as having acquired and transferred real property K because C acquired and transferred legal title to real property K. Thus, C was a qualified intermediary. This result is reached for purposes of this section regardless of whether C was B's agent under state law.

(iii) Because the escrow holder was not a disqualified person and the escrow agreement expressly limited B's rights to receive, pledge, borrow, or otherwise obtain the benefits of money or other property in escrow as provided in paragraph (g)(6) of this section, the escrow account was a qualified escrow account. For purposes of section 1031 and this section, therefore, B is determined not to be in actual or constructive receipt of the funds in escrow before B received real property K.

(iv) The exchange agreement between B and C expressly limited B's rights to receive, pledge, borrow, or otherwise obtain the

Federal Register / Vol. 56, No. 84 / Wednesday, May 1, 1991 / Rules and Regulations **19945**

benefits of any money held by C as provided in paragraph (g)(6) of this section. Because C was a qualified intermediary, for purposes of section 1031 and this section B is determined not to be in actual or constructive receipt of any funds held by C before B received real property K. In addition, B's transfer of real property X and acquisition of real property K qualify as an exchange under section 1031. See paragraph (j) of this section for determining the amount of gain or loss recognized.

(v) If the escrow agreement had expressly limited C's rights to receive, pledge, borrow, or otherwise obtain the benefits of money or other property as provided in paragraph (g)(6) of this section, but had not expressly limited B's rights to receive, pledge, borrow, or otherwise obtain the benefits of that money or other property, the escrow account would not have been a qualified escrow account. Consequently, paragraph (g)(3)(i) of this section would not have been applicable in determining whether B was in actual or constructive receipt of that money or other property before B received real property K.

Example 4. (i) On May 1, 1991, B enters into an agreement to sell real property X to D for $100,000 on May 17, 1991. However, D is unwilling to participate in a like-kind exchange. B thus enters into an exchange agreement with C whereby B retains C to facilitate an exchange with respect to real property X. C is not a disqualified person as described in paragraph (k) of this section. In the exchange agreement between B and C, B assigns to C all of B's rights in the agreement with D. The exchange agreement expressly limits B's rights to receive, pledge, borrow, or otherwise obtain the benefits of money or other property held by C as provided in paragraph (g)(6) of this section. On May 17, 1991, B notifies D in writing of the assignment. On the same date, B executes and delivers to D a deed conveying real property X to D. D pays $10,000 to B and $90,000 to C. On June 1, 1991, B identifies real property L as replacement property. On July 5, 1991, B enters into an agreement to purchase real property L from E for $90,000, assigns its rights in that agreement to C, and notifies E in writing of the assignment. On August 9, 1991, C pays $90,000 to E, and E executes and delivers to B a deed conveying real property L to B.

(ii) The exchange agreement entered into by B and C satisfied the requirements of paragraph (g)(4)(iii)(B) of this section. Because B's rights in its agreements with D and E were assigned to C, and D and E were notified in writing of the assignment on or before the transfer of real properties X and L, respectively, C is treated as entering into those agreements. Because C is treated as entering into an agreement with D for the transfer of real property X and, pursuant to that agreement, real property X was transferred to D, C is treated as acquiring and transferring real property X. Similarly, because C is treated as entering into an agreement with E for the transfer of real property K and, pursuant to that agreement, real property K was transferred to B, C is treated as acquiring and transferring real property K. This result is reached for

purposes of this section regardless of whether C was B's agent under state law and regardless of whether C is considered, under general tax principles, to have acquired title or beneficial ownership of the properties. Thus, C was a qualified intermediary.

(iii) The exchange agreement between B and C expressly limited B's rights to receive, pledge, borrow, or otherwise obtain the benefits of the money held by C as provided in paragraph (g)(6) of this section. Thus, B did not have the immediate ability or unrestricted right to receive money or other property held by C before B received real property L. For purposes of section 1031 and this section, therefore, B is determined not to be in actual or constructive receipt of the $90,000 held by C before B received real property L. In addition, the transfer of real property X by B and B's acquisition of real property L qualify as an exchange under section 1031. See paragraph (j) of this section for determining the amount of gain or loss recognized.

Example 5. (i) On May 1, 1991, B enters into an agreement to sell real property X to D for $100,000. However, D is unwilling to participate in a like-kind exchange. B thus enters into an agreement with C whereby B retains C to facilitate an exchange with respect to real property X. C is not a disqualified person as described in paragraph (k) of this section. The agreement between B and C expressly limits C's rights to receive, pledge, borrow, or otherwise obtain the benefits of money or other property held by C as provided in paragraph (g)(6) of this section. C neither enters into an agreement with D to transfer real property X to D nor is assigned B's rights in B's agreement to sell real property X to D. On May 17, 1991, B transfers real property X to D and instructs D to transfer the $100,000 to C. On June 1, 1991, B identifies real property M as replacement property. On August 9, 1991, C purchases real property L from E for $100,000, and E executes and delivers to C a deed conveying real property M to C. On the same date, C executes and delivers to B a deed conveying real property M to B.

(ii) Because B transferred real property X directly to D under B's agreement with D, C did not acquire real property X from B and transfer real property X to D. Moreover, because C did not acquire legal title to real property X, did not enter into an agreement with D to transfer real property X to D, and was not assigned B's rights in B's agreement to sell real property X to D, C is not treated as acquiring and transferring real property X. Thus, C was not a qualified intermediary and paragraph (g)(4)(i) of this section does not apply.

(iii) B did not exchange real property X for real property M. Rather, B sold real property X to D and purchased, through C, real property M. Therefore, the transfer of real property X does not qualify for nonrecognition of gain or loss under section 1031.

(h) *Interest and growth factors*—(1) *In general.* For purposes of this section, the taxpayer is treated as being entitled to receive interest or a growth factor with respect to a deferred exchange if the amount of money or property the

taxpayer is entitled to receive depends upon the length of time elapsed between transfer of the relinquished property and receipt of the replacement property.

(2) *Treatment as interest.* If, as part of a deferred exchange, the taxpayer receives interest or a growth factor, the interest or growth factor will be treated as interest, regardless of whether it is paid to the taxpayer in cash or in property (including property of a like kind). The taxpayer must include the interest or growth factor in income according to the taxpayer's method of accounting.

(i) [Reserved]

(j) *Determination of gain or loss recognized and the basis of property received in a deferred exchange*—(1) *In general.* Except as otherwise provided, the amount of gain or loss recognized and the basis of property received in a deferred exchange is determined by applying the rules of section 1031 and the regulations thereunder. See §§ 1.1031(b)–1, 1.1031(c)–1, 1.1031(d)–1, 1.1031(d)–1T, 1.1031(d)–2, and 1.1031(j)–1.

(2) *Coordination with section 453.* [Reserved].

(3) *Examples.* This paragraph (j) may be illustrated by the following examples. Unless otherwise provided in an example, the following facts are assumed: B, a calendar year taxpayer, and C agree to enter into a deferred exchange. Pursuant to their agreement, B is to transfer real property X to C on May 17, 1991. Real property X, which has been held by B for investment, is unencumbered and has a fair market value on May 17, 1991, of $100,000. B's adjusted basis in real property X is $40,000. On or before July 1, 1991 (the end of the identification period), B is to identify replacement property that is of a like kind to real property X. On or before November 13, 1991 (the end of the exchange period), C is required to purchase the property identified by B and to transfer that property to B. To the extent the fair market value of the replacement property transferred to B is greater or less than the fair market value of real property X, either B or C, as applicable, will make up the difference by paying cash to the other party after the date the replacement property is received. The replacement property is identified as provided in paragraph (c) of this section and is of a like kind to real property X (determined without regard to section 1031(a)(3) and this section). B intends to hold any replacement property received for investment.

Example 1. (i) On May 17, 1991, B transfers real property X to C and identifies real

19946   Federal Register / Vol. 56, No. 84 / Wednesday, May 1, 1991 / Rules and Regulations

property R as replacement property. On June 3, 1991, C transfers $10,000 to B. On September 4, 1991, C purchases real property R for $90,000 and transfers real property R to B.

(ii) The $10,000 received by B is "money or other property" for purposes of section 1031 and the regulations thereunder. Under section 1031(b), B recognizes gain in the amount of $10,000. Under section 1031(d), B's basis in real property R is $40,000 (i.e., B's basis in real property X ($40,000), decreased in the amount of money received ($10,000), and increased in the amount of gain recognized ($10,000) in the deferred exchange).

Example 2. (i) On May 17, 1991, B transfers real property X to C and identifies real property S as replacement property, and C transfers $10,000 to B. On September 4, 1991, C purchases real property S for $100,000 and transfers real property S to B. On the same day, B transfers $10,000 to C.

(ii) The $10,000 received by B is "money or other property" for purposes of section 1031 and the regulations thereunder. Under section 1031(b), B recognizes gain in the amount of $10,000. Under section 1031(d), B's basis in real property S is $50,000 (i.e., B's basis in real property X ($40,000), decreased in the amount of money received ($10,000), increased in the amount of gain recognized ($10,000), and increased in the amount of the additional consideration paid by B ($10,000) in the deferred exchange).

Example 3. (i) Under the exchange agreement, B has the right at all times to demand $100,000 in cash in lieu of replacement property. On May 17, 1991, B transfers real property X to C and identifies real property T as replacement property. On September 4, 1991, C purchases real property T for $100,000 and transfers real property T to B.

(ii) Because B has the right on May 17, 1991, to demand $100,000 in cash in lieu of replacement property, B is in constructive receipt of the $100,000 on that date. Thus, the transaction is a sale and not an exchange, and the $60,000 gain realized by B in the transaction (i.e., $100,000 amount realized less $40,000 adjusted basis) is recognized. Under section 1031(d), B's basis in real property T is $100,000.

Example 4. (i) Under the exchange agreement, B has the right at all times to demand up to $30,000 in cash and the balance in replacement property instead of receiving replacement property in the amount of $100,000. On May 17, 1991, B transfers real property X to C and identifies real property U as replacement property. On September 4, 1991, C purchases real property U for $100,000 and transfers real property U to B.

(ii) The transaction qualifies as a deferred exchange under section 1031 and this section. However, because B had the right on May 17, 1991, to demand up to $30,000 in cash, B is in constructive receipt of $30,000 on that date. Under section 1031(b), B recognizes gain in the amount of $30,000. Under section 1031(d), B's basis in real property U is $70,000 (i.e., B's basis in real property X ($40,000), decreased in the amount of money that B received ($30,000), increased in the amount of gain recognized ($30,000), and increased in the amount of additional consideration paid by B ($30,000) in the deferred exchange).

Example 5. (i) Assume real property X is encumbered by a mortgage of $30,000. On May 17, 1991, B transfers real property X to C and identifies real property V as replacement property, and C assumes the $30,000 mortgage on real property X. Real property V is encumbered by a $20,000 mortgage. On July 5, 1991, C purchases real property V for $90,000 by paying $70,000 and assuming the mortgage and transfers real property V to B with B assuming the mortgage.

(ii) The consideration received by B in the form of the liability assumed by C ($30,000) is offset by the consideration given by B in the form of the liability assumed by B ($20,000). The excess of the liability assumed by C over the liability assumed by B, $10,000, is treated as "money or other property." See § 1.1031(b)–1(c). Thus, B recognizes gain under section 1031(b) in the amount of $10,000. Under section 1031(d), B's basis in real property V is $40,000 (i.e., B's basis in real property X ($40,000), decreased in the amount of money that B is treated as receiving in the form of the liability assumed by C ($30,000), increased in the amount of money that B is treated as paying in the form of the liability assumed by B ($20,000), and increased in the amount of the gain recognized ($10,000) in the deferred exchange).

(k) *Definition of disqualified person.*
(1) For purposes of this section, a disqualified person is a person described in paragraph (k)(2), (k)(3), or (k)(4) of this section.

(2) The person is the agent of the taxpayer at the time of the transaction. For this purpose, a person who has acted as the taxpayer's employee, attorney, accountant, investment banker or broker, or real estate agent or broker within the 2-year period ending on the date of the transfer of the first of the relinquished properties is treated as an agent of the taxpayer at the time of the transaction. Solely for purposes of this paragraph (k)(2), performance of the following services will not be taken into account—

(i) Services for the taxpayer with respect to exchanges of property intended to qualify for nonrecognition of gain or loss under section 1031; and

(ii) Routine financial, title insurance, escrow, or trust services for the taxpayer by a financial institution. title insurance company, or escrow company.

(3) The person and the taxpayer bear a relationship described in either section 267(b) or section 707(b) (determined by substituting in each section "10 percent" for "50 percent" each place it appears).

(4) The person and a person described in paragraph (k)(2) of this section bear a relationship described in either section 267(b) or section 707(b) (determined by substituting in each section "10 percent" for "50 percent" each place it appears).

(5) This paragraph (k) may be illustrated by the following examples.

Unless otherwise provided, the following facts are assumed: On May 1, 1991, B enters into an exchange agreement (as defined in paragraph (g)(4)(iii)(B) of this section) with C whereby B retains C to facilitate an exchange with respect to real property X. On May 17, 1991, pursuant to the agreement, B executes and delivers to C a deed conveying real property X to C. C has no relationship to B described in paragraphs (k)(2), (k)(3), or (k)(4) of this section.

Example 1. (i) C is B's accountant and has rendered accounting services to B within the 2-year period ending on May 17, 1991, other than with respect to exchanges of property intended to qualify for nonrecognition of gain or loss under section 1031.

(ii) C is a disqualified person because C has acted as B's accountant within the 2-year period ending on May 17, 1991.

(iii) If C had not acted as B's accountant within the 2-year period ending on May 17, 1991, or if C had acted as B's accountant within that period only with respect to exchanges intended to qualify for nonrecognition of gain or loss under section 1031, C would not have been a disqualified person.

Example 2. (i) C, which is engaged in the trade or business of acting as an intermediary to facilitate deferred exchanges, is a wholly owned subsidiary of an escrow company that has performed routine escrow services for B in the past. C has previously been retained by B to act as an intermediary in prior section 1031 exchanges.

(ii) C is not a disqualified person notwithstanding the intermediary services previously provided by C to B (see paragraph (k)(2)(i) of this section) and notwithstanding the combination of C's relationship to the escrow company and the escrow services previously provided by the escrow company to B (see paragraph (k)(2)(ii) of this section).

Example 3. (i) C is a corporation that is only engaged in the trade or business of acting as an intermediary to facilitate deferred exchanges. Each of 10 law firms owns 10 percent of the outstanding stock of C. One of the 10 law firms that owns 10 percent of C is M. J is the managing partner of M and is the president of C. J, in his capacity as a partner in M, has also rendered legal advice to B within the 2-year period ending on May 17, 1991, on matters other than exchanges intended to qualify for nonrecognition of gain or loss under section 1031.

(ii) J and M are disqualified persons. C, however, is not a disqualified person because neither J nor M own, directly or indirectly, more than 10 percent of the stock of C. Similarly, J's participation in the management of C does not make C a disqualified person.

(1) [Reserved]

(m) *Definition of fair market value.* For purposes of this section, the fair market value of property means the fair market value of the property without

Federal Register / Vol. 56, No. 84 / Wednesday, May 1, 1991

regard to any liabilities secured by the property.

(n) *No inference with respect to actual or constructive receipt rules outside of section 1031.* The rules provided in this section relating to actual or constructive receipt are intended to be rules for determining whether there is actual or constructive receipt in the case of a deferred exchange. No inference is intended regarding the application of these rules for purposes of determining whether actual or constructive receipt exists for any other purpose.

(o) *Effective date.* This section applies to transfers of property made by a taxpayer on or after June 10, 1991. However, a transfer of property made by a taxpayer on or after May 16, 1990, but before June 10, 1991, will be treated as complying with section 1031 (a)(3) and this section if the deferred exchange satisfies either the provision of this section or the provisions of the notice of proposed rulemaking published in the **Federal Register** on May 16, 1990 (55 FR 20278).

Dated: April 12, 1991.

Approved:

Fred T. Goldberg, Jr.,

Commissioner of Internal Revenue.

Kenneth W. Gideon,

Assistant Secretary of the Treasury.

[FR Doc. 91–10170 Filed 4–25–91; 3:49 pm]

BILLING CODE 4830-01-M

Internal Revenue Service (T.D. 8343)

DEPARTMENT OF THE TREASURY

Internal Revenue Service

26 CFR Part 1

[T.D. 8343]

RIN 1545-AN38

Like-Kind Exchanges; Additional Rules for Exchanges of Personal Property and for Exchanges of Multiple Properties

AGENCY: Internal Revenue Service, Treasury.

ACTION: Final regulations.

SUMMARY: This document contains final regulations relating to exchanges of personal property and multiple properties under section 1031 of the Internal Revenue Code. The regulations affect persons who exchange personal property or multiple properties. The regulations are necessary to provide persons who exchange these properties with the guidance necessary to comply with the law.

EFFECTIVE DATE: The final regulations are effective for exchanges occurring on or after April 11, 1991.

FOR FURTHER INFORMATION CONTACT: _____ 202-377-9581 (not a toll-free number).

SUPPLEMENTARY INFORMATION:

Background

On April 25, 1990, the Federal Register published a Notice of Proposed Rulemaking (55 FR 17635) under section 1031 of the Internal Revenue Code of 1986, relating to exchanges of personal property and multiple properties. Those regulations proposed to amend §§ 1.1031(a)–1 and 1.1031(b)–1(c) of the Income Tax Regulations and to add new §§ 1.1031(a)–2 and 1.1031(f)–1.

After issuance of the proposed regulations, the Internal Revenue Service received public comments on the proposed regulations and held a public hearing on September 6, 1990. Six commentators spoke at the hearing. After fully considering the comments and the statements made at the hearing, the Service adopts the proposed regulations as revised by this Treasury decision. Descriptions of the revisions to the proposed regulations are included in the discussion of the public comments below. Proposed regulation § 1.1031(f)–1 has been renumbered § 1.1031(j)–1 in the final regulations.

Product Class Coding System

Under the proposed and final regulations, depreciable tangible personal property held for productive use in a business is exchanged for property of a "like kind" under section 1031 if the property is exchanged for property that is either of a like kind or of a like class. An exchange of properties of a like kind may qualify under section 1031 regardless of whether the properties are also of a like class. In determining whether exchanged properties are of a like kind, no inference is to be drawn from the fact that the properties are not of a like class.

Under the proposed regulations, depreciable tangible personal property held by the taxpayer for productive use in its business is of a like class to other depreciable tangible personal property to be held by the taxpayer for productive use in its business if the exchanged properties are within either the same "General Business Asset Class" or the same "Product Class." A General Business Asset Class consists of depreciable tangible personal property described in one of asset classes 00.11 through 00.28 and 00.4 of Rev. Proc. 87–56, 1987–2 C.B. 674. Under the final regulations, the term "General Business Asset Class" has been changed to "General Asset Class."

Under the proposed regulations, Product Classes consist of depreciable tangible personal property listed in a Product Code. A property's Product Code is its 5-digit product class under the product coding system of the U.S. Department of Commerce, Bureau of the Census, 1987 Census of Manufactures and Census of Mineral Industries, 1989 Reference Series: Numerical List of Manufactured and Mineral Products (Issued February 1989) (Numerical List).

Under the proposed regulations, in the case of depreciable tangible personal property that is not listed in a Product Code, or that is listed in a Product Code ending in a "9" (i.e., a miscellaneous category), the determination of whether the exchanged properties are of a like class is made based on all the facts and circumstances.

Several commentators suggested that the regulations provide a different approach to determine whether property is of a like class. The two most commonly suggested approaches were (1) expanding the use of categories contained in Rev. Proc. 87–56, and (2) using the 4-digit product coding system of the Numerical List.

The final regulations adopt a 4-digit coding system for classifying depreciable tangible personal property. Specifically, the regulations adopt the 4-digit product coding system within Division D of the Standard Industrial Classification codes, set forth in Executive Office of the President, Office of Management and Budget, Standard Industrial Classification Manual (1987) (SIC Manual). Division D contains a listing of manufactured products and equipment. The SIC Manual provides the framework for the Numerical List.

Adoption of the 4-digit SIC Manual coding system approach improves the administrability and certainty of these regulations in several ways. As a practical matter, the SIC Manual is much more readily available (e.g., at many public libraries) than the alternative Numerical List. In addition, the SIC Manual is referenced by other federal regulations. With respect to section 1031 exchanges, use of the 4-digit SIC Manual coding system will likely result in fewer categories (and fewer exchange groups), thus simplifying the administration of this provision in transactions involving a number of items of depreciable tangible personal property. Furthermore, properties will more often be of a like class and thus fewer taxpayers will have to demonstrate that depreciable tangible personal properties exchanged are of a like kind. For example, under the 5-digit Numerical List, dairy equipment is in Product Code 35232 and haying machinery is in Product Code 35236. Thus, under the Numerical List these properties would not be of a like class. Under the 4-digit SIC Manual, however, dairy equipment and haying machinery are both within the same Product Class (SIC Code 3523), and are of a like class.

Under the final regulations, property that is listed in a 4-digit product class ending in a "9" (i.e., a miscellaneous

category) is not considered property within a Product Class. Accordingly, that property, and property that is not listed in a 4-digit product class, cannot be of a like class based on the 4-digit SIC Manual classification. Taxpayers may still demonstrate the these properties are of a like kind.

The final regulations provide that the Commissioner may, by guidance published in the Internal Revenue Bulletin, supplement the guidance provided in the final regulations relating to classification of properties. For example, the Commissioner may determine that two properties that are listed in separate product classes each ending in a "9" are of a like class, or that property that is not listed in any product class is of a like class to property that is listed in a product class.

Personal Property Held for Investment

The proposed regulations did not provide like classes for personal property that is held for investment rather than for productive use in a business. Under the proposed regulations, therefore, an exchange of personal property held for investment could qualify for nonrecognition under section 1031 only if the exchanged properties were of a like kind. Many commentators pointed out that certain types of depreciable tangible personnal property are held for investment. Examples of depreciable tangible personal property held for investment are the lamps, carpets and other furnishings in a building that is held for investment. The commentators stated that it would facilitate compliance with and administration of the regulations not to restrict taxpayers holding such property for investment to the less objective like-kind standard.

Upon further consideration, the Service has concluded that it is appropriate to extend the like-class provisions of the proposed regulations to depreciable tangible personal property held for investment, and the final regulations so provide. As under the proposed regulations, no like classes are provided for intangible personal property or for nondepreciable personal property. Exchanges of these types of properties qualify under section 1031 only if the properties are of a like kind. Nondepreciable personal property held for investment generally includes items considered to be collectibles, for example, works of art, antiques, gems, stamps, precious metals, coins, and historical objects.

Goodwill

Under the proposed regulations, neither the goodwill nor going concern value of dissimilar businesses is of a like kind. The proposed regulations also proposed treating goodwill or going concern value of similar businesses as being of a like kind only in rare and unusual circumstances.

After considering comments received on this issue, the Internal Revenue Service has concluded that the nature and character of goodwill and going concern value of a business are so inherently unique and inseparable from the business that goodwill or going concern value of one business can never be of a like kind to goodwill or going concern value of another business.

Accordingly, under the final regulations, goodwill or going concern value of a business activity are not of a like kind to goodwill or going concern value of another business activity.

Several commentators suggested that the rule would be inappropriate because section 1031(a)(2), which provides exceptions to property eligible for nonrecognition treatment under section 1031(a)(1), does not list goodwill or going concern value. The legislative history of section 1031(a)(2) demonstrates, however, that these exceptions were provided for reasons unrelated to whether the enumerated properties could be of a like kind to any other property. The fact that goodwill or going concern value is not listed in section 1031(a)(2) therefore does not establish that goodwill or going concern value can be of a like kind.

De minimis Exception

Several commentators suggested that the regulations provide an exception from the multiple property rules for items of personal property that have de minimis value. The suggestions generally were premised on the argument that the exception would eliminate small dollar exchange groups, thus simplifying the application of the regulations.

The commentators suggesting a section 1031 de minimis rule did not address the application of section 1245 to section 1031 exchanges. In cases in which a section 1031 de minimis rule typically would apply, section 1245 (a)(1) and (b)(4) would also apply. Section 1245(a)(1) generally requires the "recapture" of prior depreciation or amortization deductions as ordinary income. Although section 1245(b)(4) provides an exception from the recapture requirement for like-kind exchanges, this exception is limited: a taxpayer who transfers section 1245

property in a section 1031 exchange must recognize recapture gain to the extent of (i) any gain recognized on the exchange (determined without regard to section 1245) plus (ii) the fair market value of property acquired which is like-kind property under section 1031 but which is not section 1245 property. See § 1.1245–4(d). Thus, a de minimis rule under section 1031 generally would neither relieve taxpayers from gain recognition nor simplify the application of the regulations. Accordingly, the final regulations do not contain a de minimis exception.

Netting of Liabilities—Debt in Anticipation

Section 1.1031(b)–1(c) of the existing regulations provides that consideration received in the form of an assumption of a liability (or a transfer of property subject to a liability) is to be treated as "other property or money" for purposes of section 1031(b). Further, in determining the amount of "other property or money" for purposes of section 1031(b), consideration given in the form of an assumption of a liability (or a receipt of property subject to a liability) is offset against consideration received in the form of an assumption of a liability (or a transfer of property subject to a liability). Section 1.1031(d)–2, examples (1) and (2), provides additional rules.

The proposed regulations would have amended § 1.1031(b)–1(c) to clarify that, in determining the amount of "other property or money" for purposes of section 1031(b), consideration received by the taxpayer in the form of an assumption of a liability (or a transfer of property subject to a liability) may not be offset by consideration given by the taxpayer in the form of an assumption of a liability (or a receipt of property subject to a liability) with respect to a liability incurred by the taxpayer in anticipation of an exchange under section 1031.

Commentators demonstrated that the proposed rule could create substantial uncertainty in the tax results of exchange transactions involving liabilities on both relinquished and replacement properties. The final regulations do not include this proposed amendment.

Other Liabilities Issues

Under the proposed regulations, all liabilities of which the taxpayer is relieved are offset against all liabilities assumed by the taxpayer in the exchange, regardless of whether the liabilities are recourse or nonrecourse and regardless of whether the liabilities are secured by or otherwise relate to

specific property transferred or received as part of the exchange. If the taxpayer assumes excess liabilities as part of the exchange (i.e., the amount of liabilities the taxpayer assumes exceeds the amount of the liabilities of which the taxpayer is relieved), the excess is allocated to the properties received in all the exchange groups, based on their fair market values and to the extent of their fair market values.

Several commentators suggested that these proposed rules not be adopted. In general, those commentators suggested that excess liabilities be allocated instead to property, if any, securing the indebtedness. This rule could be manipulated, however, in any case in which the lender permitted substitution of, or additions to, loan security in contemplation of the exchange transaction. It would put a premium on sophisticated tax planning and would not improve the administrability of the regulations. The final regulations do not change either § 1.1031(d)–2 of the existing regulations or the proposed regulations on allocating excess liabilities.

Effective Date

The regulations contained in this Treasury decision are effective for exchanges occurring on or after April 11, 1991. For exchanges occurring prior to April 11, 1991, the Internal Revenue Service will take into account whether the properties exchanged would be of a like class under these regulations in determining whether those properties are of a like kind.

Special Analyses

It has been determined that these final rules are not major rules as defined in Executive Order 12291. Therefore, a Regulatory Impact Analysis is not required. Although this Treasury decision was preceded by a notice of proposed rulemaking that solicited public comments, the notice was not required by 5 U.S.C. 553 because the regulations proposed in that notice and adopted by this Treasury decision are interpretative. Therefore, a final Regulatory Flexibility Analysis is not required by the Regulatory Flexibility Act (5 U.S.C. chapter 6). In accordance with section 7805(f) of the Internal Revenue Code, the Proposed regulations were submitted to the Chief Counsel for Advocacy of the Small Business Administration for comment on their impact on small business.

Drafting Information

The principal authors of these final regulations are Debra L. Fischer and

Arthur E. Davis III of the Office of Assistant Chief Counsel, Income Tax & Accounting. However, personnel from other offices of the Treasury Department and from the Internal Revenue Service participated in developing the regulations on matters of both substance and style.

List of Subjects 26 CFR 1.1001–1 through 1.1102–3

Banks, Banking, Holding companies, Income taxes, Radio, Reporting and Recordkeeping requirements.

Adoption of Amendments to the Regulations

For the reasons set forth in the preamble, title 26, chapter I of the Code of Federal Regulations is amended as set forth below:

PART 1—INCOME TAX; TAXABLE YEARS BEGINNING AFTER DECEMBER 31, 1953

Paragraph 1. The authority for part 1 continues to read in part:

Authority: 26 U.S.C. 7805 * * *

Par. 2. Section 1.1031(a)-1 is amended by adding a new sentence at the end of paragraph (b) to read as follows:

§ 1.1031(a)–(1)   Property held for productive use in trade or business or for investment.

*   *   *   *   *

(b) * * * For additional rules for exchanges of personal property, see § 1.1031 (a)–2.

*   *   *   *   *

Par. 3. Section 1.1031 (a)-2 is added to read as follows:

§ 1.1031(a)-2   Additional rules for exchanges of personal property.

(a) *Introduction.* Section 1.1031(a)–1(b) provides that the nonrecognition rules of section 1031 do not apply to an exchange of one kind or class of property for property of a different kind or class. This section contains additional rules for determining whether personal property has been exchanged for property of a like kind or like class. Personal properties of a like class are considered to be of a "like kind" for purposes of section 1031. In addition, an exchange of properties of a like kind may qualify under section 1031 regardless of whether the properties are also of a like class. In determining whether exchanged properties are of a like kind, no inference is to be drawn from the fact that the properties are not of a like class. Under paragraph (b) of this section, depreciable tangible personal properties are of a like class if they are either within the same General Asset Class (as defined in paragraph

(b)(2) of this section) or within the same Product Class (as defined in paragraph (b)(3) of this section). Paragraph (c) of this section provides rules for exchanges of intangible personal property and nondepreciable personal property.

(b) *Depreciable tangible personal property*—(1) *General rule.* Depreciable tangible personal property is exchanged for property of a "like kind" under section 1031 if the property is exchanged for property of a like kind or like class. Depreciable tangible personal property is of a like class to other depreciable tangible personal property if the exchanged properties are either within the same General Asset Class or within the same Product Class. A single property may not be classified within more than one General Asset Class or within more than one Product Class. In addition, property classified within any General Asset Class may not be classified within a Product Class. A property's General Asset Class or Product Class is determined as of the date of the exchange.

(2) *General Asset Classes.* Except as provided in paragraphs (b)(4) and (b)(5) of this section, property within a General Asset Class consists of depreciable tangible personal property described in one of asset classes 00.11 through 00.28 and 00.4 of Rev. Proc. 87–56, 1987–2 C.B. 674. These General Asset Classes describe types of depreciable tangible personal property that frequently are used in many businesses. The General Asset Classes are as follows:

(i) Office furniture, fixtures, and equipment (asset class 00.11),
(ii) Information systems (computers and peripheral equipment) (asset class 00.12),
(iii) Data handling equipment, except computers (asset class 00.13),
(iv) Airplanes (airframes and engines), except those used in commercial or contract carrying of passengers or freight, and all helicopters (airframes and engines) (asset class 00.21),
(v) Automobiles, taxis (asset class 00.22),
(vi) Buses (asset class 00.23),
(vii) Light general purpose trucks (asset class 00.241),
(viii) Heavy general purpose trucks (asset class 00.242),
(ix) Railroad cars and locomotives, except those owned by railroad transportation companies (asset class 00.25),
(x) Tractor units for use over-the-road (asset class 00.26),
(xi) Trailers and trailer-mounted containers (asset class 00.27),
(xii) Vessels, barges, tugs, and similar water-transportation equipment, except

those used in marine construction (asset class 00.28), and
(xiii) Industrial steam and electric generation and/or distribution systems (asset class 00.4).

(3) *Product Classes.* Except as provided in paragraphs (b)(4) and (b)(5) of this section, property within a Product Class consists of depreciable tangible personal property that is listed in a 4-digit product class within Division D of the Standard Industrial Classification codes, set forth in Executive Office of the President, Office of Management and Budget, Standard Industrial Classification Manual (1987) (SIC Manual). Copies of the SIC Manual may be obtained from the National Technical Information Service, an agency of the U.S. Department of Commerce. Division D of the SIC Manual contains a listing of manufactured products and equipment. For this purpose, any 4-digit product class ending in a "9" (*i.e.,* a miscellaneous category) will not be considered a Product Class. If a property is listed in more than one product class, the property is treated as listed in any one of those product classes. A property's 4-digit product classification is referred to as the property's "SIC Code."

(4) *Modifications of Rev. Proc. 87–56 and SIC Manual.* The asset classes of Rev. Proc. 87–56 and the product classes of the SIC Manual may be updated or otherwise modified from time to time. In the event Rev. Proc. 87–56 is modified, the General Asset Classes will follow the modification, and the modification will be effective for exchanges occurring on or after the date the modification is published in the Internal Revenue Bulletin, unless otherwise provided. Similarly, in the event the SIC Manual is modified, the Product Classes will follow the modification, and the modification will be effective for exchanges occurring on or after the effective date of the modification. However, taxpayers may rely on the unmodified SIC Manual for exchanges occurring during the one-year period following the effective date of the modification. The SIC Manual generally is modified every five years, in years ending in a 2 or 7 (e.g., 1987 and 1992). The effective date of the modified SIC Manual is announced in the Federal Register and generally is January 1 of the year the SIC Manual is modified.

(5) *Modified classification through published guidance.* The Commissioner may, by guidance published in the Internal Revenue Bulletin, supplement the guidance provided in this section relating to classification of properties. For example, the Commissioner may

determine not to follow, in whole or in part, any modification of Rev. Proc. 87–56 or the SIC Manual. The Commissioner may also determine that two types of property that are listed in separate product classes each ending in a "9" are of a like class, or that a type of property that has a SIC Code is of a like class to a type of property that does not have a SIC Code.

(6) *No inference outside of Section 1031.* The rules provided in this section concerning the use of Rev. Proc. 87–56 and the SIC Manual are limited to exchanges under section 1031. No inference is intended with respect to the classification of property for other purposes, such as depreciation.

(7) *Examples.* The application of this paragraph (b) may be illustrated by the following examples:

Example 1. Taxpayer A transfers a personal computer (asset class 00.12) to B in exchange for a printer (asset class 00.12). With respect to A, the properties exchanged are within the same General Asset Class and therefore are of a like class.

Example 2. Taxpayer C transfers an airplane (asset class 00.21) to D in exchange for a heavy general purpose truck (asset class 00.242). The properties exchanged are not of a like class because they are within different General Asset Classes. Because each of the properties is within a General Asset Class, the properties may not be classified within a Product Class. The airplane and heavy general purpose truck are also not of a like kind. Therefore, the exchange does not qualify for nonrecognition of gain or loss under section 1031.

Example 3. Taxpayer E transfers a grader to F in exchange for a scraper. Neither property is within any of the General Asset Classes, and both properties are within the same Product Class (SIC Code 3533). With respect to E, therefore, the properties exchanged are of a like class.

Example 4. Taxpayer G transfers a personal computer (asset class 00.12), an airplane (asset class 00.21) and a sanding machine (SIC Code 3553) to H in exchange for a printer (asset class 00.12), a heavy general purpose truck (asset class 00.242) and a lathe (SIC Code 3553). The personal computer and the printer are of a like class because they are within the same General Asset Class: the sanding machine and the lathe are of a like class because neither property is within any of the General Asset Classes and they are within the same Product Class. The airplane and the heavy general purpose truck are neither within the same General Asset Class nor within the same Product Class, and are not of a like kind.

(c) *Intangible personal property and nondepreciable personal property*—(1) *General rule.* An exchange of intangible personal property of nondepreciable personal property qualifies for nonrecognition of gain or loss under section 1031 only if the exchanged properties are of a like kind. No like

classes are provided for these properties. Whether intangible personal property is of a like kind to other intangible personal property generally depends on the nature or character of the rights involved (*e.g.,* a patent or a copyright) and also on the nature or character of the underlying property to which the intangible personal property relates.

(2) *Goodwill and going concern value.* The goodwill or going concern value of a business is not of a like kind to the goodwill or going concern value of another business.

(3) *Examples.* The application of this paragraph (c) may be illustrated by the following examples:

Example (1). Taxpayer K exchanges a copyright on a novel for a copyright on a different novel. The properties exchanged are of a like kind.

Example (2). Taxpayer J exchanges a copyright on a novel for a copyright on a song. The properties exchanged are not of a like kind.

(d) *Effective date.* Section 1.1031(a)–2 is effective for exchanges occurring on or after April 11, 1991.

Par. 4. Section 1.1031(j)–1 is added to read as follows:

§ 1.1031(j)–1   Exchanges of multiple properties.

(a) *Introduction*—(1) *Overview.* As a general rule, the application of section 1031 requires a property-by-property comparison for computing the gain recognized and basis of property received in a like-kind exchange. This section provides an exception to this general rule in the case of an exchange of multiple properties. An exchange is an exchange of multiple properties if, under paragraph (b)(2) of this section, more than one exchange group is created. In addition, an exchange is an exchange of multiple properties if only one exchange group is created but there is more than one property being transferred or received within that exchange group. Paragraph (b) of this section provides rules for computing the amount of gain recognized in an exchange of multiple properties qualifying for nonrecognition of gain or loss under section 1031. Paragraph (c) of this section provides rules for computing the basis of properties received in an exchange of multiple properties qualifying for nonrecognition of gain or loss under section 1031.

(2) *General Approach.* (i) In general, the amount of gain recognized in an exchange of multiple properties is computed by first separating the properties transferred and the properties received by the taxpayer in the exchange into exchange groups in the

manner described in paragraph (b)(2) of this section. The separation of the properties transferred and the properties received in the exchange into exchange groups involves matching up properties of a like kind of like class to the extent possible. Next, all liabilities assumed by the taxpayer as part of the transaction are offset by all liabilities of which the taxpayer is relieved as part of the transaction, with the excess liabilities assumed or relieved allocated in accordance with paragraph (b)(2)(ii) of this section. Then, the rules of section 1031 and the regulations thereunder are applied separately to each exchange group to determine the amount of gain recognized in the exchange. See §§ 1.1031(b)–1 and 1.1031(c)–1. Finally, the rules of section 1031 and the regulations thereunder are applied separately to each exchange group to determine the basis of the properties received in the exchange. See §§ 1.1031(d)–1 and 1.1031(d)–2.

(ii) For purposes of this section, the exchanges are assumed to be made at arms' length, so that the aggregate fair market value of the property received in the exchange equals the aggregate fair market value of the property transferred. Thus, the amount realized with respect to the properties transferred in each exchange group is assumed to equal their aggregate fair market value.

(b) *Computation of gain recognized*—(1) *In general.* In computing the amount of gain recognized in an exchange of multiple properties, the fair market value must be determined for each property transferred and for each property received by the taxpayer in the exchange. In addition, the adjusted basis must be determined for each property transferred by the taxpayer in the exchange.

(2) *Exchange groups and residual group.* The properties transferred and the properties received by the taxpayer in the exchange are separated into exchange groups and a residual group to the extent provided in this paragraph (b)(2).

(i) *Exchange groups.* Each exchange group consists of the properties transferred and received in the exchange, all of which are of a like kind or like class. If a property could be included in more than one exchange group, the taxpayer may include the property in any of those exchange groups. Property eligible for inclusion within an exchange group does not include money or property described in section 1031(a)(2) (*i.e.,* stock in trade or other property held primarily for sale, stocks, bonds, notes, other securities or evidences of indebtedness or interest,

14856 Federal Register / Vol. 56, No. 71 / Friday, April 12, 1991 / Rules and Regulations

interests in a partnership, certificates of trust or beneficial interests, or choses in action). For example, an exchange group may consist of all exchanged properties that are within the same General Asset Class or within the same Product Class (as defined in § 1.1031(a)–2(b)). Each exchange group must consist of at least one property transferred and at least one property received in the exchange.

(ii) *Treatment of liabilities.* (A) All liabilities assumed by the taxpayer as part of the exchange are offset against all liabilities of which the taxpayer is relieved as part of the exchange, regardless of whether the liabilities are recourse or nonrecourse and regardless of whether the liabilities are secured by or otherwise relate to specific property transferred or received as part of the exchange. See §§ 1.1031 (b)–1(c) and 1.1031(d)–2. For purposes of this section, liabilities assumed by the taxpayer as part of the exchange consist of liabilities of the other party to the exchange assumed by the taxpayer and liabilities subject to which the other party's property is transferred in the exchange. Similarly, liabilities of which the taxpayer is relieved as part of the exchange consist of liabilities of the taxpayer assumed by the other party to the exchange and liabilities subject to which the taxpayer's property is transferred.

(B) If there are excess liabilities assumed by the taxpayer as part of the exchange (*i.e.,* the amount of liabilities assumed by the taxpayer exceeds the amount of liabilities of which the taxpayer is relieved), the excess is allocated among the exchange groups (but not to the residual group) in proportion to the aggregate fair market value of the properties received by the taxpayer in the exchange groups. The amount of excess liabilities assumed by the taxpayer that are allocated to each exchange group may not exceed the aggregate fair market value of the properties received in the exchange group.

(C) If there are excess liabilities of which the taxpayer is relieved as part of the exchange (*i.e.,* the amount of liabilities of which the taxpayer is relieved exceeds the amount of liabilities assumed by the taxpayer), the excess is treated as a Class I asset for purposes of making allocations to the residual group under paragraph (b)(2)(iii) of this section.

(D) Paragraphs (b)(2)(ii) (A), (B), and (C) of this section are applied in the same manner even if section 1031 and this section apply to only a portion of a larger transaction (such as a transaction described in section 1060(c) and § 1.1060–1T(b)). In that event, the amount of excess liabilities assumed by the taxpayer or the amount of excess liabilities of which the taxpayer is relieved is determined based on all liabilities assumed by the taxpayer and all liabilities of which the taxpayer is relieve as part of the larger transaction.

(iii) *Residual group.* If the aggregate fair market value of the properties transferred in all of the exchange groups differs from the aggregate fair market value of the properties received in all of the exchange groups (taking liabilities into account in the manner described in paragraph (b)(2)(ii) of this section), a residual group is created. The residual group consists of an amount of money or other property having an aggregate fair market value equal to that difference. The residual group consists of either money or other property transferred in the exchange or money or other property received in the exchange, but not both. For this purpose, other property includes property described in section 1031(a)(2) (*i.e.,* stock in trade or other property held primarily for sale, stocks, bonds, notes, other securities or evidences of indebtedness or interest, interests in a partnership, certificates of trust or beneficial interests, or choses in action), property transferred that is not of a like kind or like class with any property received, and property received that is not of a like kind or like class with any property transferred. The money and properties that are allocated to the residual group are considered to come from the following assets in the following order: first from Class I assets, then from Class II assets, then from Class III assets, and then from Class IV assets. The terms Class I assets, Class II assets, Class III assets, and Class IV assets have the same meanings as in § 1.1060–1T(d). Within each Class, taxpayers may choose which properties are allocated to the residual group.

(iv) *Exchange group surplus and deficiency.* For each of the exchange groups described in this section, an "exchange group surplus" or "exchange group deficiency," if any, must be determined. An exchange group surplus is the excess of the aggregate fair market value of the properties received (less the amount of any excess liabilities assumed by the taxpayer that are allocated to that exchange group), in an exchange group over the aggregate fair market value of the properties transferred in that exchange group. An exchange group deficiency is the excess of the aggregate fair market value of the properties transferred in an exchange group over the aggregate fair market value of the properties received (less the amount of any excess liabilities assumed by the taxpayer that are

allocated to that exchange group) in that exchange group.

(3) *Amount of gain recognized.*—(i) For purposes of this section, the amount of gain or loss realized with respect to each exchange group and the residual group is the difference between the aggregate fair market value of the properties transferred in that exchange group or residual group and the properties' aggregate adjusted basis. The gain realized with respect to each exchange group is recognized to the extent of the lesser of the gain realized and the amount of the exchange group deficiency. Losses realized with respect to an exchange group are not recognized. See section 1031 (a) and (c). The total amount of gain recognized under section 1031 in the exchange is the sum of the amount of gain recognized with respect to each exchange group. With respect to the residual group, the gain or loss realized (as determined under this section) is recognized as provided in section 1001 or other applicable provision of the Code.

(ii) The amount of gain or loss realized and recognized with respect to properties transferred by the taxpayer that are not within any exchange group or the residual group is determined under section 1001 and other applicable provisions of the Code, with proper adjustments made for all liabilities not allocated to the exchange groups or the residual group.

(c) *Computation of basis of properties received.* In an exchange of multiple properties qualifying for nonrecognition of gain or loss under section 1031 and this section, the aggregate basis of properties received in each of the exchange groups is the aggregate adjusted basis of the properties transferred by the taxpayer within that exchange group, increased by the amount of gain recognized by the taxpayer with respect to that exchange group, increased by the amount of the exchange group surplus or decreased by the amount of the exchange group deficiency, and increased by the amount, if any, of excess liabilities assumed by the taxpayer that are allocated to that exchange group. The resulting aggregate basis of each exchange group is allocated proportionately to each property received in the exchange group in accordance with its fair market value. The basis of each property received within the residual group (other than money) is equal to its fair market value.

(d) *Examples.* The application of this section may be illustrated by the following examples

Federal Register / Vol. 56, No. 71 / Friday, April 12, 1991 / Rules and Regulations 14857

Example 1. (i) K exchanges computer A (asset class 00.12) and automobile A (asset class 00.22), both of which were held by K for productive use in its business, with W for printer B (asset class 00.12) and automobile B (asset class 00.22), both of which will be held by K for productive use in its business. K's adjusted basis and the fair market value of the exchanged properties are as follows:

	Adjusted basis	Fair market value
Computer A	$375	$1,000
Automobile A	1,500	4,000
Printer B		2,050
Automobile B		2,950

(ii) Under paragraph (b)(2) of this section, the properties exchanged are separated into exchange groups as follows:

(A) The first exchange group consists of computer A and printer B (both are within the same General Asset Class) and, as to K, has an exchange group surplus of $1050 because the fair market value of printer B ($2050) exceeds the fair market value of computer A ($1000) by that amount.

(B) The second exchange group consists of automobile A and automobile B (both are within the same General Asset Class) and, as to K, has an exchange group deficiency of $1050 because the fair market value of automobile A ($4000) exceeds the fair market value of automobile B ($2950) by that amount.

(iii) K recognizes gain on the exchange as follows:

(A) With respect to the first exchange group, the amount of gain realized is the excess of the fair market value of computer A ($1000) over its adjusted basis ($375), or $625. The amount of gain recognized is the lesser of the gain realized ($625) and the exchange group deficiency ($0), or $0.

(B) With respect to the second exchange group, the amount of gain realized is the excess of the fair market value of automobile A ($4000) over its adjusted basis ($1500), or $2500. The amount of gain recognized is the lesser of the gain realized ($2500) and the exchange group deficiency ($1050), or $1050.

(iv) The total amount of gain recognized by K in the exchange is the sum of the gains recognized with respect to both exchange groups ($0 + $1050), or $1050.

(v) The bases of the property received by K in the exchange, printer B and automobile B, are determined in the following manner:

(A) The basis of the property received in the first exchange group is the adjusted basis of the property transferred within the exchange group ($375), increased by the amount of gain recognized with respect to that exchange group ($0), increased by the amount of the exchange group surplus ($1050), and increased by the amount of excess liabilities assumed allocated to that exchange group ($0), or $1425. Because printer B was the only property received within the first exchange group, the entire basis of $1425 is allocated to printer B.

(B) The basis of the property received in the second exchange group is the adjusted basis of the property transferred within that exchange group ($1500), increased by the amount of gain recognized with respect to that exchange group ($1050), decreased by the amount of the exchange group deficiency ($1050), and increased by the amount of excess liabilities assumed allocated to that exchange group ($0), or $1500. Because automobile B was the only property received within the second exchange group, the entire basis of $1500 is allocated to automobile B.

Example 2. (i) F exchanges computer A (asset class 00.12) and automobile A (asset class 00.22), both of which were held by F for productive use in its business, with G for printer B (asset class 00.12) and automobile B (asset class 00.22), both of which will be held by F for productive use in its business, and corporate stock and $500 cash. The adjusted basis and fair market value of the properties are as follows:

	Adjusted basis	Fair market value
Computer A	$375	$1,000
Automobile A	3,500	4,000
Printer B		800
Automobile B		2,950
Corporate stock		750
Cash		500

(ii) Under paragraph (b)(2) of this section, the properties exchanged are separated into exchange groups as follows:

(A) The first exchange group consists of computer A and printer B (both are within the same General Asset Class) and, as to F, has an exchange group deficiency of $200 because the fair market value of computer A ($1000) exceeds the fair market value of printer B ($800) by that amount.

(B) The second exchange group consists of automobile A and automobile B (both are within the same General Asset Class) and, as to F, has an exchange group deficiency of $1050 because the fair market value of automobile A ($4000) exceeds the fair market value of automobile B ($2950) by that amount.

(C) Because the aggregate fair market value of the properties transferred by F in the exchange groups ($5,000) exceeds the aggregate fair market value of the properties received by F in the exchange groups ($3750) by $1250, there is a residual group in that amount consisting of the $500 cash and the $750 worth of corporate stock.

(iii) F recognizes gain on the exchange as follows:

(A) With respect to the first exchange group, the amount of gain realized is the excess of the fair market value of computer A ($1000) over its adjusted basis ($375), or $625. The amount of gain recognized is the lesser of the gain realized ($625) and the exchange group deficiency ($200), or $200.

(B) With respect to the second exchange group, the amount of gain realized is the excess of the fair market value of automobile A ($4000) over its adjusted basis ($3500), or $500. The amount of gain recognized is the lesser of the gain realized ($500) and the exchange group deficiency ($500), or $500.

(C) No property transferred by F was allocated to the residual group. Therefore, F does not recognize gain or loss with respect to the residual group.

(iv) The total amount of gain recognized by F in the exchange is the sum of the gains recognized with respect to both exchange groups ($200 + $500), or $700.

(v) The bases of the properties received by F in the exchange (printer B, automobile B, and the corporate stock) are determined in the following manner:

(A) The basis of the property received in the first exchange group is the adjusted basis of the property transferred within that exchange group ($375), increased by the amount of gain recognized with respect to that exchange group ($200), decreased by the amount of the exchange group deficiency ($200), and increased by the amount of excess liabilities assumed allocated to that exchange group ($0), or $375. Because printer B was the only property received within the first exchange group, the entire basis of $375 is allocated to printer B.

(B) The basis of the property received in the second exchange group is the adjusted basis of the property transferred within that exchange group ($3500), increased by the amount of gain recognized with respect to that exchange group ($500), decreased by the amount of the exchange group deficiency ($1050), and increased by the amount of excess liabilities assumed allocated to that exchange group ($0), or $2950. Because automobile B was the only property received within the second exchange group, the entire basis of $2950 is allocated to automobile B.

(C) The basis of the property received within the residual group (the corporate stock) is equal to its fair market value or $750. Cash of $500 is also received within the residual group.

Example 3. (i) J and H enter into an exchange of the following properties. All of the property (except for the inventory) transferred by J was held for productive use in J's business. All of the property received by J will be held by J for productive use in its business.

J Transfers:			H Transfers:	
Property	Adjusted basis	Fair market value	Property	Fair market value
Computer A	$1,500	$5,000	Computer Z	$4,500
Computer B	500	3,000	Printer Y	2,500
Printer C	2,000	1,500	Real Estate X	1,000
Real Estate D	1,200	2,000	Real Estate W	4,000

J Transfers:			H Transfers:	
* Property	Adjusted basis	Fair market value	Property	Fair market value
Real Estate E	0	1,800	Grader V	2,000
Scraper F	3,500	2,500	Truck T	1,700
Inventory	1,000	1,700	Cash	1,800
Total	9,500	17,500		17,500

(ii) Under paragraph (b)(2) of this section, the properties exchanged are separated into exchange groups as follows:

(A) The first exchange group consists of computer A, computer B, printer C, computer Z, and printer Y (all are within the same General Asset Class) and, as to J, has an exchange group deficiency of $2500 (($5000 + $3950 + $1500) − ($4500 + $2500)).

(B) The second exchange group consists of real estate D, E, X and W (all are of a like kind) and, as to J, has an exchange group surplus of $1200 (($1900 − $4000) − ($2800 + $3180)).

(C) The third exchange group consists of scraper F and grader V (both are within the same Product Class (SIC Code 3531)) and, as to J, has an exchange group deficiency of $300 ($2500 − $2800).

(D) Because the aggregate fair market value of the properties exchanged by J in the exchange groups ($15,800) exceeds the aggregate fair market value of the properties received by J in the exchange groups ($14,000) by $1800, there is a residual group in that amount consisting of the $1800 cash (a Class I asset).

(E) The transaction also includes a taxable exchange of inventory (which is property described in section 1031(a)(2)) for truck T (which is not of a like kind or like class to any property transferred in the exchange).

(iii) J recognizes gain on the transaction as follows:

(A) With respect to the first exchange group, the amount of gain realized is the excess of the aggregate fair market value of the properties transferred in the exchange group ($9500) over the aggregate adjusted basis ($4000). The amount of gain recognized is the lesser of the gain realized ($5500) and the exchange group deficiency ($2500), or $2500.

(B) With respect to the second exchange group, the amount of gain realized is the excess of the aggregate fair market value of the properties transferred in the exchange group ($2800) over the aggregate adjusted basis ($1200), or $2600. The amount of gain recognized is the lesser of the gain realized ($2600) and the exchange group deficiency ($0), or $0.

(C) With respect to the third exchange group, a loss is realized in the amount of $800 because the fair market value of the property transferred in the exchange group ($2500) is less than its adjusted basis ($3300). Although a loss of $800 was realized, under section 1031(a) and (c) losses are not recognized.

(D) No property transferred by J was allocated to the residual group. Therefore, J does not recognize gain or loss with respect to the residual group.

(E) With respect to the taxable exchange of inventory for truck T, gain of $700 is realized

and recognized by J (amount realized of $1700 (the fair market value of truck T) less the adjusted basis of the inventory ($1000)).

(iv) The total amount of gain recognized by J in the transaction is the sum of the gains recognized under section 1031 with respect to each exchange group ($2500 + $0 + $0) and any gain recognized outside of section 1031 ($700), or $3200.

(v) The bases of the property received by J in the exchange are determined in the following manner:

(A) The aggregate basis of the properties received in the first exchange group is the adjusted basis of the properties transferred within that exchange group ($4000), increased by the amount of gain recognized with respect to that exchange group ($2500), decreased by the amount of the exchange group deficiency ($2500), and increased by the amount of excess liabilities assumed allocated to that exchange group ($0), or $4000. This $4000 of basis is allocated proportionately among the assets received within the first exchange group in accordance with their fair market values: Computer Z's basis is $2571 ($4000 × $4500/$7000); printer Y's basis is $1429 ($4000 × $2500/$7000).

(B) The aggregate basis of the properties received in the second exchange group is the adjusted basis of the properties transferred within that exchange group ($1200), increased by the amount of gain recognized with respect to that exchange group ($0), increased by the amount of the exchange group surplus ($1200), and increased by the amount of excess liabilities assumed allocated to that exchange group ($0), or $2400. This $2400 of basis is allocated proportionately among the assets received within the second exchange group in accordance with their fair market values: Real estate X's basis is $480 ($2400 × $1000/$5000); real estate W's basis is $1920 ($2400 × $4000/$5000).

(c) The basis of the property received in the third exchange group is the adjusted basis of the property transferred within that exchange group ($3300), increased by the amount of gain recognized with respect to that exchange group ($0), decreased by the amount of the exchange group deficiency ($500), and increased by the amount of excess liabilities assumed allocated to that exchange group ($0), or $2800. Because grader V was the only property received within the third exchange group, the entire basis of $2800 is allocated to grader V.

(D) Cash of $1800 is received within the residual group.

(E) The basis of the property received in the taxable exchange (truck T) is equal to its cost of $1700.

Example 4. (i) B exchanges computer A (asset class 00.12), automobile A (asset class 00.22) and truck A (asset class 00.241), with C

for computer R (asset class 00.12), automobile R (asset class 00.22), truck R (asset class 00.241) and $400 cash. All properties transferred by either B or C were held for productive use in the respective transferor's business. Similarly, all properties to be received by either B or C will be held for productive use in the respective recipient's business. Automobile A, automobile R and truck R are each secured by a nonrecourse liability and are transferred subject to such liability. The adjusted basis, fair market value, and liability secured by each property, if any, are as follows:

	Adjusted basis	Fair market value	Liability
B transfers:			
Computer A	$800	$1,500	$0
Automobile A	900	2,500	500
Truck A	700	2,000	0
C transfers:			
Computer R	1,100	1,600	0
Automobile R	2,100	3,100	750
Truck R	600	1,400	250
Cash		400	

(ii) The tax treatment to B is as follows:

(A)(1) The first exchange group consists of computers A and R (both are within the same General Asset Class).

(2) The second exchange group consists of automobiles A and R (both are within the same General Asset Class).

(3) The third exchange group consists of trucks A and R (both are in the same General Asset Class).

(B) Under paragraph (b)(2)(ii) of this section, all liabilities assumed by B ($1000) are offset by all liabilities of which B is relieved ($500), resulting in excess liabilities assumed of $500. The excess liabilities assumed of $500 is allocated among the exchange groups in proportion to the fair market value of the properties received by B in the exchange groups as follows:

(1) $131 of excess liabilities assumed ($500 × $1600/$6100) is allocated to the first exchange group. The first exchange group has an exchange group deficiency of $31 because the fair market value of computer A ($1500) exceeds the fair market value of computer R less the excess liabilities assumed allocated to the exchange group ($1600−$131) by that amount.

(2) $254 of excess liabilities assumed ($500 × $3100/$6100) is allocated to the second exchange group. The second exchange group has an exchange group surplus of $346 because the fair market value of automobile

R less the excess liabilities assumed allocated to the exchange group ($3100–$254) exceeds the fair market value of automobile A ($2500) by that amount.

(3) $115 of excess liabilities assumed ($500 × $1400/$6100) is allocated to the third exchange group. The third exchange group has an exchange group deficiency of $715 because the fair market value of truck A ($2000) exceeds the fair market value of truck R less the excess liabilities assumed allocated to the exchange group ($1400–$115) by that amount.

(4) The difference between the aggregate fair market value of the properties transferred in all of the exchange groups, $6000, and the aggregate fair market value of the properties received in all of the exchange groups (taking excess liabilities assumed into account), $5600, is $400. Therefore there is a residual group in that amount consisting of $400 cash received.

(C) B recognizes gain on the exchange as follows:

(1) With respect to the first exchange group, the amount of gain realized is the excess of the fair market value of computer A ($1500) over its adjusted basis ($800), or $700. The amount of gain recognized is the lesser of the gain realized ($700) and the exchange group deficiency ($31), or $31.

(2) With respect to the second exchange group, the amount of gain realized is the excess of the fair market value of automobile A ($2500) over its adjusted basis ($900), or $1600.

The amount of gain recognized is the lesser of the gain realized ($1600) and the exchange group deficiency ($0), or $0.

(3) With respect to the third exchange group, the amount of gain realized is the excess of the fair market value of truck A ($2000) over its adjusted basis ($700), or $1300. The amount of gain recognized is the lesser of gain realized ($1300) and the exchange group deficiency ($715), or $715.

(4) No property transferred by B was allocated to the residual group. Therefore, B does not recognize gain or loss with respect to the residual group.

(D) The total amount of gain recognized by B in the exchange is the sum of the gains recognized under section 1031 with respect to each exchange group ($31 + $0 + $715), or $746.

(E) the bases of the property received by B in the exchange (computer R, automobile R, and truck R) are determined in the following manner:

(1) The basis of the property received in the first exchange group is the adjusted basis of the property transferred within that exchange group ($800), increased by the amount of gain recognized with respect to that exchange group ($31), decreased by the amount of the exchange group deficiency ($31), and increased by the amount of excess liabilities assumed allocated to that exchange group ($131), or $931. Because computer R was the only property received within the first exchange group, the entire basis of $931 is allocated to computer R.

(2) The basis of the property received in the second exchange group is the adjusted basis of the property transferred within that exchange group ($900), increased by the

amount of gain recognized with respect to that exchange group ($0), increased by the amount of the exchange group surplus ($346), and increased by the amount of excess liabilities assumed allocated to that exchange group ($254), or $1500. Because automobile R was the only property received within the second exchange group, the entire basis of $1500 is allocated to automobile R.

(3) The basis of the property received in the third exchange group is the adjusted basis of the property transferred within that exchange group ($700), increased by the amount of gain recognized with respect to that exchange group ($715), decreased by the amount of the exchange group deficiency ($715), and increased by the amount of excess liabilities assumed allocated to that exchange group ($115), or $815. Because truck R was the only property received within the third exchange group, the entire basis of $815 is allocated to truck R.

(F) Cash of $400 is also received by B.

(iii) The tax treatment to C is as follows:

(A) (1) The first exchange group consists of computers R and A (both are within the same General Asset Class).

(2) The second exchange group consists of automobiles R and A (both are within the same General Asset Class).

(3) The third exchange group consists of trucks R and A (both are in the same General Asset Class).

(B) Under paragraph (b)(2)(ii) of this section, all liabilities of which C is relieved ($1000) are offset by all liabilities assumed by C ($500), resulting in excess liabilities relieved of $500. This excess liabilities relieved is treated as cash received by C.

(1) The first exchange group has an exchange group deficiency of $100 because the fair market value of computer R ($1600) exceeds the fair market value of computer A ($1500) by that amount.

(2) The second exchange group has an exchange group deficiency of $600 because the fair market value of automobile R ($3100) exceeds the fair market value of automobile A ($2500) by that amount.

(3) The third exchange group has an exchange group surplus of $600 because the fair market value of truck A ($2000) exceeds the fair market value of truck R ($1400) by that amount.

(4) The difference between the aggregate fair market value of the properties transferred by C in all of the exchange groups, $6100, and the aggregate fair market value of the properties received by C in all of the exchange groups, $6000, is $100. Therefore, there is a residual group in that amount, consisting of excess liabilities relieved of $100, which is treated as cash received by C.

(5) The $400 cash paid by C and $400 of the excess liabilities relieved which is treated as cash received by C are not within the exchange groups of the residual group.

(C) C recognizes gain on the exchange as follows:

(1) With respect to the first exchange group, the amount of gain realized is the excess of the fair market value of computer R ($1600) over its adjusted basis ($1100), or $500. The amount of gain recognized is the lesser of the gain realized ($500) and the exchange group deficiency ($100), or $100.

(2) With respect to the second exchange group, the amount of gain realized is the excess of the fair market value of automobile R ($3100) over its adjusted basis ($2100), or $1000. The amount of gain recognized is the lesser of the gain realized ($1000) and the exchange group deficiency ($600), or $600.

(3) With respect to the third exchange group, the amount of gain realized is the excess of the fair market value of truck R ($1400) over its adjusted basis ($600), or $800. The amount of gain recognized is the lesser of gain realized ($800) and the exchange group deficiency ($0), or $0.

(4) No property transferred by C was allocated to the residual group. Therefore, C does not recognize any gain with respect to the residual group.

(D) The total amount of gain recognized by C in the exchange is the sum of the gains recognized under section 1031 with respect to each exchange group ($100 + $600 + $0), or $700.

(E) The bases of the properties received by C in the exchange (computer A, automobile A, and truck A) are determined in the following manner:

(1) The basis of the property received in the first exchange group is the adjusted basis of the property transferred within that exchange group ($1100), increased by the amount of gain recognized with respect to that exchange group ($100), decreased by the amount of the exchange group deficiency ($100), and increased by the amount of excess liabilities assumed allocated to that exchange group ($0), or $1100. Because computer A was the only property received within the first exchange group, the entire basis of $1100 is allocated to computer A.

(2) The basis of the property received in the second exchange group is the adjusted basis of the property transferred within that exchange group ($2100), increased by the amount of gain recognized with respect to that exchange group ($600), decreased by the amount of the exchange group deficiency ($600), and increased by the amount of excess liabilities assumed allocated to that exchange group ($0), or $2100. Because automobile A was the only property received within the second exchange group, the entire basis of $2100 is allocated to automobile A.

(3) The basis of the property received in the third exchange group is the adjusted basis of the property transferred within that exchange group ($600), increased by the amount of gain recognized with respect to that exchange group ($0), increased by the amount of the exchange group surplus ($600), and increased by the amount of excess liabilities assumed allocated to that exchange group ($0), or $1200. Because truck A was the only property received within the third exchange group, the entire basis of $1200 is allocated to truck A.

Example 5. (i) U exchanges real estate A, real estate B, and grader A (SIC Code 3531) with V for real estate R and railroad car R (General Asset Class 00.25). All properties transferred by either U or V were held for productive use in the respective transferor's business. All properties to be received by either U or V will be held for productive use in the respective recipient's business. Real estate R is secured by a

14360   Federal Register / Vol. 56, No. 71 / Friday, April 12, 1991 / Rules and Regulations

recourse liability and is transferred subject to that liability. The adjusted basis, fair market value, and liability secured by each property, if any, are as follows:

	Adjusted basis	Fair market value	Liability
U Transfers:			
Real Estate A	$2000	$5000	
Real Estate B	8000	13,500	
Grader A	500	2000	
V Transfers:			
Real Estate R	$20,000	$26,500	$7000
Railroad car R	1200	1000	

(ii) The tax treatment to U is as follows:

(A) The exchange group consists of real estate A, real estate B, and real estate R.

(B) Under paragraph (b)(2)(ii) of this section, all liabilities assumed by U ($7000) are excess liabilities assumed. The excess liabilities assumed of $7000 is allocated to the exchange group.

(1) The exchange group has an exchange group surplus of $1000 because the fair market value of real estate R less the excess liabilities assumed allocated to the exchange group ($26,500–$7000) exceeds the aggregate fair market value of real estate A and B ($18,500) by that amount.

(2) The difference between the aggregate fair market value of the properties received in the exchange group (taking excess liabilities assumed into account), $19,500, and the aggregate fair market value of the properties transferred in the exchange group, $18,500, is $1000. Therefore, there is a residual group in that amount consisting of $1000 (or 50 percent of the fair market value) of grader A.

(3) The transaction also includes a taxable exchange of the 50 percent portion of grader A not allocated to the residual group (which is not of a like kind or like class to any property received by U in the exchange) for railroad car R (which is not of a like kind or like class to any property transferred by U in the exchange).

(C) U recognizes gain on the exchange as follows:

(1) With respect to the exchange group, the amount of the gain realized is the excess of the aggregate fair market value of real estate A and B ($18,500) over the aggregate adjusted basis ($10,000), or $8500. The amount of the gain recognized is the lesser of the gain realized ($8500) and the exchange group deficiency ($0), or $0.

(2) With respect to the residual group, the amount of gain realized and recognized is the excess of the fair market value of the 50 percent portion of grader A that is allocated to the residual group ($1000) over its adjusted basis ($250), or $750.

(3) With respect to the taxable exchange of the 50 percent portion of grader A not allocated to the residual group for railroad car R, gain of $750 is realized and recognized by U (amount realized of $1000 (the fair market value of railroad car R) less the adjusted basis of the 50 percent portion of

grader A not allocated to the residual group ($250)).

(D) The total amount of gain recognized by U in the transaction is the sum of the gain recognized under section 1031 with respect to the exchange group ($0), any gain recognized with respect to the residual group ($750), and any gain recognized with respect to property transferred that is not in the exchange group or the residual group ($750), or $1500.

(E) The bases of the property received by U in the exchange (real estate R and railroad car R) are determined in the following manner:

(1) The basis of the property received in the exchange group is the aggregate adjusted basis of the property transferred within that exchange group ($10,000), increased by the amount of gain recognized with respect to that exchange group ($0), increased by the amount of the exchange group surplus ($1000), and increased by the amount of excess liabilities assumed allocated to that exchange group ($7000), or $18,000. Because real estate R is the only property received within the exchange group, the entire basis of $18,000 is allocated to real estate R.

(2) The basis of railroad car R is equal to its cost of $1000.

(iii) The tax treatment to V is as follows:

(A) The exchange group consists of real estate R, real estate A, and real estate B.

(B) Under paragraph (b)(2)(ii) of this section, the liabilities of which V is relieved ($7000) results in excess liabilities relieved of $7000 and is treated as cash received by V.

(1) The exchange group has an exchange group deficiency of $8000 because the fair market value of real estate R ($26,500) exceeds the aggregate fair market value of real estate A and B ($18,500) by that amount.

(2) The difference between the aggregate fair market value of the properties transferred by V in the exchange group, $26,500, and the aggregate fair market value of the properties received by V in the exchange group, $18,500, is $8000. Therefore, there is a residual group in that amount, consisting of the excess liabilities relieved of $7000, which is treated as cash received by V, and $1000 (or 50 percent of the fair market value) of grader A.

(3) The transaction also includes a taxable exchange of railroad car R (which is not of a like kind or like class to any property received by V in the exchange) for the 50 percent portion of grader A (which is not of a like kind or like class to any property transferred by V in the exchange) not allocated to the residual group.

(C) V recognizes gain on the exchange as follows:

(1) With respect to the exchange group, the amount of the gain realized is the excess of the fair market value of real estate R ($26,500) over its adjusted basis ($20,000), or $6500. The amount of the gain recognized is the lesser of the gain realized ($6500) and the exchange group deficiency ($8000), or $6500.

(2) No property transferred by V was allocated to the residual group. Therefore, V does not recognize gain or loss with respect to the residual group.

(3) With respect to the taxable exchange of railroad car R for the 50 percent portion of grader A not allocated to the exchange group or the residual group, a loss is realized and

recognized in the amount of $200 (the excess of the $1200 adjusted basis of railroad car R over the amount realized of $1000 (fair market value of the 50 percent portion of grader A)).

(D) The basis of the property received by V in the exchange (real estate A, real estate B, and grader A) are determined in the following manner:

(1) The basis of the property received in the exchange group is the adjusted basis of the property transferred within that exchange group ($20,000), increased by the amount of gain recognized with respect to that exchange group ($6500), and decreased by the amount of the exchange group deficiency ($8000), or $18,500. This $18,500 of basis is allocated proportionately among the assets received within the exchange group in accordance with their fair market values: real estate A's basis is $5000 ($18,500 × $5000/$18,500); real estate B's basis is $13,500 ($18,500 × $13,500/$18,500).

(2) The basis of grader A is $2000.

(e) *Effective date.* Section 1.1031 (j)–1 is effective for exchanges occurring on or after April 11, 1991.

Fred T. Goldberg,

Commissioner of Internal Revenue.

Approved: March 12, 1991.

Kenneth W. Gideon

Assistant Secretary of the Treasury.

[FR Doc. 91–8172 Filed 4–11–91; 8:45 am]

BILLING CODE 4830–01–M

Documents

NCR (No Carbon Required)   **EXCHANGE AGREEMENT**

DEFINITIONS

The **MASCULINE** includes the feminine. The **SINGULAR** includes the plural. **BROKER** includes cooperating brokers and all salespersons. **DAYS** means calendar days unless otherwise specified. **DATE OF ACCEPTANCE** means the date the Offeree accepts the offer or the Offeror accepts the counter offer. **UNUSED DEPOSITS** means earnest money deposits less expenses incurred to the date of termination of the agreement. **DELIVERED** means personally delivered or transmitted by facsimile machine or mailed by certified mail. In the event of mailing, delivery shall be deemed to have been made on the date following the day of mailing, evidenced by the postmark on the envelope containing the delivered material.

_____, the **First Party**, offers to exchange
the real property situated in the City of _____, County of _____, State of _____,
commonly known as _____
consisting of _____, herein called **Property #1**,
for the real property owned by _____, the **Second Party**,
which property is situated in the City of _____, County of _____, State of _____,
commonly known as _____
consisting of _____, herein called **Property #2**.

1. EXISTING LOANS OF RECORD

☐ **First Party** to take **Property #2**: ☐ subject to, ☐ Conditioned upon **First Party's** ability to assume:
   ☐ **First Loan** with an approximate balance of $_____ payable at $_____ p/mo., with interest currently at _____%,
   ☐ Fixed Rate, ☐ Other:_____ Assumption fee, if any, not to exceed _____% plus $_____
   ☐ **Second Loan** with an approximate balance of $_____, payable at $_____ p/mo., with interest currently at _____%,
   ☐ Fixed Rate, ☐ Other:_____ Assumption fee, if any, not to exceed _____
☐ **Second Party** to take **Property #1**: ☐ subject to, ☐ Conditioned upon **Second Party's** ability to assume:
   ☐ **First Loan** with an approximate balance of $_____, payable at $_____ p/mo., with interest currently at _____%,
   ☐ Fixed Rate, ☐ Other:_____ Assumption fee, if any, not to exceed _____% plus $_____
   ☐ **Second Loan** with an approximate balance of $_____, payable at $_____ p/mo., with interest currently at _____%,
   ☐ Fixed Rate, ☐ Other:_____ Assumption fee, if any, not to exceed _____

The Conveying Party shall, **within _____ days of acceptance,** provide the Acquiring Party with copies of all Notes and Deeds of Trust or Mortgages to be assumed or taken subject to, and **within _____ days of receipt** thereof the Acquiring Party shall in writing notify the Conveying Party of his approval or disapproval of such terms, which shall not be unreasonably withheld. The Conveying Party shall furnish the Acquiring Party a current Beneficiary Statement on the above loan(s) **within _____ days of acceptance.**

In the event of ASSUMPTION, the Acquiring Party shall use his best efforts to obtain the consent of the lender to assume the above loan(s) or waive this condition in writing **within _____ days of acceptance.** All charges related to such assumption shall be paid by the Acquiring Party.

2. ADDITIONAL CONSIDERATION

☐ **Cash:**
   Upon exchange of the properties ☐ **First Party,** ☐ **Second Party** shall pay to the other party cash in the amount of $_____
☐ **Note:**
   ☐ **First Party,** ☐ **Second Party** shall deliver a promissory note in the amount of $_____, bearing interest at the rate of
   _____%, payable _____. Said note shall be secured by
   ☐ **Property #1,** ☐ **Property #2,** and the lien of such encumbrances shall be subject to prior liens as follows: _____
   _____
   _____
   _____

   Within three (3) days of acceptance the mortgagor shall furnish a customary financial statement for the sole purpose of credit approval, which approval shall not be unreasonably withheld. Authorization is hereby granted to engage the services of a reputable credit reporting agency for this purpose. Notice of approval or disapproval shall be given **within ten (10) days of receipt of the financial statement.**

☐ **Other consideration:**
   Upon exchange of the properties the ☐ **First Party,** ☐ **Second Party** shall _____
   _____
   _____
   _____

3. ADJUSTMENT. Any net difference between the approximate loan balances shown herein and the actual remaining balances of said loans **at closing** shall be adjusted as follows: ☐ Cash, ☐ Other: _____
Said loans shall not be reduced in excess of obligatory payments to principal made **after this date** without the written consent of the other party to this agreement.

4. NEW LOAN BY FIRST PARTY. The obligations of the **First Party** are conditioned upon his ability to obtain a new loan, to be secured by **Property #2,** in the amount of $_____ payable at approximately $_____ per month, with interest not to exceed _____%, at ☐ Fixed Rate ☐ Other: _____
with the balance due **not less than** _____ years. Loan fee not to exceed _____% plus $_____. **First Party** shall use his best efforts to obtain such loan or waive this condition in writing **within _____ days of acceptance.**

5. NEW LOAN BY SECOND PARTY. The obligations of the **Second Party** are conditioned upon his ability to obtain a new loan, to be secured by **Property #1,** in the amount of $_____ payable at approximately $_____ per month, with interest not to exceed _____%, at ☐ Fixed Rate ☐ Other: _____
with the balance due **not less than** _____ years. Loan fee not to exceed _____% plus $_____. **Second Party** shall use his best efforts to obtain such loan or waive this condition in writing **within _____ days of acceptance.**

6. BONDS AND ASSESSMENTS. In the event there is a Bond or Assessment which has an outstanding principal balance and is a lien upon the property, such principal shall be ☐ paid by the Conveying Party, ☐ assumed by the Acquiring Party. In the event of assumption, said obligation(s) ☐ shall, ☐ shall not be credited to the Acquiring Party **at closing.**

7. CONDITIONS (CONTINGENCIES) SATISFIED IN WRITING. Each condition contained herein shall be satisfied according to its terms or waived in writing by the party responsible **within the time specified or any extension thereof** agreed to by the parties in writing, or this agreement shall be terminated and all unused deposits returned. Failure to give written notice of approval of any condition requiring such approval **within the time provided** shall entitle the other party to terminate this agreement. Each party shall use his best efforts to satisfy each condition.

First Party's Initials: [_____]   Second Party's Initials: [_____]   Page 1 of 4 pages

FORM 102.1 (10-91)   COPYRIGHT © 1991, BY PROFESSIONAL PUBLISHING CORP. 122 PAUL DR., SAN RAFAEL, CA 94903 (415)472-1964   **PROFESSIONAL PUBLISHING**

Parties: _____

8. EXAMINATION OF TITLE. In addition to any encumbrances referred to herein, the parties shall convey title to the property subject only to: [1] Real Estate Taxes not yet due, and [2] Covenants, Conditions, Restrictions, Rights of Way and Easements of Records, if any, which do not materially affect the value or intended use of the property. **Fifteen (15) days from acceptance** are allowed each of the parties for examination of title to the properties to be acquired by them and to report in writing any valid objections thereto. Any exceptions to title, which would be disclosed by examination of the records, shall be deemed to have been accepted unless reported in writing **within said _____ days.** If any objections are reported, the Conveying Party shall use all due diligence to remove such exceptions at his own expense **within sixty (60) days thereafter.** But if such exceptions cannot be removed **within the number of days allowed,** all rights and obligations hereunder shall terminate, unless the party acquiring the property so affected elects to accept the property subject to such exceptions. If the Conveying Party concludes he is unwilling or unable to remove such objections, the Conveying Party shall so notify the Acquiring Party **within ten (10) days of receipt of said objections.** In that event the Acquiring Party may terminate this agreement and all unused deposits shall be returned.

9. EVIDENCE OF TITLE. Evidence of title shall be in the form of ☐ a Policy of Title Insurance, ☐ Other: _____ _____, to be paid for by the parties on the properties they are ☐ conveying, ☐ acquiring.

10. CLOSING. Within _____ days of acceptance, or upon removal of any exceptions to title as provided above, whichever is later, both parties shall deposit in escrow all funds and instruments necessary to complete the exchange.
Escrow fees to be paid by _____.
Documentary transfer tax, if any, to be paid by _____
Escrow holder shall be _____.

11. SURVIVAL. The omission from escrow instructions of any provision herein shall not waive the right of any party. All representations or warranties shall survive the conveyance of the property.

12. PHYSICAL POSSESSION. Physical possession of both properties to be delivered upon recordation of the deeds.

13. PRORATIONS. Rents, taxes and other expenses of the properties to be prorated as of the date of recordation of the deeds. Security deposits, advance rentals, or considerations involving future lease credits shall be credited to the party acquiring title.

14. INSURANCE. Each party hereto is to obtain hazard insurance on the property to be acquired, **prepaid for one year** in an amount satisfactory to the loan holders and covering one hundred percent replacement cost of improvements and to name holders of the secured loans as additional payees.
The mortgagor agrees further to annually increase said insurance if necessary, to relate to the value of the property during the term of mortgage.
The mortgagor shall instruct the insurance carrier to deliver to the mortgagees **before closing** a certificate providing for **30 days written notice in the event of cancellation.**

15. DUE ON SALE CLAUSE. If the note and deed of trust or mortgage for any existing loan contains an acceleration or "due on sale" clause, the lender may demand full payment of the entire loan balance as a result of this transaction. Both parties acknowledge that they are not relying on any representation by the other party or the Broker with respect to the enforceability of such a provision in existing notes and deeds of trust or mortgages, or deeds of trust or mortgages to be executed in accordance with this agreement. Both parties have been advised by the Broker to seek independent legal advice with respect to these matters.

16. BALLOON PAYMENT. Both parties acknowledge that they have not received or relied upon any statements or representations made to them by the Broker regarding availability of funds, or rate of interest at which funds might be available, at the time a party becomes obligated to refinance or pay off the remaining balance of any loan pursuant to the terms of this agreement.

17. DISCLAIMER. Both parties acknowledge that they have not received or relied upon any statements or representations made to them by the Broker(s) herein, regarding the effect of this transaction upon their respective tax liabilities. Both parties further acknowledge that the broker(s) will not be investigating the status of permits, zoning, location of property lines, and/or code compliance. Square footage of structures is approximate and neither the parties nor the broker(s) guarantee accuracy. The parties need to satisfy themselves concerning these issues.

18. NOTICES. Both parties warrant that they have no notice of violations relating to their respective properties from City, County, or State agencies.

19. MAINTENANCE. Conveying party covenants that the heating, air conditioning, electrical, solar, septic system, gutters and downspouts, sprinkler, and plumbing systems including water heater, pool and spa systems, as well as built-in appliances and other mechanical apparatus shall be in **working order** on the **date possession is delivered.** The Conveying party shall replace any cracked or broken glass including windows, mirrors, shower and tub enclosures. **Until possession is delivered** the Conveying Party shall maintain all structures, landscaping, grounds and pool. Conveying party agrees to deliver the property in a neat and clean condition with all debris and personal belongings removed. **The following items are specifically excluded from the above:** _____
_____
Acquiring party and the Conveying Party understand and acknowledge that broker shall not in any circumstances be liable for any breach in this clause.

20. ACCESS TO PROPERTY. Both parties agree to provide reasonable access to their respective properties to each other, and to inspectors representing them, and to representatives of lending institutions for appraisal purposes.

21. PROVISIONS ON THE REVERSE SIDE. The provisions *initialed below,* printed in full on the reverse side, are included in this agreement.

[____] A. Income and Expense Statements	[____] I. City and County Inspections
[____] B. Existing Leases	[____] J. Smoke Detector Ordinance
[____] C. Changes during Transaction	[____] K. Operating Permit
[____] D. Personal Property in furnished units of Property #1	[____] L. Occupancy Permit
[____] E. Personal Property in furnished units of Property #2	[____] M. Flood Hazard Zone — Property #1
[____] F. Pest Control Inspection	[____] N. Flood Hazard Zone — Property #2
[____] G. Waiver of Pest Control Inspection	[____] O. Rent Control Ordinance
[____] H. Inspections of property condition to be approved or disapproved within _____ days of acceptance	

22. DEFAULT. In the event that either party shall default in the performance of this agreement, the other party may, subject to any rights of the Broker herein, retain the defaulting party's deposit, if any, on account of damages sustained and may take such actions as he deems appropriate to collect such additional damages as may be been actually sustained, and the defaulting party shall have the right to take such action as he deems appropriate to recover such portion of the deposit as may be allowed by law. In the event that either party shall so default, the defaulting party agrees to pay the Broker(s) entitled thereto such fees as would be payable in the absence of such default. The parties' obligations to said Broker(s) shall be in addition to any rights which said Broker(s) may have against them in the event of default. In the event legal action is instituted by the Broker(s) or any party to this agreement, to enforce the terms of this agreement, or arising out of the execution of this agreement or the sale, or to collect fees, the prevailing party shall be entitled to receive from the other party a reasonable attorney fee to be determined by the court in which such action is brought.

23. F.I.R.P.T.A. (Foreign Investment and Real Property Tax Act). The Foreign Investment and Real Property Tax Act requires the Acquiring Party of real property to withhold ten percent (10%) of the sale price and to deposit that amount with the Internal Revenue Service **upon closing,** if the Conveying Party is a foreign person, foreign corporation or partnership, or non-resident alien, unless the property qualifies for an exemption under the act.
Unless it is established that the transaction is exempt because the purchase price is $300,000 or less and the Acquiring Party intends to use the property as his primary residence, the Conveying Party agrees to:
a. Provide Broker with a Non-Foreign Seller Affidavit (PPC Form 101-V), stating under penalty of perjury that the Conveying Party is not a foreign person; or
b. Provide Broker with a Certificate from the Internal Revenue Service establishing that no federal income tax withholding is required.
c. Subparagraphs (a) or (b) to be provided to Acquiring Party **within _____ days of acceptance** or the Conveying Party consents to withholding ten percent (10%) from the sale price, to be deposited with the Internal Revenue Service.

First Party's Initials: [_____]   Second Party's Initials: [_____]

PROVISIONS:

_____**21-A. INCOME AND EXPENSE STATEMENTS.** Each party shall submit to the other party a true and complete statement of rental income and expenses **within seven (7) days of acceptance.** The parties shall be deemed to have approved said statements unless written notice to the contrary is delivered to the other party's agent **within seven (7) days of receipt of said statements.**

_____**21-B. EXISTING LEASES.** Each party shall take title subject to existing leases and rights of parties in possession under month-to-month tenancies, if any, as listed on Exhibit attached hereto. **Within seven (7) days of acceptance,** each party shall deliver to the other party copies of said leases and rental agreements, as well as copies of all outstanding notices sent to tenants, and a written statement of all oral agreements with tenants, incured defaults by owner or tenants, claims made by or to tenants, and a statement of all tenants' deposits held by owner. The parties shall be deemed to have approved said documents unless written notice to the contrary is delivered to the other party's agent **within seven (7) days of receipt of said documents.** Each party warrants to the other party that the copies of said documents and other agreements relating to the respective parties are true copies of leases and agreements in effect and that there are no written or oral modifications with respect thereto.

_____**21-C. CHANGES DURING TRANSACTION.** During the pendency of this transaction each party agrees that no changes in the existing leases or rental agreements shall be made, nor new leases or rental agreements entered into, nor shall any substantial alterations or repairs be made or undertaken without the written consent of the other party.

_____**21-D. PERSONAL PROPERTY IN FURNISHED UNITS OF PROPERTY #1.** All furniture and furnishings and any other personal property owned by the **First Party** and used in the operation of **Property #1** per attached signed inventory shall be transferred by Bill of Sale to the **Second Party** at closing. Said inventory has been made an integral part of this agreement **prior to its execution.**

_____**21-E. PERSONAL PROPERTY IN FURNISHED UNITS OF PROPERTY #2.** All furniture and furnishings and any other personal property owned by the **Second Party** and used in the operation of **Property #2** per attached signed inventory shall be transferred by Bill of Sale to the **First Party** at closing. Said inventory has been made an integral part of this agreement prior to its execution.

_____**21-F. PEST CONTROL INSPECTION.** Within ten (10) days of acceptance the Conveying party shall furnish the Acquiring party, at its expense, a current written inspection report by a registered structural pest control operator, covering the main building and garage. (Said inspection report shall **not** include roof coverings, which are included under the heading INSPECTIONS OF PHYSICAL CONDITION OF PROPERTY.)

If further inspection of inaccessible areas is recommended in the report, the Acquiring party may require that said areas be inspected. If any infestation or infection is discovered by such inspection, the additional cost of such inspection and additional required work shall be paid by the Conveying Party. If no infestation or infection is found, the additional cost of inspecting such inaccessible areas and the work required to return the property to its original condition shall be paid by the Acquiring Party.

The inspector shall be requested to separately report:

Section (1) — Work recommended (a) to correct infestation and/or infection of wood destroying pests or organisms, (b) to repair damage caused by such infestation and infection, and (c) to repair plumbing and other leaks, including repair of leaking shower stalls and pans.

Section (2) — Work recommended to correct conditions which are deemed likely to lead to infestation or infection, but where no infestation or infection exists at the time.

If no infestation or infection of wood destroying pests or organisms is found, the report shall include a written Certification that on the date of inspection "no evidence of active infestation or infection was found."

Work recommended in said report for the property to be conveyed shall be paid by the Conveying Party, unless otherwise specified herein.

Funds for work specified in said reports, to be done at the Conveying Party's expense, shall be held in escrow and disbursed by escrow holder upon receipt of a Certification statement by a licensed structural pest control operator, certifying that the properties are free of evidence of active infestation or infection.

As soon as the same are available, copies of the reports and any certification or other proof of completion of the work shall be delivered to the agents of the parties who are authorized to receive the same on behalf of their principals.

_____**21-G. WAIVER OF PEST CONTROL INSPECTION.** Both parties have satisfied themselves about the condition of the properties and agree to acquire the respective properties in their present condition without the benefit of a structural pest control inspection. Each party acknowledges that he has not received or relied upon any representations by either Broker or the other party with respect to the physical condition of the property.

_____**21-H. INSPECTIONS OF PHYSICAL CONDITION OF PROPERTY.** Each party shall have the right to retain, at his expense, licensed experts including but not limited to engineers, geologists, architects, contractors and specialty contractors, to inspect the property for any structural and non-structural conditions including but not limited to matters concerning roofing, electrical, plumbing, heating, cooling, electrical appliances, well, septic system, pool, survey, geological and environmental hazards including but not limited to toxic wastes or substances, radon gas, formaldehyde, asbestos, lead-based paint, and radioactive substances. **Within the number of days specified in Item 21-H on the reverse side** each party shall notify the other party in writing of approval or disapproval of all inspection reports obtained. If the party receiving such notice fails to agree to correct any unacceptable conditions **within five (5) days of receipt of such notice,** the disapproving party may terminate this agreement and all unused deposits shall be returned.

_____**21-I. CITY AND COUNTY INSPECTIONS.** Local ordinance requires that the property be inspected for compliance with local building and permit regulations, standards and ordinances as a condition to sale or transfer. **Within five (5) days of acceptance** the Conveying Party shall notify the appropriate local agency to cause the property to be inspected **at the earliest practicable date.** If the Conveying Party is unable or unwilling to remedy any violations, this agreement shall terminate unless the Acquiring Party agrees to pay the cost of corrections required.

_____**21-J. SMOKE DETECTORS.** In accordance with local ordinance smoke detectors shall be installed by the Conveying Party. If required, said smoke detectors shall be inspected by the appropriate local agency **prior to closing** and a compliance report obtained.

_____**21-K. OPERATING PERMIT.** Each party warrants to the other party that an operating permit for the property is in effect.

_____**21-L. OCCUPANCY PERMIT.** Each party warrants to the other party that an occupancy permit for the property is in effect.

_____**21-M. FLOOD HAZARD ZONE — PROPERTY #1.** The **Second Party** has been advised that **Property #1** is located in an area which the Secretary of HUD has found to have special flood hazards and that it will be necessary to purchase flood insurance in order to obtain any loan secured by the property from any federally regulated financial institution or a loan insured or guaranteed by an agency of the U.S. Government.

The purpose of the program is to provide flood insurance at reasonable cost. For further information consult your lender or insurance carrier. The Acquiring Party shall be deemed to be satisfied with the result of such inquiries unless written notice to the contrary is delivered to the Conveying Party or his agent **within seven (7) days of acceptance,** in which case the Acquiring Party may terminate this agreement and all unused deposits shall be returned.

_____**21-N. FLOOD HAZARD ZONE — PROPERTY #2.** The First Party has been advised that **Property #2** is located in an area which the Secretary of HUD has found to have special flood hazards and that it will be necessary to purchase flood insurance in order to obtain any loan secured by the property from any federally regulated financial institution or a loan insured or guaranteed by an agency of the U.S. Government.

The purpose of the program is to provide flood insurance at reasonable cost. For further information consult your lender or insurance carrier. The Acquiring Party shall be deemed to be satisfied with the result of such inquiries unless written notice to the contrary is delivered to the Conveying Party or his agent **within seven (7) days of acceptance,** in which case the Acquiring Party may terminate this agreement and all unused deposits shall be returned.

_____**21-O. RENT CONTROL ORDINANCE.** The Acquiring Party is aware that a local ordinance is in effect which regulates the rights and obligations of property owners. It may also affect the manner in which future rents can be adjusted.

Parties: _____

24. ENVIRONMENTAL HAZARDS BOOKLET. [_____] The Acquiring Party acknowledges receipt of the "Environmental Hazards Booklet".

25. HAZARDOUS MATERIALS. Hazardous Materials Addendum (PPC Form 110.61) ☐ is, ☐ is not attached hereto.

26. ADDITIONAL TERMS AND CONDITIONS:

_____
_____
_____
_____
_____
_____
_____
_____
_____
_____
_____
_____
_____
_____
_____
_____
_____

27. ADDENDA. The following addenda are attached and made a part of this agreement:_____
_____
_____

28. EXPIRATION OF OFFER. This offer shall expire unless a copy hereof with written acceptance is delivered to the **First Party** or his agent **within** _____ **days from date.**

29. TIME. Time is of the essence of this agreement.

30. COUNTERPARTS. This agreement may be executed in one or more counterparts, each of which is deemed to be an original hereof, and all of which shall together constitute one and the same instrument.

31. FAX TRANSMISSION. The facsimile transmission of a signed copy hereof or any counter offer to the other party or his/her agent, followed by faxed acknowledgement of receipt, shall consitute delivery of said signed document. The parties agree to confirm such delivery by mailing or personally delivering a signed copy to the other party or his/her agent.

32. ENTIRE AGREEMENT. This document contains the entire agreement of the parties and supersedes all prior agreement or representations with respect to the property which are not expressly set forth herein. This agreement may be modified only by a writing signed and dated by both parties. **Both parties acknowledge that they have not relied on any statements of the real estate agent or broker which are not herein expressed.**

33. BROKERAGE FEE. Upon acceptance hereof the undersigned **First Party** hereby agrees to pay a brokerage fee for services rendered to _____, as follows:_____.

The Broker is hereby authorized to cooperate with other brokers and to divide the fees in any manner satisfactory to them.

34. AGENCY RELATIONSHIP CONFIRMATION. The following agency relationship is hereby confirmed for this transaction:

BROKER: _____ is the agent of (check one):
          (Print Name of Firm)

          ☐ the First Party exclusively; or ☐ the Second Party exclusively; or ☐ both the First Party and Second Party.

BROKER: _____ is the agent of (check one):
          (Print Name of Firm)

          ☐ the First Party exclusively; or ☐ the Second Party exclusively; or ☐ both the First Party and Second Party.

Note: This confirmation DOES NOT take the place of any AGENCY DISCLOSURE form which may be required by law.

The undersigned First Party acknowledges receipt of a copy hereof and acknowledges further that he has not received or relied upon any statements or representations by the Broker which are not herein expressed.

_____ Real Estate Company   Dated: _____ Time: _____

By _____   _____ **First Party**

Broker's Initials: _____ Dated: _____   _____ **First Party**

ACCEPTANCE

The undersigned **Second Party** accepts the foregoing offer and agrees to exchange the herein described properties on the terms and conditions herein specified; [_____] subject to attached Counter Offer, [_____] not subject to any Counter Offer.

35. BROKERAGE FEE. The undersigned **Second Party** agrees to pay a brokerage fee for services rendered to _____ as follows: _____

The undersigned Second Party acknowledges receipt of a copy hereof and acknowledges further that he has not received or relied upon any statements or representations by the Broker which are not herein expressed.

_____ Real Estate Company   Dated: _____ Time: _____

By _____   _____ **Second Party**

Broker's Initials: _____ Dated: _____   _____ **Second Party**

FORM 102.3 (10-91)   COPYRIGHT © 1991, BY PROFESSIONAL PUBLISHING CORP. 122 PAUL DR. SAN RAFAEL, CA 94903 (415) 472-1964   **PROFESSIONAL PUBLISHING**

NCR (No Carbon Required)

ADDENDUM TO EXCHANGE AGREEMENT

In reference to Exchange Agreement between _____

and _____,

dated _____, and accepted on _____, covering the real
properties commonly known as _____

and _____

the undersigned parties to said Exchange Agreement herewith agree to _____

_____
_____
_____
_____
_____
_____
_____
_____
_____
_____
_____
_____
_____
_____
_____
_____
_____
_____

The herein agreement, upon its execution by both parties hereto, is herewith made an integral part of the aforementioned Exchange Agreement.

DATED: _____   DATED: _____

_____ First Party   _____ Second Party

_____ First Party   _____ Second Party

_____ First Party   _____ Second Party

_____ First Party   _____ Second Party

Witness _____ Agent   Witness _____ Agent

FORM 102-B (1-86) COPYRIGHT 1986. BY PROFESSIONAL PUBLISHING CORP. 122 PAUL DR. SAN RAFAEL, CA 94903 (415) 472-1964   PROFESSIONAL PUBLISHING

EXCHANGE COMMISSION AGREEMENT

In reference to Exchange Agreement dated _____, the undersigned ☐ **First Party,** ☐ **Second Party:**

_____

hereby agrees to pay to:

_____

the broker in this transaction, for services rendered in the exchange of the real property described as:

_____

for the real property described as:

_____

the sum of $_____ (_____ dollars),

due upon the execution of said Exchange Agreement by both parties thereto, in the form of:

1) ☐ Cash

2) ☐ A note secured by a deed of trust (mortgage) upon the property described as:

_____

to be executed by the undersigned in favor of above broker, payable at $_____ or more per month including interest at _____%

per annum, with the entire balance due _____ **years from date of note.**

3) ☐ Other: _____

_____

_____

_____

_____

_____

_____

Dated _____

Broker _____ Client _____

By _____ Client _____

Address _____ Address _____

Phone _____ Phone _____

Internal Revenue Service Forms

appendix **E**

1991

 Department of the Treasury
Internal Revenue Service

Instructions for Form 8824

Like-Kind Exchanges

(Section references are to the Internal Revenue Code unless otherwise noted.)

General Instructions

Paperwork Reduction Act Notice

We ask for the information on this form to carry out the Internal Revenue laws of the United States. You are required to give us the information. We need it to ensure that you are complying with these laws and to allow us to figure and collect the right amount of tax.

The time needed to complete and file this form will vary depending on individual circumstances. The estimated average time is:

Recordkeeping . . . . . 27 min.

**Learning about
the law or the form** . . . . 22 min.

Preparing the form . . . . 54 min.

**Copying, assembling, and
sending the form to the IRS** . 27 min.

If you have comments concerning the accuracy of these time estimates or suggestions for making this form more simple, we would be happy to hear from you. You can write to both the IRS and the Office of Management and Budget at the addresses listed in the instructions for the tax return with which this form is filed.

Purpose of Form

Use Parts I and II of Form 8824 to report the exchange of business or investment property for property that is of a like kind (section 1031). Use Part III of Form 8824 to report the nonrecognition of gain from conflict-of-interest sales by certain members of the executive branch of the Federal Government (section 1043).

Form 8824 is used as a supporting statement for like-kind exchanges reported on other forms, including **Form 4797**, Sales of Business Property, and the **Schedule D** for your tax return. Complete and attach a separate Form 8824 for each exchange. See the instructions for Form 4797 or Schedule D for how to report the exchange on those forms.

Additional Information.—For more information on like-kind exchanges, see section 1031 and Regulations section 1.1031, and **Pub. 544**, Sales and Other Dispositions of Assets.

When To File

File Form 8824 for the tax year in which you transferred the property you gave up to the other party in the exchange.

Related Party Exchanges.—Special rules apply to section 1031 exchanges made with a **related party**. A related party includes your spouse, child, grandchild, parent, brother or sister, or a related corporation, S corporation, partnership (for exchanges after 8/3/90), or trust. See section 1031(f).

If the exchange was made with a related party, you must file Form 8824 for the year of the exchange and also for the 2 years following the year of the exchange. For any of these years, if either you or the related party disposes of the property received in the exchange, the deferred gain or (loss) from line 21 must be reported on your return unless one of the exceptions shown on line 11 applies. See the instructions for line 21.

If you are filing this form for 1 of the 2 years following the year of the exchange, complete lines 1 through 10. If both lines 9 and 10 are "No," stop there and attach the form to your return. If either line 9 or line 10 is "Yes" and one of the exceptions on line 11 applies, check the applicable box on line 11, stop there, and attach the form to your return. If none of the exceptions on line 11 applies, complete Part II. The deferred gain or (loss) from line 21 must be included in income on your return for this tax year. Report the deferred gain or (loss) in the same manner as if the exchange had been a sale.

An exchange that is structured to avoid the related party rules is not eligible for like-kind exchange treatment. See section 1031(f)(4).

Like-Kind Exchanges

Generally, if you exchange business or investment property solely for business or investment property of a like kind, no gain or loss is recognized under section 1031. If you also receive other property or money, then the gain, if any, is recognized to the extent of the other property or money received, but a loss is not recognized.

Section 1031 does not apply to exchanges of inventory, stocks, bonds, notes, other securities or evidence of indebtedness, and certain other assets. See section 1031(a)(2).

Like-Kind Property

Properties are of a like kind if they are of the same nature or character, even if they differ in grade or quality. Personal properties of a like class are also considered to be of a like kind. Real property is of the same kind as other real property, regardless of whether the properties are improved or unimproved. However, real property located in the United States and real property located outside the United States are **not** property of a like kind.

Deferred Exchanges

A deferred exchange is one in which the property received in the exchange is not received immediately upon the transfer of the property you gave up in the exchange. For a deferred exchange to qualify as a like-kind exchange, the following requirements must be met:

1. The replacement property to be received by you in the exchange must be identified within 45 days after the date on which you transferred the property given up, and

2. You must receive the new property by the earlier of 180 days after the date on which you transferred the property given up or the due date of your tax return for the year of the transfer (including extensions).

Property is properly identified by notifying another party to the exchange (other than a related party) of your selection of the property. The identification may also be made in a written agreement for the exchange of properties.

Multi-Asset Exchanges

Exchanges of Multiple Properties.—An exchange of multiple properties occurs if the properties exchanged consist of more than one group of like-kind properties being transferred and received. For example, an exchange of land, vehicles, and cash for land and vehicles would be an exchange of multiple properties. An exchange of land, vehicles, and cash for only land would not be an exchange of multiple properties.

In addition, an exchange is an exchange of multiple properties if only one group of like-kind properties is created but there is more than one property being transferred or received within that group.

Special rules apply when figuring the amount of gain recognized and the basis of properties received in an exchange of multiple properties. See Regulations section 1.1031(j)-1 for details.

**Transfer and Receipt of Both
Like-Kind and Other Property.**—

Cat. No. 12311A

Special rules also apply when figuring the amount of gain recognized and the basis of property received in an exchange involving the transfer and receipt of both like-kind and other property that does not qualify as an exchange of multiple properties. See Regulations section 1.1031(d)-1 for details.

Reporting of Multi-Asset Exchanges.— If you transferred and received (a) more than one group of like-kind properties, or (b) cash or other (not like-kind) property, do not complete lines 12 through 18 of Form 8824. Instead, attach a statement showing the computation of the realized and recognized gain, and enter the correct amount for lines 19 through 22. Report any gain recognized on Schedule D, Form 4797, or **Form 6252,** Installment Sale Income, whichever applies.

Specific Instructions

Lines 1 and 2.—For real property, show the address, type of property, and include the country if located outside the United States. For personal property, enter a short description.

Line 5.—See **Deferred Exchanges,** on page 1.

Line 7.—See **Related Party Exchanges,** on page 1, for the definition of a related party.

Line 11.—If you believe that you can establish to the satisfaction of the IRS that tax avoidance was not a principal purpose of both the exchange and the disposition, attach an explanation. See **Pub. 537,** Installment Sales, for exceptions where tax avoidance is not a principal purpose.

Lines 12, 13, and 14.—If you gave up other property in the exchange in addition to the like-kind property, enter the fair market value and your adjusted basis of the other property on lines 12 and 13. If you did not give up other property, skip lines 12 through 14, and go to line 15. The gain or (loss) from this property is figured on line 14 and must be reported on your return. Report the gain or (loss) in the same manner as if the exchange had been a sale.

Line 15.—Include on line 15 the sum of the following:

● Any cash paid to you by the other party,

● The FMV of other (not like-kind) property you received, if any, AND

● Net liabilities assumed by the other party—the excess, if any, of any liabilities assumed by the other party (including any mortgages to which the property you gave up was subject) **over** the **total** of: (1) any liabilities you assumed (or to which the property you

received was subject), (2) cash you paid to the other party, and (3) the FMV of other property you gave up.

Reduce the sum of the above amounts (but not below zero) by any exchange expenses you incurred.

See the example below the line 18 instructions.

Line 18.—Include on line 18 the sum of the following:

● The adjusted basis of the like-kind property you gave up,

● Exchange expenses, if any (except for expenses used to reduce the amount reported on line 15), AND

● Net amount paid to other party—the excess, if any, of the **total** of: (1) any liabilities you assumed, (2) cash you paid to the other party, and (3) the FMV of the other property you gave up, **over** any liabilities assumed by the other party.

See the example below for how to figure the amounts to be entered on lines 15 and 18. Also see Regulations section 1.1031(d)-2.

Example. D owns an apartment house with an FMV of $220,000, an adjusted basis of $100,000, and subject to a mortgage of $80,000. E owns an apartment house with an FMV of $250,000, an adjusted basis of $175,000, and subject to a mortgage of $150,000. D transfers his apartment house to E, and receives in exchange the apartment house owned by E and $40,000 in cash. Each apartment house is transferred subject to the mortgage on it.

D would enter on line 15 only the $40,000 of cash received from E. The $80,000 of liabilities assumed by E is not included because it does not exceed the $150,000 of liabilities D assumed. D would enter $170,000 on line 18—the $100,000 adjusted basis, plus the $70,000 excess of the liabilities D assumed over the liabilities assumed by E ($150,000 – $80,000).

E would enter $30,000 on line 15—the excess of the $150,000 of liabilities assumed by D over the total of the $80,000 of liabilities E assumed and the $40,000 of cash E paid. E would enter on line 18 only the adjusted basis of $175,000, because the total of the $80,000 of liabilities E assumed and the $40,000 of cash E paid ($120,000) does not exceed the $150,000 of liabilities assumed by D.

Line 20—Recognized gain.—If line 20 is more than zero, include the gain from line 20 on the form or schedule on which this exchange is reported.

If you are reporting the recognized gain on the installment method, see section 453(f)(6) to determine the

amount taxable this year, and report it on Form 6252. If the exchange involved a related party, write "Related Party Like-Kind Exchange" at the top of Form 6252.

Line 21—Deferred gain or (loss).—If line 19 is a loss, enter on line 21 the loss from line 19. Otherwise, subtract the amount on line 20, if any, from the amount on line 19 and enter the result.

If the exchange was made with a related party, and either you **or** the related party disposes of the property received in the exchange within 2 years after the last transfer of property that was part of the exchange, the deferred gain or (loss) must be reported on your return in the year of the disposition (unless one of the exceptions on line 11 applies). Report the gain or (loss) in the same manner as if the exchange had been a sale. See **Related Party Exchanges** under **When To File,** on page 1.

Line 22—Basis of like-kind property received.—The amount on line 22 is your basis in the like-kind property you received in the exchange. The basis of other property received in the exchange, if any, is its fair market value.

Part III—Section 1043 Conflict-of-Interest Sales

If you sell property at a gain according to a certificate of divestiture issued by the Office of Government Ethics, you may elect to recognize gain on the sale only to the extent that the amount realized on the sale exceeds the cost of replacement property (permitted property) purchased within 60 days after the sale. Complete Part III of Form 8824 only if the cost of the replacement property exceeds the basis of the divested property.

Basis in the replacement property is reduced by the amount of the gain not recognized. If more than one purchase of replacement property is made, reduce the basis of the replacement property in the order that the property was acquired.

Permitted property is any obligation of the United States or any diversified investment fund approved by the Office of Government Ethics.

Report the sale on Form 4797 or Schedule D, where the transaction would be reported if section 1043 did not apply. For the description, write "Form 8824, section 1043." If Form 8824, line 30, is zero, write "EGA 89" in the gain column, but if line 30 is more than zero, enter the gain. Complete all other columns as appropriate.

Line 26.—Enter the amount you received from the sale of the divested property, minus any selling expenses.

Form 8824

Like-Kind Exchanges

(and nonrecognition of gain from conflict-of-interest sales)

▶ See separate instructions.   ▶ Attach to your tax return.
▶ Use a separate form for each like-kind exchange.

Department of the Treasury
Internal Revenue Service

OMB No. 1545-1190

1991

Attachment
Sequence No. **49**

Name(s) shown on tax return

Identifying number

Part I Information on the Like-Kind Exchange

Note: *If the property described on line 1 or line 2 is real property located outside the United States, indicate the country.*

1 Description of like-kind property given up ▶ ....

2 Description of like-kind property received ▶ ....

3	Date like-kind property given up was originally acquired (month, day, year)	**3** / /
4	Date you actually transferred your property to other party (month, day, year)	**4** / /
5	Date the like-kind property you received was identified (month, day, year). See instructions	**5** / /
6	Date you actually received the like-kind property from other party (month, day, year)	**6** / /

7 Was the exchange made with a related party (see instructions)?

a ☐ Yes, in this tax year   b ☐ Yes, in a prior tax year   c ☐ No *(If "No," go to Part II.)*

8 Enter the following information about the related party:

Name	Identifying number
Address (no., street, and apt. or suite no., rural route, or P.O. box no. if mail is not delivered to street address)	
City or town, state, and ZIP code	Relationship to you

9 During this tax year, did the related party sell or dispose of the like-kind property received from you in the exchange? . . . . . ☐ Yes ☐ No

10 During this tax year, did you sell or dispose of the like-kind property you received? . . . . . ☐ Yes ☐ No

If both lines 9 and 10 are "No," go to Part II. If either line 9 or line 10 is "Yes," the deferred gain or (loss) from line 21 must be reported on your return this tax year, **unless** one of the exceptions on line 11 applies. See instructions.

11 If one of the exceptions below applies to the disposition, check the applicable box:

☐ The disposition was after the death of either of the related parties.

☐ The disposition was an involuntary conversion, and the threat of conversion occurred after the exchange.

☐ You can establish to the satisfaction of the IRS that neither the exchange nor the disposition had tax avoidance as its principal purpose. If this box is checked, attach an explanation. See instructions.

Part II Realized Gain or (Loss), Recognized Gain, and Basis of Like-Kind Property Received

Caution: *If you transferred and received (a) more than one group of like-kind properties, or (b) cash or other (not like-kind) property, see instructions under Multi-Asset Exchanges.*

Note: *Complete lines 12 through 14 ONLY if you gave up property that was not like-kind. Otherwise, go to line 15 now.*

12	Fair market value (FMV) of other property given up	**12**
13	Adjusted basis of other property given up	**13**
14	Gain or (loss) recognized on other property given up. Subtract line 13 from line 12. See instructions for where to report the gain or (loss) on your tax return	**14**
15	Cash received, FMV of other property received, plus net liabilities assumed by other party, reduced (but not below zero) by any exchange expenses you incurred (see instructions)	**15**
16	FMV of like-kind property you received	**16**
17	Add lines 15 and 16	**17**
18	Adjusted basis of like-kind property you gave up, net amounts paid to other party, plus any exchange expenses **not** used on line 15 (see instructions)	**18**
19	**Realized gain or (loss).** Subtract line 18 from line 17	**19**
20	**Recognized gain.** Enter the smaller of line 15 or line 19, but not less than zero. Report this amount on the form or schedule on which this exchange is reported. See instructions	**20**
21	Deferred gain or (loss). Subtract line 20 from line 19. If a related party exchange, see instructions	**21**
22	**Basis of like-kind property received.** Subtract line 15 from the sum of lines 18 and 20	**22**

For Paperwork Reduction Act Notice, see separate instructions.   Cat. No. 12311A   Form **8824** (1991)

Form 8824 (1991)   Page **2**

| Name(s) shown on tax return. (Do not enter name and social security number if shown on other side.) | Your social security number |

Part III **Section 1043 Conflict-of-Interest Sales.** See instructions. (Attach a copy of your certificate of divestiture.)

Note: *This part is only to be used by officers or employees of the executive branch of the Federal Government for reporting nonrecognition of gain under section 1043 on the sale of property to comply with the conflict-of-interest requirements.*

23   Description of divested property ▶ ....

24   Description of replacement property ▶ ....

25   Date divested property was sold (month, day, year) . . . . **25** / /

26   Sales price of divested property. See instructions **26**

27   Basis of divested property **27**

28   **Realized gain.** Subtract line 27 from line 26 . . . . **28**

29   Cost of replacement property purchased within 60 days after date of sale **29**

30   **Recognized gain.** Subtract line 29 from line 26. If zero or less, enter -0-. If more than zero, enter this amount on the line on Schedule D or Form 4797 on which this transaction is reported . . **30**

31   Gain not recognized. Subtract line 30 from line 28 . . . . . . **31**

32   **Basis of replacement property.** Subtract line 31 from line 29 . . . . **32**

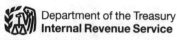

**Department of the Treasury
Internal Revenue Service**

Instructions for Form 6252

Installment Sale Income

(Section references are to the Internal Revenue Code unless otherwise noted.)

General Instructions

Paperwork Reduction Act Notice

We ask for the information on this form to carry out the Internal Revenue laws of the United States. You are required to give us the information. We need it to ensure that you are complying with these laws and to allow us to figure and collect the right amount of tax.

The time needed to complete and file this form will vary depending on individual circumstances. The estimated average time is:

Recordkeeping	1 hr., 25 min.
Learning about the law or the form	35 min.
Preparing the form	56 min.
Copying, assembling, and sending the form to the IRS .	20 min.

If you have comments concerning the accuracy of these time estimates or suggestions for making this form more simple, we would be happy to hear from you. You can write to both the IRS and the Office of Management and Budget at the addresses listed in the instructions for the tax return with which this form is filed.

Purpose of Form

Use Form 6252 to report income from casual sales of real or personal property (other than inventory) if you will receive any payments in a tax year after the year of sale.

If any part of an installment payment you received is for interest, be sure to report that interest on the appropriate form or schedule. Do not report interest received, carrying charges received, or unstated interest on this form. Get **Pub. 537,** Installment Sales, for details on unstated interest.

You cannot use the installment method for sales after 1986 of stock or securities traded on an established securities market. See section 453(k).

Do not use Form 6252 if you elect not to report the sale on the installment method. To elect out, see the Instructions for **Schedule D (Form 1040),** Capital Gains and Losses, or **Form 4797,** Sales of Business Property. If you do not use the installment method, report the sale on Schedule D or Form 4797, whichever applies.

Note: Generally, once you file Form 6252, you cannot later elect out of the installment method. See Pub. 537 for details.

Report the ordinary income from sections 1245, 1250, 179, and 291 in full in the year of sale even if no payments were received. Figure the ordinary income to be recaptured on Form 4797, Part III.

Which Parts To Complete

For the Year of Sale—Complete items A through E, Part I, and Part II.

For Years After the Year of Sale—Complete items A through E, and Part II, for any year you receive a payment from an installment sale.

Related Party Sales—If you sold marketable securities to a related party, complete Form 6252 for each year of the installment agreement even if you did not receive a payment. See **Installment Sales to Related Party,** below, for the definition of a related party. For any year after the year of sale, complete items A through E, and Part III. (If you received a payment, also complete Part II.)

If you sold property other than marketable securities to a related party, complete the form for the year of sale and for 2 years after the year of sale even if you did not receive a payment. If during this 2-year period you did not receive an actual or deemed payment, complete items A through E, and Part III. After this 2-year period, see **For Years After the Year of Sale,** above.

Installment Sales to Related Party

A special rule applies to a first disposition (sale or exchange) of property under the installment method to a related party who then makes a second disposition (sale, exchange, gift, or cancellation of installment note) before making all payments on the first disposition. For this purpose, a related party includes your spouse, child, grandchild, parent, brother, sister, or a related corporation, S corporation, partnership, estate, or trust. See section 453(f)(1) for more details.

Under this rule, you treat part or all of the amount the related party realized (or the fair market value if the disposed property is not sold or exchanged) from the second disposition as if you received it from the first disposition at the time of the second disposition. Figure the gain, if any, on lines 23 through 30. This rule does not apply to any of the exceptions listed in item H of Part III.

Sale of Depreciable Property to Related Person

Generally, if you sell depreciable property to a related person (as defined in section 453(g)(3)), you may not report the sale using the installment method. For this purpose, depreciable property is any property that can be depreciated by the person or entity to whom you transfer it.

However, you may use the installment method if you can show to the satisfaction of the IRS that avoidance of Federal income taxes was not one of the principal purposes of the sale (e.g., no significant tax deferral benefits will result from the sale).

If the installment method does not apply, report the sale on Schedule D or Form 4797, whichever applies. Treat all payments you will receive as if they were received in the year of sale. Use fair market value for any payment that is contingent as to amount. If the fair market value cannot be readily determined, basis is recovered ratably.

Pledge Rule

If an installment obligation from a nondealer disposition of real property used in a trade or business or held for the production of rental income with a sales price over $150,000 is pledged as security on debt after December 17, 1987, treat the net proceeds of the secured debt as a payment on the installment obligation. This rule applies to the disposition of any property under the installment method after 1988 with a sales price over $150,000, except for farm property and personal use property disposed of by an individual. The amount treated as a payment cannot exceed the excess of the total contract price over any payments received under the contract before the secured debt was obtained.

The pledge rule does not apply to pledges made after December 17, 1987, if the debt is incurred to refinance the principal amount of a debt that was outstanding on December 17, 1987, AND was secured by nondealer real property installment obligations on that date and at all times after that date until the refinancing occurred. However, this exception does not apply to the extent that the principal amount of the debt resulting from the refinancing exceeds the principal amount of the refinanced debt immediately

Cat. No. 64262Q

before the refinancing. Also, the pledge rule does not affect refinancing due to the calling of a debt by the creditor as long as the debt is then refinanced by a person other than this creditor or someone related to the creditor.

Interest on Deferred Tax

Interest must be paid on the deferred tax from certain installment obligations. (The rules generally apply to dispositions of real property after 1987, and to dispositions of personal property after 1988.) The interest applies to any installment obligation arising from the disposition of any property under the installment method if:

● The property had a sales price over $150,000 AND

● The aggregate balance of those obligations arising during, and outstanding at the close of, the tax year is more than $5 million.

Exception: *These rules do not apply to dispositions of farm property or dispositions of personal use property by an individual.*

Interest must be paid in subsequent years if installment obligations, which originally required interest to be paid, are still outstanding at the close of a tax year.

How To Report the Interest.—The interest is not figured on Form 6252. See section 453A to figure the interest. Enter the interest as an additional tax on your tax return. Include it in the amount to be entered on the total tax line after credits and other taxes. For individuals, this is line 53 of the 1991 Form 1040. For corporations, it is line 10 of Schedule J (Form 1120). Write "Section 453A(c) interest" to the left of the amount.

Corporations may deduct the interest in the year it is paid or accrued. For individuals and other taxpayers, this interest is not deductible.

Additional Information

See Pub. 537 for details about reductions in selling price, the single sale of several assets, like-kind exchanges, dispositions of installment obligations, and repossessions.

Specific Instructions

Partnerships and S corporations that pass through a section 179 expense deduction to their partners or shareholders should not include this amount on lines 5 and 8.

For the Year of Sale.—If this is the year of sale and you sold section 1245, 1250, 1252, 1254, or 1255 property, you may have ordinary income. Complete Part III of Form 4797 to figure the ordinary income. See the instructions for Part IV of Form 4797 before starting Part I of Form 6252.

Line 1—Selling price.—Enter the total of any money, face amount of the installment

obligation, and the fair market value of other property that you received or will receive in exchange for the property sold. Include on line 1 any existing mortgage or other debt the buyer assumed or took the property subject to.

If there is no stated maximum selling price, such as in a contingent sale, attach a schedule showing the computation of gain. Enter the taxable part on line 20 (and also line 28 if Part III applies). See Temporary Regulations section 15A.453.

Line 2—Mortgages and other debts.—Enter only mortgages (or other debts) the buyer assumed from the seller or took the property subject to. Do not include new mortgages the buyer gets from a bank, the seller, or other sources.

Line 4—Cost or other basis of property sold.—Enter the original cost and other expenses you incurred in buying the property. Add the cost of improvements, etc., and subtract any casualty losses previously allowed. For more details, get **Pub. 551**, Basis of Assets.

Line 5—Depreciation allowed or allowable.—Enter all depreciation or amortization you deducted or should have deducted from the date of purchase until the date of sale. Add any deduction you took under section 179 and the downward basis adjustment under section 50(c) or the corresponding provision of prior law, if any. Subtract any investment tax credit recapture amount if the basis of the property was reduced under section 50(c) or the corresponding provision of prior law and any section 179 or 280F recapture amount included in gross income in a prior tax year.

Line 7—Commissions and other expenses of sale.—Enter sales commissions, advertising expenses, attorney and legal fees, etc., in selling the property.

Line 8—Ordinary income recapture.—See the instructions for Parts III and IV of Form 4797 to figure the recapture. Enter the part of the gain from the sale of depreciable property recaptured under sections 1245 and 1250 (including sections 179 and 291) here and on line 13 of Form 4797.

Line 15—Gross profit percentage.—Enter the gross profit percentage determined for the year of sale even if you did not file Form 6252 for that year.

Line 17—Payments received during year.—Enter all money and the fair market value of any property you received in 1991. Include as payments any amount withheld to pay off a mortgage or other debt, such as broker and legal fees. Do not include the buyer's note, any mortgage, or other liability assumed by the buyer. If you did not receive any payments in 1991, enter -0-.

If in prior years an amount was entered on the equivalent of line 25 of the 1991 form, do not include it on this line. Instead, enter it on line 19.

See **Pledge Rule** on page 1 for details about proceeds that must be treated as payments on installment obligations.

Line 19—Payments received in prior years.—Enter all money and the fair market value of property you received before 1991 from the sale. Include allocable installment income and any other deemed payments from prior years.

Lines 21 and 29.—Report on line 21 or line 29 any ordinary income recapture on section 1252, 1254, and 1255 property. This includes recapture for the year of sale or any remaining recapture from a prior year sale. See section 453(i). Also report on these lines any ordinary income recapture remaining from prior years on section 1245 and 1250 property sold before June 7, 1984. Do not enter ordinary income from a section 179 deduction. If this is the year of sale, see the instructions for Part IV of Form 4797.

The amount on these lines should not exceed the total of the amounts on lines 20 and 28.

Lines 22 and 30—Trade or business property.—Enter this amount on Form 4797, line 4, if the property was held more than 1 year. If the property was held 1 year or less, or if you have an ordinary gain from a noncapital asset (even if the holding period is more than 1 year) enter the amount on Form 4797, line 10, and write "From Form 6252."

Capital assets.—Enter this amount on Schedule D as a short-term or long-term gain. Use the lines identified as from Form 6252.

Item H.—If one of the exceptions apply, check the appropriate box. Skip lines 23 through 30. If you checked the last box, attach an explanation. Generally, the nontax avoidance exception will apply to the second disposition if:

● The disposition was involuntary, (e.g., a creditor of the related person foreclosed on the property, or the related person declared bankruptcy), or

● The disposition was an installment sale under which the terms of payment were substantially equal to or longer than those for the first sale. However, the resale terms must not permit significant deferral of recognition of gain from the first sale (e.g., amounts from the resale are being collected sooner).

Line 23.—If the related party sold all or part of the property from the original sale in 1991, enter the selling price of the part resold. If part was sold in an earlier year and part was sold this year, enter the cumulative amount of the selling price.

Form **6252**	**Installment Sale Income**	OMB No. 1545-0228
Department of the Treasury Internal Revenue Service	▶ See separate instructions. ▶ Attach to your tax return. Use a separate form for each sale or other disposition of property on the installment method.	**19̄91** Attachment Sequence No. **79**
Name(s) shown on return		Identifying number

A Description of property ▶ ....

B Date acquired (month, day, and year) ▶ ⌊___/___/___⌋   **C** Date sold (month, day, and year) ▶ ⌊___/___/___⌋

D Was the property sold to a related party after May 14, 1980? See instructions . . . . ☐ Yes ☐ No

E If the answer to D is "Yes," was the property a marketable security? If "Yes," complete Part III. If "No,"
complete Part III for the year of sale and for 2 years after the year of sale . . . . ☐ Yes ☐ No

Part I	Gross Profit and Contract Price *(Complete this part for the year of sale only.)*				
1	Selling price including mortgages and other debts. Do not include interest whether stated or unstated			**1**	
2	Mortgages and other debts the buyer assumed or took the property subject to, but not new mortgages the buyer got from a bank or other source. .	**2**			
3	Subtract line 2 from line 1.	**3**			
4	Cost or other basis of property sold	**4**			
5	Depreciation allowed or allowable	**5**			
6	Adjusted basis. Subtract line 5 from line 4	**6**			
7	Commissions and other expenses of sale.	**7**			
8	Income recapture from Form 4797, Part III. See instructions . .	**8**			
9	Add lines 6, 7, and 8			**9**	
10	Subtract line 9 from line 1. If zero or less, do not complete the rest of this form			**10**	
11	If the property described in question A above was your main home, enter the total of lines 9f and 15 from Form 2119. Otherwise, enter -0-			**11**	
12	**Gross profit.** Subtract line 11 from line 10			**12**	
13	Subtract line 9 from line 2. If zero or less, enter -0-			**13**	
14	**Contract price.** Add line 3 and line 13			**14**	

Part II	Installment Sale Income *(Complete this part for the year of sale and any year you receive a payment or have certain debts you must treat as a payment on installment obligations.)*			
15	Gross profit percentage. Divide line 12 by line 14. For years after the year of sale, see instructions		**15**	
16	**For year of sale only**—Enter amount from line 13 above; otherwise, enter -0-		**16**	
17	Payments received during year. See instructions. Do not include interest whether stated or unstated		**17**	
18	Add lines 16 and 17		**18**	
19	Payments received in prior years. See instructions. Do not include interest whether stated or unstated	**19**		
20	**Installment sale income.** Multiply line 18 by line 15		**20**	
21	Part of line 20 that is ordinary income under recapture rules. See instructions		**21**	
22	Subtract line 21 from line 20. Enter here and on Schedule D or Form 4797		**22**	

Part III	Related Party Installment Sale Income *(Do not complete if you received the final payment this tax year.)*			

F Name, address, and taxpayer identifying number of related party ....

....

G Did the related party, during this tax year, resell or dispose of the property ("second disposition")? . . . ☐ Yes ☐ No

H **If the answer to question G is "Yes," complete lines 23 through 30 below unless one of the following conditions is met (check only the box that applies).**

☐ The second disposition was more than 2 years after the first disposition (other than dispositions of marketable securities). If this box is checked, enter the date of disposition (month, day, year). . ▶ ⌊___/___/___⌋

☐ The first disposition was a sale or exchange of stock to the issuing corporation.

☐ The second disposition was an involuntary conversion where the threat of conversion occurred after the first disposition.

☐ The second disposition occurred after the death of the original seller or buyer.

☐ It can be established to the satisfaction of the Internal Revenue Service that tax avoidance was not a principal purpose for either of the dispositions. If this box is checked, attach an explanation. See instructions.

23	Selling price of property sold by related party	**23**	
24	Enter contract price from line 14 for year of first sale	**24**	
25	Enter the **smaller** of line 23 or line 24	**25**	
26	Total payments received by the end of your 1991 tax year. Add lines 18 and 19	**26**	
27	Subtract line 26 from line 25. If zero or less, enter -0-	**27**	
28	Multiply line 27 by the gross profit percentage on line 15 for year of first sale	**28**	
29	Part of line 28 that is ordinary income under recapture rules. See instructions	**29**	
30	Subtract line 29 from line 28. Enter here and on Schedule D or Form 4797	**30**	

For Paperwork Reduction Act Notice, see separate instructions.   Cat. No. 13601R   Form **6252** (1991)

*U.S. Government Printing Office: 1991 — 285-378

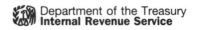

Instructions for Form 2119

Sale of Your Home

Paperwork Reduction Act Notice.—We ask for the information on this form to carry out the Internal Revenue laws of the United States. You are required to give us the information. We need it to ensure that you are complying with these laws and to allow us to figure and collect the right amount of tax.

The time needed to complete and file this form will vary depending on individual circumstances. The estimated average time is:

Recordkeeping	. 46 min.
Learning about the law or the form	. 13 min.
Preparing the form	. 44 min.
Copying, assembling, and sending the form to the IRS	. 20 min.

If you have comments concerning the accuracy of these time estimates or suggestions for making this form more simple, we would be happy to hear from you. You can write to both the **Internal Revenue Service,** Washington, DC 20224, Attention: IRS Reports Clearance Officer, T:FP; and the **Office of Management and Budget,** Paperwork Reduction Project (1545-0072), Washington, DC 20503. **Do not** send this form to either of these offices. Instead, see **When and Where To File** on this page.

General Instructions

Purpose of Form

Use Form 2119 to report the sale of your main home. If you replaced your main home, use Form 2119 to postpone all or part of the gain. Form 2119 is also used by people who were age 55 or older on the date of sale to elect a one-time exclusion of the gain on the sale.

Caution. *If the home you sold was financed (in whole or in part) from a mortgage credit certificate or the proceeds of a tax-exempt qualified mortgage bond, you may owe additional tax. Get Form 8828, Recapture of Federal Mortgage Subsidy, for details.*

Main Home.—Your main home is the one you live in most of the time. It can be a house, houseboat, housetrailer, cooperative apartment, condominium, etc.

Additional Information

You may want to get **Pub. 523,** Tax Information on Selling Your Home, for more details.

Who Must File

You must file Form 1040 with Form 2119 for the year in which you sell your main home, even if the sale resulted in a loss or you are electing the one-time exclusion for people

age 55 or older. There may be additional filing requirements as well. See **When and Where To File** below.

If part of your home was rented out or used for business in the year of sale, report that part of the sale on **Form 4797,** Sales of Business Property. See the instructions for line 3.

If you sold your home on the installment method, complete Form 2119 and **Form 6252,** Installment Sale Income.

If your home was damaged by fire, storm, or other casualty, see **Form 4684,** Casualties and Thefts, and its separate instructions, and **Pub. 547,** Nonbusiness Disasters, Casualties, and Thefts.

If your home was condemned for public use, you can choose to postpone gain under the rules for a condemnation, or you can choose to treat the transaction as a sale of your home. For details, see Pub. 523.

If your home was sold in connection with a divorce or separation, see Pub. 523. Also, get **Pub. 504,** Tax Information for Divorced or Separated Individuals.

Which Parts To Complete

Parts I and II.—You must complete Parts I and II.

Part III.—Complete this part only if you qualify for the **One-Time Exclusion for People Age 55 or Older** (explained later), and you want to make the election for this sale.

Part IV.—Complete line 10 even if you did not take the exclusion in Part III. Complete lines 11 through 16 only if line 10 is more than zero and you answered "Yes" on line 2.

When and Where To File

File Form 2119 with your tax return for the year of sale.

Additional Filing Requirements.—If you have not replaced your home, but plan to do so within the replacement period (defined on page 2), you will also have to complete a second Form 2119.

● You must file the second Form 2119 by itself if:

1. You planned to replace your home within the replacement period, **and**

2. You later replaced your home within the replacement period, **and**

3. Your taxable gain (line 14c on the second Form 2119) is zero.

If your taxable gain is zero, no tax is due, but you must still file the second form to show that you replaced your home within the replacement period. Enter your name and address, and sign and date the second form. If a joint return was filed for the year of sale,

both you and your spouse must sign the second Form 2119. Send the form to the place where you would file your next tax return based on the address where you now live.

● You must file **Form 1040X,** Amended U.S. Individual Income Tax Return, for the year of sale with the second Form 2119 attached if:

1. You planned to replace your home when you filed your tax return, you later replaced your home within the replacement period, **and** you had a taxable gain on line 14c of the second Form 2119; **or**

2. You planned to replace your home when you filed your tax return, but did **not** do so within the replacement period; **or**

3. You did **not** plan to replace your home when you filed your tax return and included the gain in income, but later you did replace your home within the replacement period.

Report the correct amount of gain from Form 2119 on Schedule D (Form 1040) and attach both forms to Form 1040X. Interest will be charged on any additional tax due. If tax is to be refunded to you, interest will be included with the refund.

One-Time Exclusion for People Age 55 or Older

Generally, you can elect to exclude from your income up to $125,000 ($62,500 if married filing a separate return) of the gain from one sale of any main home you choose. However, for sales after July 26, 1978, the exclusion is available only once. To make the election for this sale, complete Part III and answer "Yes" on line 9c. You qualify to make the election if you meet **ALL** of the following tests:

1. You or your spouse were age 55 or older on the date of sale,

2. Neither you nor your spouse have ever excluded gain on the sale of a home after July 26, 1978, and

3. The person who was age 55 or older owned and lived in the home for periods adding up to at least 3 years within the 5-year period ending on the date of sale.

For purposes of test 3, if you were physically or mentally unable to care for yourself, count as time living in your main home any time during the 5-year period that you lived in a facility such as a nursing home. The facility must be licensed by a state (or political subdivision) to care for people in your condition. For this rule to apply, you must have owned and used your residence as your main home for a total of at least 1 year during the 5-year period. See Pub. 523 for more details.

The gain excluded is never taxed. But, if the gain is more than the amount excluded, complete Part IV to figure whether the excess

Cat. No. 18038W

gain is included in your income or postponed. If the gain is less than $125,000 ($62,500 if married filing a separate return), the difference **cannot** be excluded on a future sale of another main home. Generally, you can make or revoke the election within 3 years from the due date of your return (including extensions) for the year of sale. To make or revoke the election, file Form 1040X with Form 2119 attached.

Married Taxpayers.—If you and your spouse owned the property jointly and file a joint return, only one of you must meet the age, ownership, and use tests to be able to make the election. If you did not own the property jointly, the spouse who owned the property must meet these tests.

If you were married at the time of sale, both you and your spouse must agree to exclude the gain. If you do not file a joint return with that spouse, your spouse must agree to exclude the gain by signing a statement saying, "I agree to the Part III election." The statement and signature may be made on a separate piece of paper or in the bottom margin of Form 2119.

If you sell a home while you are married, and one spouse already made the election prior to the marriage, neither of you can exclude gain on the sale.

The election to exclude gain does not apply separately to you and your spouse. If you elect to exclude gain during marriage and later divorce, neither of you can make the election again.

Postponing Gain

If you buy or build another main home and move into it within the replacement period (defined below), you must postpone all or part of the gain in most cases. The amount of gain postponed is shown on line 15.

If one spouse dies after the old home is sold and before the new home is bought, the gain from the sale of the old home is postponed if the above requirements are met, the spouses were married on the date of death, and the surviving spouse uses the new home as his or her main home. This rule applies regardless of whether the title of the old home is in one spouse's name or is held jointly. For more details, see Pub. 523.

If you bought more than one main home during the replacement period, only the last one you bought qualifies as your new main home for postponing gain. If you sold more than one main home during the replacement period, any sale after the first one does not qualify for postponing gain. However, these rules do not apply if you sold your home because of a job change that qualifies for a moving expense deduction. If this is the case, file a Form 2119 for each sale, for the year of the sale, and attach an explanation for each sale (except the first) for the year of the sale. For more details on qualifications for moving expenses, get **Pub. 521,** Moving Expenses.

Replacement Period.—Generally, the replacement period starts 2 years before and ends 2 years after the date you sell your former main home. The replacement period may be longer if you are on active duty in the U.S. Armed Forces for more than 90 days, or

if you live and work outside the U.S. For more details, see Pub. 523.

Applying Separate Gain to Basis of New Home.—If you are married and the old home was owned by only one spouse, but you and your spouse own the new home jointly, you and your spouse may elect to divide the gain and the adjusted basis. If you owned the old home jointly, and you now own new homes separately, you may elect to divide the gain to be postponed. In either situation, you both must:

1. Use the old and new homes as your main homes, and

2. Sign a statement that says, "We agree to reduce the basis of the new home(s) by the gain from selling the old home." This statement can be made in the bottom margin of Form 2119 or on an attached sheet.

If you both do not meet these two requirements, you must report the gain in the regular way without allocation.

Line Instructions

You may not take double benefits. For example, you cannot use the moving expenses that are part of your moving expense deduction on **Form 3903,** Moving Expenses, to lower the amount of gain on the sale of your old home or to add to the cost of your new home.

Line 1b.—If you report the gain from the sale of your home on Form 6252 using the installment method, complete Form 2119 first. When completing Form 6252, be sure to enter the total of lines 9f and 15 of Form 2119 on line 11 of Form 6252. Do not enter the gain from Form 2119 on Schedule D (Form 1040).

Note: Report interest you receive on a note (or other financial instrument) as interest income for the tax year in which you receive it.

Line 3.—If any part of either home was rented out or used for business for which a deduction is allowed, check "Yes."

● If part of your former main home was rented out or used for business in the year of sale, treat the sale as two separate sales. Report the part of the sale that applies to the rental or business use on Form 4797. Report only the part of the sale that represents your main home on Form 2119. You must allocate the sales price, expense of sale, and the basis of the property sold between Forms 2119 and 4797.

Note: Only the part of the fixing-up expenses that applies to your main home may be included on line 11. These amounts are not allowed on Form 4797.

Attach a statement showing the total selling price of the property and the method used to allocate the amounts between Forms 2119 and 4797. You cannot postpone or take the one-time exclusion on the part of the gain that is reported on Form 4797.

● If part of your new main home is rented out or used for business, enter on line 13b only

the part of the total cost of the property that is allocable to your new main home. Attach a statement showing the total cost of the property and the allocation between the part that is your new main home and the part that is rented out or used for business.

Line 4—Selling Price of Home.—Enter the gross sales price of your old home. Generally, this includes the amount of money you received, plus all notes, mortgages, or other debts that are part of the sale, and the fair market value of any other property you received.

Line 5—Expense of Sale.—Enter your expense of sale, such as commissions, advertising expenses, and attorney and legal fees, that you paid in selling your old home. Loan charges, such as points charged to the seller, are also selling expenses. Do not include fixing-up expenses on this line, but see the instructions for line 11.

Line 7—Basis of Home Sold.—Include the cost of any capital improvements, and subtract any depreciation, casualty losses, or energy credits you reported on your tax return(s) that were related to your old home.

If you filed a Form 2119 when you originally bought your old home (to postpone gain on a previous sale of a home), use the adjusted basis of the new home from the last line of that Form 2119 as the starting point to figure the basis of your old home. If you did not file a Form 2119 to postpone gain when you originally bought your old home, use the cost of the home including any expenses incurred to buy the home as the starting point.

For more details or if you acquired your home other than by purchase, such as by gift, inheritance, or trade, see Pub. 523 and **Pub. 551,** Basis of Assets.

Line 11—Fixing-up Expenses.—Enter the amount paid for work performed on your old home in order to help sell it. Do not include amounts that are otherwise deductible, or selling expenses included on line 5. The expenses must be for work performed within 90 days before the contract to sell the home was signed and paid within 30 days after the sale. Do not include expenses for permanent improvements or replacements, which should be added to the basis of the property sold.

Line 13b—Cost of New Home.—The cost of your new home includes one or more of the following:

1. Cash payments,

2. The amount of any mortgage or other debt on the new home,

3. Commissions and other purchase expenses you paid that were not deducted as moving expenses, and

4. Any capital expenses incurred within 2 years before or 2 years after the sale of your old home.

If you build your new home, include all construction costs incurred within 2 years before and 2 years after the sale of the old home. Do not include the value of your own labor.

Page 2

Form **2119**	**Sale of Your Home**	OMB No. 1545-0072
Department of the Treasury Internal Revenue Service	▶ Attach to Form 1040 for year of sale. ▶ See separate instructions. ▶ Please print or type.	**1991** Attachment Sequence No. **20**

Your first name and initial. (If joint return, also give spouse's name and initial.)	Last name	Your social security number
Fill in Your Address Only If You Are Filing This Form by Itself and Not With Your Tax Return	Present address (no., street, and apt. no., rural route, or P.O. box no. if mail is not delivered to street address)	Spouse's social security number
	City, town or post office, state, and ZIP code	

Caution: *If the home sold was financed (in whole or part) from a mortgage credit certificate or the proceeds of a tax-exempt qualified mortgage bond, you may owe additional tax. Get* **Form 8828,** *Recapture of Federal Mortgage Subsidy, for details.*

Part I General Information

1a Date your former main home was sold (month, day, year) . . . . ▶	**1a**	/ /
b Face amount of any mortgage, note (e.g., second trust), or other financial instrument on which you will get periodic payments of principal or interest from this sale (see instructions) . . .	**1b**	
2 Have you bought or built a new main home?	☐ Yes ☐ No	
3 Is or was any part of either main home rented out or used for business? (If "Yes," see instructions.) . .	☐ Yes ☐ No	

Part II Gain on Sale (Do not include amounts you deduct as moving expenses.)

4 Selling price of home. (Do not include personal property items that you sold with your home.)	**4**	
5 Expense of sale. (Include sales commissions, advertising, legal, etc.)	**5**	
6 Amount realized. Subtract line 5 from line 4	**6**	
7 Basis of home sold (see instructions)	**7**	
8a **Gain on sale.** Subtract line 7 from line 6	**8a**	

  • If line 8a is zero or less, stop here and attach this form to your return.
  • If line 2 is "Yes," you **must** go to Part III or Part IV, whichever applies. Otherwise, go to line 8b.

b If you haven't replaced your home, do you plan to do so within the replacement period (see instructions)?	☐ Yes ☐ No	

  • If "Yes," stop here, attach this form to your return, and see **Additional Filing Requirements** in the instructions.
  • If "No," you **must** go to Part III or Part IV, whichever applies.

Part III One-Time Exclusion of Gain for People Age 55 or Older (If you are not taking the exclusion, go to Part IV now.)

9a Who was age 55 or older on date of sale?	☐ You ☐ Your spouse ☐ Both of you	
b Did the person who was age 55 or older own and use the property as his or her main home for a total of at least 3 years (except for short absences) of the 5-year period before the sale? (If "No," go to Part IV now.)	☐ Yes ☐ No	
c If line 9b is "Yes," do you elect to take the one-time exclusion? (If "No," go to Part IV now.) . . .	☐ Yes ☐ No	
d At time of sale, who owned the home?	☐ You ☐ Your spouse ☐ Both of you	
e Social security number of spouse at time of sale if you had a different spouse from the one above at time of sale. (If you were not married at time of sale, enter "None.") . . . . . . ▶	**9e**	
f **Exclusion.** Enter the **smaller** of line 8a or $125,000 ($62,500, if married filing separate return)	**9f**	

Part IV Adjusted Sales Price, Taxable Gain, and Adjusted Basis of New Home

10 Subtract line 9f from line 8a	**10**	

  • If line 10 is zero, stop here and attach this form to your return.
  • If line 2 is "Yes," go to line 11 now.
  • If you are reporting this sale on the installment method, stop here and see the line 1b instructions.
  • All others, stop here and **enter the amount from line 10 on Schedule D, line 2 or line 9.**

11 Fixing-up expenses (see instructions for time limits)	**11**	
12 **Adjusted sales price.** Subtract line 11 from line 6	**12**	
13a Date you moved into new home (month, day, year) ▶ ___ / ___ / ___ **b** Cost of new home	**13b**	
14a Add line 9f and line 13b	**14a**	
b Subtract line 14a from line 12. If the result is zero or less, enter -0-	**14b**	
c **Taxable gain.** Enter the **smaller** of line 10 or line 14b	**14c**	

  • If line 14c is zero, go to line 15 and attach this form to your return.
  • If you are reporting this sale on the installment method, see the line 1b instructions and go to line 15.
  • All others, **enter the amount from line 14c on Schedule D, line 2 or line 9,** and go to line 15.

15 Postponed gain. Subtract line 14c from line 10	**15**	
16 **Adjusted basis of new home.** Subtract line 15 from line 13b	**16**	

Sign Here Only If You Are Filing This Form by Itself and Not With Your Tax Return	Under penalties of perjury, I declare that I have examined this form, including attachments, and to the best of my knowledge and belief, it is true, correct, and complete.	
	Your signature Date	Spouse's signature Date
▶	(If a joint return, both must sign.)	

For Paperwork Reduction Act Notice, see separate instructions.   Cat. No. 11710J   Form **2119** (1991)

Court Rulings

OUTLINE SUMMARY OF AUTHORITIES FROM

EXCHANGING REAL ESTATE

ALPHABETICAL

by

Dr. Mark Lee Levine

NAME OF CASE	SUCCESSFUL PARTY	ISSUE	RULE	COMMENTS
Alderson, James v. Comm. 63-2 USTC 9499, 317 F.2d 790 (5th Cir. 1963), rev'd T.C. 215	Tp.	Can Tp. intend sale and switch to an exchange?	Yes	See L. Coupe
Allen, Joyce M. v. Comm. TCM 1982-188	Gov.	Tp. actually sold real estate used for rental purposes, placing cash in escrow, and subsequently transferring prop. through escrow, this did not qualify as §1031. Discussed infra.	No	
Levere Anderson, TC Memo 1985-205		Sale and purchase not within §1031		
J. H. Baird 39 TC 608 (1962)	Tp.	Was exchange of real estate for real estate and building to be built within §1031?	Yes	
Barker, Earlene T. v. Comm. 74 TC #555 (1980)	Tp.	Can Tp. avoid boot with $$ coming in at closing to pay off loan without Tp. control of the same?	Yes	See L.R. 8003004.
Bernard, George v. Comm. 26 TCM 858, TC Memo 1967-176	Gov.	Acquiring w/intent to resell or transfer is not within §1031?	Yes	Tp. lost as an acquisition to retransfer is not within 1031.
Bezdjian, v. Comm. T.C. Memo 1987-140 (1987)	Gov.	Was this a valid non-simultane-ous exchange, with escrow?	No	This was a sale!

NAME OF CASE	SUCCESSFUL PARTY	ISSUE	RULE	COMMENTS
Biggs, Franklin B. v. Comm. 632 F.2d 1171 (5th Cir. 1980) aff' g 69 TC 905 (1978) USTC 9114	Tp.	Can Tp. use 3rd party to acquire real estate; Tp. advanced $$ & controls within §1031?	Yes	
Black, Ethel v. Comm. 35 TC 90 (1960)	Gov.	Can a property acquired for personal use and/or resale come within Code §1031?	No	
Bloomington Coca-Cola v. Comm. 51-1 USTC 9320, 189 F.2d Gov. 14 (7th Cir. 1951)	Gov.	Was this a §1031 transaction? (It was held to be a sale.)	No	Tp. wanted abandonment so he could take the loss. Denied.
Boise Cascade v. Comm. 33 TCM #1443, TC Memo 1974-315	Gov.	Exchange of fee with Lease and/ option and still be like kind?	Yes	See also Leslie Lease affects grade or quality, not nature of property character.
Bolker, Joseph R. v. Comm. 81 TC #48 (1983)	Tp.	Will Code §1031 apply where there is a transfer followed by a retransfer?	Yes	Tp. had a liquidation of a corp., by an exchange. Order of events was not important. Thus, a transfer from the entity and then an exchange as in Bolker or from a party and then into an entity, the partnership, in Magneson, was not important. These were steps to an end result contemplated.

NAME OF CASE	SUCCESSFUL PARTY	ISSUE	RULE	COMMENTS
Bolker v. Comm., 760 F.2d 1039 (1985), aff'd on App. 85-1 USTC 9400	Tp.	Corp. transfer and then exchange within §1031	Yes	
Borchard, Antone v. Comm. 24 TCM #1643, TC Memo 1965-297	Tp.	Can Tp. come within §1031 if he agrees to take cash if he loses a 1031 attempt?	Yes	See also Leslie Coupe; Alderson, etc.
Bowers, Estate of 94 T.C. No. 34 (1990)	Gov.	Will a transaction structured as a sale constitute an exchange?	No	This sale was "substantially implemented" before it was restructured.
Brauer, Arthur E. 74 TC 1134 (1980)	Tp.	Is direct deeding o.k.?	Yes	See also Haden, L.R. 8003004; but see to contrary Halpern & Carlton.
Calif. Fed. Life Ins. Co. v. Comm., 78 TC #107 (1981)	Gov.	Is exchange of Swiss francs held as inventory property for Double Eagle gold coins, w/in §1031?	No	1) Swiss francs are still currency in Switzerland, but Gold Eagles are not currency; 2) Tp's economic situation changed after exchange.
Carlton, June v. U.S. 67-2 USTC 9625, 385 F.2d 238 (5th Cir. 1967)	Gov.	Can Tp. take direct deed in multiple party deal within §1031?	No	But see Brauer; Halpern.
Century Electric Co. v. Comm. 51-2 USTC 9482, 192 F.2d 155	Gov.	(1) Is loss deductible? (2) Is it within §1031?	No Yes	— (8th Cir. 1951).

NAME OF CASE	SUCCESSFUL PARTY	ISSUE	RULE	COMMENTS
Chase v. Comm., 92 TC #53 (1989)	Gov.	Can §1031 interplay within an installment sale?	Yes	But, this was held to be a sale, not an exchange.
Clemente, Inc., TC Memo 1985-367		Exchange of land for limited right to extract gravel not within §1031		
Click, D. v. Comm., 78 TC 225 (1982)	Gov.	Tax Court held that §1031 was not applicable where Tp. acquired prop. with intent to make a gift of prop. This does not meet the requirement of "intent" to hold the property		See Wagensen.
Coastal Terminals, Inc. v. U.S. 63-2 USTC 9623, 320 F.2d 333 (4th Cir. 1963)	Tp.	Can you come within §1031 if an acquisition, if there is an acquisition, then improvements, than exchange with Tp.?	Yes	See also J.H. Baird; 124 Front St.; See So. Pacific.
Coleman v. Comm. 180 F.2d 758 (8t h Cir., 1950)				
Coupe, Leslie Q. v. Comm. 52 TC 394 (1969), acq. 1970 2 C.B. 19	Tp.	Can Tp. switch, before closing, from a sale to exchange deal, or make it contingent?	Yes	See Alderson.

NAME OF CASE	SUCCESSFUL PARTY	ISSUE	RULE	COMMENTS
Crenshaw, Emory K. v. U.S. 450 F.2d 472 (5th Cir. 1971) acq. 1970 2 C.B. 19	Gov.	Substance was a sale under §731 and not §1031?	Yes	—
Crooks, Richard W. v. Comm. 92 T.C. #49 (1989), 92 TC 816				
Crowley, Milner and Co. v. Comm., 76 U.S.T.C. #1030 (1981)	Tp.	Was it a valid sale with leaseback?	Yes	Tp. received benefit of a loss deduction; see above re: Leslie case (new case-not in text).
Davis, Alan S. v. U.S. 411 F. Supp. 964 (U.S. D.C. HA 1976)	Tp.	This involved a Code §1033 involuntary conversion, w/in the like-kind test	—	This was a condemnation case; thus, the like-kind standard applied.
Detroit Egg Biscuit & Specialty Co. v. Comm., 9 BTA 1365 (1928)	Gov.	Is intent for a §1031 enough?	No	Tp. sold & reinvested.
Antonio D. D'Onofrio v. Comm., TC Memo 1983-632	Gov.	Was the activity a sale or exchange within Code §1031?	Sale	Facts supported Tp's activity constituting a sale and not an exchange; the sale and reinvestment does not constitute an exchange.
Everett, Cary A. 37 TCM 274, TC Memo 1978-53	Tp.	Tax deferred on exchange of investment timber for other investment timber?	Yes	—

NAME OF CASE	SUCCESSFUL PARTY	ISSUE	RULE	COMMENTS
Federal National Mortgage Assn., 896 F.2d 580 (1990)	Gov.	Can Tp. claim an exchange dealing with mortgages?	No	Thus, losses were not recognized.
GCM 39536 (1985)		Exchange of land for stock in ditch company not within §1031		
Garcia, Phillip v. Comm. 80 TC #491 (3/17/83)	Tp.	Was this an exchange within §1031?	W/in	Held for Tp. as not boot; (1) Tp. did not have control over the cash; (2) Tp. was involved in inter-dependent transactions.
Gibson, Stuart L. v. Comm. TC Memo 1982-342	Gov.	Held that §1031 transaction did not apply where a sale took place and Tp. reinvested part of proceeds on day following disposition		
Gulfstream Land and Development Corp. v. Comm., 71 TC #587 (1979)	—	Is exchange of joint venture interest for joint venture interest within §1031?	—	Dismissed without resolution of issue.
Haden Co. v. Comm. 48-1 USTC 9147, 165 F.2d 588 (5th Cir. 1948)	Gov.	Is direct deeding on multiple properties sufficient to exclude §1031?	No	Tp. denied loss deduction; see also Brauer.
Halpern v. U.S. 68-1 USTC 9308, 286 F. Supp. 255 (D.C. Ga. 1968)	Gov.	Does direct deeding, without interdependent contract, mean no §1031?	Yes	See Contra, Brauer and Haden; see also, consistent with Halpern, Carlton.

NAME OF CASE	SUCCESSFUL PARTY	ISSUE	RULE	COMMENTS
Harr v. MacLaughlin 36-2 USTC 9447, 15 F. Supp. 1004 (D.C. Pa. 1936)	Tp.	Holding for resale?	Yes	No §1031 - Tp. wanted sale, as loss recog.
Hayden, Dick v. U.S., 82-2 USTC #9604 (Wyo. 1981) 82-2 USTC ¶9604 (1981)	Tp.	Tp. involved in 3-way transaction involving exchange of real estate, ranch, land, or other ranch land. Other party involved was oil company willing to pay cash in case and act to acquire prop. favored by Hayden, Tp. Since Tp. conveyed his prop. into escrow, with that deed remaining in escrow until simultaneous transfer of prop. to the Tp., through escrow, an exchange of releasing deed out of escrow, this qualified as §1031 transaction. Court said intent of Tp. was irrelevant. Issue is strictly whether transaction qualified under §1031. Held for Tp.; Gov't filed for appeal but dismissed action. (Wagensen was mentioned in the case, but this was the son of F. Wagensen; see letter to Levine from attorneys).		

NAME OF CASE	SUCCESSFUL PARTY	ISSUE	RULE	COMMENTS
Koch v. Comm. 71 TC 54 (1978)	Tp.	Is exchange of property for real estate w/long-term leases w/in §1031?	Yes	
Lee v. Comm., TC Memo 1986-294 (1986)	Gov.	Could Tp. convert a sale/ reinvestment into an exchange?	No	
Leslie Co. 76-2 USTC 9553, 539 F.2d 943 (3rd Cir. 1976), aff'g 64 TC #247 (1976)	Tp.	Was it a valid sale with leaseback?	Yes	Tp. gets loss; follows Jordan Marsh and contrary to R.R.76-301.
Long, Arthur E. v. Comm. 77 TC 1045 (1981)	Tp.	Can Tp. come w/in §1031 in the Gov. on boot exchange of joint venture for general partnership interest?	Yes	Tp./Gov. had 5 issues: 1) W/in l031 ? = yes See also Miller, Myer, Rev. Rul. 78-135 and Gulfstream.
		(2nd) If there is debt relief, is it still taxed - partnership debt issue	Yes	See l03l; Levine article Tp.d/Gov. had 5 issues: 1) W/in l031 ? = yes 2) Recog. gain ? = yes.
Magneson v. Comm., 55 AFTR 2d 85-9ll, aff'd 81 TC 67 (1983), aff'd 753 F.2d 1490 (9th Cir. 1985)		Exchange transfer followed by transfer to partnership still within Code §l03l		But, now see Code §1031(f) (related parties).

NAME OF CASE	SUCCESSFUL PARTY	ISSUE	RULE	COMMENTS
Norman J. Magneson V. Comm., 81 TC 67 (1983) 753 F.2d 1490 (1985) 85-1 USTC ¶9205	Tp.	Will Code §1031 apply where there is a transfer followed by a retransfer?	Yes	Subject to comments: Taxpayer exchange fee simple for undivided interest; upon acquisition, Tp. contributed property to a partnership for an interest in a general partnership; Held qualified.
Maloney v. Comm., 93 TC #9 (1989)	Tp.	Can there be a §1031 followed by a Corp. 333 liquidation, all w/in §1031?	Yes	But, now see elimination of Code §333 and 1989 Legislation as to related parties under §1031.
Mars v. Comm., TC Memo 1987-481	Gov.	Will a sale be restructured as an exchange?	No	
Jordan Marsh Co. v. Comm. 59-2 USTC 9641, 269 F.2d 453 (2nd Cir. 1959)	Tp.	Was it a sale and leaseback or 1031 transaction?	Yes No	Thus, Tp. took loss write off.
Mason v. Comm., TC Memo 1988-273	Tp.	Will a liquidation of a partnership followed by §1031	Yes	But, now see new Rule under Code §1031(f), to deny §1031. transfer come w/in §1031?
Maxwell, Mark v. U.S. 88-2 U.S.T.C. 9560 (1988), 62 AFTR 2d 88-5406	Gov.	Will constructive receipt destroy the exchange?	Yes	

NAME OF CASE	SUCCESSFUL PARTY	ISSUE	RULE	COMMENTS
Mays, W.A. v. Campbell, Ellis 66-1 USTC 9147, 246 F. Supp. 375 (D. Tex. 1966)	Tp.	Was this within §1031? Was transfer of money boot?	Yes No	(only $ received is in boot, not payment of $).
Meadows, Byron Wayne v. Comm. TCM 1981-417	Gov.	Will a sale and reinvestment come w/in §1031?	No	Basic concept of "no sale" structure issue.
Mercantile Trust Co. of Baltimore, et al., v. Comm. 32 BTA 82 (1935)	Tp.	OK to structure for §1031?	Yes	—
Meyer, Sr., Estate of, et al. v. Comm., 74-2 USTC 9676, 503 F.2d 5567 (9th Cir. 1974)	Tp.	Exchange of general for general within §1031? Exchange of general for limited within §1031?	Yes No	—
MHS Company, Inc. v. Comm. 575 F.2d 1177 (6th Cir. 1978), 78-1 USTC ¶9442	Gov.	Is there a distinction of personalty or realty as to ownership as a partner or a joint venturer?	Yes	Tp., in partnership, owned personalty, not realty.
Milbrew, Inc., et al. v. Comm. TC Memo 1981-610	Gov.	Can Tp. sell property and reinvest with independent transaction and postpone gain?	No	Basic law.
Miller, Norman A. v. Comm. 63-2 USTC 9606 (D.C. Ind. 1963)	Tp.	It is within §1031 to exchange a general partnership interest in a tavern for auto parts?	Yes	—

NAME OF CASE	SUCCESSFUL PARTY	ISSUE	RULE	COMMENTS
Nixon v. Comm., TC Memo 1987-318	Gov.	Can constructive receipt destroy the exchange?	Yes	
124 Front St., Inc. v. Comm. 65 TC #6 (1975), nonacq. in part and acq. in part, 1976-2 CB 2&3	Tp.	Can Tp. use 3rd party funds to acquire property re: exchange and still be within §1031?	Yes	Question by Gov. did not raise 75-291 et al; see also Biggs; L.R. 8110028.
Comm. v. North Shore Bus. Co. 44-1 USTC 9345, 143 F.2d 114 (2nd Cir. 1944)	Tp.	Does Tp. receive boot if used at closing to pay debt are not within control of Tp.?	No	See also Barker.
Peter Pappas v. Comm., 78 TC 1078 (1982)	Tp.	Tp. claimed valid §1031 transaction where there was an exchange of interests in partnership. Held that §1031 can apply to exchange of general partnership interests involving real estate. Court held §1031 and §741 were not in conflict. §741 held to be characterization provision to determine whether asset is capital asset. Poor analysis by Court on this issue and questions of acquisitions with intent to transfer. §1031 held applicable, but Tp. still taxed for other reasons.		

NAME OF CASE	SUCCESSFUL PARTY	ISSUE	RULE	COMMENTS
Red Wing Carriers, Inc., et al. v. Tomlinson, Laurie W. 68-2 USTC 9540, 399 F.2d 652 (5th Cir. 1968)	Gov.	Is a non-simultaneous exchange of automobiles within §1031?	Yes	See Rev. Rul. 61-119 automobiles - non-simultaneous; see Rutherford; Starker.
Regals Realty v. Comm., 123 F.2d 931 (2nd Cir. 1942)	Gov.	Will property purchased w/out the intent for reinvestment use or trade or business come w/in §1031?	No	
Rezendes, Edwin v. Comm. 26 TCM 858, TC Memo 1967-176	Gov.	Will property held for resale fall w/in §1031?	No	
Rogers, John M. v. Comm. 44 TC 126 (1965) aff'd per curiam 67-1 USTC 9419, 377 F.2d 534 (9th Cir. 1967)	Gov.	Is this within §1031 if Tp. gives X an option on real estate; then Y enters and there is an exchange deal with Tp., but before exchange, X exercises option on the real estate?	No	Should have exchanged first then X exercised the option.
Rutherford, Bennie D. v. Comm. 37 TCM 1851-77, TC Memo 1978-505	Gov.	Can heifers now existing be exchanged for those to be born & come within §1031	Yes	Tp. did not want 1031 as Tp. wanted new adjusted basis (ITC/depreciation).
Rutland, Hubert and Ruth 36 TCM 40, TC Memo 1977-008	Tp.	Is this within §1031 in part? Can you structure §1031 for tax benefit purposes?	Yes Yes	—

NAME OF CASE	SUCCESSFUL PARTY	ISSUE	RULE	COMMENTS
Smith, Juhl v. Comm. 76-2 USTC 954l, 537 F.2d 972 (8th Cir. 1976)		Court focused on importance of intent to hold prop. for investment or use in trade or business. This was not Tp. intent; thus did not qualify as §1031 transaction		
Southern Pacific Railway, 75 TC #477 (Tenn. 1980)	Tp.	Can Tp. have §1031 even if the Tp., railroad, performed all necessary work to relocate rail-road lines from the property surrendered in exchange for properties received in the exchange? Tp. reimbursed other party for relocation costs incurred	Yes	See cases, herein, that concur.
Starker I (Starker, Bruce v. U.S.) 75-1 USTC 9443 (D.C. Ore. 1975)	Tp.	Is non-simultaneous exchange of a Tp. property with long view within §1031?	Yes	See also Redwing; Rutherford.
Starker II (Starker, T.J. v. U.S.) 77-2 USTC 95l2, 432 F. Supp. 864 (D.C. Ore. 1977)	Gov.	Is non-simultaneous exchange of a Tp. property with long view within §1031? (with Crown as opposed to Longview, on issue)	No	—

NAME OF CASE	SUCCESSFUL PARTY	ISSUE	RULE	COMMENTS
Starker II (appeal) (Starker, T.J. v. U.S.), 79-2 USTC 9541, 602 F.2d 1341 (9th Cir. 1979), aff'g and rem'g 77-2 USTC 9512, 432 F. Supp. 864 (D.C. Ore. 1977)	Tp.	Is a non-simultaneous exchange within §1031?	Yes 8/79	8/24/79.
Swaim, Emsy H. v. U.S., 79-2 USTC 9462, (D.C., N.D., Tex. 1979)	Gov.	Is the sale and exchange within §1031?	No	—
Von Muff, Carl G., TC Memo 1983-514	Gov.	Was the activity a sale or exchange within Code §1031?	Sale	Facts supported Tp's activity as constituting a sale and not an exchange; the fact that form is important will not violate equal protection, constitutionally speaking.
Wagensen, Fred S. v. Comm. 74 TC #653 (1980)	Tp.	Can Tp. acquire and later give gift without §1031 problem?	Yes	But not within 75-291, etc.
Wakeham v. Comm., [not designed for publication] [94 F.2d 265 (1990)]	—	Can sale followed by reinvestment fall within Code §1031?	No	See Bezdjian case.
Wilhelm, Mary R., T.C. Memo 1983-274 (1983)	Tp.	Could the IRS assert Tp. carried over a negative basis on 1031 pr. where the Tp. depreciated the trade car more than the business portion of the auto?	No	Held for Tp.: No negative basis can be carried over. They cited Tufts.

NAME OF CASE	SUCCESSFUL PARTY	ISSUE	RULE	COMMENTS
Young, Robert v. Comm., TC Memo 1985-221	Gov.	Sale followed by investment not within §1031		
§1245 & §1250	Gov.	Move from §1245 or §1250 to non-1245 or non-1250 can generate gain?	Yes	Still question of 1250 acceleration or just 1250. Corresponding change with 1031 due to ACRS?
§1031	—	—	-	See Appendix A-1.
§1031(a)	—	Basic §1031 rule	-	See Appendix A-1 and 5-12.
§1031(b)	—	Amount of gain to recognize	-	See Appendix A-1 and 5-43.
§1031(c)	—	Amount of losses	-	See Appendix A-1 and 5-60.
§1031(d)	—	Basis on §1031	-	See Appendix A-1 and 5-61.
§1031(e)	—	Livestock - different sexes	-	See Appendix A-1 and 5-62.
§1031(f)	—	Related parties	-	See Appendix A-1.
§1031(g)	—	—	-	See Appendix A-1.
§1031(h)	—	U.S./foreign realty	-	See Appendix A-1.
Regs. 1.1031(a)-1	—	General rules		See Appendix A-1.

NAME OF CASE	SUCCESSFUL PARTY	ISSUE	RULE	COMMENTS
Regs. 1.1031(a)-1(c)	—	Is leasehold of 30 years or more within §1031?		Yes —
Regs. 1.1031(b)-1	—	Gain to recognize		
Regs. 1.1031(b)(6)	—	Gain to recognize		
Regs. 1.1031(c)-1	—	Losses		
Reg. 1.1031(d)-2	Tp.	Is assumption of interest an offset to debt relief? Subject to or assume?	Yes	—
Regs. 1.1031(e)-1	—	Livestock, different sexes		
Reg. 1.1245-1(a)(5)		Holds that §1031 will not apply in some instances where recapture is otherwise applicable		
Reg. 1.1250-1(b)(6)		Holds that §1031 will not apply in some instances where recapture is otherwise applicable		

NAME OF CASE	SUCCESSFUL PARTY	ISSUE	RULE	COMMENTS
Final REGUALTIONS	—	—		
Rev. Rul. 55-749, 1955-2 CB 295		Ruling takes position that where water rights are the equivalent of real prop., such water rights could be exchanged for a fee interest in real estate and be within §1031(a), assuming other elements of this Section are met		
Rev. Rul. 57-244 1957-1 C.B. 247	Tp.	Can 3 people exchange lots within §1031, undivided interest?	Yes	—
Rev. Rul. 57-365 1957-2 CB 521	Tp.	Will it come within §1031 if a taxpayer exchanges between related parties and the related parties involve a parent and a subsidiary corporation? Will this be valid within 1031?	Yes	—
Rev. Rul. 57-469, 1957-2 CB 521	Tp.	Is an exchange treatment allowed for sale with an incompetent?	No	State does not allow an exchange with an incompetent.
Rev. Rul. 59-229, 1959-2 CB 180	—	Is it within §1031 for: (1) exchange of farm with unharvested crop; (2) reciprocal assumptions of mortgages, and (3) §1034 exchange?	Yes Yes No	Not within §1031; use §1034.

NAME OF CASE	SUCCESSFUL PARTY	ISSUE	RULE	COMMENTS
Rev. Rul. 61-119, 1961-1 CB 395	Gov.	Can you avoid §1031 by equipment (1) sale and (2) separate purchase?	No	See also Red Wing Carriers.
Rev. Rul. 65-155, 1965-1 CB 356	Gov.	Can you use §453 and §1031 without a problem for the combination?		But now see ERTA which allows this. No
Rev. Rul. 66-209, 1966-2 C.B. 299	Gov.	Is an exchange of lot for executing a lease w/in Code §1031?	No	Was not lot for lease; it was a lot for agreement to rent.
Rev. Rul. 67-255, 1967-2 C.B. 270	Gov.	Can Tp. come w/in §1031 by reinvest (building) on realty already owned by the Tp.?	No	But, some cases are to the contrary.
Rev. Rul. 67-380, 1967-1 C.B. 291	Tp.	Can exchange of baseball contracts come w/in §1031?	Yes	—
Rev. Rul. 68-36, 1968-1 CB 357	—	Do we allocate adjusted basis in §1031 with multiple properties based on fair market values?	Yes	—
Rev. Rul. 68-331, 1968-1 CB 352	Tp.	Exchange of producing oil lease for fee simple improved ranch can be within §1031?	Yes	

NAME OF CASE	SUCCESSFUL PARTY	ISSUE	RULE	COMMENTS
Rev. Rul. 68-363, 1968-2 CB 336	Tp.	Can exchange come within §1031 if U.S. real estate is exchanged for foreign real estate?	Yes	—
Rev. Rul. 72-151, 1972-1 CB 225	Tp.	Will §1031 exchanges between related parties create problems?	No	Assuming 100% 1031(a) treatment, no problem; if you are within 1031(b), a partially tax-deferred exchange, see limitation.
Rev. Rul. 72-456, 1972-2 CB 468	Tp.	Can Tp. look only to net cash received as boot if Tp. pays closing costs from boot received?	Yes	—
Rev. Rul. 72-515, 1972-2 CB 466		Exchange of unencumbered fee for timberlands, different qualify and quantity, qualified for nonrecognition under §1031 if otherwise exchanged for like-kind prop. Exchange between Tp. and U.S.		
Rev. Rul. 72-601, 1972-2 CB 467	Gov.	If a 7-year old transfers his remainder interest in exchange for a life estate, is this within §1031?	No	Life expectancy of father less than 30 years, so not within the Regs.

NAME OF CASE	SUCCESSFUL PARTY	ISSUE	RULE	COMMENTS
Rev. Rul. 73-476, 1973-2 CB 300	Tp.	3 individual Tps., not dealers, who owned undivided interests as tenants-in-common in 3 parts of real estate, could be involved in §1031 transaction with their undivided interests. Each ended with 100% interest in one parcel		
		Can an undivided interest in real estate be exchanged within §1031?	Yes	—
Rev. Rul. 74-7, 1974-1 CB 198	—	Is an exchange of foreign currency within §1031?		See also where item is not used No for legal tender in exchange for Swiss $$ for U.S. currency.
Rev. Rul. 75-291, 1975-2 CB 332	Gov.	Is an exchange of foreign currency within §1031?	No	See also where item is not used for legal tender in exchange for Swiss $$ for U.S. currency.
Rev. Rul. 75-292, 1975-2 CB 333	Gov.	Is an exchange of foreign currency within §1031?	No	See also where item is not used for legal tender in exchange for Swiss $$ for U.S. currency.
Rev. Rul. 76-214,		Exchanging Mexican peso non-Australian 100-Corona non-currency bullion comes within §1031(a)		1976-1 CB 218 currency bullion gold coins for

NAME OF CASE	SUCCESSFUL PARTY	ISSUE	RULE	COMMENTS
Rev. Rul. 76-301, 1976-2 CB 241	Gov.	Sale of leasehold by tenant & sublet back within §1031?	Yes	Thus, contrary to Jordan Marsh.
Rev. Rul. 77-297, 1977-2 CB 304		Prearranged prohibition rule on transferring prop. under §1031 does not apply because of clause in contract that sale may take place, but does not take place. However, acquiring with intent to retransfer destroys §1031 treatment		(But see Magneson and Bolker to the contrary.)
Rev. Rul. 77-337, 1977-2 CB 305	Gov.	Is this within §1031 to have an exchange with the intent to retransfer?	No	Not 1031; see Rev. Rul. 77-297; 75-291; 75-292.
Rev. Rul. 78-4, IRB 1978-1, 9	Tp.	Exchange of remainder interest in 1/2 piece of real estate for same within §1031?	Yes	Need not be fee simple absolute.
Rev. Rul. 78-135, IRB 1978-15	Gov.	Exchange of partnership interest within §1031?	No	—
Rev. Rul. 78-163, 1978-18, 9	Tp.	Is the transfer of $400 × real estate to State for $100 × real estate from State to Tp.: (2) within §1031?	Yes	

NAME OF CASE	SUCCESSFUL PARTY	ISSUE	RULE	COMMENTS
Rev. Rul. 79-44, 1969-1 C.B. 265	Tp.	Can tenants in common do an exchange to separate their interests?	Yes	But, if therre is debt relief, there can be taxable gain.
Rev. Rul. 79-143, 1979-1 CB 264		Holds that where there is exchange of US $20 gold pieces, numismatic, for South African Krugerrand gold coins, bullion, it will not qualify under §1031		
Rev. Rul. 80-96	—	Holds that a valid deferred exchange exists where there is exchange of gold bullion for Canadian Maple Leaf gold coins		
Rev. Rul. 82-166, IRB 1982-40		Does an exchange of gold bullion held for investment, when exchanged for silver bullion, held for investment, qualify for non-recognition of gain under §1031?	No	No. Theory is that numismastic-type coins and builion-type coins represent totally different types of underlying investments/not like-kind prop.
Rev. Rul. 84-121, IRB 1984-23		Exchange of property to "exercise" an option for property is within §1031		
Rev. Rul. 85-135		Exchange of assets of two t.v. stations within §1031		

NAME OF CASE	SUCCESSFUL PARTY	ISSUE	RULE	COMMENTS
Rev. Rul. 89-121,	Gov.	When exchanging assets in a business, do you look at the individual assets involved?	Yes	—
Rev. Rul. 90-34	Tp.	Can Tp. transfer his property to Y and receive the like-kind property back from someone other than Y? §1.1031(a)-(3), Example 4.	Yes	Direct deeding was allowed in this case. However, see Proposed Treas. Regs.
L.R. 7852022		Where parties intended tax-deferred exchange but were unable to complete because of title problem, subsequent sale prevented exchange even though parties took proceeds and immediately purchased the other prop. in question. Did not qualify for exchange		
L.R. 7906061		Holds that where partnership has coal mining operations and it desires to exchange certain of those qualifying interests and lease bonus payments for fee interest in other real estate, this can qualify w/in §I031		

NAME OF CASE	SUCCESSFUL PARTY	ISSUE	RULE	COMMENTS
L.R. 7938087 (6/22/79) but see L.R. 8046122 (was suspended by L.R. 8005049)	Tp.	Is this a valid non-simultaneous transfer of real estate where X transfers his property to a trust with Y transferring $$ to the trust and land then going out of the trust to Y with the $$ in the trust to be used to acquire property?	Yes	—
L.R. 7948063 (8/29/79)		Conversion of general partnership to limited partnership would not constitute sale or exchange		
L.R. 8003004 (8/19/79)		Tps. were allowed to offset boot received as result of assumption of mortgages by other party to the exchange, by boot paid to other party by the Tp. in form of refinancing of other party's mortgage		
L.R. 8005049 (but see L.R. 8046122)	Gov.	Does this suspend L.R. 7938087?	Yes	— (11/8/79).

NAME OF CASE	SUCCESSFUL PARTY	ISSUE	RULE	COMMENTS
L.R. 8008113 (11/29/79) (revoked L.R. 7938087)		Addresses the issue as to whether real estate investment trusts will receive tax-deferred treatment when it desired to transfer its interest in certain buildings in a shopping center to a third party. After transfer, the REIT would lease land under buildings to buyer for 35 years. Buyer had no specific props. in question, but it was agreed REIT would identify certain props. to have third party acquire those props. and make the exchagne. Was w/in §1031		
L.R. 8035049		Holds that where steel company agreed to transfer its plant and facilities to a tool manufacturer, subject to agreement that manufacturer had to locate land and plant facilities in another location, properly structured, this could qualify for exchange. The manufacturer purchased a tract of land and contracted for construction of plant facilities on behalf of future exchange with steel company. After construction finished, the steel company and manufacturer undertook simultaneous transfer of their interests. Did qualify for tax-deferred exchange		

NAME OF CASE	SUCCESSFUL PARTY	ISSUE	RULE	COMMENTS
L.R. 8046l22 (revoked L.R. 7938087)	Gov.	Does this revoke L.R. 7938087?	Yes	— (8/25/80).
L.R. 8103l17		The Gov't stated where Tp. owns 2 interests in real estate, with one piece containing house used as rental rental unit, and other being unimproved, the Tp. could exchange the 2 interests for a house and lot, where part of use of this Property would be for investment		
L.R. 8ll0028 (12/l0/80)	Tp.	Can a Tp. use §l03l exchange even when the other side is to build on the property and the Tp. is to receive it in a §l03l transaction, with Tp.'s approval re: the building work?	Yes	Supports prior law; see also PLR 8l32l26, Rev. Rul. 75-29l; Southern Pacific, infra.
L.R. 8ll7053		Where corp. exchanges gold bullion held for investment for South African Kruggerrands, the weight of gold for trade is different because of minting fees. However, Ruling holds the transaction qualifies §l03l		

NAME OF CASE	SUCCESSFUL PARTY	ISSUE	RULE	COMMENTS
L.R. 8126070	Tp.	Can property rec. by a Trust in exchange come w/in §1031 even if the Trust terminates in near future? An exchange or prop. can come w/in 1031 even when there is a termina- Facts indicate that trust agreement provided for certain real estate for children of decedent. The farm land in question in trust was to be exchanged for other ground. Even though the trust would terminate by terms of trust shortly after exchange, it nevertheless qualified under 1031. Trust termination was caused by a provision in trust to terminate when youngest child reached age 35, approx. 6 months after the exchange	Yes	Apparently still held for use in trade or business or for investment; No intent to retransfer; see Wagensen. tion of trust tha
L.R. 8132126 (5/18/81)	Tp.	Is an exchange of a golf course by Tp. (X) a deferred exchange for like property to be acquired and developed by (Y) w/in §1031?	Yes	See also Rev. Rul. 75-291; Southern Pacific; PLR 8110028; no agency of Y for X.

NAME OF CASE	SUCCESSFUL PARTY	ISSUE	RULE	COMMENTS
L.R. 8135048	Tp.	If Corp. owns mineral interests overriding royalty and Corp. owns apartment, office bldg. and 1/2 condo, can it trade real estate to the Corp's shareholder for shareholder's royalty interest w/in §1031?	Yes	1) Was valid 1031; 2) not problem of shareholder owning corp.; 3) not anticipatory assignment of income.
L.R. 8141112	Gov.	Can Tp. exchange "right to prohibit development of farm land? (state subsidy w/in §1031)?	No	This was/is not property w/in §1031.
L.R. 8150134		When converting a general partnership involving real estate into a limited partnership, this will not constitute a sale or exchange of the partnership interest, and therefore gain will not be generated. Thus, it is a tax-free conversion		
L.R. 8206109		Holds that a tax-deferred transaction did not occur where Tp. invests proceeds received from disposition of rental prop. into another type of investment, namely real estate investment trust		

NAME OF CASE	SUCCESSFUL PARTY	ISSUE	RULE	COMMENTS
L.R. 8237017				
L.R. 8328011	Tp.	Will security deposits and/or rent deposits constitute debt relief	No	This Ruling cites R.R. 75-363, regarding security deposits and R.R. 73-301 regarding rental deposits. When property is transferred follow grantor trust rules, which means that it would not be debt. It was simply a transferring of monies of other parties.
L.R. 8429039		Exchange, with intent to transfer in 2 years or more is within §1031		
L.R. 8434015		Exchange of realty for personalty not within §1031		
L.R. 8445010	Tp.	Can you exchange, w/in §1031, stock in a cooperative?	Yes	—
L.R. 8453034		Exchange of motel (s) for leasehold (c) is within §1031		
L.R. 8508095		Exchange of investment real estate		
L.R. 851012 (but see L.R. 854005)		Basis question after exchange		

NAME OF CASE	SUCCESSFUL PARTY	ISSUE	RULE	COMMENTS
L.R. 8515016		Exchange of real estate by corp. for realty from shareholders qualifies		
L.R. 8526038		Exchange of property not previously held for use in trade or business or for investment		
L.R. 8540005		Exchange between shareholders and corp. within §1031		
L.R. 8803053	Tp.	Can you exchange, w/in §1031, between related parties?	Yes	But, watch 1989 legislative limits.
L.R. 8810034	—	Exchanges, w/in §1031, may involve cooperatives	Yes	—
L.R. 8818034	Tp.	Can timberland for timberland come w/in §1031?	Yes	—
L.R. 8836006	—	Can you exchange, w/in §1031, between tenants in common?	Yes	Watch out forr 1989 legislation §1031(f).
L.R. 8847042 (revoked by L.R. 8921058)	Tp.	Can you exchange you property for your property?	Yes	But, now see PLR 8921058.

NAME OF CASE	SUCCESSFUL PARTY	ISSUE	RULE	COMMENTS
L.R. 8852031 (see also L.R. 8923050)	—	Direct deeding issues	OK	In some cases; see also Barker and Haden; revoked here by PLR 8923050.
L.R. 8912023 (revoked by L.R. 8944043)	Tp.	Exchanging interests in the same partnership can come w/in §1031	Yes	But, revoked by PLR 8944043.
L.R. 8915032	Tp.	This PLR illustrates a non-simultaneous exchange with escrow/letter of credit	—	CAREFUL!
L.R. 8921058 (revoked by L.R. 8847042)	—	Is exchanging your realty for your realty1 w/in §1031?	No	See PLR 8847042.
L.R. 8923050	—	Revoking PLR 8852031 as to direct deeding	—	—
L.R. 8929039	Tp.	Can a trust exchange a beach house for a house?	Yes	—
L.R. 8933019	Tp.	Division of property by tenants in common	—	—
L.R. 8938045	Tp.	Can you exchange commercial bldg. for commercial condo?	Yes	—

NAME OF CASE	SUCCESSFUL PARTY	ISSUE	RULE	COMMENTS
L.R. 8944043 (revoked L.R. 8912023)	Gov.	Can you exchange partnership interest in the same partnership, limited for general, w/in §1031?	No	Revoked PLR 8912023.
L.R. 8950034	Tp.	Whether a nonpossessory fee can come within Code §1031(a)?	Yes	
L.R. 9003011	Gov.	Can one exchange an entire business?	No	One must look to each individual asset. See Rev. Rul. 89-121.
L.R. 9003012	Gov.	Can one exchange an entire business?	No	One must look to each individual asset. See Rev. Rul. 89-121.
L.R. 9003040	Tp.	Will revocation of a Private Letter Rul. be retroactive?	No	This assumes good faith action by Tp.
L.R. 9028055	Tp.	Can Tp. exchange stock interest?	No	Not possible under Code §1031 Is possible under other Sections.
L.R. 9031015	Gov.	Can Tp. exchange for property to be constructed?	No	It is possible to exchange in such circumstances. However, the facts were not structured properly in this Ruling.

NAME OF CASE	SUCCESSFUL PARTY	ISSUE	RULE	COMMENTS
L.R. 9038030	Tp.	Can Tp. exchange under Code §1031 and not be blocked by Code §1031(h) if Tp. receives property located in the U.S. Virgin Islands?	Yes	This constituted property within the United States.

Commercial Investment Real Estate Institute Forms

Alternative Cash Sales Worksheet

Pg _____ of _____

Mortgage Balances

	Year:	Year:	Year:	Year:	Year:
Principal Balance - 1st Mortgage					
Principal Balance - 2nd Mortgage					
TOTAL UNPAID PRINCIPAL					

Calculation of Sale Proceeds

PROJECTED SALES PRICE

CALCULATION OF ADJUSTED BASIS:

1	Basis at Acquisition		
2	+ Capital Additions		
3	− Cost Recovery (Depreciation) Taken		
4	− Basis in Partial Sales		
5	= Adjusted Basis at Sale		

CALCULATION OF EXCESS COST RECOVERY:

6	Total Cost Recovery Taken (Line 3)		
7	− Straight Line Cost Recovery		
8	= Excess Cost Recovery		

CALCULATION OF CAPITAL GAIN ON SALE:

9	Sale Price		
10	− Costs of Sale		
11	− Adjusted Basis at Sale (Line 5)		
12	− Participation Payments		
13	= Total Gain		
14	− Excess Cost Recovery (Line 8)		
15	− Suspended Losses		
16	= Capital Gain or (Loss)		

ITEMS TAXED AS ORDINARY INCOME:

17	Excess Cost Recovery (Line 8)		
18	− Unamortized Loan Points		
19	= Ordinary Taxable Income		
20	X Tax Rate on Ordinary Income		
21	= Tax (Savings) on Ordinary Income		

ITEMS TAXED AS CAPITAL GAIN:

22	Capital Gain (Line 16)		
23	X Percentage of Capital Gain Reportable		
24	= Taxable Capital Gain		
25	X Tax Rate on Capital Gain		
26	= Tax on Capital Gain		

CALCULATION OF SALE PROCEEDS AFTER TAX:

27	Total Sale Price (Line 9)		
28	− Costs of Sale (Line 10)		
29	− Participation Payments (Line 12)		
30	− Mortgage Balance(s) (from top of form)		
31	= Sale Proceeds Before Taxes		
32	− Tax (Savings) on Ordinary Income (Line 21)		
33	− Tax on Capital Gain (Line 26)		
34	− Recapture of Investment Tax Credits		
35	= SALE PROCEEDS AFTER TAX		

The statements and figures herein while not guaranteed
are secured from sources we believe authoritative

Prepared by _____

Cash Flow Analysis Worksheet

Property Name _____   Purchase Price _____

Prepared For _____   Costs of Acquisition _____

Prepared By _____   Loan Points _____

Date Prepared _____   Down Payment _____

Mortgage Data			Cost Recovery Data		
	1st Mortgage	2nd Mortgage		Improvements	Personal Property
Amount			Value		
Interest Rate			C. R. Method		
Term			Useful Life		
Payments / Year			In Service Date		
Periodic Payment			Recapture (All / None / Excess)		
Annual Debt Service					
Comments			Investment Tax Credit ($$ or %)		

Taxable Income

Year: _____ Year: _____ Year: _____ Year: _____ Year: _____

1 Potential Rental Income
2 − Vacancy & Credit Losses
3 = Effective Rental Income
4 + Other Income
5 = Gross Operating Income
6 − Operating Expenses
7 = NET OPERATING INCOME
8 − Interest - 1st Mortgage
9 − Interest - 2nd Mortgage
10 − Cost Recovery - Improvements
11 − Cost Recovery - Personal Property
12 − _____
13 − _____
14 = Real Estate Taxable Income
15 Tax Liability (Savings) @ _____ %

Cash Flow

16 NET OPERATING INCOME (Line 7)
17 − Annual Debt Service
18 − _____
19 − _____
20 = CASH FLOW BEFORE TAXES
21 − Tax Liability (Savings) (Line 15)
22 + Investment Tax Credit
23 = CASH FLOW AFTER TAXES

Annual Property Operating Data

Name _____

Location _____

Type of Property _____

Size of Property _____ ☐ Sq.Ft. ☐ Units

Purpose:

☐ Owner's Statement ☐ Broker's Reconstructed ☐ Forecast

☐ Existing Financing ☐ Potential Financing

☐ Seller's Position ☐ Buyer's Position

Assessed / Appraised Values

Land	$ _____	_____ %
Improvement	$ _____	_____ %
Personal Property	$ _____	_____ %
Total	$ _____	100 %

Adjusted Basis as of _____ $ _____

Date _____

Price $ _____

Existing Loan _____

Equity _____

		Balance	Payment	#Pmts/Yr.	Interest	Term
Existing						
1st	$					
2nd	$					
3rd	$					
Potential:						
1st	$					
2nd	$					

	ALL FIGURES ANNUAL	$/SQ.FT. or $/Unit %	COMMENTS/FOOTNOTES
1	POTENTIAL RENTAL INCOME		
2	Less: Vacancy & Cr. Losses	(_____ % of $ _____)	
3	EFFECTIVE RENTAL INCOME		
4	Plus: Other Income		
5	GROSS OPERATING INCOME		
	OPERATING EXPENSES:		
6	Real Estate Taxes		
7	Personal Property Taxes		
8	Property Insurance		
9	Off Site Management		
10	Payroll - Onsite Personnel		
11	Expenses / Benefits		
12	Taxes / Worker's Compensation		
13	Repairs and Maintenance		
	Utilities:		
14			
15			
16			
17			
18	Accounting and Legal		
19	Real Estate Leasing Commissions		
20	Advertising / Licenses / Permits		
21	Supplies		
22	Miscellaneous		
	Contract Services:		
23			
24			
25			
26			
27			
28			
29	TOTAL OPERATING EXPENSES		
30	NET OPERATING INCOME		
31	Less: Annual Debt Service		
32	CASH FLOW BEFORE TAXES		

The statements and figures herein while not guaranteed are secured from sources we believe authoritative   Prepared by _____

Pg _____ of _____

Installment Sale Worksheet

Date _____

Prepared for _____

Property _____

Sale Price _____

- Down Payment _____

- Existing Loan _____

= Purchase Money Note _____

Amortization of Purchase Money Note

Amount _____ Rate _____ Term _____ Pmt _____ A.D.S. _____

Year	Annual Debt Service	Interest	Principal	Remaining Balance
1				
2				
3				
4				
5				
6				

Calculation of Gain

1	Gross Sale Price		
2	Adjusted Cost Basis at Sale		
3	+ Costs of Sale		
4	+ Excess Cost Recovery to be Recaptured		
5	= Adjusted Basis Including Sale Costs & Recapture		
6	Gain to be Spread over Contract Term (Line 1 minus Line 5)		

Calculation of Excess of Mortgage over Basis

7	Existing Loan(s)
8	− Adjusted Basis Including Sale Costs & Recapture (Line 5)
9	= Excess of Mortgage over Basis (Must be 0 or greater - Negative # not allowed)

Principal Received at Closing and in Year of Sale

PRINCIPAL ACTUALLY RECEIVED:

10	Down Payment
11	+ Option Money Applied to Purchase Price

PRINCIPAL DEEMED TO BE RECEIVED:

12	+ Excess of Mortgage over Basis (Line 9)
13	+ Seller's Matured Liabilities that Buyer will Pay this Year
14	+ Buyer Forgiveness of Unrelated Debt of Seller to Buyer
15	= Principal Actually Received or Deemed to be Received at Closing by the Seller
16	Principal Received on Purchase Money Note during Year of Sale - but after Closing

Calculation of Contract Price and Profit Ratio

17	Gross Sale Price (Line 1)
18	+ Mortgage in Excess of Basis, if any (Line 9)
19	− Existing Loan(s) (Line 7)
20	= Contract Price
21	Profit Ratio = Line 6 divided by Line 20

The statements and figures herein while not guaranteed
are secured from sources we believe authoritative

Prepared by _____

Pg _____ of _____

Alternative T-Bars Worksheet

Alternative # _____		Alternative # _____		Alternative # _____	
n	$	n	$	n	$
0	(_____)	0	(_____)	0	(_____)
1	_____	1	_____	1	_____
2	_____	2	_____	2	_____
3	_____	3	_____	3	_____
4	_____	4	_____	4	_____
5	_____	5	_____	5	_____
6	_____	6	_____	6	_____
7	_____	7	_____	7	_____
8	_____	8	_____	8	_____
9	_____	9	_____	9	_____
10	_____	10	_____	10	_____
11	_____	11	_____	11	_____
12	_____	12	_____	12	_____
13	_____	13	_____	13	_____
14	_____	14	_____	14	_____
15	_____	15	_____	15	_____
IRR = _____		IRR = _____		IRR = _____	

The statements and figures herein while not guaranteed
are secured from sources we believe authoritative

Prepared by _____

Exchange Recapitulation

Date _____

Property 1	Market Value 2	Existing Loans 3	Equity 4	Cash		Paper		Comm. 9	Trans. Costs 10	Net Equity 11	New Loan 12	Old Loan 13	Net Loan Proceeds 14
				Gives (In) 5	Gets (Out) 6	Gives 7	Gets 8						

The statements and figures presented herein, while not guaranteed, are secured from sources we believe authoritative.

Prepared by _____

Installment Sale Cash Flow Analysis

Pg _____ of _____

Date _____

Prepared for _____

Property _____

Suspended Losses _____

	Closing (Mo / Yr)	(Mo / Yr)	(Mo / Yr)	(Mo / Yr)	(Mo / Yr)
	____ / ____	____ / ____	____ / ____	____ / ____	____ / ____

Taxable Income

TAXABLE INTEREST:

1   Interest Income Received

2 − Interest Expense - Paid out

3 = Net Taxable Interest

TAXABLE GAIN:

4   Principal Payments Received

5 X Reportable Profit Ratio

6 = Capital Gain

USE LINES 7 - 9 ONLY IF PROPERTY HAS SUSPENDED LOSSES

7   Line 6 as % of Worksheet Line 6

8   Suspended Losses X Line 7

9   Net Capital Gain Reportable (6 - 8)

CALCULATION OF TAX:

10   Net Taxable Interest (line 3)

11 + Cost Recovery Recapture

12 = Taxable Income @ Ordinary Rate

13 X Ordinary Tax Rate

14 = Tax on Ordinary Income

15   Capital Gain (line 6 or line 9)

16 X Capital Gain Tax Rate

17 = Tax on Capital Gain

18   Total Tax due (line 14 + line 17)

Cash Flows

CASH RECEIVED:

19   Down Payment

20 + Debt Service Received

21 = Total Cash Received

CASH PAID OUT:

22   Sale Costs

23 + Debt Service Paid Out

24 = Total Cash Paid Out

CASH FLOWS AFTER TAX:

25   Total Cash Received (line 21)

26 − Total Cash Paid Out (line 24)

27 = Cash Flow Before Tax

28 − Total Tax Due (line 18)

29 = **CASH FLOW AFTER TAX**

The statements and figures herein while not guaranteed are secured from sources we believe authoritative

Prepared By _____

EXCHANGE BASIS ADJUSTMENT FORM
Realized Gain (Loss) Computation

1. Market Value of Property Conveyed $ _____
2. Less: Disposition Costs $ _____
3. Less: Basis at Time of Disposition $ _____
4. Equals: Realized Gain (Loss) $ _____

if (loss) - skip to line 9

Recognized Gain Computation

Sum of unlike property received:

a. cash $ _____
b. boot $ _____
c. net loan relief $ _____

Sum of a, b, and c above $ _____

Lesser of

$ _____   or $ _____
Realized Gain (line 4)   Sum of a, b, and c above

Equals

5. Recognized Gain $ _____

Computation of Unrecognized Gain

6. Realized Gain (line 4) $ _____
7. Less: Recognized Gain (line 5 above) $ _____
8. Equals: Unrecognized Gain $ _____

Computation of Substitute Basis

9. Market Value of Acquired Property $ _____
10. Less: Unrecognized Gain (line 8) or
    Plus: line 4, if loss $ _____
11. Plus: Acquisition costs $ _____
12. Equals: Substitute basis (replacement prop.) $ _____

Allocation of Substitute Basis

13. Land Allocation   _____ % $ _____
14. Improvement Allocation   _____ % $ _____
15. Personal Property Allocation _____ % $ _____

The statements and figures herein,
while not guaranteed, are secured from sources
we believe authoritative   Prepared by _____

Adjustments to Real Estate Taxable Income Worksheet

Property Name _____

	YEAR:	YEAR:	YEAR:	YEAR:	YEAR:

1. Real Estate Taxable Income [Before Adjustments] (from Line 14 - Cash Flow Analysis)

2. Prior Year's Cumulative Suspended Losses Available to Offset Current Year's Income
   a) Prior Years' Cumulative Suspended Losses Available (from prior year - Line 7)
   b) Prior Years' Cumulative Suspended Losses Used to Offset Current Year's
      Positive Taxable Income: (if Line 1 is positive, enter the negative of the amount
      shown on Line 1, but not more than Line 2a; if Line 1 is negative, enter 0)
   c) Cumulative Suspended Losses Remaining (Line 2a - Line 2b)

3. Rental Allowance for Current Year:
   a) Adjusted Gross Income
   b) Phase-out of the $25,000 Allowance: (if Line 3a is greater than $150,000, enter
      $25,000; if Line 3a is less than $100,000 enter 0; if Line 3a is between $100,000 and
      $150,000, subtract $100,000 from Line 3a and enter 50% of this number on this Line;)
   c) Maximum Rental Allowance of this year's loss ($25,000 - Line 3b)
   d) Current Year's Rental Allowance: (if Line 1 is positive, enter 0; if Line 1 is
      negative, enter the least negative of Line 3c or Line 1)
   e) Current Year's Rental Allowance remaining for use against prior years' cumulative
      suspended losses (Line 3c - Line 3d)

4. Current Year's Remaining Rental Allowance Applied to Prior Years' Suspended Losses
   a) Cumulative Suspended Losses remaining (Line 2c)
   b) Rental Allowance Used (Enter the least negative of Line 3e or Line 4a)
   c) Prior Years' Cumulative Suspended Losses Remaining (Line 4a - Line 4b)

5. Phase - In of Passive Losses (Use only if property was acquired prior to 10/23/86)
   a) Current Year's Loss Remaining for Phase-in (Line 1 - Line 3d, but NOT < 0)
   b) Phase - in % Allowed (1987 = 65%; 1988 = 40%; 1989 = 20%; 1990 = 10%)
   c) Dollar Amount of Phase - in Allowed (Line 5a times Line 5b)

6. Current Year's Suspended Loss (Line 1 - Line 3d - Line 5c)

7. Cumulative Suspended Losses Carried Forward (Line 4c + Line 6)

8. Real Estate Taxable Income [after adjustments]:
   (if Line 1 is negative then Line 3d + Line 4b + Line 5c)
   (if Line 1 is positive then Line 1 - Line 2b - Line 4b)
   ENTER THIS NUMBER ON LINE 14 OF THE CASH FLOW ANALYSIS FORM

Prepared by _____   Date _____

INDEX

About the Publisher

PROBUS PUBLISHING COMPANY

Probus Publishing Company fills the informational needs of today's business professional by publishing authoritative, quality books on timely and relevant topics, including:

* Investing
* Futures/Options Trading
* Banking
* Finance
* Marketing and Sales
* Manufacturing and Project Management
* Personal Finance, Real Estate, Insurance and Estate Planning
* Entrepreneurship
* Management

Probus books are available at quantity discounts when purchased for business, educational or sales promotional use. For more information, please call the Director, Corporate/Institutional Sales at 1-800-PROBUS-1, or write:

Director, Corporate/Institutional Sales
Probus Publishing Company
1925 N. Clybourn Avenue
Chicago, Illinois 60614
FAX (312) 868-6250